The Qur᾿ān

The Clear Guidance

A Fusion of Multiple Commentaries of the Noble Qur᾿ān alongside Contemporary Research and Analysis

VOLUME TWO

Sūrah al-Baqarah (Chapter 2) - Verses 142-252

LEAD RESEARCHER and WRITER: Saleem Bhimji
ASSISTANT ADVISOR: Sabika Mithani
COPY EDITOR: Arifa Hudda
Under the Guidance of Moulana Nabi R. Mir (Abidi)

ISBN: 978-1-68312-362-0
Library of Congress Control Number: 2023915623

The Qur'ān: The Clear Guidance
VOLUME TWO
Sūrah al-Baqarah (Chapter 2): Verses 142-252

Lead Researcher and Writer: Saleem Bhimji
Assistant Advisor: Sabika Mithani
Copy Editor: Arifa Hudda
Under the Guidance of: Moulana Nabi R. Mir (Abidi)

Cover Design and Text Layout by Saleem Bhimji

Published by Al-Kisa Foundation
www.alkisafoundation.org

First Paperback Edition 2024

Dedication

This book is dedicated to the Imām of our Time عجل الله فرجه الشريف, Prophet Muḥammad ﷺ, his beloved daughter, Sayyidah Fāṭimah az-Zahrāʾ عليها السلام and the first eleven Imāms عليهم السلام.

Acknowledgments

Prophet Muḥammad ﷺ said:

يُوزَنُ يَوْمَ الْقِيَامَةِ مِدَادُ الْعُلَمَآءِ وَدِمَآءُ الشُّهَدَآءِ فَيَرْجَحُ مِدَادُ الْعُلَمَآءِ عَلَى دِمَآءِ الشُّهَدَآءِ

"On the Day of Resurrection, the ink of the scholars will be weighed against the blood of the martyrs, and the ink of the scholars will be heavier than the blood of the martyrs."[1]

The true reward lies with Allah عز وجل, but we would like to sincerely thank Shaykh Ehsan Ahmadi and Sister Zamena Momin. May Allah عز وجل bless them in this world and the next.

---

[1] Pāyānade, *Nahj al-Faṣāhah*, Saying #3,222.

Marḥumīn Dedication

Please recite a Sūrah al-Fātiḥah for the following Marḥūmīn:

Mohammed Ali Abbas

Nizar Abbas Abdul Latif

Rafia Mehdi

Sabiha Jafri

Sana-e-Fatema Khalfan Kara

Syed Mohammad Askari Baqueri

Syed Mohammad Raza Baqueri

Syed Nurul Hasan Jafri

Tausif Ahmad Shah

Zakia Askari

Transliteration Table

The method of transliteration of Islamic terminology from the Arabic language has been carried out according to the standard transliteration table mentioned below.

ء	ʾ	ر	r	ف	f
ا	a	ز	z	ق	q
ب	b	س	s	ك	k
ت	t	ش	sh	ل	l
ث	th	ص	ṣ	م	m
ج	j	ض	ḍ	ن	n
ح	ḥ	ط	ṭ	و	w
خ	kh	ظ	ẓ	ه	h
د	d	ع	ʿ	ي	y
ذ	dh	غ	gh		

Vowels

ـَ	a	ـِ	i	ـُ	u

Long Vowels

ا	ā	ي	ī	و	ū

Farsi Letters

پ	p	چ	ch
ژ	jh	گ	g

Symbols Used in This Book

Throughout this work, when taking the name of any of the revered personalities in Islamic history, including Allah عزّ وجلّ, Prophet Muḥammad صلى الله عليه وآله, his select family members, and religious scholars, we have employed the following Arabic symbols to show the reverence to each of them. As a part of Islamic culture, readers are requested to send the salutations upon these personalities when they read this work.

عزّ وجلّ

Mighty and Majestic (is He)

Used exclusively for God - Allah عزّ وجلّ

صلى الله عليه وآله

Blessings of Allah be upon him and his Immaculate Progeny

Used exclusively for Prophet Muḥammad صلى الله عليه وآله

عليه السلام

Peace be upon him

Used for one honored male

عليهما السلام

Peace be upon them both

Used for two honored men or women or a combination

عليهم السلام

Peace be upon all of them

Used for three or more honored men or women or a combination

عليها السلام

Peace be upon her

Used for one honored female

عجّل الله تعالى فرجه الشريف

May Allah, the Most High, hasten his noble return

Used exclusively for Imam al-Mahdī عجّل الله تعالى فرجه الشريف

Contents

Dedication i

Acknowledgments i

Marḥumīn Dedication iii

Transliteration Table v

Symbols Used in This Book vii

Verse 142 1

The Event of the Shift of the Qiblah 1

Keys of Guidance 2

Verse 143 3

A Balanced, Middle Nation 3

Wisdom behind the Change in Qiblah 5

Specific Meaning of The Middle Nation 6

Keys of Guidance 9

Verse 144 10

Wherever You Are, Turn Toward the Kaʿbah 10

Specifics on the Changing of the Qiblah 11

How was the Qiblah Redirected? 12

The Place 12

A Unique Challenge vis-a-vis the Congregational Prayer 13

Reasons for the Change of the Qiblah 15

Reactions and Consequences 17

Keys of Guidance 18

Verse 145 19

The Jews and Christians will Never be Pleased 19

Keys of Guidance 20

Verse 146 21

They Certainly Recognized Prophet Muḥammad ﷺ 21

Keys of Guidance 22

Verse 147 23

Keys of Guidance 23

Verse 148 .... **24**
Every Nation has a Focal Point for Prayer 25
Keys of Guidance 26

Verse 149 .... **27**
Have Reverence of Allah ﷻ Alone 27
Keys of Guidance 28

Verse 150 .... **28**
Keys of Guidance 30

Verse 151 .... **31**
Spiritual Agenda of Prophet Muḥammad ﷺ 32
Keys of Guidance 34

Verse 152 .... **34**
What is Remembrance (Dhikr) of Allah ﷻ? 35
A Life of Remembrance 35
Avoiding Ghaflah 36
Why do we Need Dhikrullāh? 37
Different Forms of Dhikr 37
Dhikr in One's Life 38
Keys of Guidance 39

Verse 153 .... **40**
Fortitude and Focus on Allah ﷻ 40
Keys of Guidance 41

Verse 154 .... **42**
History of Revelation 42
Martyrs are Alive 44
Keys of Guidance 46

Verse 155 .... **46**
This World: A Divinely-Created Testing Ground 47
Why does Allah ﷻ Test Humanity? 47
Tests of Allah ﷻ are Universal 48
Secret to Success in the Divine Tests 49
Keys of Guidance 49

Verse 156 .... **51**

What is a Misfortune/Trial (Musībah)? 51
Keys of Guidance 54

Verse 157 .... **54**
Keys of Guidance 55

Verse 158 .... **55**
Actions of the Ignorant 57
Allah ﷻ is Thankful to His Servants? 58
Two Hills of aṣ-Ṣafā and al-Marwah 59
Historical Position of aṣ-Ṣafā and al-Marwah 59
Keys of Guidance 62

Verse 159 .... **62**
History of Revelation 63
It is Impermissible to Conceal the Truth 64
Hiding the Truth as Seen in the Ḥadīth 65
Keys of Guidance 66

Verse 160 .... **66**
Keys of Guidance 67

Verse 161 .... **68**
Outcome of Those who Die as Disbelievers 68
Keys of Guidance 69

Verse 162 .... **70**
Why Remain in Punishment Forever? 70
Why will the Punishment not be Decreased or Lightened? 71
Keys of Guidance 71

Verse 163 .... **71**
Keys of Guidance 72

Verse 164 .... **72**
Manifestations of His Pure Essence in Existence 73
Keys of Guidance 75

Verse 165 .... **76**
Keys of Guidance 79

Verse 166 .... **80**
Disavowing their Devotees 80

Keys of Guidance 81

Verse 167 **81**

Keys of Guidance 82

Verse 168 **83**

History of Revelation 83

The Movements of Satan 85

Keys of Guidance 86

Verse 169 **86**

Gradual Immorality 87

Keys of Guidance 88

Verse 170 **88**

Blindly Following One's Forefathers 89

Keys of Guidance 89

Verse 171 **91**

Keys of Guidance 92

Verse 172 **92**

Pure versus Polluted 92

Keys of Guidance 93

Verse 173 **94**

Keys of Guidance 97

Verse 174 **97**

History of Revelation 98

Another Censure for Hiding the Truth 98

Keys of Guidance 100

Verse 175 **101**

Keys of Guidance 102

Verse 176 **102**

Keys of Guidance 103

Verse 177 **104**

The Source of Righteousness 105

Keys of Guidance 110

Verse 178 **111**

History of Revelation 112
There is Life in the Laws of Retribution 114
Why Blood-money? 116
Philosophy of Qiṣāṣ 118
Keys of Guidance 119

Verse 179 **120**
Keys of Guidance 121

Verse 180 **122**
Keys of Guidance 124

Verse 181 **125**
Keys of Guidance 125

Verse 182 **126**
Philosophy of the Last Will and Testament 128
Maintaining Justice in the Last Will and Testament 131
Keys of Guidance 131

Verse 183 **133**
Types and History of Fasting 133
Fast of the Month of Ramaḍān: Source of God-Consciousness 134
Keys of Guidance 135

Verse 184 **136**
Keys of Guidance 139

Verse 185 **140**
Various Outcomes of Fasting 141
Societal Benefits of Fasting 142
Medical Benefits of Fasting 143
Fasting in the Previous Nations 144
Choosing the Month of Ramaḍān 145
Keys of Guidance 145

Verse 186 **147**
History of Revelation 147
The Weapon Known as Supplication (Duʿāʾ) 148
Keys of Guidance 150

Verse 187 **151**

History of Revelation 152
Expansion in the Rules of Fasting 153
From Beginning to End - The Goal is Taqwā 156
Keys of Guidance 156

Verse 188 158
Bribes and Kickbacks - a Major Socio-Economic Problem 159
Keys of Guidance 161

Verse 189 162
History of Revelation 162
Various Questions of the People 164
Keys of Guidance 165

Verse 190 166
History of Revelation 166
Explanation of this Verse 166
Keys of Guidance 167

Verse 191 168
Connection to the Previous Verse 169
Keys of Guidance 171

Verse 192 173
Keys of Guidance 173

Verse 193 174
Jihād in Islam 175
1. Jihād: Used to Extinguish Rebellions 176
2. Defensive Jihād 178
3. Intellectual Attempt to Enlighten the World to Monotheism 179
4. Jihād: Supporting the Oppressed 180
Keys of Guidance 180

Verse 194 181
Keys of Guidance 184

Verse 195 184
Almsgiving Prevents the Destruction of Society 185
Keys of Guidance 186

Verse 196 186

Some Important Rules of Ḥajj 188
Importance of Ḥajj 190
Various Types of Ḥajj 190
Keys of Guidance 191

Verse 197 192
Keys of Guidance 195

Verse 198 195
A Few Key Points 197
Keys of Guidance 198

Verse 199 199
First Stop in Ḥajj 200
Second Stop in Ḥajj 201
Keys of Guidance 202

Verse 200 203
History of Revelation 204
Interpretation 204
Keys of Guidance 205

Verse 201 206
Keys of Guidance 207

Verse 202 208
Keys of Guidance 209

Verse 203 210
What is this Remembrance (Adhkār)? 211
Keys of Guidance 212

Verse 204 213
History of Revelation 213
Interpretation 214
Keys of Guidance 214

Verse 205 215
Keys of Guidance 216

Verse 206 216
Keys of Guidance 217

Verse 207 217

History of Revelation 217
Commentary 218
Keys of Guidance 219

Verse 208 .... **219**
World Peace in the Shadow of True Faith 220
Keys of Guidance 221

Verse 209 .... **222**
Keys of Guidance 222

Verse 210 .... **223**
Seeing Allah ﷻ 224
Keys of Guidance 224

Verse 211 .... **225**
Keys of Guidance 227

Verse 212 .... **228**
History of Revelation 228
The Beautification of this Temporal World 228
Commentary 233
Keys of Guidance 234

Verse 213 .... **235**
Keys of Guidance 239

Verse 214 .... **239**
History of Revelation 240
Commentary 240
Keys of Guidance 241

Verse 215 .... **241**
History of Revelation 242
The Reality of Infāq 242
The Benefits of Infāq 243
The Conditions for the Acceptance of Infāq 246
The Ranking of Recipients for Infāq 251
Commentary 257
Keys of Guidance 258

Verse 216 .... **260**

Connection to Previous Verses 260
Commentary 262
Keys of Guidance 263

Verse 217 **264**
History of Revelation 265
Commentary 266
Keys of Guidance 268

Verse 218 **269**
History of Revelation 269
Keys of Guidance 271

Verse 219 **272**
History of Revelation 272
Connection to the Previous Verses 272
Commentary 276
Spending in Charity for Others (Infāq) 279
Keys of Guidance 281

Verse 220 **283**
History of Revelation 284
Commentary 284
Keys of Guidance 286

Verse 221 **287**
History of Revelation 288
Commentary 289
Keys of Guidance 291

Verse 222 **292**
History of Revelation 292
Keys of Guidance 295

Verse 223 **297**
Keys of Guidance 299

Verse 224 **300**
History of Revelation 300
Commentary 300
Keys of Guidance 302

Verse 225 .... **302**
Keys of Guidance 303
Verse 226 .... **303**
Īlā' has a Unique Ruling 305
Islam and the Western World 305
Divine Attributes at the End of Each Verse 307
Keys of Guidance 307
Verse 227 .... **309**
Keys of Guidance 310
Verse 228 .... **312**
Keys of Guidance 315
Verse 229 .... **317**
History of Revelation 318
Commentary 318
Types of Divorce in Islam 321
Keys of Guidance 322
Verse 230 .... **323**
History of Revelation 324
Commentary 324
Keys of Guidance 325
Verse 231 .... **326**
Further Controls in Divorce 327
Keys of Guidance 328
Verse 232 .... **329**
History of Revelation 329
Another Cultural Chain Imprisoning Women 329
Keys of Guidance 331
Verse 233 .... **332**
Seven Directives for Breastfeeding 333
Keys of Guidance 336
Verse 234 .... **337**
Irrational Attitudes toward Women 337
Keys of Guidance 340

Verse 235 ... **340**
Keys of Guidance ... 342

Verse 236 ... **343**
Keys of Guidance ... 344

Verse 237 ... **345**
Keys of Guidance ... 347

Verse 238 ... **348**
History of Revelation ... 348
Connection to the Previous Verse ... 349
Importance of Ṣalāh, Especially the Middle Prayer ... 349
Keys of Guidance ... 350

Verse 239 ... **351**
Keys of Guidance ... 352

Verse 240 ... **353**
Connection with the Previous Verses ... 353
Keys of Guidance ... 356

Verse 241 ... **357**
Keys of Guidance ... 358

Verse 242 ... **359**
Keys of Guidance ... 359

Verse 243 ... **359**
History of Revelation ... 360
Connection with the Previous Verses ... 360
Commentary ... 361
Keys of Guidance ... 362

Verse 244 ... **362**
Keys of Guidance ... 363

Verse 245 ... **363**
History of Revelation ... 364
Connection with the Previous Verses ... 364
Commentary ... 365
Why the Phrase "A Loan to Allah ﷻ"? ... 365
Keys of Guidance ... 366

Verse 246 .... **367**
Connection with the Previous Verses 368
Lessons from the History of the Children of Isrā'īl 368
Keys of Guidance 371
Verse 247 .... **372**
Keys of Guidance 373
Verse 248 .... **374**
Keys of Guidance 375
Verse 249 .... **378**
Keys of Guidance 380
Verse 250 .... **381**
Keys of Guidance 382
Verse 251 .... **383**
Keys of Guidance 387
Verse 252 .... **388**
Keys of Guidance 388
Personalities Mentioned **393**
Glossary of Terms **395**
Index **405**
About the Board ʿĀlim **415**

Start of the Second Section *(Juzʾ)* of the Noble Qurʾān

Verse 142

سَيَقُولُ ٱلسُّفَهَآءُ مِنَ ٱلنَّاسِ مَا وَلَّىٰهُمْ عَن قِبْلَتِهِمُ ٱلَّتِى كَانُوا۟ عَلَيْهَا ۚ قُل
لِّلَّهِ ٱلْمَشْرِقُ وَٱلْمَغْرِبُ ۚ يَهْدِى مَن يَشَآءُ إِلَىٰ صِرَٰطٍ مُّسْتَقِيمٍ ﴿١٤٢﴾

The (hypocritical) fools among the people say: "What has turned them (the Muslims) from the *qiblah* (direction) which they were facing (in the prayer)?" Say (O Muḥammad ﷺ to them): "To Allah belongs the East and the West. He guides whomever He wills to a Straight Path."

The Event of the Shift of the Qiblah

An example of His Divine guidance shining on the believers. This verse and a few verses later on examine one of the most important developments in the history of Islam, which caused a commotion among the people.

As we know, Prophet Muḥammad ﷺ and the early community of believers in Mecca performed their daily prayers facing Jerusalem *(Bayt al-Muqaddas)* by the command of Allah ﷻ. This was the standard for the first 13 years during the mission in Mecca, and a few months after the migration to the city of Medina. However, in the post-migration period the *qiblah* was changed and the Muslims were directed to now face the Kaʿbah in Mecca whenever they offer their prayers.

The Jews were disappointed, and according to their previously-seen ways which the Qurʾān references in many places, they began to make more excuses why they would not accept Prophet Muḥammad ﷺ and the teachings that he was bringing.

In this verse, Allah ﷻ states that very soon, the simple-minded people will ask the Muslims to turn back to the previous *qiblah* which they used to face during their prayers.

In essence, the Jews were saying to the Muslims that: What is the rationale behind the change in your *qiblah*? If your original *qiblah* was correct then why the change; and if your new *qiblah* is the right one, then why did you pray in the direction of Jerusalem for over 13 years?

The word which Allah ﷻ uses to describe these people is 'fools' *(as-sufahā')* and it is the plural of *safīyah,* and literally it means 'a person whose body is very light and easily moves around in the wind by itself or if one is pushed.' The word gradually took on the meaning of a simple-minded person - whether it comes to religious issues or secular affairs.

Allah ﷻ then directed His Prophet ﷺ to say to everyone - the Jews who were living at that time and were constantly trying to find faults with him and his message; and also addressing the Muslims - reminding them that to Allah ﷻ belongs the East and West, and He guides whomever He wants to the Straight Path.

This verse served to put an end to those who were questioning this issue that whether it is Jerusalem or the Kaʿbah, every place and every land belongs solely to Allah ﷻ and the House of Allah ﷻ is not limited - what matters is that a person sincerely and whole-heartedly submits to His commands.

In addition, the changing of the *qiblah* was also one of the many testing stages for the Muslims, and another step in their evolutionary progress of spiritual perfection, and each one of these tests that Allah ﷻ was putting the Muslims through was an example of His Divine guidance shining on the believers.

Keys of Guidance

- Muslims need to constantly anticipate the conspiracies, rumors, and excuses of the enemies, and be prepared to respond to them in order to stop their influence and prevent the spread of such plots against Islam.
- The sanctity and dignity of both sacred times and places does not depend on the believers, but rather these are determined by Allah ﷻ.

Verse 143

وَكَذَٰلِكَ جَعَلْنَٰكُمْ أُمَّةً وَسَطًا لِّتَكُونُوا۟ شُهَدَآءَ عَلَى ٱلنَّاسِ وَيَكُونَ
ٱلرَّسُولُ عَلَيْكُمْ شَهِيدًا ۗ وَمَا جَعَلْنَا ٱلْقِبْلَةَ ٱلَّتِى كُنتَ عَلَيْهَآ إِلَّا لِنَعْلَمَ
مَن يَتَّبِعُ ٱلرَّسُولَ مِمَّن يَنقَلِبُ عَلَىٰ عَقِبَيْهِ ۚ وَإِن كَانَتْ لَكَبِيرَةً إِلَّا عَلَى
ٱلَّذِينَ هَدَى ٱللَّهُ ۗ وَمَا كَانَ ٱللَّهُ لِيُضِيعَ إِيمَٰنَكُمْ ۚ إِنَّ ٱللَّهَ بِٱلنَّاسِ لَرَءُوفٌ
رَّحِيمٌ ﴿١٤٣﴾

And in that way We have made you (Muslims) a balanced community that you may be witnesses for the people, and that the Messenger (Muḥammad ﷺ) may be a witness over you. We did not previously appoint (Jerusalem) the direction to turn in the prayer except that We may determine who truly follows the Messenger, from one who turns back on one's heels. And indeed that testing was burdensome, except for those whom Allah guided, and Allah will never let your faith go to waste. Surely Allah is for the people, All-Kind *(Ra'ūf)*, All-Merciful *(Raḥīm)*.

A Balanced, Middle Nation

This verse refers to a portion of the philosophy and secrets of why the *qiblah* was altered.

In introducing the blessings which are seen in this verse, Allah ﷻ uses the word translated as 'and in that way' *(kadhālika)*. This preposition is used to refer to 'something far away,' and here it takes on the meaning of great blessings which are given to a community - someone or something 'far away' - spiritually.

This verse has two distinct meanings - a general one and a specific one, and we will review both - starting with the general understanding.

Allah ﷻ first reminds the Muslims at the time of Prophet Muḥammad ﷺ that just as their *qiblah* is a 'middle' *qiblah*, We have made you, the

Muslims, a 'middle' nation - in moderation, between the two extremes.

The *qiblah* of the Muslims is considered to be a 'middle *qiblah*' from a geographical point of view because historians have noted that Christians would face eastwards to face their *qiblah*, the birthplace of Prophet 'Isā ﷺ in Jerusalem. The Jews, who primarily lived in Shāmāt and Babylon stood facing Jerusalem, which for them was to the west.

However the Kaʿbah, which in relation to where the Muslims of that time were living, namely Medina - was almost due south.

Interestingly, the special attention which the Muslims gave to determine the direction of the Kaʿbah caused the science of geography to flourish among Muslims at the beginning of Islam, because they needed to be able to determine the direction of the *qiblah* from anywhere in the world that they were.

Allah ﷻ then adds that being a middle-nation means that the Muslims will be a witness over the people, and that Prophet Muḥammad ﷺ will be a witness over all of them.

The Muslim nation *(ummah)* being a witness over the people of the world, and Prophet Muḥammad ﷺ being a witness over the Muslims may refer to them being exemplary role models, because witnesses are always chosen from among the best people of a group. Thus, this means that by the mere fact that the Muslims have such a balanced set of theological beliefs and teachings, they are the ideal nation for others to follow, just like Prophet Muḥammad ﷺ is an exemplary individual for all of humanity, but specifically the Muslims to take as a role model.

Allah ﷻ then points to another reason for the changing of the *qiblah* and states that this was done only to distinguish those who follow Prophet Muḥammad ﷺ from those who turn their back on him, and Allah ﷻ adds that this change was difficult for people to accept - except those whom Allah ﷻ guided.

Indeed, unless there is Divine guidance, the spirit of absolute submission to His command will not be seen in an individual.

Finally, since the luring of the enemies or the unknowing friends thought that by changing the *qiblah*, the previous good deeds and actions of worship may be rendered null and void since they were done in a different direction, Allah ﷻ adds that the prayers and acts of worship which were done facing the former *qiblah* are all valid, and Allah ﷻ would never waste one's faith - meaning the good deeds - because Allah ﷻ is All-Kind and All-Compassionate.

Wisdom behind the Change in Qiblah

During the initial stages of the birth and growth of Islam, the Kaʿbah located in the city of Mecca was the center of idolatry, and thus the Muslims were ordered to temporarily pray toward the direction of Jerusalem, ensuring a separation from the ranks of the pagans.

However, when the Muslims migrated to the city of Medina, formed a government and became a distinct group, then it was no longer required to continue praying in the direction of Jerusalem, and thus Allah ﷻ decreed that they should now turn toward the Kaʿbah in Mecca for their acts of worship - the building which is the oldest center of Monotheism *(Tawḥīd)* and the first place of worship for the past Prophets.

It should be noted that the Kaʿbah was still being used as a house of worship for the polytheists and hundreds of idols were still housed in and around the Kaʿbah, and it was not until the ninth year after the migration when the victory of Mecca took place that the house became purified of the idols and idol worshiping and all traces of idolatry were removed.

Obviously, this shift was difficult for the Muslims at two different levels:

1. Initially, they were forced to pray toward the direction of Jerusalem, knowing that the Kaʿbah was the true spiritual capital of their faith, and they had become habituated to facing Jerusalem;
2. With the shift in the *qiblah*, they now had to change their direction of prayer and face the city of Mecca, after having prayed to Allah ﷻ facing Jerusalem for so many years and becoming accustomed to it.

The Muslims were being tested through this so that whatever effects of polytheism which may have been left in their psyche would burn in this fiery furnace of obedience to the rules of Allah ﷻ.

If there remained any bonds from the past days of idol worshiping, then it would be through the spirit of absolute submission to the commands of Allah ﷻ that they could be removed.

Specific Meaning of The Middle Nation

Although Allah ﷻ referred to the Muslims as the 'middle nation,' and this is one valid interpretation of this verse, however in *Tafsīre Tasnīm*, Āyatullāh Jawādī Āmulī, presents a nuanced commentary of this verse in Volume Seven which we have summarized and present below.

There are 'chosen ones' from among the Muslim community who have been exalted by Allah ﷻ due to their relationship to Prophet Muḥammad ﷺ - not merely a blood-line relation, but more so a spiritual connection to the Noble Messenger. The most perfect and complete manifestation of those who have that deep connection with the Prophet ﷺ are the 12 Immaculate Imāms of the Ahlul Bayt ﵈ - those who are, based on the permission of Allah ﷻ, constantly in the spiritual presence of the Prophet ﷺ, and will act as witnesses over the beliefs, actions, and morals of society.

In this verse, Allah ﷻ mentions the blessings of this middle nation by using the word translated as 'and in that way' *(kadhālika)*. This preposition refers to 'something spiritually distanced' - individuals who although are physically close to the Muslim community, however whose spiritual reality is something 'far away.' This same point can be seen in the beginning of Sūrah al-Baqarah when Allah ﷻ speaks about the Qur'ān by saying: 'That *(dhālika)* is the Book (the Qur'ān) in which there is no doubt.' Allah ﷻ is using the preposition 'that' *(dhālika)* which is used in Arabic for things which are far away from a person, and despite the fact that the physical Qur'ān which we have today in our hands is with us, however the meta-physical reality of the Qur'ān is something else so Allah ﷻ refers to The Book as being "far away" from us.

Similar are the Imāms of the Ahlul Bayt ﵈. Although during the first 240 or so years of Islam, the Imāms were "close" to society since they lived in the midst of the people, however they were in some regards, distanced from the masses - or we should say that the masses had distanced themselves away from the Ahlul Bayt ﵈.

In this verse, Allah ﷻ is referring to the axis point of this middle nation as being the witnesses *(shuhadāʾ)* - however as for who they are

- at one end of the spectrum is Prophet Muḥammad ﷺ, and at the other end of the spectrum is humanity.

However, this 'middle nation' which Allah ﷻ is referring to is not as some imagine, or what some feel: that the entire collective of the Muslim *ummah* is 'in the middle' - and the Jewish community and the Christian community are on the two ends. Rather, the correct interpretation is that this 'middle nation' or the 'axis point' refers to specific individuals, as is confirmed by multiple *ḥadīth.* These individuals are witnesses over humanity with the Prophet ﷺ being a witness over them; these individuals are the axis point between Prophet Muḥammad ﷺ and the Muslim nation; these people are unique personalities which have a God-granted status to stand in between certain people and act as witnesses during the time when Prophet Muḥammad ﷺ is in his intermediary *(barzakh)* life. Based on numerous *ḥadīth* from the Imāms of the Ahlul Bayt ؑ when commenting on this verse and who this middle nation is who are the witnesses, in one tradition Imām ʿAlī as-Sajjād ؑ is quoted as having said: "We (the Imāms of the Ahlul Bayt ؑ) are them (the witnesses of Allah ﷻ over all of humanity)."[1]

The meaning of witnessing in this verse is witnessing over the deeds of the people. Those who are tasked with being witnesses in the life of this world must be given thorough knowledge about the beliefs and actions of the people, and will then convey them on the Day of Resurrection. This testimony, in regards to matters of belief, morality, and the practical deeds is based on mystical and Divine teaching, not physical witnessing - as a physical witness can only see those actions which were performed or hear those words which were said - but they have no information about the intention behind why a person did a certain action or said a particular thing. On the Day of Judgment, people will not only be judged by their words or deeds, but more importantly behind the reason why these things were done. Therefore, such witnesses must have this kind of knowledge through a Divine source and of a higher type - meaning

---

[1] ʿAllāmah Majlisī, *Biḥār al-Anwār*, Vol. 23, Pg. 350. This tradition is as follows:

فِي قَوْلِهِ تَعَالَى لِتَكُونُوا شُهَدَاءَ عَلَى النَّاسِ قَالَ: نَحْنُ هُمْ.

the inner insight. The witnesses therefore, must be aware of the inner thoughts of each person in society if they are to witness and testify for, or against them and this is not at all possible for an average individual to carry out.

The position of being the final Messenger of Allah ﷻ gives the noble Prophet Muḥammad ﷺ the right to be a witness over the actions of humanity in the most complete fashion, and for perpetuity - both during his lifetime, and also in his current other world intermediary existence *(barzakhī),* and that too in all of the areas of a believer's life. Therefore, we recognize him as *Shahīd ash-Shuhadā'* - the Ultimate Witness over all other Witnesses.

In this regard, a *ḥadīth* states: "Indeed the order of Allah has been issued that there should be no disagreement among the believers, and for this reason He has made them witnesses over people. In this way, (Prophet) Muḥammad is a witness over us (the Imāms of the Ahlul Bayt ﷺ), and we are a witness over our followers (Shīʿah), while our Shīʿah are witnesses over the people."[2]

The famous companion, Salmān al-Muḥammadī (al-Fārisī) once asked Prophet Muḥammad ﷺ in regards to the verse under review that who is Allah ﷻ referring to as being the witnesses over humanity, to which the Prophet ﷺ replied: "They are 13 specific men - me, my brother ʿAlī, and the 11 [Imāms] from his children (meaning the Divinely-ordained Leaders after him)."[3]

To conclude, we quote one final *ḥadīth*, this time from Imām ʿAlī ؑ in which he is reported to have said: "Indeed Allah, the Blessed and Exalted, has purified us, protected us (from all types of transgressions), and He has made us as the witnesses over His creations and His representatives

---

[2] Ḥuwayzī, ʿAbd ʿAli ibn Jumuʿah al-, *Tafsīr Nūr ath-Thaqalayn*, Vol. 1, Pg. 710. The initial portion of this tradition is as follows:

وَلَقَدْ قُضِىَ الْأَمْرُ أَنْ لَا يَكُونَ بَيْنَ الْمُؤْمِنِينَ اخْتِلَافٌ...

[3] Bayāḍhī, ʿAlī ibn Yūnis al-ʿĀmilī al-, *Aṣ-Ṣirāṭ al-Mustaqīm*, Vol. 2, Pg. 118. This tradition is as follows:

هُمْ ثَلَاثَةَ عَشَرَ رَجُلًا خَاصَّةً أَنَا وَأَخِى عَلِيٌّ ؑ وَأَحَدَ عَشَرَ مِنْ وُلْدِهِ.

upon His Earth; and He has made us to be with the Qur'ān and has made the Qur'ān to be with us - we will never separate ourselves from it (the Qur'ān), nor will it (the Qur'ān) ever separate itself from us."[4]

Keys of Guidance

- The saints *(awliyā')*, by the permission of Allah ﷻ, are able to see and witness all of our actions. The Qur'ān testifies in this verse and other verses that there are some human beings whom Allah ﷻ permits to have the ability to observe all of the actions and behaviors of the people - not only during their 'lives' in this world, but even after they physically pass away from this transient abode they are still allowed this honor, and have the vision to 'see' their followers and other people - thus, they continue to be witnesses over all of humanity.
- We should never become laid back or comfortable with anything - even the commandments of Allah ﷻ because it is possible that we may be obligated to perform a particular action for a time frame, and then contrary to our expectations, Allah ﷻ will change that - forcing us to break our habits.
- The rules and regulations of Islam, as the senior scholars have defined them, may change over time due to the process of independent reasoning and research *(ijtihād)*. This will not render our previous deeds worthless, as they are still accepted by Allah ﷻ, however when a scholar issues a new verdict, his followers need to accept his reasoning and submit to the laws by following the new rulings.
- All of the evolutionary and legislational changes and developments which come about in Islam are due to the Mercy and Compassion of Allah ﷻ - He does not want to make life difficult for us.

---

[4] Shaykh Kulaynī, *Al-Kāfī*, Vol. 1, Pg. 191. The initial portion of this tradition is as follows:

إِنَّ اللّٰهَ تَبَارَكَ وَتَعَالَى طَهَّرَنَا وَعَصَمَنَا وَجَعَلَنَا شُهَدَآءَ عَلَى خَلْقِهِ وَحُجَّتَهُ فِي أَرْضِهِ...

Verse 144

قَدْ نَرَىٰ تَقَلُّبَ وَجْهِكَ فِى ٱلسَّمَآءِ ۖ فَلَنُوَلِّيَنَّكَ قِبْلَةً تَرْضَىٰهَا ۚ فَوَلِّ وَجْهَكَ شَطْرَ ٱلْمَسْجِدِ ٱلْحَرَامِ ۚ وَحَيْثُ مَا كُنتُمْ فَوَلُّوا۟ وُجُوهَكُمْ شَطْرَهُۥ ۗ وَإِنَّ ٱلَّذِينَ أُوتُوا۟ ٱلْكِتَـٰبَ لَيَعْلَمُونَ أَنَّهُ ٱلْحَقُّ مِن رَّبِّهِمْ ۗ وَمَا ٱللَّهُ بِغَـٰفِلٍ عَمَّا يَعْمَلُونَ ﴿١٤٤﴾

Certainly We have seen you (O Muḥammad ﷺ) often turning your face toward heaven. (Do not worry for) We will surely turn you toward a direction *(qiblah)* that will please you. (Now the time has come so) turn your face toward the Sacred Mosque *(Masjid al-Ḥarām)*. (And you too, O believers also) turn your faces toward it wherever you are. Surely those who were given the Book do know (the coming of this Prophet and this change of *qiblah*) to be true (commandments) from their Lord, and Allah is not unaware of what they do.

Wherever You Are, Turn Toward the Kaʿbah

In this verse, in which the command to change the *qiblah* was issued, Allah ﷻ begins by telling Prophet Muḥammad ﷺ that He sees the Prophet ﷺ turning toward the sky to determine the final *qiblah* which his community will turn to, and that Allah ﷻ has finally decreed that the Muslims should stop facing Jerusalem, and instead face toward Mecca and the Sacred Mosque *(Masjid al-Ḥarām)*.

It was at this point that Allah ﷻ told Prophet Muḥammad ﷺ to turn his face toward the Sacred Mosque - not only for those who are in the city of Medina, but rather for everyone, wherever they may be.

According to the narrations, the order to change the *qiblah* was sent down during the noon *(Ẓuhr)* prayer and was to be carried out immediately.

Historians note that the Angel of Revelation, Jibrāʾīl ؑ, took the arm of the Prophet ﷺ and physically turned his body from the direction of Jerusalem which was north-west from the city of Medina, and made him face toward the Kaʿbah in Mecca which was south-east from the city of Medina. It was not only the Prophet ﷺ who made this shift, but when the Muslims saw this change occurring, they realized that they too needed to change the direction, so during the course of their noon prayer they also turned in the same direction as the Prophet.

Interestingly, the change of *qiblah* is actually one of the signs of the Final Messenger, Prophet Muḥammad ﷺ mentioned in the previous Books which Allah ﷻ revealed to the past generations, so when the People of the Book heard that the *qiblah* had changed, they realized that this was their Promised Messenger.

The Qurʾān addresses this saying that those who had previously received Books from Allah ﷻ know very well that this change is a true command issued by their Lord because they had documented evidence of this in their Books that the Final Promised Messenger of Allah ﷻ will pray toward two different directions.

Allah ﷻ concludes by reminding the non-believers who heard about this, and saw the change in *qiblah* that Allah ﷻ is not unaware of their nefarious actions in hiding these verses from their co-religionists. Instead of introducing the change of *qiblah* as a sign of the truthfulness of Prophet Muḥammad ﷺ, the Jews and Christians worked to conceal this reality which was mentioned in their own Books, and they created a controversy over it.

Specifics on the Changing of the Qiblah[5]

The change of *qiblah* took place in the month of Rajab, in the second year after the migration (624 CE) after the revelation of this verse.

According to the majority of historiographers, this event took place in *Masjid al-Qiblatayn*, which literally means Mosque of the Two *Qiblahs* in the city of Medina during the noon prayer.

An interesting point which many have questioned is in regards to

---

[5] Extracted and summarized from the article found on en.wikishia.net/view/Change_of_the_Qibla. (Last accessed on September 14, 2022)

how the redirection of the *qiblah* took place during the middle of a congregational prayer - a change in the direction in which they were praying in which they were obligated by Allah ﷻ to to turn by over 180 degrees.

How was the Qiblah Redirected?

According to some narrations, on the day of the change of the *qiblah*, Prophet Muḥammad ﷺ was performing the noon prayer in the direction of Jerusalem. As usual, the men were saying their prayers behind him, and women were saying their prayers behind the men - or in other reports, they were standing beside the men with a curtain in between them.

After performing two units *(rakaʿāt)* of the noon *(Ẓuhr)* prayer, Angel Jibrāʾīl ؑ descended to Prophet Muḥammad ﷺ by the permission of Allah ﷻ, and began to reveal verse 144 of Sūrah al-Baqarah to him, directing him to turn toward the Kaʿbah in Mecca.[6]

There are differences in the accounts of when this change was ordered, and whether or not prayers were being performed at the time of the redirection, and therefore in some accounts, it has been narrated that this occurred in the afternoon *(ʿAṣr)* prayer, while others report that it was during the morning *(Fajr)* prayer.[7]

The Place

There is no agreement among the historians as to where the redirection of the *qiblah* occurred, and therefore three places have been mentioned in the historical sources:

1. The Masjid in the area of Banū Salima in the north-western part

---

[6] Hāshimī, Abū ʿAbdillāh Muḥammad ibn Saʿd al-, *Aṭ-Ṭabaqāt al-Kubrā*, Vol. 1, Pg. 186; Shaykh Ṣadūq, *Man lā Yaḥḍuruhu al-Faqīh*, Vol. 1, Pg. 275.

[7] *Aṭ-Ṭabaqāt al-Kubrā*, Vol. 1, Pp. 186-7; Muṭṭalibī, Abū ʿAbdillāh Muḥammad ibn Isḥāq al-, *ʿUyūn al-Athar*, Vol. 1, Pg. 269.

of Medina[8] known as Masjid Dhūl Qiblatayn.[9] The majority of the historians take this to be the place where the redirection occurred.[10]

2. The Masjid of the Banū Sālim ibn ʿAwf tribe where Prophet Muḥammad ﷺ performed his first Friday *(Jumuʿah)* prayer.[11]
3. The Masjid of the Prophet ﷺ - Masjid an-Nabawī.[12]

A Unique Challenge vis-a-vis the Congregational Prayer

Jerusalem is located north-west of the city of Medina, while the Kaʿbah which is located in *Masjid al-Ḥarām* is south-east of Medina. Therefore, Prophet Muḥammad ﷺ had to turn his entire body close to 180 degrees![13]

According to some narrations, the men were standing on the right side of the room while the women were on the left side with a curtain in between them in the house of Banū Sālim. Some reports note that Imām ʿAlī ﷺ was in the last row of the congregational prayer, and thus when Prophet Muḥammad ﷺ turned, he ended up being in the last row with Imām ʿAlī ﷺ now standing in the first row, so he stepped forward and became the imām of the prayers - replacing Prophet Muḥammad ﷺ.

However, according to other reports, Prophet Muḥammad ﷺ was still 'leading' this congregational prayer. This has led some people to question how this event played out. If those praying behind Prophet Muḥammad ﷺ turned, they would now be standing in front of him, as they had all turned 180 degrees, although he was still technically leading[14]

---

[8] Qā'idān, *Tārīkh wa Āthār-i Islāmī-yi Makkah wa Madīna Munawwarah*, Pg. 268.

[9] Baghdādī, Abū ʿAbdillāh Muḥammad ibn Maḥmūd al-, *Ad-Durra ath-Thamīna*, Pg. 115; *ʿUyūn al-Athar*, Vol. 1, Pg. 308.

[10] *Aṭ-Ṭabaqāt al-Kubrā*, Vol. 1, Pg. 186; Yaʿqūbī, Aḥmad ibn Abī Yaʿqūb al-, *Tārīkh al-Yaʿqūbī*, Vol. 2, Pg. 42; Zamakhsharī, Abūl Qāsim Maḥmūd ibn ʿUmar al-, *Al-Kashshāf*, Vol. 1, Pg. 202.

[11] Qummī, Abūl Ḥasan ʿAlī ibn Ibrāhīm al-, *Tafsīr al-Qummī*, Vol. 1, Pg. 63.

[12] *Aṭ-Ṭabaqāt al-Kubrā*, Vol. 1, Pg. 185; Samhūdī, Nūr ad-Dīn ʿAlī ibn ʿAbdullāh al-, *Wafāʾ al-Wafā*, Vol. 1, Pg. 278.

[13] *Ad-Durra ath-Thamīna*, Pg. 126.

[14] The historical accounts of this event differ and so in some opinions, as we

the congregational *(jamāʿah)* prayer. As for whether the women praying beside the men with a curtain separating them became aware of this change in direction is not clear from the historical records. However, what is perplexing is that seeing as how everyone had turned around 180 degrees, this would mean that the prayer leader was now standing at the back of the congregation, and not in front of the men as was the common method.[15]

In order to understand what happened, we can refer to some historical sources which note that after the change of the *qiblah* to the Kaʿbah, Prophet Muḥammad ﷺ physically moved from his place - which would now be the back of the masjid to the other end of the masjid[16] - now considered the front - and the men and women present all turned to face the Kaʿbah.[17]

It must be noted that the prayer which Muslims perform today cannot be compared with the prayers the Muslims performed both before and after the migration to Medina. The *ṣalāh* with Muslims perform is now an established practice and no new laws can come to add or take away from the style of the *ṣalāh*.

However, during the time of the Noble Prophet of Islam ﷺ, rules were being taught to the new community in stages and this meant that there would be development of the process of worship - and *ṣalāh* was one of these areas which would undergo a transformation from the first prayers in Mecca until the time of the death of Prophet Muḥammad ﷺ.

When Allah ﷻ send the direct command *(ḥukm)* to change the direction of *qiblah*, the Noble Prophet ﷺ was obligated to establish the command of Allah immediately and to inform the Muslim community.

---

previously noted, Imām ʿAlī ؑ lead the remainder of the prayers with the Prophet ﷺ behind him; in other historical sources, Prophet Muḥammad ﷺ moved to the front to lead the prayers.

[15] Shāmī, Muḥammad ibn Yūsuf al-, *Subul al-Hudā*, Vol. 3, Pg. 370.

[16] *Ad-Durra ath-Thamīna*, Pg. 126; *Subul al-Hudā*, Vol. 3, Pg. 370.

[17] *Aṭ-Ṭabaqāt al-Kubrā*, Vol. 1, Pg. 186; *ʿUyūn al-Athar*, Vol. 1, Pg. 269; *Wafāʾ al-Wafā*, Vol. 1, Pg. 278.

The trusted Noble Prophet ﷺ is the *shāriʿ* - that is, the one obligated to establish the laws sent by Allah ﷻ, and the people trusted in him that they would follow his every movement. It is for this reason that when it came to how to pray, as the Qurʾān is silent on the methodology of how to perform the *ṣalāh*, the Noble Prophet ﷺ has been quoted as saying: "Pray! Just as you see me pray."[18]

Based on this account, Prophet Muḥammad ﷺ, the leader of the congregational prayer did not simply turn 180 degrees[19] or 160 degrees, but also physically walked to the other side of the masjid in order for there to be enough space for men and women saying their prayers behind him to move to form new rows of the congregational prayer.[20]

It should be noted that historians are not clear about how large this masjid was, or how many people were actually praying with Prophet Muḥammad ﷺ when the order to change the direction came to him.

Reasons for the Change of the Qiblah

Commentators of the Qurʾān have mentioned different reasons for the change of the *qiblah*:

1. During the time when Prophet Muḥammad ﷺ lived in Mecca, the Kaʿbah was full of idols which the polytheists used to worship. Thus, Prophet Muḥammad ﷺ complied with the Divine command to temporarily turn toward Jerusalem so as to differentiate himself, the Muslims, and their worship from the direction of worship which the polytheists where engaged in.[21]
2. When the Islamic government of Prophet Muḥammad ﷺ was established in the city of Medina, the Muslim community had gained some sense of stability and were now distinguished from others. Thus, it was not necessary for Jerusalem to be their direction

[18] *Biḥār al-Anwār*, Vol. 82, Pg. 279. This tradition is as follows:

صَلُّو كَمَا رَأَيْتُمُونِي أُصَلِّي.

[19] *Tārīkh wa Āthār-i Islāmī-yi Makkah wa Madīna Munawwarah*, Pg. 306.

[20] *Wafāʾ al-Wafā*, Vol. 3, Pg. 372.

[21] *Al-Kashshāf*, Vol. 1, Pg. 200.

of prayer anymore, and since Prophet Muḥammad ﷺ wanted there to be a redirection of the *qiblah,* the obvious choice was the Kaʿbah which was the oldest house of Monotheism *(Tawḥīd),* and the original home of the past Prophets. After the ruling of the new *qiblah*, the Muslims were now clearly distinguished from the Jews who also turned toward Jerusalem for their acts of devotion.[22]

3. When Prophet Muḥammad ﷺ migrated to the city of Medina, the Jews took his direction of worship toward Jerusalem to be evidence of a defect in Islam and the truthfulness of Judaism - as has been quoted in the Qur'ān in two instances: "Those to whom We gave the Book (before) know him (the Messenger with all of his distinguishing attributes including the direction where he will turn to in the prayer) as they know their own sons. Yet a party among them conceal the truth and they do it knowingly."[23] As well Allah ﷻ says: "Those who were given the Book (before) know him (the Messenger with all of his distinguishing attributes) as they know their own sons; yet those who ruin their own selves (by concealing this truth, being overcome by their lusts and worldly interests) - they do not believe."[24] Therefore, according to some reports, the Jews in the city of Medina claimed that the Muslims had no prayer direction of their own, so they had instructed the Muslims to turn toward Jerusalem.[25]
4. The redirection of the *qiblah* was a test for those who claimed

---

[22] Shaykh Ṭūsī, *At-Ṭibyān*, Vol. 2, Pg. 5; Rāzī, Abul Futūḥ ar-, *Rawḍ al-Jinān*, Vol. 2, Pg. 203; Ṭabarsī, Aḥmad ibn Abī Ṭālib aṭ-, *Majmaʿ al-Bayān*, Vol. 1, Pp. 412-4.

[23] Qur'ān, Sūrah al-Baqarah (2), Verse 146:

ٱلَّذِينَ ءَاتَيْنَـٰهُمُ ٱلْكِتَـٰبَ يَعْرِفُونَهُۥ كَمَا يَعْرِفُونَ أَبْنَآءَهُمْ ۖ وَإِنَّ فَرِيقًا مِّنْهُمْ لَيَكْتُمُونَ ٱلْحَقَّ وَهُمْ يَعْلَمُونَ ﴿١٤٦﴾

[24] Ibid., Sūrah al-Anʿām (6), Verse 20:

ٱلَّذِينَ ءَاتَيْنَـٰهُمُ ٱلْكِتَـٰبَ يَعْرِفُونَهُۥ كَمَا يَعْرِفُونَ أَبْنَآءَهُمُ ۘ ٱلَّذِينَ خَسِرُوٓا۟ أَنفُسَهُمْ فَهُمْ لَا يُؤْمِنُونَ ﴿٢٠﴾

[25] Ṭabarī, Abū Jaʿfar Muḥammad al-, *Jāmiʿ al-Bayān*, Vol. 1, Pg. 400.

to be sincere Muslims[26] because the true followers accepted this command without questioning or reluctance, but those who were not true believers started to ask questions, just like the Jews had done during the time of Prophet Mūsā ﵇, and even much later when Prophet Muḥammad ﷺ came on the scene and introduced himself as the Promised Messenger sent by Allah ﷻ - and it was these individuals who found it difficult to comply with this order.[27]

Reactions and Consequences

The redirection of the *qiblah* was followed by reactions and consequences.

A number of Muslims were worried about the loss of Divine rewards for their own past prayers, or the prayers of their deceased predecessors,[28] so to respond to and console them, Prophet Muḥammad ﷺ recited the following verse of the Qur'ān to them: "...And Allah will never let your faith go to waste. Surely Allah is to the people All-Kind, All-Compassionate."[29 & 30]

Thus, the biased polytheists and enemies of Islam could no longer reproach Muslims because of their turning toward Jerusalem in the early years of their conversion to Islam.

At the same time, the changing of the *qiblah* also affected many people living in the Arabian Peninsula in a positive manner because they loved the Kaʿbah and had an affinity to it. Thus, they became more sympathetic to the cause of Islam as is noted in the Qur'ān: "From wherever you go out (for journeying), turn your face (O Messenger) toward the Sacred Mosque (in prayer). Wherever you may be, (O you who believe) turn your faces toward it so that the people may not have an argument against

---

[26] *Al-Kashshāf,* Vol. 1, Pg. 200.

[27] *Jāmiʿ al-Bayān,* Vol. 2, Pg. 8.

[28] Sulaymān, Maqātil ibn, *Tafsīr Maqātil ibn Sulaymān,* Vol. 1, Pg. 146.

[29] Qur'ān, Sūrah al-Baqarah (2), Verse 143:

وَمَا كَانَ ٱللَّهُ لِيُضِيعَ إِيمَـٰنَكُمْ ۚ إِنَّ ٱللَّهَ بِٱلنَّاسِ لَرَءُوفٌ رَّحِيمٌ ﴿١٤٣﴾

[30] Bayhaqī, Abū Bakr Aḥmad ibn Ḥusayn al-, *Dalā'il an-Nubuwwah,* Vol. 2, Pg. 575; *Majmaʿ al-Bayān,* Vol. 1, Pg. 417.

you - unless they are those immersed in wrongdoing..."[31]

One of the groups opposed to the change in the *qiblah* were the Jews of the Arabian Peninsula, most notably those who lived in and around the city of Medina. They were displeased by the redirection and began to spread propaganda against the Muslims, as Allah ﷻ has referenced: "The (hypocritical) fools among the people will say: 'What has turned them from the direction which they used to face (in the prayer)?' Say (O Muḥammad): 'To Allah belongs the East and the West (and therefore the whole Earth with its Easts and Wests - in whatever direction He wants us to turn, we will turn). He guides whomsoever He wills to the Straight Path.'"[32]

Keys of Guidance

- The legislation and the change of rulings all come from Allah ﷻ, and as such Prophet Muḥammad ﷺ or his Divinely-appointed successors, the Imāms of the Ahlul Bayt ؑ do not issue any orders from themselves.
- Allah ﷻ seeks the pleasure of His Messenger ﷺ, and the pleasure of Allah ﷻ lies in the pleasure of His Messenger ﷺ.
- The orders of the religion are not harsh, and this can be seen in the verse of the change of the *qiblah* where Allah ﷻ directs the Muslims to stand facing the Sacred Mosque, but He does not say that exactly face the Kaʿbah.

---

[31] Qur'ān, Sūrah al-Baqarah (2), Verse 150:

وَمِنْ حَيْثُ خَرَجْتَ فَوَلِّ وَجْهَكَ شَطْرَ ٱلْمَسْجِدِ ٱلْحَرَامِ ۚ وَحَيْثُ مَا كُنتُمْ فَوَلُّوا وُجُوهَكُمْ
شَطْرَهُۥ لِئَلَّا يَكُونَ لِلنَّاسِ عَلَيْكُمْ حُجَّةٌ إِلَّا ٱلَّذِينَ ظَلَمُوا مِنْهُمْ...

[32] Ibid., Verse 142:

سَيَقُولُ ٱلسُّفَهَآءُ مِنَ ٱلنَّاسِ مَا وَلَّىٰهُمْ عَن قِبْلَتِهِمُ ٱلَّتِى كَانُوا عَلَيْهَا ۚ قُل لِّلَّهِ ٱلْمَشْرِقُ
وَٱلْمَغْرِبُ ۚ يَهْدِى مَن يَشَآءُ إِلَىٰ صِرَٰطٍ مُّسْتَقِيمٍ ﴿١٤٢﴾

Verse 145

وَلَئِنْ أَتَيْتَ ٱلَّذِينَ أُوتُوا۟ ٱلْكِتَـٰبَ بِكُلِّ ءَايَةٍ مَّا تَبِعُوا۟ قِبْلَتَكَ ۚ وَمَآ أَنتَ
بِتَابِعٍ قِبْلَتَهُمْ ۚ وَمَا بَعْضُهُم بِتَابِعٍ قِبْلَةَ بَعْضٍ ۚ وَلَئِنِ ٱتَّبَعْتَ أَهْوَآءَهُم مِّنۢ
بَعْدِ مَا جَآءَكَ مِنَ ٱلْعِلْمِ ۙ إِنَّكَ إِذًا لَّمِنَ ٱلظَّـٰلِمِينَ ﴿١٤٥﴾

Even if you (O Muḥammad ﷺ) were to bring to those who were given the Book (before you - the Jews and Christians) all kinds of signs and evidences, they would not follow your direction *(qiblah).* Indeed you are not a follower of their direction, nor are they followers of one another's direction. Were you to follow their fancies and desires after the knowledge has come to you, then you will surely be among the wrongdoers.

The Jews and Christians will Never be Pleased

In the interpretation of the previous verse, we read that the People of the Book knew that the changing of the *qiblah* was one of the signs of the legitimacy of Prophet Muḥammad ﷺ and his message, however their prejudices prevented them from accepting him.

Here Allah ﷻ reveals that even if Prophet Muḥammad ﷺ was to bring the Jews and Christians a sign and proof of His claims to Prophethood, they would still not accept Islam - which Allah ﷻ has respectfully noted as that they would not follow His *qiblah.*

Allah ﷻ then adds that Prophet Muḥammad ﷺ will also never follow their *qiblah* - their religions or teachings, and that the Jews and Christians should not think that it is possible to change the *qiblah* back again because now this is the permanent and final one for the Muslims.

Allah ﷻ goes on to say that the Jews and Christians which are living around Prophet Muḥammad ﷺ and the Muslims in the city of Medina are so fanatical in their beliefs that none of them will follow the *qiblah* of one another - neither will the Jews follow the Christian direction of prayer, nor will the Christians follow the Jewish direction of prayer.

To further emphasize and conclude this statement, Allah ﷻ warns Prophet Muḥammad ﷺ that if he, after having all of this awareness from Allah, ﷻ still wants to follow their whims and desires, then he and the believers will have done a great injustice to themselves!

In *Tafsīre Tasnīm*, under the commentary of this last portion of the verse, Āyatullāh Jawādī Amulī states that it is possible that although it seems that Allah ﷻ is warning Prophet Muḥammad ﷺ, however this may be an example - based on a famous Arabic proverb (إياك أعني واسمعي يا جرة) - in which a statement is made that carries a certain meaning, however it also brings with it a hidden meaning - there is something much deeper behind the words which the person speaking them intends to relate.

Thus, although Allah ﷻ is addressing Prophet Muḥammad ﷺ with these words, however the intended audience is the Muslim community.

As we know, the change of rulings is not in the hands of anyone other than Allah ﷻ which is manifest through the words of Prophet Muḥammad ﷺ and for this reason the addressee is the Prophet ﷺ himself.

Allah ﷻ uses this pattern of speech many times in the Qur'ān to warn Prophet Muḥammad ﷺ, but it is intended for the general people; for example He tells the Prophet not to follow the base desires. In other times, He warns the Prophet ﷺ that if he were to associate partners with Allah ﷻ, then all of his good actions would be destroyed, but obviously we know that Prophet Muḥammad ﷺ would never do such a thing due to his infallibility. At the same time though, he is also responsible to follow the same rules and regulations which all other Muslims are obligated to follow *(mukallaf)*.

Keys of Guidance

- In our society today, we see that those who follow falsehood have a strong conviction in what they believe, and they even promote it with pride and do not compromise. Here, Allah ﷻ is reminding us that we Muslims have the truth - *al-ḥaqq*; thus, we need to have positive pride, and never compromise our beliefs and ideals for anything!
- We must never give into the noise and clamor of the opponents of Islam, although they will try their best to divert the Muslims

from the straight path. We need to be firm and decisive in order to disappoint the enemies and stay firm on our true ways.

- Knowledge on its own is never enough to be guided to Allah ﷻ and the teachings of submission; rather a spirit of righteousness and humility is also necessary.

Verse 146

ٱلَّذِينَ ءَاتَيْنَٰهُمُ ٱلْكِتَٰبَ يَعْرِفُونَهُۥ كَمَا يَعْرِفُونَ أَبْنَآءَهُمْ ۖ وَإِنَّ فَرِيقًا مِّنْهُمْ لَيَكْتُمُونَ ٱلْحَقَّ وَهُمْ يَعْلَمُونَ ﴿١٤٦﴾

Those to whom We gave the Book (the Jews and Christians) know him (Prophet Muḥammad ﷺ) as they know their own sons. Yet a group from among them conceal the truth and they do it knowingly.

They Certainly Recognized Prophet Muḥammad ﷺ

Following the previous discussions about the stubbornness and prejudice of a group of the Jews and Christians, this verse informs the believers and non-believers living during the time of Prophet Muḥammad ﷺ about the Promised Messenger, Muḥammad ﷺ.

Those whom Allah ﷻ had given the previous Scriptures to by way of revelation, knew Prophet Muḥammad ﷺ just as they knew and recognized their own children because they had read his name and the signs of his advent in their own religious Books; however as Allah ﷻ states that some of them knowingly concealed the truth.

However, a group of them, seeing these clear signs accepted Islam - people such as ʿAbdullāh ibn Salām,[33] who was initially a Jewish scholar

---

[33] According to the researchers at IslamQuest, ʿAbdullāh ibn Salām ibn Ḥārith Isrāʾīlī was a Jewish scholar who some historians state that he converted to Islam in the first year after the migration *(hijrah)* to the city of Medina. Other scholars state that he converted to Islam two years before the death of Prophet Muḥammad ﷺ - meaning around the eighth year after migration.

but then accepted Islam; and he has been quoted as saying: "I recognize the Prophet of Islam better than I recognize my own son!"

🔑 Keys of Guidance

- If there is no spirit of truth-seeking within an individual, then just the fact that one is seeking and may gain some knowledge will never be enough to come to the path of true guidance. The Jews, with their deep knowledge of the Messenger of Allah ﷺ, being in his presence, speaking to him, seeing him giving them in-depth background about the Children of Isrāʾīl and what they had gone

---

In some of the commentaries of the Qurʾān, scholars have discussed some verses which have been interpreted as being revealed in honor of ʿAbdullāh ibn Salām, however these sorts of traditions and reports have been critiqued by Shīʿah and Sunnī commentators of the Qurʾān, as well as some historians.

ʿAbdullāh ibn Salām is an ambiguous and dubious personality in history which stems in part due to some of his actions after accepting Islam, such as his support for ʿUthmān ibn al-ʿAffān, his refusing to pledge allegiance to Imām ʿAlī ؈, and him adding many ḥadīth considered as Isrāʾīliyyāt within the texts of the interpretation of the Noble Qurʾān. Hence, it seems that there were nefarious hands at play which sought to raise his virtues in order to make it seem that he was greater than he actually was.

The term Isrāʾīliyyāt refers to those stories and concepts which have found their way into the commentary of the Qurʾān, ḥadīth, and stories of the faith however, are not rooted in the Qurʾān or the Prophetic teachings - it is also commonly referred to as the injection of Judeo-Christian Material in the Islamic source works. Rather, they are said to have originated from the Children of Isrāʾīl - the Jewish community - meaning that these were falsities which were introduced most notably by those claiming to be Muslims, having converted from Judaism. They brought their religious baggage with them and either intentionally or unintentionally, worked to corrupt Islam from within.

In any case, the Islamic sources agree that ʿAbdullāh ibn Salām became a Muslim based on his understanding of passages found in the Tawrāh or other Jewish works about the advent of the promised Messenger of Allah ﷺ; however with that said, one should not rule out the possibility that there are false reports concerning this individual. (Extracted from www.islamquest.net/fa/archive/question/fa22383. Last accessed on September 14, 2022)

through - still did not accept him.

- Muslims - who are followers of a faith which obligates its followers to be fair and just when dealing with everyone, including one's adversaries - must observe fairness with friends and foes alike. In this verse, the Qur'ān does not attribute the negative trait of intentionally concealing the truth to all of the People of the Book - because there were and still are decent and upright people among them as well.

Verse 147

ٱلۡحَقُّ مِن رَّبِّكَ فَلَا تَكُونَنَّ مِنَ ٱلۡمُمۡتَرِينَ ﴿١٤٧﴾

This is the truth from your Lord; so then be not from among the doubters.

To further emphasize what was previously mentioned in regards to the change in the *qiblah*, or rather as it can be considered as a complete shift in the practical rulings *(aḥkām)* of Islam, Allah ﷻ reiterates that the *qiblah* change is a true ruling from the Almighty - guiding the Muslims that they must never be in doubt in this, or other areas which in the future may result in changes to the Islamic rulings.

Although the direct addressee of this verse is Prophet Muḥammad ﷺ, however the actual audience is the entire Muslim community because a Prophet whose source of knowledge is spiritual witnessing *(shuhūd)* and is a recipient of revelation *(waḥī)* directly from Allah ﷻ would never have doubts or misgivings seeing as how for him, revelation *(waḥī)* is like a sixth sense, and it is the epitome of the 'Eye of Certainty' *('Ayn al-Yaqīn)*.[34]

Keys of Guidance

- The Truth *(al-Ḥaqq)* is from our Lord and Nurturer, and if we

---

[34] In the triad of the 'Knowledge of Certainty' *('Ilm al-Yaqīn)*, 'Eye of Certainty'

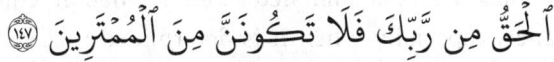

truly believe this and trust His Ability, Knowledge, Mercy, Love, and Intention to nurture us then we will not doubt His actions and wisdom - regardless of what happens in our lives. The stronger this belief and trust is, the stronger our resolve, submission, and actions will be.

- Orders and prohibitions which stem directly from Allah ﷻ and are communicated to humanity through a Prophet via revelation *(waḥī),* or through successfully transmitted narrations (*ḥadīth* that are *mutawātir)*[35] can never be disputed about, nor is there any room for denial of them.
- Leaders must be firm and determined when it comes to their governance, especially when it is determined that certain laws or traditions need to be changed, even if they go against established customs.

Verse 148

وَلِكُلٍّ وِجْهَةٌ هُوَ مُوَلِّيهَا ۖ فَاسْتَبِقُوا الْخَيْرَاتِ ۚ أَيْنَ مَا تَكُونُوا يَأْتِ بِكُمُ
اللَّهُ جَمِيعًا ۚ إِنَّ اللَّهَ عَلَىٰ كُلِّ شَيْءٍ قَدِيرٌ ﴿١٤٨﴾

And everyone has a direction toward which they turn, so strive together as if in a race, (O believers) toward all that is good. Wherever you may be, Allah will bring you all together. Surely

---

('Ayn al-Yaqīn), and the 'Truth of Certainty' *(Ḥaqq al-Yaqīn)* - the 'Eye of Certainty' can be likened to actually seeing the light of the flames of a fire, after having merely heard a description of that fire. This is the stage of knowledge before being consumed by the flames themselves which would be the 'Truth of Certainty.' The 'Eye of Certainty' is the 'inner eye or insight' and the opening of this eye only comes about through the Mercy of Allah ﷻ.

[35] A *ḥadīth* which is referred to as *mutawātir* is one which has been reported numerously by different narrators and through various chains of transmission, in a way that its authenticity is substantiated.

Allah over everything is All-Powerful.

Every Nation has a Focal Point for Prayer

This verse provides an answer to the Jewish community living during the time of Prophet Muḥammad ﷺ who caused a storm over the changing of the *qiblah* of the Muslims.

Allah ﷻ responds to them and reminds them that every group of people have their own *qiblah* - or focal point for prayers and acts of worship which He appoints for them; and it is Allah ﷻ who determines this direction, that is why the Muslims have now stopped praying in the direction of Jerusalem and have now turned to the Sacred Mosque in Mecca.

Throughout the history of the Prophets which Allah ﷻ sent to humanity, there have been different directions of prayer for each distinct group.

The direction of the *qiblah* is not like the Principles of Religion *(Uṣūl ad-Dīn)*[36] which can never change, and therefore Allah ﷻ tells the Jews that rather than directing your energies toward the change of the Muslim *qiblah* and direction of prayer, they should instead focus on excelling over one another in doing good deeds.

This is a theme which is seen later on in this chapter and will be discussed at length where Allah ﷻ says: "Godliness (and virtue) is not that you should turn your faces in the direction of the East and the West; but he is Godly who believes in Allah, and the Last Day, and the angels, and the Book, and the Prophets; and gives away of one's property with pleasure although they love it, to the relatives, and the orphans, and the destitute, and the wayfarer, and those who have to beg (or who need a loan), and for the liberation of slaves; and establishes the prayer *(ṣalāh);* and pays the (prescribed purifying) alms *(zakāh).* And those (are Godly) who fulfill their covenant when they have engaged in a covenant, and

---

[36] The *Uṣūl ad-Dīn* or Principles of Faith, also known as the Roots of Religion are a set of essential beliefs in every faith that a person claiming to follow that religion must believe in; otherwise one will not be considered as part of that faith tradition.

who are patient and persevering in misfortune, hardship, and disease, and at the time of stress (such as when there is a battle between truth and falsehood). Those are they who are true (in their faith), and those are they who have achieved righteousness, (piety and due reverence of Allah)."[37]

Then, as a warning to the critics, and an encouragement to the virtuous, Allah ﷻ reminds the people - not only the Jews living during the time of Prophet Muḥammad ﷺ but everyone - that wherever you are, Allah ﷻ will bring you all back to life one Day to present you with your rewards and punishments for the good and evil deeds that you performed in the life of this world.

Since it may be incomprehensible for certain people to understand how Allah ﷻ can collect the particles of the body of someone who has died after it may have fully decayed, and perhaps the bones which have now just turned to dust and have been blown away into various regions - how will they be gathered, covered with flesh, and brought back to life again, Allah ﷻ ends this verse by reminding humanity that this is all possible for Him because indeed Allah has Power over everything.

Keys of Guidance

- Uniformity in our faith can best be reflected in our congregational *(jamāʿah)* prayers where believers from all walks of life stand shoulder to shoulder, face the same *qiblah*, perform the same actions, recite the same *dhikr*, and are in total sync with one another in every single action and recitation.
- With life being so short, we need to let go of useless discussions,

[37] Qurʾān, Sūrah al-Baqarah (2), Verse 177:

لَّيْسَ ٱلْبِرَّ أَن تُوَلُّوا۟ وُجُوهَكُمْ قِبَلَ ٱلْمَشْرِقِ وَٱلْمَغْرِبِ وَلَـٰكِنَّ ٱلْبِرَّ مَنْ ءَامَنَ بِٱللَّهِ وَٱلْيَوْمِ
ٱلْـَٔاخِرِ وَٱلْمَلَـٰٓئِكَةِ وَٱلْكِتَـٰبِ وَٱلنَّبِيِّـۧنَ وَءَاتَى ٱلْمَالَ عَلَىٰ حُبِّهِۦ ذَوِى ٱلْقُرْبَىٰ وَٱلْيَتَـٰمَىٰ
وَٱلْمَسَـٰكِينَ وَٱبْنَ ٱلسَّبِيلِ وَٱلسَّآئِلِينَ وَفِى ٱلرِّقَابِ وَأَقَامَ ٱلصَّلَوٰةَ وَءَاتَى ٱلزَّكَوٰةَ وَٱلْمُوفُونَ
بِعَهْدِهِمْ إِذَا عَـٰهَدُوا۟ ۖ وَٱلصَّـٰبِرِينَ فِى ٱلْبَأْسَآءِ وَٱلضَّرَّآءِ وَحِينَ ٱلْبَأْسِ ۗ أُو۟لَـٰٓئِكَ ٱلَّذِينَ صَدَقُوا۟ ۖ
وَأُو۟لَـٰٓئِكَ هُمُ ٱلْمُتَّقُونَ ﴿١٧٧﴾

arguments which lead to nowhere, and words which cause hatred, animosity, and division. Instead, we must focus our time and energy on doing good deeds - actions which are endorsed by the Qur'ān, and the teachings of Prophet Muḥammad ﷺ and his Ahlul Bayt ؑ.

- In the world today, people are busy competing to try and surpass one another in material matters such as a greater net-worth, a larger mansion, luxurious cars, name-brand clothing, most expensive jewelry, latest gadgets, etc.; however more important than any of these is to compete with one another in acts of goodness and charity for the betterment of all of humanity.

Verse 149

وَمِنْ حَيْثُ خَرَجْتَ فَوَلِّ وَجْهَكَ شَطْرَ ٱلْمَسْجِدِ ٱلْحَرَامِ ۖ وَإِنَّهُۥ لَلْحَقُّ مِن

رَّبِّكَ ۗ وَمَا ٱللَّهُ بِغَٰفِلٍ عَمَّا تَعْمَلُونَ ﴿١٤٩﴾

And from wherever you go out, turn your face (O Muḥammad ﷺ) toward the Sacred Mosque. This is the truth from your Lord; and Allah is not unaware of what you do.

Have Reverence of Allah ﷻ Alone

This verse and the next one continues the theme about the changing of the *qiblah* and its consequences for the Muslims.

Allah ﷻ first focuses His attention and directs His speech to Prophet Muḥammad ﷺ, reminding him with a resolute commandment that wherever he is, when the time for prayer comes, he (and as an extension all Muslims) must turn their face toward the Sacred Mosque, and as a point of emphasis, Allah ﷻ adds that this is a true command from his Lord.

At the end of this verse, as a threat to the conspirators and a subtle piece of advice to the believers, Allah ﷻ reminds them that His Knowledge is vast, and that He is not at all unaware of what they do.

Keys of Guidance

- From such verses, Muslims throughout the ages have realized the importance of praying in the "right direction," and have excelled at geography, and the other sciences needed to ensure that their places of worship face the right direction, and that they too face Mecca when they offer their prayers. The rise of technology has allowed Muslims to create apps to accurately pinpoint the direction of the *qiblah* from any point on the Earth to ensure that they are facing the correct direction. In addition, scholars have given verdicts on how a person should pray while in a moving vehicle such as on a train or a plane, in order to ensure that a Muslim maintains the rules of facing the *qiblah* even while on a journey.

Verse 150

وَمِنْ حَيْثُ خَرَجْتَ فَوَلِّ وَجْهَكَ شَطْرَ ٱلْمَسْجِدِ ٱلْحَرَامِ ۚ وَحَيْثُ مَا كُنتُمْ
فَوَلُّوا۟ وُجُوهَكُمْ شَطْرَهُۥ لِئَلَّا يَكُونَ لِلنَّاسِ عَلَيْكُمْ حُجَّةٌ إِلَّا ٱلَّذِينَ
ظَلَمُوا۟ مِنْهُمْ فَلَا تَخْشَوْهُمْ وَٱخْشَوْنِى وَلِأُتِمَّ نِعْمَتِى عَلَيْكُمْ وَلَعَلَّكُمْ
تَهْتَدُونَ ﴿١٥٠﴾

And from wherever you go out, turn your face (O Muhammad ﷺ) toward the Sacred Mosque. And wherever you may be (O believers) turn your faces toward it, that the people may not have an argument against you - unless they be those immersed in wrongdoing; and hold not them in awe, but stand in awe of Me (Allah ﷻ) that I may complete My favor upon you, and that perhaps you may be entirely guided.

Once again in this verse, Allah ﷻ repeats the general rule of turning toward the Sacred Mosque at the time of prayers, and tells Prophet

Muḥammad ﷺ and the believers that wherever they go, they must turn themselves toward this Masjid in Mecca for their prayers.

As was seen in the previous verse, although the initial order was addressed directly to Prophet Muḥammad ﷺ, it should be clear that the intended recipients of this command are the entire community of believers because the order to face *Masjid al-Ḥarām* in Mecca during prayers is not only for Prophet Muḥammad ﷺ but for everyone, just like the change in the *qiblah* was for all Muslims to follow.

In the next portion of this verse, in order to emphasize and further clarify this ruling and its applicability, Allah ﷻ adds that whenever and wherever the believers travel or go anywhere, they must face Mecca and *Masjid al-Ḥarām.*

The next part of this verse provides three important points which Muslims need to keep in mind:

1. This verse wanted to silence the opposition as Allah ﷻ clearly states that the change in the direction of the *qiblah* was so that the oppressors - those who continued in their stubbornness against Islam - would have no claims to use in opposition to Prophet Muḥammad ﷺ because one of the signs of the Promised Prophet mentioned in their previous Scriptures was that he would pray in two different directions.
2. By Allah ﷻ referring to this stubborn group of individuals with the term of 'oppressors' *(ẓālim),* this may have frightened some believers, and therefore Allah ﷻ follows up His statement by reminding Prophet Muḥammad ﷺ and more importantly the believers that they must not be afraid of these people and that they should only have fear and awe of Allah ﷻ in their hearts. This is one of the basic principles of the Islamic Monotheism *(Tawḥīd)* in that it seeks to nurture the sense of not fearing anyone or anything other than Allah ﷻ.
3. Allah ﷻ concludes this verse by speaking about Him completing His blessings upon the believers, and affirms that the change of the *qiblah* was to allow the Muslims to spiritually and mentally evolve; and it was to free the young Muslim community from the bondage of prejudice, and that through this Allah ﷻ was actually

completing yet another round of His blessings upon the Muslims, to aide in their guidance.

In this verse, there is a portion which reads: '...that the people may not have an argument against you...' A question one may ask is: "What kind of *ḥujjah* and proof does turning toward the *qiblah* bring us?"

A *ḥujjah* is defined as: 'something which is a sign or a proof that guides us and others toward Allah ﷻ.' Praying in the direction of the *qiblah* at certain times, especially when praying in public places, creates a God-conscious atmosphere for ourselves, and is like a sign for others to be guided and reminded of Allah ﷻ.

Allah ﷻ also assures us that we must not be afraid of turning toward Him for worship in public spaces. Many times, we see that when believers are traveling and are synched with their purpose and remembrance of Allah ﷻ, they stand together to pray; in addition to the help of Allah ﷻ, both the strength in numbers and the God-conscious atmosphere that they create, gives others motivation to become stronger in their faith, and more courageous in their remembrance of Allah ﷻ and their purpose of life on this Earth.

When a person goes out to a public park in a non-Muslim majority country, and at prayer time they see a group of believers praying in a public place, other Muslims will feel comfortable to join them, or they will become motivated to pray in public as well.

This is also seen in the world around us when those who live false lifestyles ensure that they create parades and march in the streets to stand for their cause. They organize public events and engage the masses in other ways to show their pride and commitment to the cause which they believe in. Through this public display and uniformity which they present, they create "strength" - however because this is rooted in falsehood, eventually it will crumble.

Keys of Guidance

- It is important to note another message of this verse, and that is although the verse is saying to 'physically' face the *qiblah,* however much deeper than this is to instill the point in the believers to always have the remembrance of Allah ﷻ and their purpose of life in mind. This remembrance and purpose should be unified in one's existence no matter where they are, and is a trait of the God-conscious believers. Therefore, it is important to understand and realize that all believers are connected and unified all of the time. It is extremely crucial to have this uniformity in purpose during our travels. We emphasize this purpose and remembrance during travel because when one is at home, it is easier to focus on one's purpose and there are not as many challenges; but when we go out into the world, we will experience many different challenges and may even get distracted, so it becomes extremely important to keep focused on the presence of Allah ﷻ and our purpose of life at all times.

- One of the goals in life is to ensure that the Muslim community is strong and vocal, and that they are not dominated by others, rather they are able to achieve their own independence in all areas of life.
- In many instances, foreign and outside elements are not as much of a threat and danger to Islam and the Muslim community, but what is more dangerous is a lack of piety and God-consciousness *(taqwā)* of the Muslims, and when they put their trust and reliance on other than Allah ﷻ - whether it be on political systems, governments, or other people in general.
- Guidance has many stages, but one should never be satisfied when they are in relation to Allah ﷻ because we must always strive to get closer to the Almighty ﷻ, and we should continuously ask for guidance from Allah ﷻ Himself - just like we recite in Sūrah al-Fātiḥa several times a day where we are seeking and actively working to remain on this Straight Path.

Verse 151

كَمَآ أَرۡسَلۡنَا فِيكُمۡ رَسُولٗا مِّنكُمۡ يَتۡلُواْ عَلَيۡكُمۡ ءَايَٰتِنَا وَيُزَكِّيكُمۡ
وَيُعَلِّمُكُمُ ٱلۡكِتَٰبَ وَٱلۡحِكۡمَةَ وَيُعَلِّمُكُم مَّا لَمۡ تَكُونُواْ تَعۡلَمُونَ ١٥١

Just as We sent among you a Messenger from among your own

selves, reciting to you Our revelations *(āyāt)*, and purifying you (of false beliefs, doctrines, and sins), and instructing you in the Book (*Kitāb* - the Qur'ān) and the Wisdom *(Ḥikmah)*, and instructing you in whatever you do not know.

This verse is unique in how Allah ﷻ is speaking to the community. The fact that the pronoun "all of you" *(kum)* is repeated six times in this verse speaks volumes.

However, who are the "all of you" *(kum)* that Allah ﷻ is directly addressing here?

Scholars of the Qur'ān believe that this is referring to a specific group of people who are ready and willing to believe and follow Prophet Muḥammad ﷺ.

Spiritual Agenda of Prophet Muḥammad ﷺ

In the last portion of the previous verse, Allah ﷻ stated that one of the reasons for the change in the *qiblah* was for Him to complete His blessings upon the believers and guide them.

In this verse, by the usage of the word 'just' *(kamā)* at the beginning, Allah ﷻ wants to say that in reality the change in the *qiblah* was not the only blessing which He bestowed on the believers. Rather, there were many other blessings which had already been given in the past, and they will continue to be showered upon the believers in the future.

The first blessing which Allah ﷻ enumerates in this verse is by Him saying that just as by changing the *qiblah*, He completed His blessing upon the Muslims, He has also sent a Messenger, Prophet Muḥammad ﷺ to the believers from their own kind, meaning that he was a human being like them so he was able to be a teacher, leader, and role model for other humans because he was aware of their pains, needs, and problems - and this in itself was a great blessing.

Allah ﷻ then refers to four other blessings in this verse which were bestowed upon the Muslims by the blessing of being given this Prophet ﷺ:

1. He, Prophet Muḥammad ﷺ, will recite Our revelations *(āyāt)* to

the people. That is, he will prepare the hearts of the believers to accept the meanings of these Divinely-sent words. The regular and calculated recitation of the Qur'ān by Prophet Muḥammad ﷺ was meant to prepare the people for two important objectives of teaching *(taʿlīm)* and nurturing *(tarbiyah)*, which is mentioned in the next portion of this verse.

2. Prophet Muḥammad ﷺ will work to purify the people. The direct meaning of the word purifying *(tazkiyah)* means 'enhancing and progressing.' Thus, with the help of the revelations from Allah ﷻ, Prophet Muḥammad ﷺ would supplement the spiritual and material perfection which the believers were developing, and he was there to complement the improvement of the human soul.

3. Next, Prophet Muḥammad ﷺ will teach the community of believers the Book and the Wisdom. Although teaching *(taʿlīm)* inherently takes precedence over spiritually-based nurturing *(tarbiyah)*, however in order to demonstrate that the ultimate goal of all of the Prophets which were sent by Allah ﷻ and their message is founded on the correct spiritually-based nurturing, the Noble Qur'ān often mentions it before the act of teaching. The word the Book *(Kitāb)* refers to 'the verses of the Qur'ān,' and the 'Divine revelation' *(waḥī)* which was miraculously revealed to Prophet Muḥammad ﷺ; while the phrase the Wisdom *(Ḥikmah)* refers to 'the words of the Prophet ﷺ and 'his direct teachings' which are commonly referred to as the *sunnah*.[38]

4. The fourth blessing which is mentioned in this verse is where Allah ﷻ says that he, Prophet Muḥammad ﷺ, will teach the community of believers what they do not know. This means that had it not been for the Prophets which Allah ﷻ sent, many sciences would have

---

[38] The *sunnah* or the tradition consists of the 'words, deeds, and tacit, silent approval of Prophet Muḥammad ﷺ,' and as an extension the specific successors from the family of the Prophet which make up the 12 Imāms ؑ, as well as the conduct of the daughter of Prophet Muḥammad ﷺ, Sayyidah Fāṭimah az-Zahrā' ؑ. These words, deeds, and consents count as one of the four sources used in the deduction *(ijtihād)* of Islamic Laws in Jurisprudence.

remained unknown from humanity forever. In addition to being moral and social leaders, the Prophets which Allah ﷻ sent were also scientific leaders without whose leadership, human beings would not have advanced and matured.

Keys of Guidance

- Successful leadership of a community can only happen when the leader is from the people themselves, and not brought in from an outside, foreign culture - one must be from that group of people, know the language and expressions of the people, and experience the joys and feel the pains that people go through.
- Religious education must always take precedence, and be the primary axis of the lives of our children and all of the Muslims, then comes the teachings of the secular world.

Verse 152

فَٱذْكُرُونِىٓ أَذْكُرْكُمْ وَٱشْكُرُوا۟ لِى وَلَا تَكْفُرُونِ ﴿١٥٢﴾

So remember Me, I will remember you; and give thanks to Me, and do not deny (be ungrateful to) Me.

This verse outlines that believers need to be in a constant state of the remembrance of Allah ﷻ, then He in turn will continue to remember them. As well, they need to be thankful for the innumerable blessings which He constantly provides them, and show gratitude to Allah ﷻ by using the blessings correctly; and not deny or be ungrateful for what He has provided.

The phrase "remember Me" refers to a principle in nurturing *(tarbiyah)* in that when Allah ﷻ says "remember Me" it means 'to continuously bring to mind that Pure Essence which is Allah ﷻ who is the source of all goodness and virtues. It is through constantly remembering the Almighty One that will help make us become more sincere, determined, strong, and united in our activities.

The meaning of expressing gratitude *(shukr)* and not being ungrateful to Allah ﷻ for all of His gifts is that we use every blessing which He has given to us properly in the way for which it was made so that He may increase His Mercy and Blessings upon us.

What is Remembrance (Dhikr) of Allah ﷻ?

The meaning of remembrance *(dhikr)* of Allah ﷻ is not just remembering Him on the tongue by a verbal declaration - although the tongue is the translator of the heart; but rather, it is much deeper than this.

It has been narrated in several *ḥadīth* from the Immaculate leaders of Islam, the 12 Imāms of the Ahlul Bayt ﷺ that *dhikr* is a practical remembrance of Allah ﷻ. As such, we read in a tradition from Prophet Muḥammad ﷺ that he advised Imām ʿAlī ؑ in the following manner: "O ʿAlī! There are three things which this nation shall not be able to bear: equality with their brothers/sisters in regards to their wealth; giving people their rights; and remembering Allah in any state - and this does not simply mean saying: "Glory be to Allah" *(Subḥanallah)* and "All Praise belongs to Allah" *(Walḥamdulillāh)* and "There is no creature worthy of worship except for Allah" *(Subḥanallah walḥamdulillāh wa lā ilāhā illa Allah wallahu Akbar).*" Rather, whenever they encounter something which they are prohibited from, they fear Allah, the Noble and Grand, in regards to that thing and refrain from it."[39]

A Life of Remembrance

What does an individual do when one misses or remembers a person you care about?

When we remember someone who we are close to, we try to let them know. For example, if we miss our friends or remember them, we might call to talk to them, or message them, or physically spend time with them.

In the pre-Islamic Era of Ignorance, people used to perform the

---

[39] Shaykh Ṣadūq, *Al-Khiṣāl*, Vol. 1, Pg. 125, Chapter on Traditions which Make Note of the Number Three. The initial portion of this tradition is as follows:

يَا عَلِيُّ ثَلَاثٌ لَا تُطِيقُهَا هٰذِهِ الْأُمَّةُ: أَلْمُوَاسَاةُ لِلْأَخِ فِي مَالِهِ، وَإِنْصَافُ النَّاسِ مِنْ نَفْسِهِ...

ritual of *Ḥajj*, but it had become filled with pagan customs. One of these customs was that after people would finish the *Ḥajj*, they would sit and remember their ancestors. They would brag to each other by comparing the accomplishments of one another's ancestors and act arrogantly because of this.

In the Qur'ān, Allah ﷻ corrected this invalid custom. He instructed those who completed the *Ḥajj* as follows: "And when you finish your rites, then remember Allah as you would remember your fathers, or with a more ardent remembrance."[40]

People might miss their parents, grandparents, or ancestors who have left this world, and remember them. But the feeling that we need to have toward Allah ﷻ should be more ardent and intense, because everything that our parents, ancestors, or anyone else has given to us is actually from Allah ﷻ!

Whether one is feeling happy after finishing something difficult like *Ḥajj*, or a person in the midst of performing one's tasks, Allah ﷻ reminds everyone about the importance of remembering Him at all times.

Even in a situation as complex and dangerous as a battle, the Qur'ān reminds us not to forget Allah ﷻ: "O you who have faith! When you encounter a force [in battle or some enemy], then stand firm, and remember Allah much so that perhaps you may be felicitous."[41]

Avoiding Ghaflah

There are two types of *dhikr* or remembrance. The first type is when you remember after previously having forgotten, or being heedless. This forgetting, or state of heedlessness *(ghaflah)*, is the opposite of remembrance. We do not want to be heedless and ever forget Allah ﷻ. Imām ʿAlī ؑ said: "It is by the constant remembrance of Allah that heedlessness is avoided."

---

[40] Qur'ān, Sūrah al-Baqarah (2), Verse 200:

فَإِذَا قَضَيْتُم مَّنَٰسِكَكُمْ فَٱذْكُرُوا۟ ٱللَّهَ كَذِكْرِكُمْ ءَابَآءَكُمْ أَوْ أَشَدَّ ذِكْرًا ۗ ...

[41] Ibid., Sūrah al-Anfāl (8), Verse 45:

يَٰٓأَيُّهَا ٱلَّذِينَ ءَامَنُوٓا۟ إِذَا لَقِيتُمْ فِئَةً فَٱثْبُتُوا۟ وَٱذْكُرُوا۟ ٱللَّهَ كَثِيرًا لَّعَلَّكُمْ تُفْلِحُونَ ﴿٤٥﴾

Why do we Need Dhikrullāh?

Dhikr means remembrance, and it is often referred to as *dhikrullāh*, or 'the remembrance of Allah ﷻ.'

The second type of *dhikr* is called *murāqabah*, which is a higher level of *dhikr*. It is when a person is constantly mindful of something that is worthy of giving attention to. This means that one tries to never fall into a state of *ghaflah*.

Imām aṣ-Ṣādiq ﵇ has told us that when we neglect to remember Allah ﷻ, we are like a bird flying in the air who has been targeted by a hunter and will be taken down from the sky.

We human beings are constantly being hunted by both the inner and outer devils *(Shayāṭīn)*. As soon as a person falls into negligence and does not have that remembrance of Allah ﷻ, then *Shayṭān* can attack them very easily. They will fall into a state of heedlessness which can lead to sin and spiritual pollution.

Different Forms of Dhikr

What are some ways that a person can do *dhikrullāh*?

Dhikr can be of different types: the heart (silent), the tongue (verbal), or in actions (practical).

Some verbal recitations include:

1. The literal recitation of the beautiful Names of Allah ﷻ *(Asmāʾ al-Ḥusnā)*.
2. The recitation of Qur'ān or supplications *(duʿās)*.
3. The daily prayers *(ṣalāh)* are a form of *dhikr*.

Practical *dhikr* is that when a person is tempted with a sin, one abstains from committing that sin due to the remembrance of Allah ﷻ. This may be the desire to indulge in a forbidden pleasure, or it may be the temptation to speak ill about someone, or to express unnecessary anger, or to backbite, or lie, etc. Remembering Allah ﷻ in such a situation will bring about a shame of sinning in the presence of the Almighty and in essence deter a person from committing the forbidden.

If a person knows and recognizes that without being alert and present with the *dhikr* of Allah ﷻ, one's heart can be preyed upon by *Shayṭān* who is always lurking around to catch the heedless ones, then why do people not always remain present with the remembrance of Allah ﷻ in their hearts?

The combination of practical *dhikr* and verbal *dhikr* will help an individual strengthen the remembrance of Allah ﷻ in one's heart.

This 'internal *dhikr*' in the heart is mentioned in the Qur'ān: "And remember your Lord within yourself humbly and reverentially (i.e. with awe), without being loud in the words - in the mornings and in the evenings - and do not be among the heedless ones."[42]

Dhikr in One's Life

What are some of the ways in which a person can incorporate *dhikr* into one's daily life?

When someone wants to try to incorporate any habit into one's daily life, one should start off by building small, consistent habits. Here are some examples of habits which can help instill the *dhikr* of Allah ﷻ in an individual:

1. Saying *Bismillāh* (in the Name of Allah) before starting any action such as eating, drinking, traveling, coming in and out of home, etc.
2. Saying *Alḥamdulillāh* (all Praise belongs to Allah) after an action like eating, drinking, finishing an exam, etc.
3. Reciting a consistent amount of the Qur'ān everyday, such as 10 verses *(āyāt)* or 5 minutes daily.
4. Reciting *Ṣalawāt (Allāhumma ṣalli ʿalā Muḥammad wa Āl Muḥammad)* and other such recitations.
5. Conveying your greetings to the Messenger of Allah ﷺ and the Imām of the time ʿaj everyday, preferably in the morning soon after waking up.
6. Performing the *Tasbīḥ* of Sayyidah Fāṭimah az-Zahrā' ʿa.
7. Whenever a person feels tempted by the inner or outer *Shayṭān* to

---

[42] Qur'ān, Sūrah al-Aʿrāf (7), Verse 205:

وَٱذْكُر رَّبَّكَ فِى نَفْسِكَ تَضَرُّعًا وَخِيفَةً وَدُونَ ٱلْجَهْرِ مِنَ ٱلْقَوْلِ بِٱلْغُدُوِّ وَٱلْآصَالِ وَلَا تَكُن مِّنَ ٱلْغَافِلِينَ ۝

disobey Allah ﷻ, then one should verbally remember Allah ﷻ by seeking refuge in Him from the *Shayṭān*, and practically remember Him by removing one's self from the place or thing which is tempting the person.

8. When a person is really busy, take short but regular breaks to feel grateful to Allah ﷻ for everything He has done and continues to do for everyone.
9. Regularly, perform intentional - but not random - acts of kindness and charity.
10. Be committed to the practice of Islam in order to further the love of Allah ﷻ within an individual.

Therefore, in conclusion it must be noted that Allah ﷻ always remembers His creations and is constantly giving them abundant blessings, such as the blessing of life and everything needed for it, as well as countless other essential necessities. If a servant can give one's complete attention to Allah ﷻ in every moment of one's life, then one will receive more of the blessings of Allah ﷻ as this kind of remembrance is a much higher level, and will help a person get closer to Allah ﷻ and reach the ultimate purpose and goal of one's existence.

Keys of Guidance

- Allah ﷻ is such a generous and loving God that it is He alone who gives status to a human being, and He gives it to such an extent that He has proudly said that if humans take the time to remember Him - not just once or twice - but if we are in a constant state of remembrance of our Creator, then He will bless us more and more. Remembrance here means having a constant awareness of the presence of Allah ﷻ with us at all times. We can be doing anything at all in our lives such as working, studying, helping others, resting, etc.; but the important thing is that we remain connected to Him at every moment of our lives, and realize our purpose of existence, and stay away from those things which can cause spiritual heedlessness.
- It is through remembering Allah ﷻ, and the countless, never-ending blessings which He provides us with that can pave the way for us to

show gratitude and appreciation to Him, because it is when we fall into neglect and fail to recognize the blessings which He constantly showers us with that can lead us down the path of denial of His favors and bounties.

Verse 153

يَـٰٓأَيُّهَا ٱلَّذِينَ ءَامَنُوا۟ ٱسْتَعِينُوا۟ بِٱلصَّبْرِ وَٱلصَّلَوٰةِ ۚ إِنَّ ٱللَّهَ مَعَ ٱلصَّـٰبِرِينَ ﴿١٥٣﴾

O you who believe! Seek assistance (against all kinds of hardships and tribulations) through patience *(ṣabr)* and prayer *(ṣalāh)*; surely Allah is with the patient ones.

Fortitude and Focus on Allah ﷻ

In the previous verses, the discussion centered on education *(taʿlīm)*, correct nurturing *(tarbiyah)*, remembrance of Allah ﷻ *(dhikr)* and thanksgiving *(shukr);* in this verse, the focus is on what is referred to as endurance or patience *(ṣabr)*, and without this important trait, the previously mentioned four stages will not be able to take shape. Therefore in this verse, Allah ﷻ guides the believers that as people of true faith, they must seek help through patience and prayer.

It is with the two forces of endurance which is developed through patience, and focus on Allah ﷻ which takes place through *ṣalāh* that the believers will be able to dive into the battle of hardships and difficult events in their lives, knowing that victory will be theirs, because just as Allah ﷻ states at the end of this verse, indeed He is with those who have patience.

Contrary to popular belief, patience has never meant to endure misery, submit to humiliation, accept oppression, or surrender to the causes of failure. Rather, patience means perseverance and endurance in the face of any problem, and the outcomes which may come about for an individual as a result of a difficulty.

The concept of patience has true meaning only when there are ups and downs in life, but it means little to nothing in regular situations.

It is when a trial or some kind of discomfort comes in one's path, or something happens that this trait actually is valued.

When a person has faith, they have certain standards they abide by and are accountable to Allah ﷻ for. In life everyone will naturally go through different challenges; and in order for our faith to be healthy and be able to grow and flourish, we need to have patience and a strong connection with Allah ﷻ.

A better way to understand faith and patience is like a bottle of water. The bottle symbolizes a person's humanity and servitude, while the cap is a person's faith. As long as the bottle is on the table and the table is not moving, everything is fine - even if the cap is not on the bottle. However if someone bumps the table, then we need to ensure that the cap is placed tightly on the bottle to ensure that the water does not spill out. Such is patience in the life of a believer.

Another point that this verse emphasizes on is the important support which goes along with forbearance, and that is the prayers. We read in the *aḥādīth* that whenever Imām ʿAlī ﵇ was faced with a problem, he would go and perform *ṣalāh,* then go forth to try and solve the dilemma while reciting this verse under review.

The above verse recommends two core principles which we must implement in our lives: one is reliance on Allah ﷻ which is through the manifestation of prayers *(ṣalāh),* and the other is the issue of forbearance and persistence which is mentioned as patience *(ṣabr).*

It is worthy to note that there are almost 70 instances in the Noble Qur'ān where Allah ﷻ speaks about patience and endurance, and more than ten of these are dedicated to and addressed directly to Prophet Muḥammad ﷺ.

Keys of Guidance

- Faith *(īmān)* in itself is a praiseworthy state to be in, however it will be much more beneficial when it is accompanied by action *(ʿamal),* trust *(tawakkul),* and endurance *(ṣabr).*
- *Ṣalāh* can be described as a lever[43] - it is not a burden. It is there to

[43] A lever is defined as a rigid bar which rests on a pivot, and it can be used to

help us out in times of ease and difficulty, not to cause us additional stress or trouble.

- Although Allah ﷻ is present with everyone and is everywhere, just like He says elsewhere in the Qur'ān that He is closer to us than our jugular vein, however there is a unique type of closeness and presence which Allah ﷻ speaks about in this verse when it comes to those who have patience and that is a special type of grace, love, and assistance which He confers upon those who exhibit fortitude, and have patience during the different trials and tribulations that everyone will go through in this transient world.

Verse 154

وَلَا تَقُولُوا۟ لِمَن يُقْتَلُ فِى سَبِيلِ ٱللَّهِ أَمْوَٰتٌۢ ۚ بَلْ أَحْيَآءٌ وَلَٰكِن لَّا تَشْعُرُونَ ﴿١٥٤﴾

And do not say about those who are killed in Allah's path: "They are dead." Rather they are alive, but you are not aware.

History of Revelation

It has been narrated from Ibn ʿAbbās that this verse was revealed about those who were killed in the battle of Badr[44] and there were a total of 14

help move a heavy or firmly fixed load with one end when pressure is applied to the other.

[44] The battle of Badr was the first and most important battle between the Muslims and the polytheists of Quraysh during the early history of Islam. This battle took place on the 17th of the month of Ramaḍān in the 2nd year after the migration in the area of Badr which is around 96 miles from the city of Medina, and about 192 miles from the city of Mecca. Although the Muslims were limited in number and had scant resources, with the heavenly guidance that they received, their own inner courage and strength which they had developed, and with the unique valor of brave warriors such as Imām ʿAlī ؑ and Hamzah *Sayyid ash-Shuhadā'* ؑ (Leader of the Martyrs), the Muslims gained a decisive victory.

people who were killed - six from the side of the immigrants *(muhājirūn),* and eight from the helpers *(anṣār).*

At the end of the war, some people said that those who were killed in the battle of Badr had 'died.' In response to their statement, Allah ﷻ revealed this verse, forbidding them from using the word 'dead' for those who were considered as martyrs *(shuhadā').*[45]

---

[45] *Shuhadā'* is the plural of *shahīd* which denotes a martyr in Islam. Although the word *shahīd* occurs frequently in the Qur'ān in the generic sense of a 'witness,' it never comes in the Qur'ān in the meaning of a person who dies for one's faith, or a 'martyr.' This latter sense acquires wider use in the *ḥadīth.* The term which the Qur'ān uses frequently to describe those who are martyred for the sake of religion is: 'those killed in the way of Allah - *fī sabīlillāh.'* As for why Muslims use the term *shahīd* for a martyr, it may be due to the following reasons:

1. The angels of Divine mercy witness the sacrifice and martyrdom of an individual;
2. Allah ﷻ and the angels testify to this person's entry into Heaven;
3. When an individual who is killed in the way of Allah ﷻ falls to the ground and breathes his last breath, he does so by falling on the *shāhida* which is another name for the ground;
4. They are alive and present *(shāhid)* with their Lord;
5. They see or witness *(shāhid)* the Divine Kingdom *(al-Mulk wa al-Malakūt)* of Allah ﷻ.

This term is commonly used as a posthumous title for those who are considered to have accepted, or even consciously sought out their own death in order to bear witness to their Islamic beliefs.

The first male martyr in the path of Islam was Yāsir ibn 'Āmir 'Ansī, the famous companion of Prophet Muḥammad ﷺ, and the first female martyr in Islam was his wife, Sumayyah, the daughter of Khabāṭ. These were the parents of the well-known companion, 'Ammār al-Yāsir. Yāsir and his wife Sumayyah were among the first converts to Islam, and despite their old age they resisted the most severe tortures and remained steadfast on the path of Islam. Eventually, they were martyred as a result of the tortures that were inflicted upon them by Abū Jahl.

Martyrs are Alive

Following the topic of perseverance, the verse under review speaks about the eternal life which the martyrs enjoy which is closely related to their perseverance and patience while in this world, and dealing with the difficulties of this transient life.

The first point which Allah ﷻ tells the believers with respect to those who are killed in His way is that we are not permitted to refer to them as being dead. He goes on to add that in actuality, they are alive, however we do not understand!

Essentially, in any movement, a group of easy-going, cowardly people step aside from the challenges of life, and not only do they do nothing for the cause, they also try to discourage others from taking an active role in a movement.

Such people were also present in the formative years of Islam, and anytime a Muslim achieved martyrdom in the defensive struggles *(jihād)*, they would loudly proclaim that so and so died! By very openly lamenting the death, they made others anxious as if they were trying to dissuade them from giving up their own lives to safeguard Islam.

In response to these detrimental words, Allah ﷻ explicitly says in the Qur'ān that those who give up their lives in the way of Allah ﷻ are actually alive, immortal, and enjoying spiritual sustenance in the presence of Allah ﷻ, and those who are imprisoned in the limited walls of this material world cannot understand this reality because of their lack of faith *(īmān)*, spiritual negligence *(ghaflah)*, and their tunnel vision. In addition, their mindset and paradigm is completely materialistic, so they cannot even start to comprehend what is beyond this world.

This verse also wanted to mention the continued existence of the soul and the post-Earthly life in the realm before the Day of Judgment which is known as the *barzakh*.[46]

[46] *Barzakh* is 'a domain of existence between this world and the hereafter;' it is also called the 'imaginal world' or the 'world of the grave.' *Barzakh* exists for both believers and non-believers, and it is kind of similar to Heaven for the former, and Hell for the latter - those who were the obstinate, sinful ones in this world. In Arabic, the word *barzakh* literally means 'an interval or a barrier

Further details on this subject, as well as the issue of the eternal life of between two things,' and technically it means 'an interval between the end of this worldly life, death, and the beginning of the hereafter.'

The word *barzakh* has been mentioned three times in the Qur'ān: Sūrah al-Furqān (25), Verse 53, Sūrah al-Mu'minūn (23), Verse 100, and Sūrah ar-Rahmān (55), Verse 20 and it is only in this last reference that it has been used in the meaning in question:

$$\text{لَعَلِّي أَعْمَلُ صَالِحًا فِيمَا تَرَكْتُ كَلَّا إِنَّهَا كَلِمَةٌ هُوَ قَائِلُهَا وَمِنْ وَرَائِهِمْ بَرْزَخٌ إِلَى يَوْمِ يُبْعَثُونَ}$$ ﴿١٠٠﴾

'That I may act righteously with respect to whatever I have left undone in the world.' No, never! It is merely a word that he utters over and over again before those (who are dead) is an intermediate world (of the grave, where they will stay) until the Day when they will be raised up.

According to this verse, at the time of death some people will ask if they can return to the world to perform good deeds which they had not done previously, however they will be in a barrier or an interval - a *barzakh* - until the Day of Judgment. The phrase "...until the Day when they will be raised up," indicates that *barzakh* is an interval between this world and the hereafter which everyone will experience after death and before the Day of Judgment.

According to a tradition from Imām Ja'far aṣ-Ṣādiq 🕮, all (true) Shī'ah will go to Heaven in the hereafter, however the tradition goes on to say that: "I take an oath by Allah that I fear for you in the *barzakh*." A person asked the Imām about *barzakh* and he replied: "[It is] the grave, from one's death until the Day of Judgment."

This statement implies that the world of the grave is the world of *barzakh* - keeping in mind that the word 'grave' in this tradition does not mean a specific hole in the earth in which a body is normally buried, but rather it is a metaphor for the world after this world - the *barzakh*.

The human soul attaches itself to an illusory or *barzakhī* body. An illusory body is not material, yet it enjoys some of the characteristics of material objects, such as shape and size, and in these respects the illusory body is like one's natural body. A better understanding of what this *barzakhī* body will be like is if we think about the forms or images that we observe while we are dreaming. That which we see in our dreams are undoubtedly non-material - those things do not occupy any space, nor do they have any mass, yet they have shapes, sizes, and forms like other material objects in this world.

the martyrs *(shuhadā')*, and the rewards and high position of those killed in the way of Allah ﷻ will be discussed in the commentary of: "And do not think of those who have been killed in Allah's cause as dead; rather, they are alive with their Lord, receiving sustenance."[47]

After death, the inevitable reality is that the body will perish while the soul will be transferred into another realm of existence. The word 'life' which Allah ﷻ speaks about in this verse refers to 'the quality of life after death for the martyrs' as they receive a special type of sustenance from Allah ﷻ.

Keys of Guidance

- Our limited understanding of this world which we live in is based solely on the material aspect of it, and therefore it must be supplemented and tweaked by our belief in Allah ﷻ and what the Immaculates have taught us about our religion. We must let the teachings of Islam shape the limited understanding which we have about this temporal world.
- Dying is inevitable, and we will all experience death at least once in our "life" - however it is when a person struggles in the way of Allah ﷻ and sacrifices oneself in this worldly life that one will have the greatest status in the sight of Allah ﷻ.
- The physical body will definitely die, however the soul will remain alive after death; and when it comes to the *shuhadā'*, not only do their souls live on long after they leave this world, but they continue to live on in the hearts and memories of the believers who remember them and their heroic sacrifices.

Verse 155

وَلَنَبۡلُوَنَّكُم بِشَيۡءٖ مِّنَ ٱلۡخَوۡفِ وَٱلۡجُوعِ وَنَقۡصٖ مِّنَ ٱلۡأَمۡوَٰلِ وَٱلۡأَنفُسِ

---

[47] Qur'ān, Sūrah Āl 'Imrān (3), Verse 169:

وَلَا تَحۡسَبَنَّ ٱلَّذِينَ قُتِلُواْ فِي سَبِيلِ ٱللَّهِ أَمۡوَٰتَۢاۚ بَلۡ أَحۡيَآءٌ عِندَ رَبِّهِمۡ يُرۡزَقُونَ ﴿١٦٩﴾

وَٱلثَّمَرَٰتِۗ وَبَشِّرِ ٱلصَّٰبِرِينَ ﴿١٥٥﴾

And We will certainly test you all with something of fear and hunger, and loss of wealth and lives and fruits (earnings); but give glad tidings to the patient ones.

This World: A Divinely-Created Testing Ground

Following the discussion on martyrdom in the way of Allah ﷻ and the eternal life that the martyrs will enjoy, Allah ﷻ turns the focus to different kinds of tests and trials which humanity will go through in this world and its various expressions.

Allah ﷻ starts off by saying that without a doubt, He will test everyone with some kind of fear, hunger, reduction in wealth, personal lives, and their 'fruits' which refers to earnings, children, etc.

Since victory in these examinations is not possible except under the shadow of perseverance, Allah ﷻ adds that those who endure and show patience will be given good tidings from Him.

Such people, the ones with endurance are able to withstand the ordeals which they are put through, and therefore the good news of victory belongs to them, while the spiritually-weak who are not able to fulfill their covenants will be ruined by the ordeals of life.

Why does Allah ﷻ Test Humanity?

Tests are normally taken from a person so that something which is vague or unknown can be known and recognized, thus reducing one's ignorance. For example, a teacher will give a test or exam to the students to see if they have correctly understood the material which was taught; or a person may get a blood test done so that the doctor can diagnose various types of diseases - in both of these cases, the test is in order to clarify the unknown.

If the very nature of a test is this, then why does Allah ﷻ test people? He is Aware of everything and Knows the unseen of the heavens and the Earth. Is there anything which is hidden from Him that needs to be revealed by a test?

In response, one must understand that the concept of a test as it relates to Allah ﷻ is vastly different from its meaning as it relates to human beings.

When we conduct tests, it is for us to know more about something or someone like in the case of a student; or it is to remove ambiguity and ignorance, or be able to come to a certain conclusion such as a medical test. However, when it comes to why Allah ﷻ examines human beings, it is to aide in their growth and correct their upbringing.

Allah ﷻ makes this clear in the Qurʾān where He says: "...(All of this happened as it did) so that He may test what (thoughts, intentions, inclinations, etc.) is in your hearts, and purify what is in your hearts (the faith); and Allah has full knowledge of what is (hidden) in the hearts..."[48]

It has been narrated in *Nahj al-Balāghah* that the Commander of the Faithful, Imām ʿAlī ؑ said the following in regards to the philosophy of tests which Allah ﷻ puts humanity through: "...Even though Allah, the Glorified, knows them more than they know themselves, however He lets people perform their actions through which they earn rewards or punishments..."[49]

Tests of Allah ﷻ are Universal

Since the system of life is one of progression toward perfection and all living beings follow this path, when it comes to the human being, according to this general law everyone from the Prophets ؑ down to the common people must be tested in order to be able to develop their talents and reach their full potential.

The Divine tests are distinct for all people. Sometimes they may take form through Allah ﷻ providing an abundance of blessings and success to someone; at other times, they are seen by a person falling into hardships

---

[48] Qurʾān, Sūrah Āl ʿImrān (3), Verse 154:

...وَلِيَبْتَلِيَ اللَّهُ مَا فِي صُدُورِكُمْ وَلِيُمَحِّصَ مَا فِي قُلُوبِكُمْ...

[49] *Nahj al-Balāghah*, Short Saying 93. The initial portion of this tradition is as follows:

وَإِنْ كَانَ سُبْحَانَهُ أَعْلَمَ بِهِمْ مِنْ أَنْفُسِهِمْ وَلَكِنْ...

and misfortunes.

Occasionally, the tests will be more severe with extreme difficulties; while for others, their tests will be relatively easy.

Ultimately, even the outcomes will all yield different results, however the main issue remains the same - everyone will be put through some kind of test and trial by Allah ﷻ.

Secret to Success in the Divine Tests

Now that we understand that all of humanity is sharing in a vast Divine exam, a question remains: "What is the best way to succeed in these tests?"

The answer is given in the last part of this verse:

1. The first and most important step to victory is mentioned in the portion of this verse where Allah ﷻ says: "...and give glad tidings to the patient ones."

This sentence explicitly states that the key to victory is patience and perseverance, and it is for this reason that good news is given only to the patient and steadfast ones.

2. The second thing to keep in mind is in regards to the transience of difficulties and hardships in this world. This temporal life which we lead is nothing more than a passage into another world, and when we recognize and accept this reality, then that will be another factor for victory, as Allah ﷻ reminds us: "Surely we belong to Allah, and to Him we will return."[50]

Keys of Guidance

- As a roadmap for us to follow, we must recognize:
  1. The purpose of life: This is encapsulated in the phrase *qurbatan ilallāh* - meaning 'for the sake of attaining proximity to Allah ﷻ' and to become the best version of ourselves that can only be achieved by getting closer to Allah ﷻ and following His guidelines.
  2. One of the ways to achieve success in this purpose of life is being

[50] Qur'ān. Sūrah al-Baqarah (2), Verse 156.

tested by Allah ﷻ.

- The Mercy of Allah ﷻ is embedded in tests from the Divine - it is not a punishment.
- The method of testing is unique and different for each individual depending on one's capacity.
- The outcome of tests is not limited to this world - and this point is a game-changer if we understand it. Having a broader scope will help a believer get through the challenges of this life easier and have a better mindset. For example, if a person is hospitalized for a few days, they need to realize that those few hard days will give them positive results that will manifest themselves after they are discharged in that they will be able to live a longer and healthier life. In the same way, this life of a few days compared to the infinite life of the world to come will show a majority of its results in the hereafter.
- The tests which Allah ﷻ implements belong to the category of actions which are within the realm of *Sunnatullāh* - the immutable constants of the System of Allah ﷻ - they are a definite and Divinely-planned program and tradition which everyone has to go through - Prophets ﷺ, Messengers ﷺ, Imāms ﷺ, Saints, and common people.
- Going through adversities gives rise to the power of resistance, and moral and spiritual growth. There are many human traits such as patience *(ṣabr)*, gratification *(riḍā)*, submission *(taslīm)*, contentment *(qanāʿah)*, asceticism *(zuhd)*, piety *(taqwā)*, self-sacrifice *(īthār)*, and many others which can flourish and mature under the shadow of hardships and misfortunes.
- Just like the Mercy and Compassion of Allah ﷻ are unlimited and indescribable, so too are the "good tidings" *(bishārah)* of Allah ﷻ. He does not mention what these "glad tidings" are - He leaves it open to imply that they can include all types of different blessings.

Verse 156

ٱلَّذِينَ إِذَآ أَصَٰبَتۡهُم مُّصِيبَةٞ قَالُوٓاْ إِنَّا لِلَّهِ وَإِنَّآ إِلَيۡهِ رَٰجِعُونَ ١٥٦

Those who, when a misfortune befalls them, say: "Surely we belong to Allah, and surely to Him we will return."

In continuation of the previous verse, this verse introduces one of the unique qualities of those who have patience, where Allah ﷻ says that when a calamity befalls them, they say: "Surely We belong to Allah, and surely to Him we will return *(innā lillāhī wa innā ilayhī rāji'ūn).*"

Paying attention to the fact that we are all from Allah ﷻ, teaches us that we should never be saddened by a decrease in blessings from Him because all of the gifts which He provides, especially our lives, belong to Him - they are not ours! One day He may give something to us, and another day He may take it back - but both are good for us.

In addition, realizing the fact that we will all return back to Allah ﷻ emphasizes to us that this Earth is not our eternal abode, the declines and surges in blessings from Allah ﷻ are all short-lived. In reality, these gifts from Allah ﷻ are merely tools that we must use as we traverse the stages of spiritual evolution, and by keeping these two principles of life in front of us - meaning our origin and our end - they will evoke a profound effect on nurturing a spirit of patience within us.

The meaning of "saying" the phrase: "Surely we belong to Allah, and to Him we will return" when a trial or difficulty occur, should not just be a verbal declaration; rather, we must pay attention to this reality and the spirit of this phrase, due to the fact that the world of Monotheism *(Tawḥīd)* and true faith *(īmān)* lie deep within this statement.

What is a Misfortune/Trial (Musībah)?

The word *musībah* can be defined as 'hardships or difficulties.' The way we react and respond to these will be life-changing decisions and paths which we create for ourselves.

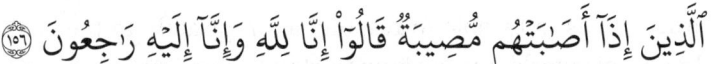

This verse refers to a mindset that people who go through these tests and are believers have: simply put, they truly recognize that their beginning is from Allah ﷻ and that their end is back to Allah ﷻ.

In order for us to be able to respond appropriately to the challenges of the life of this world, we must understand the six worlds of existence:

1. *ʿĀlam adh-Dharr*: The World of Particles. From the time our soul was created until we are placed in the womb of our mother - as believers, we do not know too much about this realm because the Qurʾān is silent on this world and what transpired there.
2. *ʿĀlam al-Baṭn*: The World of the Womb. From the time we are in our mother's womb until birth - this can be for a minimum of a six-month period of gestation up to a maximum of approximately nine months or so.
3. *ʿĀlam an-Nāsūt*: The World of Physical Bodies. From birth until death. For some people, this may only be a brief moment; for others: a minute, an hour, a day, a month, a year, a decade, a century, etc. Human beings are meant to progress and work hard in this world to see good results in the upcoming worlds of existence.
4. *ʿĀlam al-Barzakh*: The World of the Grave. The time of this differs for people because it begins from that point of one's physical death / martyrdom, and will continue up until the Day of Resurrection when everyone will be given a new life when they are raised up from their graves, and made to stand in the presence of Allah ﷻ for judgment.
5. *ʿĀlam al-Maʿād*: The World of the Hereafter. We know how long this day is: simply, it is one day, however we do not know how long that one day will be. There are multiple *ḥadīth* which say that this one day could be as long as 50,000 years.
6. *ʿĀlam al-Khulūd*: The World of Eternity. Those who were righteous individuals in this world will reside in Paradise forever; while those who led lives of uncontrollable sins and never asked forgiveness from anyone - including Allah ﷻ - will be sent to Hell to reside there for eternity.

Many of these worlds are not in our control, and as such the only two that we have some control over are the third, *ʿĀlam an-Nāsūt*, and to a limited extent, the fourth, *ʿĀlam al-Barzakh.* Whatever we do in life in the third world will impact our life in the fourth world. If we have a good understanding of these realms, and perform the correct deeds in this world, then we can then control our destiny in the following worlds to allow us the best state in the final abode - the world of perpetuity.

In short, whatever we want to attain has to be acquired in *ʿĀlam an-Nāsūt* because after this world, nothing can be gained in the *barzakh* realm by ourselves - we simply reap what we sow. Yes, there are ways to continue to have blessings in this world such as through good acts of charity which we did in the temporal world which continue to provide goodness to others - such as facilitating clean, potable water; leaving behind knowledge which others benefit from and when others do good deeds in our name and for our rewards, however we personally are not able to do anything for ourselves while in the grave. Therefore, it is our choice if we want to work and earn solely for this world, or if we wish to attain goodness for this world and the next. The choice is ours.

It is just like the life of this world. When someone gets sick and is admitted to the hospital, it is their choice to accept the treatment or not. They can be seen by the doctor, have tests run on their body, and be given the prognosis. If they decide to accept the treatment and spend some time in the hospital, or in therapy for a few weeks going through some difficulties, but they are told that they will then be on the road to recovery and more or less have a lifetime of good health - then that is their decision to accept this. On the other hand, they can refuse treatment and perhaps enjoy life for the next week or two, however their future health after that will not be guaranteed. In either case, they are free to choose what they want to do.

Thus, it is our choice in this life as it relates to what we want to do in this world to build our next worlds: Do we want to flourish only in this world; or both in this world and the next, and therefore have an everlasting life of happiness in the hereafter?

Thus, a smart believer is one who recognizes that one's beginning did not start from birth, and one's end will not terminate with death. A believer understands that one's life between birth and death is a place to shape the eternal life after death.

Therefore, any trial or difficulty *(musībah)* is a blessing in disguise because it will help a true believer strengthen one's faith, and develop certain qualities that will allow the person to return to Allah ﷻ manifesting His qualities and dwell in eternal peace, tranquility, and comfort.

In conclusion we realize that going through hardships and difficulties in this temporal world is a great blessing, and that is why in regards to the tragedy of Karbalāʾ, Lady Zaynab ؑ, daughter of Imām ʿAlī ؑ and Sayyidah Fāṭimah az-Zahrāʾ ؑ said: "I saw nothing but beauty;" and when Imām Ḥusayn ؑ went through all that he did on the day of ʿĀshūrāʾ, he turned to his Creator and said: "O my Lord! Accept (this) from me."

Keys of Guidance

- The root of patience is to have a strong, unwavering faith in Allah ﷻ and the Day of Resurrection; and also to be hopeful of receiving rewards from Allah ﷻ both in this world and the next, based on our actions and His never-ending Mercy.

Verse 157

أُوْلَٰٓئِكَ عَلَيْهِمْ صَلَوَٰتٌ مِّن رَّبِّهِمْ وَرَحْمَةٌۖ وَأُوْلَٰٓئِكَ هُمُ ٱلْمُهْتَدُونَ ١٥٧

Such are those upon whom are blessings from their Lord and mercy; and they are the rightly guided ones.

Before we can review this verse, we need to define three key points and words which Allah ﷻ has used here:

1. *Ṣalawāt*: This refers to constant blessings and elevation of status.
2. *Raḥmah*: The constant mercy and love that leads to peace, tranquility, and comfort.
3. *Hidāyah*: Being on the right path and direction in order to be able to fulfill the ultimate purpose of life.

Imagine if someone has the proper mindset and understands that these three strengths are what Allah ﷻ will help them with, then they will never lose hope or motivation in life.

Here, Allah ﷻ recounts the Divine gifts reserved for those who show perseverance after having passed through trials and tribulations in their lives, and states that these are the people upon whom the grace and mercy of Allah ﷻ will be showered upon.

The grace and mercy which comes from Allah ﷻ strengthens the true believers so that they do not fall into error and deviation because they are aware of and dread the dangerous paths which can diverge a person away from Allah ﷻ. At the end of this verse, Allah ﷻ concludes by stating that since **He** is personally taking care of them, they will be the guided ones.

Keys of Guidance

- Allah ﷻ actually gives encouragement to those who exhibit patience, and this should teach us that we too must be ready to show extra respect and honor to those who are struggling in the way of Allah ﷻ *(mujāhidīn)*, and those who are going through difficulties yet bearing them with patience, knowing that they are being blessed by Allah ﷻ.
- Those who go through difficulties in life and show patience are not only receiving a reward for these trials and bearing them with fortitude, but they are also individuals who are on the actual path of true guidance from Allah ﷻ. There are many people who think that they are guided, others who are trying to be guided, and yet others who wish that they were guided - but in the case of those with patience, Allah ﷻ guarantees that they are guided and on the right path in life.

Verse 158

إِنَّ ٱلصَّفَا وَٱلۡمَرۡوَةَ مِن شَعَآئِرِ ٱللَّهِۖ فَمَنۡ حَجَّ ٱلۡبَيۡتَ أَوِ ٱعۡتَمَرَ فَلَا جُنَاحَ
عَلَيۡهِ أَن يَطَّوَّفَ بِهِمَاۚ وَمَن تَطَوَّعَ خَيۡرٗا فَإِنَّ ٱللَّهَ شَاكِرٌ عَلِيمٌ ١٥٨

Indeed (the mountains of) aṣ-Ṣafā and al-Marwah are among the emblems *(shaʿāʾir)* that Allah has appointed (to represent Islam). Therefore whoever performs *Ḥajj*[51] (the major pilgrimage) to the House (of Allah ﷻ) or the *ʿUmrah*[52] (the minor pilgrimage), there is no blame on him to run between these two (mountains). And whoever does a good work voluntarily (such as additional acts of *ṭawāf*[53] around the Kaʿbah, or running between aṣ-Ṣafā and al-Marwah, or other actions), surely Allah is All-Responsive to Thankfulness *(Shākir)*, All-Knowing *(ʿAlīm)*.

In many narrations narrated by the Shīʿah and Sunnī scholars, we read that in the Age of Ignorance *(Jāhiliyyah)*,[54] the polytheists had installed

[51] *Ḥajj* is an act of worship, and one of the most important sacraments in Islam which consists of pilgrimage to the city of Mecca and its surrounding areas to perform specific rituals. In addition to the spiritual aspect of worship, *Ḥajj* also has social, economic, and political aspects to it, and it is one of the largest gatherings of Muslims which happens once a year, and it takes place from around the 8th day to the 12th day of the last lunar month which is Dhūl Ḥijjah.

All Muslims are in agreement that it is an obligation to undertake the *Ḥajj* at least once in a person's lifetime for all able-bodied Muslims who are physically and financially able to make this journey.

[52] The *ʿUmrah* is a non-compulsory, but recommended pilgrimage to the city of Mecca in order to perform certain rituals in the vicinity of the Kaʿbah; and this can be performed at almost any time of the year. There are two types of *ʿUmrahs*: *ʿUmrah al-Mufradah* and *ʿUmrah at-Tamattuʿ*.

[53] The word *ṭawāf* means 'to surround something or turn around something on foot' and in Islamic jurisprudence it means 'to circumambulate around the Kaʿbah.' *Ṭawāf* around the Kaʿbah is an obligatory ritual of *Ḥajj* and *ʿUmrah* in which a pilgrim circumambulates around the Kaʿbah seven times counter-clockwise, while fulfilling some specific conditions which are detailed in the books of Islamic Laws.

[54] The Era or Age of Ignorance *(Jāhilīyyah)* is a term which the Qurʾān and *ḥadīth* use to speak about the lifestyle, conducts, and beliefs of the Arabs before the emergence of Islam in Arabia.

an idol named *Asāf* on the top of the mountain of aṣ-Ṣafā, and another idol called *Nāila* on top of the mountain of al-Marwah.

When they would walk *(saʿī)*[55] between these two mountains during their acts of worship, they used to rub their hands on the heads of these two idols, seeking blessings from them. Due to this action of the polytheists, the Muslims did not want to walk between these two mountains of aṣ-Ṣafā and al-Marwah when they performed the acts of worship, and thought that in such circumstances as long as these idols were present it was not the right thing to do.

In order to clarify the verdict, this verse was revealed in which Allah ﷻ declared that the two mountains of aṣ-Ṣafā and al-Marwah are among the emblems of Allah ﷻ, and that if the ignorant people of Mecca have defiled them through installing these idols, then this is not a reason for the Muslims to abandon the duty of performing the walking *(saʿī)* between aṣ-Ṣafā and al-Marwah.

Actions of the Ignorant

Given the unique psychological condition which existed in the early Muslims in regards to acts of worship performed around the Sacred Mosque and their defilement by the polytheists, Allah ﷻ clarified that aṣ-Ṣafā and al-Marwah are among the rites and signs of Allah ﷻ.

The Almighty went on to stress the importance of these two emblems and told the Muslims that there is no problem if during the course of

---

The word *jāhiliyyah* is derived from the word *jahl* which means 'ignorance' and along with its cognates, these different words were used in the Arabic poetry before Islam. The word literally means 'lack of knowledge,' but its usage in regards to the specific Era in which the Qur'ān used it does not have such implications. Rather, it refers to a sort of conduct that was so arrogant and self-centered that the people of that time who had this mindset did not obey any power or authority - be it human or be it Divine.

[55] The act of *saʿī* consists of walking between the two mountains of aṣ-Ṣafā and al-Marwah a total of seven times with the intention of doing an action which is required as part of the obligatory rituals for *Ḥajj* or *ʿUmrah*. Each round of this action, meaning walking from one mountain to the other, is called a *shawt*.

performing the rites of worship to the House of Allah, whether it be for *Ḥajj* or *'Umrah* if they make their way between these two mountains for the act of *sa'ī*.

At the end of this verse, Allah ﷻ tells the believers that whoever obeys His commands as it relates to doing good deeds will find Allah ﷻ thankful to that person, and that He is fully Aware of all of their actions.

Allah ﷻ is Thankful to His Servants?

This phrase which Allah ﷻ uses about Him being 'thankful' to His servants is described by commentators of the Qur'ān as a very subtle and emotionally touching phrase. However, we must realize that we should not equate the human emotion and process of thanking others when they do something for us to the method of Allah ﷻ showing thanks, nor the rationale behind why He would do so.

At one level, the thanks which Allah ﷻ shows is understood as being the highest level of respect which He has for the good deeds His servants perform. In such a scenario, He becomes grateful to them for their righteous actions - not that He requires them to do so. Note that when it is said that Allah ﷻ becomes grateful, He does not go through changes in Himself or in His state - rather, Him being grateful means that the individual who has acted appropriately is given the opportunity to earn something of Paradise just as when we talk about the anger of Allah ﷻ, it does not mean a spiritual change in Him, but rather, His including the individual who had acted inappropriately into the punishment of hell in the world to come.

In return of their obedience and good deeds, Allah ﷻ thanks the servants and reminds the believers that He is All-Aware of their intentions - He knows who is interested in serving the idols and who is disgusted with them, and despite their presence in the Sacred Mosque, they should continue to worship the One True God, even though the revered space is polluted with false gods.

Two Hills of aṣ-Ṣafā and al-Marwah

Aṣ-Ṣafā and al-Marwah are the names of two small mountains[56] in Mecca, which today, due to the development of the Sacred Mosque, are on the eastern side of the building on the side where the Black Stone and the *Maqām-e Ibrāhīm* are located.

The word *aṣ-Ṣafā* literally means 'a solid and smooth stone that is not mixed with soil and sand,' while *al-marwah* means 'a solid and rough stone.'

The word 'emblems' *(shaʿāʾir)* is the plural of *shaʿīrah* and it means 'a sign or insignia,' and thus the meaning of the phrase: 'the emblems of Allah' *(shaʿāʾirullāh)* are 'those signs which remind a person about Allah ﷻ and renew a memory of sacred reminiscences in the heart of an individual.'

Another word which Allah ﷻ uses in this verse, *iʿtamara*, comes from the root *ʿamarah* and its original meaning was 'an addition which someone would build to a house or another building, allowing the structure to reach its full completion,' however in the terminology of religion *(sharīʿah)* it refers to 'special acts which are added to the Ḥajj rituals.'

Historical Position of aṣ-Ṣafā and al-Marwah

History narrates that Prophet Ibrāhīm ؑ had reached old age, but still had no children. He prayed to Allah ﷻ to bless him with offspring, and around the same time that this supplication was made, his slave-girl/wife, Hājar ؑ, was blessed with a son who was fathered by Prophet Ibrāhīm ؑ that he named Ismāʿīl ؑ.[57]

---

[56] The distance between these two mountains, referred to in Arabic as *masʿa* is about 1,295 feet. These mountains used to be quite tall, however due to numerous factors, including the expansion of the Sacred Mosque, they reduced in height - with the Mountain of aṣ-Ṣafā being around 26 feet high, while only traces of the Mountain of al-Marwah remaining with the majority of it having been completely leveled flat.

[57] Historians have stated that his name was not Arabic, and is made up of two words, *ismaʿ* and *īl* - which literally means 'Allah heard' and it was such because

As a test from Allah ﷻ commanded Prophet Ibrāhīm ؑ to take his second wife, Hājar, and their child Ismā'īl ؑ to Mecca, which at that time was a dry, barren desert land and leave them there. Prophet Ibrāhīm ؑ obeyed the command of Allah ﷻ and took them to Mecca.

As he planned to return back home alone, his wife Hājar ؑ began to cry and ask Prophet Ibrāhīm ؑ what she and her infant son would do in this waterless and unfertile desert.

The heart of Prophet Ibrāhīm ؑ was so moved due to the tears of his infant son, so along with his own burning tears, he prayed to Allah ﷻ and said: "Our Lord! I have settled some of my offspring (Ismā'īl ؑ and his descendants) in an uncultivable valley near Your Sacred House, our Lord, that they may establish the prayer *(ṣalāh)*; so make the hearts of people incline toward them, and provide for them the fruits (produce of earth by such means as trade), so that they may give thanks (constantly from the heart, and in speech, and action by fulfilling Your commandments)."[58]

Prophet Ibrāhīm ؑ went on to say: "Lord, because of your command, I will leave my wife and child alone in this desert, so that Your Name may be Exalted, and Your House may be settled."

Prophet Ibrāhīm ؑ said these words, bid his farewells to his wife and infant son, then amid deep sorrow and love, left them alone there.

Shortly thereafter, Hājar ؑ ran out of food and water, and the milk in her body had also stopped, and her infant's impatience and begging gazes made her so anxious that she ended up forgetting her own thirst as she struggled to find water for her young baby, Ismā'īl ؑ.

Allah ﷻ heard the supplication of Prophet Ibrāhīm ؑ and granted him a child. Ismā'īl is mentioned a total of 12 times in the Noble Qur'ān in regards to various subjects, such as helping his father build the Ka'bah, having revelation come to him, and in passages where other Prophets which Allah ﷻ sent for humanity are mentioned. For references about Prophet Ismā'īl ؑ in the Qur'ān refer to: 2:125, 2:127, 2:133, 2:136, 2:140, 3:84, 4:163, 6:86, 14:39, 19:54, 21:85, 38:48.

[58] Qur'ān, Sūrah Ibrāhīm (14), Verse 37:

رَبَّنَآ إِنِّيٓ أَسْكَنتُ مِن ذُرِّيَّتِي بِوَادٍ غَيْرِ ذِي زَرْعٍ عِندَ بَيْتِكَ ٱلْمُحَرَّمِ رَبَّنَا لِيُقِيمُوا۟ ٱلصَّلَوٰةَ
فَٱجْعَلْ أَفْـِٔدَةً مِّنَ ٱلنَّاسِ تَهْوِىٓ إِلَيْهِمْ وَٱرْزُقْهُم مِّنَ ٱلثَّمَرَٰتِ لَعَلَّهُمْ يَشْكُرُونَ ﴿٣٧﴾

Lady Hājar ☙ first made her way to the mountain of aṣ-Ṣafā but there was no trace of water there.

A mirage from the side of the mountain of al-Marwah caught her eyes and she thought she saw water there so she rushed toward it, however upon reaching that small mountain, she saw that no water was to be found there either.

She looked back toward where she had just come from, and now saw a mirage at the mountain of aṣ-Ṣafā, so she returned to it, and this effort to fight for the survival of her dear child played out seven times.

In the concluding moments in which her infant son was going through perhaps the final minutes of his young life, a fountain of water began to gush from beneath the feet of Ismā'īl ☙ - it was the water of *zamzam* - and what an unexpected surprise it must have been! The mother and child drank from it and were saved from an imminent death.

The traverse between the mountains of aṣ-Ṣafā and al-Marwah teach us that in order to revive the truth and realize the greatness of Allah's ☙ pure teachings, everyone - even an infant child - must stand to the end, ready to give up one's life.

The journey of Lady Hājar ☙ from aṣ-Ṣafā to al-Marwah teaches us that even in times of despair there should be hope. This expedition also expresses that we must appreciate religion, and the center of Monotheism (*Tawḥīd*) which is the city of Mecca. There are some individuals who have reached the brink of death in order to preserve this sacred place for us, and others who have even sacrificed their lives for it.

It is for this reason that Allah ☙ made it obligatory upon each pilgrim to His House to walk between these two mountains seven times in order to renew these historical legacies - and that too, wearing special clothing (*iḥrām*) in the form of a pilgrim's garb. Every individual must walk from one mountain to the other in a unique way, free from any special privileges or recognition - regardless of who the person is.

Those people who due to arrogance and pride refuse to walk on public sidewalks, or do not want to be seen in public walking around with the 'common people,' or would never be seen walking at a brisk pace in the streets - are now being ordered by Allah ☙ to walk at a slow pace in one area, then walk hurriedly at another portion during the act of the *saʿī* between the mountains of aṣ-Ṣafā and al-Marwah.[59]

When we look into the narrations about why *saʿī* takes on this unique process of first walking at a standard pace, then a light jog for a few feet, followed by reverting back to walking at a standard pace again, *ḥadīth* mention that this should be done in order to ensure that the inner core of the arrogant ones is awoken and that they humble themselves.

Keys of Guidance

- The special focus which Allah ﷻ gives to certain places, times, and people causes them to transform from being in a normal state to one of Divine sanctification, and being raised to be Signs of Allah ﷻ - *Shaʿāʾirullāh.*
- If a center which is disseminating the truth is infected by people who start performing strange things or following illogical superstitions, then the religiously-minded and knowledgeable people must not stop going to that place; rather, they must attend those centers, and through their active presence work to purify them, and ensure that the deviants who have introduced unfounded practices are not allowed to continue their behaviors.

Verse 159

إِنَّ ٱلَّذِينَ يَكۡتُمُونَ مَآ أَنزَلۡنَا مِنَ ٱلۡبَيِّنَٰتِ وَٱلۡهُدَىٰ مِنۢ بَعۡدِ مَا بَيَّنَّٰهُ
لِلنَّاسِ فِي ٱلۡكِتَٰبِ أُوْلَٰٓئِكَ يَلۡعَنُهُمُ ٱللَّهُ وَيَلۡعَنُهُمُ ٱللَّٰعِنُونَ ١٥٩

Surely those who conceal anything of the clear truths and (the revelations conveying) the guidance which We have sent down,

---

[59] The Muslim Jurists note that when performing the *saʿī* between the two mountains of aṣ-Ṣafā and al-Marwa, it is recommended for men to perform an act known as *harwala* - which can be defined as a brisk jog. This is performed both when going from aṣ-Ṣafā to al-Marwa, and also back from al-Marwa to aṣ-Ṣafā. Today, the *Ḥajj* authorities have labeled the area where this act should be done by green light markers.

after We have made them clear in the Book, Allah curses[60] such people (meaning that they themselves have turned their backs from the Mercy of Allah), and so do all (of those) who (have any authority to) curse.

History of Revelation

It has been narrated that Ibn ʿAbbās said that several Muslims, such as Muʿādh ibn Jabal, Saʿd ibn Muʿādh, and Khārijah ibn Zayd asked a group of Jewish scholars some questions in regards to the advent of Prophet Muḥammad ﷺ as mentioned in the Tawrāh. These Jews hid the truth and refused to explain what was mentioned in their Books, and thus this verse was revealed, reminding them about their responsibility that they

---

[60] In the Noble Qurʾān, the damnation *(laʿn)* which Allah ﷻ speaks about is attributed to Himself, His angels, and some of His Prophets ﷺ. A damned human is said to be either in Hell, or living in a state wherein one is divorced from Heaven, and/or in a state of disgrace from the favors of Allah ﷻ. Such individuals are in this state they find themselves in is due to their own actions.

Rāghib al-Iṣfahānī states that: "Malediction *(laʿn)* means 'the rejection and distancing of oneself [from something] - angrily.' If malediction is practiced by Allah ﷻ, then its meaning is that in the next life, one will face the Divine retribution; while in this transient world, it means that the individual will be cut off from being able to accept the Mercy [of Allah ﷻ] and the Divine providence. If malediction is employed by an individual, then it means that one makes supplication and imprecation, and entreats [Allah ﷻ] to bring about damage to the person whom one is praying against." (*Al-Mufradāt* of Rāghib, Vol. 2, Pg. 339)

The verses which employ this term speak about damnation against: Shayṭān, the disbelievers, those who leave Islam, the disbelievers from the tribe of ʿĀd, the disbelievers from among the people of Pharaoh, the disbelievers from the Tribes of Isrāʾīl, disbelievers from among the People of the Book, the Jews who disregarded the Sabbath, and many other groups.

Therefore not only here, but even in other verses of the Qurʾān in which the removal of the Mercy of Allah ﷻ is spoken about, we must understand that it means that such people have turned their back on the Mercy of Allah ﷻ which is always there, so in reality, this is their own doing.

should not hide the truth.

It is Impermissible to Conceal the Truth

In previous verses, Allah ﷻ spoke about *Ḥajj* and how it is a proof of Allah ﷻ. In addition, we must recognize that He has given us enough signs all around us to guide us to Him. In this verse, we see that after all He has done to provide us guidance, if people recognize the truth and still choose to conceal it, not abide by it, reject it, or fight against it, then the only natural result is that they have separated themselves from Allah ﷻ and His Mercy.

Although according to the history of revelation, this verse was revealed in regards to some Jewish scholars who lived during the time of Prophet Muḥammad ﷺ, however this does not mean that we should limit the meaning of this verse to just them.

In addition to its historical relevance, it also provides the reader with a general rule about those who conceal the truth in every era and rebukes such people. The verse tells us that those who conceal the clear proofs and means of guidance which Allah ﷻ sends down to the people after He clearly outlined these proofs in the Books which were revealed to the past Prophets will earn the damnation of Allah ﷻ - meaning the removal of His Mercy.

Not only does Allah ﷻ rebuke them, but He goes on to say that there are others - referring to the believers - who are permitted to call on this damnation of Allah ﷻ upon such people - keeping in mind that the meaning of damnation here is that the believers too should distance themselves from these people due to their sinful nature and actions. If at any time they decide to change their ways and repent, then there is no need for the believers to distance themselves from these people anymore.

Once again, we must reiterate this extremely important point that the damnation from Allah ﷻ a direct result of a person themselves deciding to remove themselves from the vast Mercy of Allah ﷻ due to their own actions. The Mercy of Allah ﷻ is always there, and if the sinners repent and return to Allah ﷻ, then they will once again benefit from His vast Mercy, as it is they who had turned their back on the Mercy of the One True God - otherwise His Mercy has not gone anywhere.

The concealment of the truth is an act which should also provoke the anger of the followers of the truth, and it is not limited to concealing the revelations of Allah ﷻ, or the proofs which would lead someone to better understand the Prophethood of Prophet Muḥammad ﷺ - or any other Prophet which Allah ﷻ sent for the guidance of humanity.

In fact, this concealment can relate to anything which can bring people to the point of knowing and accepting the truth - and all of this is contained within this phrase.

Even when silence is used to hide the truth such that a person should speak out and expose the truth but does not do so, allowing falsehood to perpetuate due to one's silence is also another example of concealing the truth.

Hiding the Truth as Seen in the Ḥadīth

We see very stern warnings in the *ḥadīth* which are aimed at those religious scholars who know the truth but hide it from the masses.

As an example, Prophet Muḥammad ﷺ has been quoted as saying: "Whoever benefits from the knowledge of a scholar but then hides that knowledge [which he gained] from others, Allah will restrain that person with a bridle of fire over their mouth on the Day of Resurrection."[61]

In another tradition it is mentioned that the Commander of the Faithful, Imām ʿAlī ؑ was asked: "Who is the worst creation of Allah after Satan and the Pharaoh?" Imām ʿAlī ؑ replied: "The religious scholars who are corrupt, reveal falsehoods, or hide the truths; and they are the ones about whom Allah, the Most High has said: 'Indeed it is these people whom Allah has cursed, and all of those who are permitted to evoke the damnation of Allah should do so [to them as well].'"[62]

---

[61] Ṭabarsī, Abū Manṣūr, *Majmaʿ al-Bayān*, under the verse in review. *Biḥār al-Anwār*, Vol. 7, Pg. 217 (with slight variations), Vol. 57, Pg. 301; and also Vol. 89, Pg. 111. The initial portion of this tradition is as follows:

مَنْ سُئِلَ عَنْ عِلْمٍ يَعْلَمُهُ فَكَتَمَهُ لُجِمَ يَوْمَ الْقِيَامَةِ...

[62] Ṭabarsī, Abū Manṣūr, *Al-Iḥtijāj* according the narration found in *Tafsīr Nūr ath-Thaqalayn*, Vol. 3, Pg. 139; *Biḥār al-Anwār*, Vol. 2, Pg. 88, *Tuḥaf al-ʿUqūl*, Pg.

Keys of Guidance

- Hiding the truth is considered as one of the major sins in Islam because it works as a catalyst to prevent people from being guided to Allah ﷻ, and could even result in many generations of people deviating from the true path of servitude to the Almighty ﷻ.
- Concealment of the truth in whichever form or shape it takes place - whether it be by an individual or a government, verbally or digitally, through the media or another outlet - is considered to be a serious act of oppression against the religion of Allah ﷻ and human rights because everyone has a God-given right to guidance - just like one has a right to food, clothing, shelter, and security. Therefore, anyone who conceals the truth will find oneself at the receiving end of the damnation of Allah ﷻ and society.

Verse 160

إِلَّا ٱلَّذِينَ تَابُواْ وَأَصۡلَحُواْ وَبَيَّنُواْ فَأُوْلَٰٓئِكَ أَتُوبُ عَلَيۡهِمۡ وَأَنَا ٱلتَّوَّابُ ٱلرَّحِيمُ ١٦٠

Except those who repent and mend their ways, and openly declare (those signs and Revelations); for those, I (Allah ﷻ) will return their repentance with forgiveness (and include them in My special Mercy). And I am the One Who accepts Repentance *(at-Tawwāb)*, the All-Merciful *(ar-Raḥīm)*.

Previously, we spoke about the actions of people, and how everything a person does has consequences. We touched upon concealing the truth, rejecting it, and fighting against it, and how this will lead to eternal damnation *(laʿn)* which is them turning their backs to the Mercy of Allah

---

35. The initial portion of this tradition is as follows:

مَنْ شَرُّ خَلْقِ اللّٰهِ بَعْدَ إِبْلِيسَ وَفِرْعَونَ؟ قَالَ: أَلْعُلَمَاءُ إِذَا فَسَدُوا هُوَ الْـمُظْهِرُونَ...

ﷻ, and thus being away from His Compassion.

The verse under review seeks to emphasize that this *laʿn* is because of the actions of the people themselves, and for them to realize that the door to repentance is always open for everyone, and the moment that anyone repents and seeks the Mercy of Allah ﷻ, it will reach them and they will be showered with His Grace, Blessings, and Compassion.

The Qurʾān, as a Book of guidance, never closes the door of hope to the sinners and those who have erred. It continuously provides a way back to Allah ﷻ for those who made mistakes in their lives, and never allows people to live in despair or become hopeless in the Mercy of Allah ﷻ - no matter how tainted with sins they may be.

This verse offers us a glimpse into the way of achieving salvation in the face of sins which a person has performed. Allah ﷻ guides humanity and tells them that if they have transgressed His laws, and later on recognize their mistakes, then they can always repent and turn back to Allah ﷻ in remorse. They should correct their evil deeds by making amends and performing good deeds, then Allah ﷻ will turn back to them - metaphorically speaking - and accept them and their repentance.

Not only in this verse, but in countless other instances in the Qurʾān, Allah ﷻ confirms that He continuously turns back toward His penitent servants *(at-Tawwāb)*, and He is the All-Merciful *(ar-Raḥīm)*.

Keys of Guidance

- Allah ﷻ has provided people with an opportunity to repent and turn back to Him, and this is available for any wrongdoer, no matter what situation they find themselves in with regards to Allah ﷻ.
- The repentance of every sin is commensurate with the sin performed. The repentance of hiding the truth is to openly declare it; the true repentance of sins like stealing is to return the stolen things back to their rightful owner; the sin of backbiting (openly expressing someone's shortcomings, faults, or defects) is to spread good words and speak highly about that individual who was spoken ill of.
- Allah ﷻ is such a Loving and Benevolent God that the return of His Grace and Pardon is always available for those who sin, but then

repent for their evil actions, turn back to Him, and make amends for their shortcomings.

Verse 161

إِنَّ ٱلَّذِينَ كَفَرُواْ وَمَاتُواْ وَهُمْ كُفَّارٌ أُوْلَٰٓئِكَ عَلَيْهِمْ لَعْنَةُ ٱللَّهِ وَٱلْمَلَٰٓئِكَةِ
وَٱلنَّاسِ أَجْمَعِينَ ﴿١٦١﴾

Indeed those who reject the truth (after knowing it as the truth) and die as unbelievers have earned the curse of Allah, and the angels, and all of humankind.

Outcome of Those who Die as Disbelievers

In the previous verses, we saw the outcome of those who knew the truth and still concealed it, while in this verse and the next one this discussion is furthered, and Allah ﷻ refers to the obstinate disbelievers *(kuffār)* who continue to be stubborn and conceal the truth, thus enter into disbelief by denying the truth until they leave this world.

Before we move on, we must make it clear that this verse and other similar verses in the Qur'ān are not addressing the common people who may not know much about the truth and are just following the rest of the people in society, or those who have no access to the truth due to the influx of fake news propaganda against the One True God and Islam. Rather, this and similar verses are addressing those who really understand the truth but choose to reject it or conceal it.

In the first portion of this verse Allah ﷻ states that those who disbelieve and die in a state of open disbelief and obstinacy to the truth, even though they knew that it was from Allah ﷻ but still decided to reject it, are cursed by Allah ﷻ - meaning they have turned their backs on His special Mercy which was reserved for those who were on the truth, and therefore they have actually brought upon the damnation on themselves.

This act of removing the special Mercy of Allah ﷻ is not limited to

Him, but rather even the angels will supplicate to Allah ﷻ and ask Him to remove His Mercy from those people, and in addition all of humanity who are entitled to evoke the damnation upon such people will also appeal this to Allah ﷻ.

We must note that when *la'n* is attributed to the angels, and the Qur'ān states that they curse the rejecters of the truth, it means that they are asking Allah ﷻ for permission to limit the Mercy of Allah ﷻ that goes through them to these people.

When *la'n* is attributed to humanity, it means that a person cuts ties and detaches oneself from these people due to their actions.

Just like those who conceal the truth, this group of people are also caught in damnation with this slight difference that since they insisted on leading a life of disbelief *(kufr)* until the end of their lives, there is no return for them, and there will be no room for them to avail the Mercy and Compassion of Allah ﷻ unless and until they decide to leave this path and to go back to the servitude of Allah ﷻ. Once a person realizes that they have done wrong and feel inner remorse, they will make a pledge to change their ways, and immediately the Mercy of Allah ﷻ will reach them again - it was always there waiting to cover them, however they had placed a barrier between themselves and His Mercy.

Keys of Guidance

- Insisting on disbelief *(kufr)* and rejecting the truth after it has become clear, and dying in a state of denial of Allah ﷻ seals a person's fate, and will result in eternal separation from the Divine Mercy of Allah.
- If a person were to die in this state before one has the time to return to Allah ﷻ and engage in *tawbah* and accept the truth, then their situation would be quite drastic. However we must realize that the way to Allah ﷻ is always open and there is no 'dead-end' in life to turn back to Allah ﷻ - it is never too late to repent and believe in Allah ﷻ - and the only thing which seals a person's fate is death.

Verse 162

خَٰلِدِينَ فِيهَا لَا يُخَفَّفُ عَنْهُمُ ٱلْعَذَابُ وَلَا هُمْ يُنظَرُونَ ۝

They will remain in it (forever) and their punishment shall not be lightened, nor will they be granted any respite.

Allah ﷻ adds to the description of the obstinate disbelievers by stating that not only will they be deprived of His All-Encompassing Mercy, but they will abide in the fire of Hell forever, and will not be relieved of their torment whatsoever, nor will they have any respite while they are in it.

Why Remain in Punishment Forever?

There are some actions which do not only have a lifetime effect, rather they affect the entire future of humanity for generations to come. A person who oppresses others in such a way that the aftermath of it will affect even the future generations after knowing what they have done and the ramifications of it needs to spend eternity in Hell just like the outcome of their actions lasted for a protracted period of time.

It is very important to note that such people are very specific and few in number. The level of their stubbornness in rejecting the truth and insisting on a life of sin fighting against the One True God and His teachings which are meant to help humanity is so great that even if they went to Hell, then came back, they would continue their evil ways.

In this regard, there is a clear *ḥadīth* from Imām aṣ-Ṣādiq ؈ in which he has been quoted as saying: "The people of the fire will permanently be kept in the fire because their intentions in this world were such that if they were to live forever therein, they would have disobeyed Allah forever; and verily the people of Paradise will also be made to remain in Paradise permanently because their intentions in this world were to obey Allah even if they were only to live here forever. So, it is due to the intentions of these people that they have their permanent residence." Then the Imām ؈ recited the words of Allah, the Exalted: "Say: 'Everyone acts according to one's character' and said that this means according to one's intention."[63]

Why will the Punishment not be Decreased or Lightened?

Allah ﷻ is All-Just and All-Compassionate. When these disbelievers, even after being punished are still adamant on their cruel ways, and they themselves chose this path and are not looking for a decreased punishment or lightened chastisement, there is no need for Allah ﷻ to provide it to them.

Keys of Guidance

- A reduction in punishment, or even its delay is something which is strictly related to the life of this world, because on the Day of Judgment once the accounts have been settled, there will neither be any reduction in the punishment, nor any way to delay the inevitable anguish.

Verse 163

وَإِلَٰهُكُمۡ إِلَٰهٞ وَٰحِدٞۖ لَّآ إِلَٰهَ إِلَّا هُوَ ٱلرَّحۡمَٰنُ ٱلرَّحِيمُ ١٦٣

And your God is One Allah; there is no god-except for Him, the All-Compassionate *(ar-Raḥmān)*, the All-Merciful *(ar-Raḥīm)*.

Since the principle of Monotheism *(Tawḥīd)* puts an end to all of the misfortunes which Allah ﷻ spoke about in the previous verses, at this point He reminds the disbelievers that their God is the One True God - Allah ﷻ; and to further emphasize this, He states that there is no god worthy of worship except for Him.

The last portion of this verse goes on to further elaborate about Allah ﷻ as He reminds the people, specifically those living during the time of Prophet Muḥammad ﷺ who previously denied Allah ﷻ and the message

---

[63] *Al-Kāfī*, Vol. 2, Pg. 85, Ḥadīth 5. The initial portion of this tradition is as follows:

إِنَّمَا خُلِّدَ أَهْلُ النَّارِ فِي النَّارِ لِأَنَّ نِيَّاتِهِمْ كَانَتْ فِي الدُّنْيَا...

of His Prophet ﷺ, or those who were hiding the truth from others that if they were to repent and accept Allah ﷻ as the One True God, and Prophet Muḥammad ﷺ as the Promised Messenger, then He will forgive them as He is the All-Compassionate, the All-Merciful.

Yes, the One whose general Mercy *(Raḥmāniyyah)* encompasses everything and everyone, and Who provides special Mercy *(Raḥīmiyyah)* for the believers is worthy of worship and adoration - and no one and nothing else at all deserves this.

Keys of Guidance

- After speaking about perpetuity in punishment and anguish, it is the way of Allah ﷻ that He always brings His general Mercy *(Raḥmāniyyah)* and special Mercy *(Raḥīmiyyah)* as a conclusion to give hope and purpose to the human being. Therefore, with this verse and similar verses in the Qur'ān, the way of Allah ﷻ is that He always specifically speaks about His Mercy because His main purpose is to constantly guide humanity so that the eventual outcome of everyone will be Paradise, not a continuous residence in the fire of Hell - as He wants us to be on the right path and do good.

Verse 164

إِنَّ فِي خَلْقِ ٱلسَّمَٰوَٰتِ وَٱلْأَرْضِ وَٱخْتِلَٰفِ ٱلَّيْلِ وَٱلنَّهَارِ وَٱلْفُلْكِ ٱلَّتِي
تَجْرِي فِي ٱلْبَحْرِ بِمَا يَنفَعُ ٱلنَّاسَ وَمَآ أَنزَلَ ٱللَّهُ مِنَ ٱلسَّمَآءِ مِن مَّآءٍ
فَأَحْيَا بِهِ ٱلْأَرْضَ بَعْدَ مَوْتِهَا وَبَثَّ فِيهَا مِن كُلِّ دَآبَّةٍ وَتَصْرِيفِ ٱلرِّيَٰحِ
وَٱلسَّحَابِ ٱلْمُسَخَّرِ بَيْنَ ٱلسَّمَآءِ وَٱلْأَرْضِ لَأٓيَٰتٍ لِّقَوْمٍ يَعْقِلُونَ ١٦٤

Surely in the creation of the heavens and the earth, and the alternation of the night and the day, and the vessels sailing in the sea with profits for the people, and the water that Allah sends down from the sky, therewith reviving the earth after its death, and dispersing therein all kinds of living creatures, and His disposal of the winds, and the clouds subservient between the sky and the earth - surely there are signs for people who use their intellect.

Manifestations of His Pure Essence in Existence

Since the previous verse spoke about the Oneness *(Tawḥīd)* of the One True God - Allah ﷻ, this verse provides some of the proofs about His existence.

Wherever we find order and cohesion in the world of creation, this points to the presence of knowledge - as such order could not have come about through ignorance; and everywhere we find harmony in the world of creation, this points to unity and oneness.

Based on this principle, when dealing with the manifestations of order in the universe on one hand, and the harmony and unity of action of these orderly systems on the other, we realize that the source of this unique knowledge and power all come from One Being - Allah ﷻ.

In this verse, six components related to the workings of the order in the universe are mentioned, each of which is a sign of that great Originator - Allah ﷻ, and they are the following:

1. Creation of the heavens and the earth: Scientists have stated that there are thousands of galaxies in existence, and that our solar system is just one of them.[64] There are hundreds of millions of bright suns and stars in our galaxy alone, among which scientists estimate are millions of habitable planets[65] with billions of living

---

[64] Although the estimates among different experts vary, an acceptable range is between 100 billion and 200 billion galaxies, says Mario Livio, an astrophysicist at the Space Telescope Science Institute in Baltimore, Maryland. When the James Webb Space Telescope launched in 2020, the observatory was expected to reveal even more information about early galaxies in the universe. (Taken from www.space.com/25303-how-many-galaxies-are-in-the-universe.html. Last accessed on September 21, 2022)

[65] In November 2013, astronomers reported, based on Kepler space mission data, that there could be as many as 40 billion Earth-sized planets orbiting in the

creatures.

2. Alternation of the night and the day: The transformation of the night into the day, and the "coming and going" of light and darkness[66] with its unique, gradual order through which the four seasons come about[67] provides living beings with all that they need to go through their evolutionary stages, and this is another sign of Allah ﷻ and His transcendent nature.
3. Ships that sail in the sea for the benefit of people: Human beings sail across oceans and seas[68] by the use of both large and small ships, and travel to different parts of the earth in order to fulfill various tasks such as carrying people and cargo from one country to another.
4. Water which Allah ﷻ sends down from the sky, and through it revives the earth after its death, and spreads in it all kinds of creatures: Life-giving drops of rain which fall onto the earth

---

habitable zones of Sun-like stars and red dwarfs in the Milky Way, 11 billion of which may be orbiting Sun-like stars.

[66] Earth's axis is an imaginary pole going right through the center of Earth from "top" to "bottom." Earth spins around this pole, making one complete turn each day. That is why we have day and night, and why every part of the Earth's surface gets some of each. (Extracted from www.spaceplace.nasa.gov/seasons/en/. Last accessed on September 21, 2022)

[67] Earth's tilted axis causes the seasons. Throughout the year, different parts of Earth receive the Sun's most direct rays. So, when the North Pole tilts toward the Sun, it is summer in the Northern Hemisphere, and when the South Pole tilts toward the Sun, it is winter in the Northern Hemisphere.

[68] The explanation behind how ships which may weigh thousands of pounds can sail on top of the water and not sink has been described through the use of Archimedes' Principle which states that the force exerted on an object in a fluid is equal to the weight of fluid displaced (moved out of the way) by the object. This force is called buoyant force. The buoyant force pushes upwards against an object. Gravity exerts a downward force on the object (its weight) which is determined by the object's mass. So if the force exerted downward on the object by gravity is less than the buoyant force, then the object will float.

through the unique system[69] that is in place is extraordinary because although water in itself is "lifeless" - it provides life to creations on earth, and this is yet another point to show us the Power and Greatness of Allah ﷻ.

5. Changes in the direction of the wind: Not only does the wind blow over the seas, oceans, and allows the ships to move, it also aids in the pollination of plants by helping to move male pollen to the female parts of plants in order to fertilize them.[70] In addition, we also benefit from the wind because it moves polluted and deoxygenated air from the cities to the deserts and forests, which helps provide a means of purification of the air, and a form of ventilation for human beings and animals. Therefore, the winds with these and countless other benefits is also another sign of the Almighty's infinite Wisdom and Grace.
6. Clouds which are subservient between the earth and the sky: The dense clouds that hover over our heads and hold billions of tons of water which are suspended between the earth and the sky seem to contravene the law of gravity, so they are another sign of the greatness of Allah ﷻ.

All of these are signs of Allah ﷻ and His Oneness - however, these are signs for people who reflect and ponder deeply on them, and wonder about who put all of this precision into the world, and contemplate that could it have been a random coincidence that all of this happened by chance, or on its own?

---

[69] What causes rain? Clouds are made of water droplets. Within a cloud, water droplets condense into one another causing the droplets to grow. When these water droplets get too heavy to stay suspended in the clouds, they fall onto the earth as rain.

[70] Anemophily is a process when pollen is transported by air currents from one individual plant to another. About 12% of the world's flowering plants are wind-pollinated, including grasses, cereal crops, many trees, and the infamous allergenic ragweeds. (Extracted from www.ucanr.edu/sites/PollenNation/Meet_The_Pollinators/Wind/. Last accessed on September 21, 2022)

Keys of Guidance

- Again and again in the Qur'ān, Allah ﷻ tells us to use our intellect as it is a tool which if used appropriately, will allow us to receive guidance from Allah ﷻ, and help us reach Allah ﷻ and the purpose that we were created for. It is for this reason that in a *ḥadīth* from Imām aṣ-Ṣādiq ؑ, he says: "Thinking for an hour is better than worshiping for a year, for 'Only those who possess intellect take admonition.'"[71 & 72]
- Studying nature and the wonderful processes which exist is one of the ways to get to know and recognize Allah ﷻ, and can enable a person to realize His Power, Wisdom, Greatness, and Oneness.
- It is only a wise person who will look at one's surroundings; the order which exists around the universe; the way in which everything in nature fits so perfectly with each other - and then come to the conclusion that there can only be One True God who has put all of this into motion and that is Allah ﷻ.

Verse 165

وَمِنَ ٱلنَّاسِ مَن يَتَّخِذُ مِن دُونِ ٱللَّهِ أَندَادًا يُحِبُّونَهُمْ كَحُبِّ ٱللَّهِ ۖ وَٱلَّذِينَ
ءَامَنُوٓا۟ أَشَدُّ حُبًّا لِّلَّهِ ۗ وَلَوْ يَرَى ٱلَّذِينَ ظَلَمُوٓا۟ إِذْ يَرَوْنَ ٱلْعَذَابَ أَنَّ ٱلْقُوَّةَ
لِلَّهِ جَمِيعًا وَأَنَّ ٱللَّهَ شَدِيدُ ٱلْعَذَابِ ١٦٥

And from among humankind are those who take to themselves objects of worship as rivals to Allah, loving them with a love like that which is the due for Allah only - while those who truly

[71] *Biḥār al-Anwār,* Vol. 71, Pg. 327, Ḥadīth 22. This tradition is as follows:

تَفَكُّرُ سَاعَةٍ خَيْرٌ مِنْ عِبَادَةِ سَنَةٍ: إِنَّمَا يَتَذَكَّرُ أُولُوا الْأَلْبَابِ.

[72] Qur'ān. Sūrah az-Zumar (39), Verse 9:

...إِنَّمَا يَتَذَكَّرُ أُو۟لُوا۟ ٱلْأَلْبَٰبِ ٩

believe are firmer in their love for Allah. If only those who do this (greatest) wrong could see - as they will see when they behold the punishment - that the power altogether belongs to Allah, and that Allah is severe in punishing.

In previous verses, Allah ﷻ invoked the innate nature within humanity, reminding people about the signs of creations that will lead them to knowing the One True God who is worthy of worship. These signs were given to us by Allah ﷻ as part of our human nature to aid in knowing and worshiping Him.

In this verse, Allah ﷻ is talking about those who have this innate nature, however instead of worshiping the One True God - Allah ﷻ, they are trying to fulfill and quench their innate nature through something else, i.e. the idols.

In the past, idols were most often statues carved out of wood or stone, and fashioned by peoples' hands. However today, these idols take on different forms from the traditional statues to excessive worship of materialistic things to excessive love of personalities such as celebrities, or politicians, etc.

All of this is done because there are some people who do not want to accept the Truth after acknowledging it, and thus want to maintain their stubborn attitude, while for some it may be due to their sheer ignorance.

In this verse, the focus is on those who reject the proofs which demonstrate the existence of Allah ﷻ and have taken the path of polytheism, idolatry, and belief in multiple gods. This verse speaks about those who bow down before the empty gods and love them, a love that is only worthy of being shown to Allah ﷻ who is the Source of all perfection and the Giver of all blessings.

Allah ﷻ states here that there are some who choose idols as their gods rather than submitting to Him, and not only have they chosen idols as their gods, but they are devoted to them just like those who believe in and submit to Allah ﷻ show their love to Him. However, Allah ﷻ makes a note that the love which the idol worshipers show for their false gods is short lived, and those who believe have a greater love for Allah ﷻ than the idolaters have for the statues that they submit to.

True love always aspires for a type of perfection, and a person can never fall in love with someone or something which has shortcomings and deficiencies as a person always seeks existence and perfection - even in that which they love. It is for this reason that the Being whose existence and perfection is superior to all, meaning Allah ﷻ, deserves to be loved more than anyone or anything else. In addition, as human beings, we have been created with the 'Breath of Allah ﷻ' infused inside of us, as the Qur'ān states: "When I have fashioned him (Prophet Ādam) in due proportions and breathed into him out of My Spirit, then fall down prostrating before him (as a token of respect for him and his superiority)."[73] Thus, we have the potential to be infinite through reconnecting with Allah ﷻ during the life of this world. We need to realize that the finite - everything in this transient world - cannot satisfy one unless they are connected to the infinite; and the only thing which can satisfy such a person is the One True God - the Infinite Allah ﷻ.

The love which believers have in their hearts comes from reason *('aql)*, knowledge *('ilm)*, and cognizance *(ma'rifah)*; while the love which disbelievers demonstrate is based on ignorance *(jahl)*, superstition, and fantasy, and therefore it is not stable or long lasting at all.

Allah ﷻ continues and says in this verse that those who did wrong by choosing a god to worship and submit to other than the One True God - Allah ﷻ, when they see the punishment of Allah ﷻ, they will know that all power belongs to the Almighty alone, and not the false gods which they worshiped because if their idols had power, then they could have helped those who worshiped them.

They are also reminded in the life of this world that Allah ﷻ has a severe punishment waiting for those who knowingly do not submit to Him, and that the idols which they worshiped as gods have absolutely no power to help them whatsoever.

Another interpretation has also been given for this verse which is

---

[73] Qur'ān, Sūrah al-Ḥijr (15), Verse 29:

فَإِذَا سَوَّيْتُهُۥ وَنَفَخْتُ فِيهِ مِن رُّوحِى فَقَعُواْ لَهُۥ سَٰجِدِينَ ﴿٢٩﴾

based on a *ḥadīth* from Imām Muḥammad al-Bāqir in which it is stated: "Jābir said: 'I asked Abū Jaʿfar about the words of Allah, Mighty and Majestic: 'And from the people there are ones who take for themselves objects of worship besides Allah, whom they love as they love Allah.' The Imām replied: 'By Allah! They are the friends of so and so, and so and so. They are taking them as Imāms (leaders) besides whom Allah had made to be as the Imāms for the people. Thus, due to that, He said: 'And if those who are unjust had seen the punishment when they see it, that the power is wholly Allah's and that Allah is Severe in requiting (evil). (Sūrah al-Baqarah (2), Verse 165);' and 'When those who were followed shall renounce those who followed (them), and they see the Punishment and their ties are cut asunder. (Sūrah al-Baqarah (2), Verse 166);' and He said: 'And those who followed shall say: 'Had there been for us a return, then we would renounce them as they have renounced us. Thus will Allah show them their deeds to be intense regret to them, and they shall not come out from the fire. (Sūrah al-Baqarah (2), Verse 167).'' Then Abū Jaʿfar said: 'By Allah! They are the unjust imāms (leaders) and their adherents.'"[74]

This statement of the fifth Imām becomes clear when we realize that the pronoun of 'them' *(hum)* contained within the word 'they love them' *(yuḥibūnahum)* is used for living creations, not inanimate objects.

Keys of Guidance

- Love is a natural part of all human beings. Our love is especially drawn to perfection, and those who care for us and nurture us, naturally we have a love toward them, and these include: our parents, our family members, our teachers, fellow believers, the Prophets, Imāms, etc. However, true love can only be toward a Being who is pure and has true perfection, and that can be none other than Allah; therefore, eventually we need to learn and understand that all other love is merely a reflection of the love we have for Allah.

[74] *Al-Kāfī*, Vol. 1, Pg. 374, Ḥadīth 11. The initial portion of this tradition is as follows:

سَأَلْتُ أَبَا جَعْفَرٍ عليه السلام عَنْ قَوْلِ اللهِ عزّ وجلّ وَمِنَ النَّاسِ مَنْ يَتَّخِذُ مِنْ دُونِ اللهِ أَنْدَاداً...

- Some people do not realize the emptiness and futility of their ways and belief systems, and only when the curtains are lifted and the Day of Judgment will come about will those people realize the errors in their ways while they were in this transient world.

Verse 166

إِذْ تَبَرَّأَ ٱلَّذِينَ ٱتُّبِعُواْ مِنَ ٱلَّذِينَ ٱتَّبَعُواْ وَرَأَوُاْ ٱلْعَذَابَ وَتَقَطَّعَتْ بِهِمُ ٱلْأَسْبَابُ ﴿١٦٦﴾

When those who were followed will disown the followers and declare themselves innocent of their evil deeds, and they will see the punishment, and their relations between them will be cut off.

Disavowing their Devotees

Continuing the discussion from the previous verse, Allah ﷻ reminds those who used to worship false gods and setup idols as their point of worship that once death comes, their veils of ignorance, pride, and negligence will be removed, and they will be forced to confess that their beliefs and lifestyle were deviant.

However, since they will have no support or refuge, they will resort to try and pin the blame on their leaders - the same ones whom they followed in the life of this transitory world - due to the severe state of misery that they will find themselves in. But Allah ﷻ says in this verse that those leaders who were themselves misled and busy misleading others in the life of this world will try and distance themselves from those devotees who followed them!

The meaning of idols in this verse does not simply relate to the stone and wooden idols which people make, but rather even the tyrants and despots which the pagans gave themselves to and blindly accepted whatever they were told to do are also referred to in this verse.

At the end of this verse, Allah ﷻ makes it clear that a time will come when they will see the punishments of Allah ﷻ, and the relationships between these individuals will be severed; and everyone will be on their own to deal with the judgment of Allah ﷻ.

Keys of Guidance

- Every love and affection which an individual has for another thing or person, if it is not based on intellect, then sooner or later it will lead to enmity and separation; however, love that is built on the foundation of Allah ﷻ and what He wants for His servants will by its very nature, everlasting - in this world and the world to come.
- Love leads to obedience - and this can either be positive or negative depending on numerous factors. If a person loves another human being for other than the sake of Allah ﷻ, then this can have the potential to deviate one causing a person to fall into sin if they are asked by their beloved to do something contrary to the laws of Allah ﷻ. However, if an individual loves another person for the sake of Allah ﷻ, then if one is asked to do something by their beloved, they will first check to ensure that it is something which Allah ﷻ has permitted.

Verse 167

وَقَالَ ٱلَّذِينَ ٱتَّبَعُوا۟ لَوْ أَنَّ لَنَا كَرَّةً فَنَتَبَرَّأَ مِنْهُمْ كَمَا تَبَرَّءُوا۟ مِنَّا ۗ كَذَٰلِكَ
يُرِيهِمُ ٱللَّهُ أَعْمَـٰلَهُمْ حَسَرَٰتٍ عَلَيْهِمْ ۖ وَمَا هُم بِخَـٰرِجِينَ مِنَ ٱلنَّارِ ١٦٧

And those who followed others (their deviant leaders) say: "Had there been another turn for us, we would disown them as they disown us (now)." Thus, Allah will show them their deeds in a manner that will cause them bitter regrets, but they will not leave the fire.

This verse presents a unique view into the psyche of people who blindly followed others in the life of this transient world that on the Day of Judgment, they will actually run after those whom they followed in this world in order to seek refuge and beg for intercession from them. However, as we saw in the previous verse, those same leaders will run in the opposite direction and tell Allah ﷻ that they have nothing to do with what their supposed followers are attributing to them.

It will be at that time when these blind followers will wish that they could return to the world so they can disavow and renounce the misguided, deviant leaders, just like on the Day of Judgment the so-called leaders will be rejecting any relationship with those whom they caused to deviate!

However, what benefit will their pleas bring as there will be absolutely no way for them to return back to this world to relive their lives and make different choices.

At the end of this verse, Allah ﷻ states that they will have immense remorse and regret because this is how the nature of these kinds of actions are, but it will be too late in the next world to change anything. Indeed, the natural consequences of these kinds of actions will be the fire of Hell. However, this regret will be useless because the Day of Judgment will not be a time or place for actions, nor can any amends or changes be made; and the only outcome for such people will be the punishment they themselves created.

Keys of Guidance

- We must have the courage to break free from the despots and autocrats in this world. Sometimes this is very difficult to do, however we must recognize them as being detrimental to our current lives, and more importantly our other-worldly existence; and we need to realize that they are not committed to their followers and will gladly throw them under the bus to save themselves in the life of this world, and they will also do the same in the world to come. We must leave them now and let them suffer their own fate in this world with the same political and judicial systems that they have so much confidence in, and let them deal with Allah ﷻ on the Day of Ultimate Justice.

- On the Day of Resurrection, human beings will see the truth as it is and they will regret their actions; they will wish that they could return to this world to change and better their actions, however that will not be possible, and they will need to fess up to their crimes and pay the penalties for them.

Verse 168

يَا أَيُّهَا النَّاسُ كُلُوا مِمَّا فِي الْأَرْضِ حَلَالًا طَيِّبًا وَلَا تَتَّبِعُوا خُطُوَاتِ الشَّيْطَانِ ۚ إِنَّهُ لَكُمْ عَدُوٌّ مُّبِينٌ

O humankind! Eat from what is on the earth provided that it is lawful, pure, and wholesome; and do not follow in the footsteps of Satan (who deceives); indeed he (Satan) is an open enemy to you.

History of Revelation

It has been narrated from Ibn ʿAbbās that some Arab tribes such as:

1. Thaqīf,[75]

[75] Initially, the tribe of Thaqīf who hailed from the area of Ṭā'if on the Arabian Peninsula were polytheists, just like many of the Arab tribes before the coming of Prophet Muḥammad ﷺ were. They worshiped an idol named Lāt, which is referenced in the Noble Qur'ān.

After the death of his greatest supporter, Abū Ṭalib ؑ, Prophet Muḥammad ﷺ went to Ṭā'if to visit this tribe and invite them to Islam, however historians write that they outright rejected him and his invitation.

As they were allies to the tribes of the Quraysh, they fought alongside them against the Muslims in the Battles of Uḥud and Ḥudaybiyyah, however after the various victories of the Muslim army, slowly some of the members of the Thaqīf tribe began to accept Islam.

Finally, in the ninth year after the migration of the Muslims to Medina, during the month of Ramaḍān, the leaders and chiefs of the tribe of Thaqīf met with Prophet Muḥammad ﷺ and accepted Islam.

They returned back to Ṭā'if, spent some time convincing their people that Islam was the way forward for them, and after a few days destroyed the house

2. Khuzāʿī[76]

and others made certain types of crops which they used to grow, and various types of animal meat forbidden *(ḥarām)* upon themselves without any religious backing. They took it a step further and tried to attribute this prohibition to Allah ﷻ, and thus this verse was revealed to Prophet Muḥammad ﷺ, reprimanding them for their wrongdoing.

We must realize that what these individuals did was for their own benefit. We see this theme in many of the previous verses regarding the Jews, and even in other communities such as the Hindu community who make up various rules about the cow and its usage when it is to their own benefit - not that these rules have been revealed by God to them.

As this verse has a connection to the previous verses, we recognize that those who are misguided and regret their actions on the Day of Judgment and wish that they could come back, have different types of leaders which they follow:

---

of worship which they had constructed for their idol Lāt; and came into full submission to Allah ﷻ through Prophet Muḥammad ﷺ.

[76] According to the historians, the Tribe of Khuzāʿī lived in various regions of the Arabian Peninsula, most notably around areas which had fresh, flowing water, and mountains. In addition, some of the people of this tribe also lived outside of the Arabian Peninsula around Baghdād in Iraq, Iṣfahān in Iran, and other areas.

Before the coming of Islam, they were in charge of the affairs in the city of Mecca, however due to their excessive corruption, they were forcibly removed from this position.

After the arrival of Islam, they fought against Prophet Muḥammad ﷺ, however they were present and signed the Peace Treaty of Ḥudaybiyyah in the sixth year after the migration and eventually converted to Islam. They maintained their Islam, but during the Battle of the Camel (al-Jamal) in which ʿĀʾishah, the daughter of Abū Bakr and wife of Prophet Muḥammad ﷺ launched a war against the rightful caliph, Imām ʿAlī ؑ, in which she was responsible for the deaths of thousands of people, the Tribe of Khuzāʿī became divided into two factions where some supported ʿĀʾishah, while others supported and fought alongside the Commander of the Faithful, Imām ʿAlī ؑ.

The Tribe of Khuzāʿī also supported Imām ʿAlī ؑ during the Battle of Ṣiffīn which was fought against Muʿāwiyah, son of Abū Ṣufyān.

1. Deviant leaders - such as their political, religious, and social media influencers; as well as the rich and famous, etc.
2. Their own personal desires.

In this verse, Allah ﷻ is providing a principle that people cannot use religion for their own personal benefits, or to justify pursuing their own desires, and those who do so will face the ultimate level of remorse on the Day of Judgment.

The Movements of Satan

In the previous verses, Allah ﷻ strongly condemned the actions of the polytheists.

We should note however that one type of polytheism is to consider anything or anyone other than Allah ﷻ as a legislator of law, and the verse under review describes this as a Satanic act.

Although in this verse, Allah ﷻ addresses humanity, however the direct target were those Muslims living during the time of Prophet Muḥammad ﷺ - and the Muslims who will come after them - and Allah ﷻ tells them to eat what is lawful *(ḥalāl)* and clean *(ṭayyib)* from that which is on the earth, and that they must not follow the footsteps of Satan, for he is as Allah ﷻ has declared: a well-defined, open, and exposed enemy.

The phrase which Allah ﷻ uses: "...Indeed he (Satan) is your open and manifest enemy..." is mentioned multiple times in the Qur'ān, and it should awaken and encourage humanity to fight this threat.[77]

The Qur'ān uses certain terms when related to food and they are: permissible *(ḥalāl)* and pure *(ṭayyib)* - the first one refers to 'something which is not prohibited to use;' while the second term refers to 'things which are in harmony with the healthy nature that human beings have been created for.'

The word 'footsteps' *(khutuwāt)* seen in this verse relates to 'the different ways of Satan' or 'step by step,' and in this verse, the meaning of Satan's footsteps are 'the numerous methods which Satan uses to achieve his goal of seducing people away from the path of Allah ﷻ and His obedience.'

[77] See Qur'ān: 2:168, 2:208, 6:142, 7:22, 12:5, 17:53, 36:60, and 43:62.

Keys of Guidance

- The natural needs which a human being has been created to fulfill in their lives are the very means that Satan uses to deviate and dominate a person - things such as: food and drink, fulfilling the sexual desires, and other necessary requirements of life. Therefore, a believer has to be extra vigilant when it comes to satisfying these needs that one does not allow Satan and his temptations to get the best of them.
- Satan enters into our lives in various different ways in order to try and divert us from the path of Allah ﷻ - he will not use clear and obvious ways of diversion, but rather he will use stealth measures and seek to get us on the path of 'minor' violations of the laws of Allah ﷻ, and then slowly step by step, he will begin his process of getting the believers to leave the countless things which are permissible to indulge in the few things which are impermissible.

Verse 169

إِنَّمَا يَأْمُرُكُم بِٱلسُّوٓءِ وَٱلْفَحْشَآءِ وَأَن تَقُولُوا۟ عَلَى ٱللَّهِ مَا لَا تَعْلَمُونَ ﴿١٦٩﴾

Only he (Satan) commands you to evil and indecency, and that you should speak against Allah things which you have no (concrete) knowledge about (out of ignorance, so that you can make an excuse for your ugly actions).

This verse provides us with clear proof about Satan's enmity of humanity, and that his goal is to drag us into misery and agony in this life and the world to come, through enticing us to perform iniquity and open lewdness.

The meaning of the word 'indecency' *(faḥshā')* comes from the root *fa-ḥa-sha* and it refers to 'any act which goes beyond moderation and takes on an outward form,' and it includes those actions which Islam has deemed as impermissible that are clearly immoderate and outwardly shameless.

The human nature *(fiṭrah)* does not accept indecency, and therefore when a person commits these ugly actions, the soul is not at ease. It loses its peace and feels uncomfortable.

For example, those who lie, backbite, or kill an innocent person - or even an animal - their guilty conscience will destroy them unless they find a way to calm it down. To ease the guilt and bad feeling and cover up the *fiṭrah*, they will try and make excuses such as saying to themselves: "It was my right to do what I did," or "They deserved it," and other such weak validations.

Another excuse some may make is where they try to convince themselves that their actions were what Allah ﷻ wanted from them - for example they may say: "I need to bring justice here, and that is what Allah ﷻ expects from me, so I am justified in doing what I just did," or: "We are told to get rid of evil, so I am justified in doing whatever I can to rid the world of such wickedness."

Another thing which Satan tries to get us to do is attribute things to Allah ﷻ which we have no knowledge of - things which are irrational, or go against the very existence of Allah ﷻ.

Gradual Immorality

The phrase: "...the steps of the devil" *(khuṭuwāt ash-shayṭān)* which was seen in the previous verse refers to the negative spiritual training which the demonic forces engage in. This Satanic nurturing is one where the deviations and wrongdoings which a person engages in gradually penetrate into them - they do not happen instantaneously and overnight - rather they take time.

To be more precise, Satan's temptations lead a person, step by step, to follow him into the dark abyss of sin. This tactic is not limited to that 'original' devil - the initial individual who tempted Prophet Ādam ﷺ and his wife in the garden which was spoken about early in Sūrah al-Baqarah, the one who is known as Iblīs. Rather, all evil and spiritually-contaminated apparatuses use the same 'step by step' method to carry out their sinister plans - whether they be the devils from among the *jinn* or humanity; or the various forms of "entertainment" which are pumped into our homes and hearts by the major producers of television shows, movies, the music industry, video games, or countless smartphone applications which promote a shameless, immoral lifestyle of music, dancing, and other types of debauchery.

Therefore, the Qur᾽ān warns that everyone - especially the believers - must be alert and cautious from the very first step that they take in life, and never associate with the devil at any time on any level.

Keys of Guidance

- The promise of Satan's enmity against humanity began with his expulsion from the Kingdom of Allah ﷻ after he refused to submit to His orders in bowing down to the representative of Allah ﷻ; and Satan pledged to tempt human beings to commit open sins, lewdness, and slander against Allah ﷻ.
- Satan is unique in that not only does he entice and command human beings to perform sins, but he goes a step further and shows them the various ways to try and justify those sins.
- Even when we are in a position of doubt, nothing should ever be attributed to Allah ﷻ - let alone in cases in which we know for certain that what we are about to say has not emanated from Allah ﷻ. We must be extremely careful in interpreting the Noble Qur᾽ān, and commenting on the rules *(aḥkām)* of Islam, so as to not follow the footsteps of Satan in accrediting false things to Allah ﷻ, the Qur᾽ān, Prophet Muḥammad ﷺ, the Ahlul Bayt (عليهم السلام), or even the faith of Islam in general.

Verse 170

وَإِذَا قِيلَ لَهُمُ ٱتَّبِعُوا۟ مَآ أَنزَلَ ٱللَّهُ قَالُوا۟ بَلْ نَتَّبِعُ مَآ أَلْفَيْنَا عَلَيْهِ ءَابَآءَنَآ ۗ
أَوَلَوْ كَانَ ءَابَآؤُهُمْ لَا يَعْقِلُونَ شَيْـًٔا وَلَا يَهْتَدُونَ ﴿١٧٠﴾

And when it is said to them (those who follow in the footsteps of Satan): "Follow what Allah has sent down (external guides

- the Prophet and the Qur'ān, as well as internal guides - our innate nature)" they respond: "No, but we follow that which we found our forefathers in." What, even if their forefathers had no understanding of anything, and were not rightly guided?

Blindly Following One's Forefathers

In this verse, Allah ﷻ refers to the weak logic of the polytheists in the matter of their unjustified prohibition about certain foods which were permissible *(ḥalāl)* for them, or it may relate to the illogical reasons why they practiced idolatry.

In either case, Allah ﷻ states that when it was said to those people that they should follow what Allah ﷻ has sent down, they would immediately respond that they would rather follow what their forefathers had done in the past.

The Qur'ān outright condemns this illogical train of thought and blind imitation of a person's ancestors by posing a rhetorical question that if their forefathers did not understand anything and were not guided, then how could they really follow them!? Is this not a case of the blind leading the blind?

The Qur'ān wants us to understand that if their ancestors were learned scholars and people who were spiritually guided, then it may have been appropriate to follow them; but still with thought, reflection, and a heart-felt acceptance of what they had learned from their predecessors. However in the case of the polytheists, their precursors were neither sensible people, nor did they have a knowledgeable leader and guide, such as a Prophet sent by Allah ﷻ who they could have accepted and followed the path that he would have led them on.

Keys of Guidance

- Much of what we have today is what we have built upon from the hard work and knowledge of our ancestors which has passed down to us. Everything from our lifestyle, clothing, food, art, etc., are all positive aspects of culture and customs. Islam has no problem with such things as long as they do not violate the teachings of the faith, and thus as Muslims, we must value these things and appreciate the hard work of the earlier generations to provide these to us. For example, Islam has mandated modest clothing for men and women but has not specified the styles, fabric, color, or specifics of what this clothing must look like. As long as the required parts of the body are covered in an appropriate manner, the culture of an individual can step in to provide these specifics; the same goes for food, art, and all other areas of life.

- The only time when Islam is concerned with believers following the traditions, customs, and ways of their ancestors and deems it as unacceptable is when they go directly against the teachings of Islam. We need to analyze the traditions we follow in order to ensure that they fit with Islamic logic and reason, and that they do not contradict the teachings of our faith. In some cultures, it is considered highly disrespectful that when two people meet, they do not shake hands. However in Islamic law, a man and woman who are not related to one another are not permitted to engage in any form of physical contact - even as little as a hand shake. In such a scenario, although the culture one lives in encourages and almost requires a handshake between two people, however since Islam does not permit this, a believer must ensure that the culture they are brought up with, or live within does not supercede the Islamic teachings.
- The customs and beliefs of past generations have a strong impact on the people who come in the future, and as such we need to ensure that whatever we do in our houses or religious centers is based on the teachings of Islam, as taught by Prophet Muḥammad ﷺ and his Ahlul Bayt ﷺ. Perhaps when we pass away, those customs that we performed may continue on, and they can earn us either a reward for the good that we left behind, or a punishment for the impermissible innovations which we brought into the religion.
- The transfer of experience and knowledge from one generation to the next is valuable, and therefore the elders and seniors of a family or religious community need to ensure that they convey what they

have learned in their lives to the next generation; however the transfer of superstitions from one generation to the next is of no value, and can actually be detrimental - so it must not be allowed to disseminate.

Verse 171

وَمَثَلُ ٱلَّذِينَ كَفَرُواْ كَمَثَلِ ٱلَّذِى يَنْعِقُ بِمَا لَا يَسْمَعُ إِلَّا دُعَآءً وَنِدَآءً ۚ
صُمٌّۢ بُكْمٌ عُمْىٌ فَهُمْ لَا يَعْقِلُونَ ﴿١٧١﴾

And the parable of the faithless is that of someone who shouts after that which (one) does not hear (anything) except a call and cry (as they are careless of what they hear), they are deaf, dumb, and blind, so they do not exercise their reason.

In this verse, Allah ﷻ explains why these people - those who reject the truth *(al-ḥaqq)* - do not show any flexibility when they are presented with clear proofs for the existence of God, and continue to insist on remaining in their state of misguidedness and disbelief.

In describing them, Allah ﷻ provides a parable in which He depicts the invitation that Prophet Muḥammad ﷺ was giving to the disbelievers to study the Qur'ān like a person who calls out to his flock of sheep or another animal about an impending danger. Although the animals hear sounds, they perceive it as nothing more than noise and clatter - because obviously they do not understand human speech. However, one would think that they should at least recognize the sound of their owner and look toward him because perhaps something does not seem right.

In the same way, the disbelievers heard the words which Prophet Muḥammad ﷺ was saying, but did not even try to understand them.

In order to add emphasis and make things clearer, Allah ﷻ adds that these kinds of disbelievers are in fact, deaf, dumb, and blind; and there is no way for them to understand, and it is for this reason that they cling to false superstitions and the backward traditions of their forefathers, leaving the valuable invitation that Prophet Muḥammad ﷺ was bringing to them.

Keys of Guidance

- Our eyes, ears, and tongue only have value when they are used in the path of reflection and contemplation on the world around us, otherwise even animals have eyes and ears, but one must analyze what is the difference between them and us?
- The way to truly understand the realities of anything - especially religion - is to ask the right questions from the right people, listen to what they and others who are qualified to speak about a certain topic are saying, and then use our power of sight to look around us; when all of this is accompanied by a person of thought and reflection, then one will be able to gain a better understanding.

Verse 172

يَـٰٓأَيُّهَا ٱلَّذِينَ ءَامَنُوا۟ كُلُوا۟ مِن طَيِّبَـٰتِ مَا رَزَقْنَـٰكُمْ وَٱشْكُرُوا۟ لِلَّهِ إِن كُنتُمْ إِيَّاهُ تَعْبُدُونَ ﴿١٧٢﴾

O you who believe! Eat of the pure, wholesome things which We (Allah ﷻ) have provided for you, and (in return) give thanks to Allah, if you truly worship Him alone.

Pure versus Polluted

Since the Qur'ān continuously highlights the roots of deviation within the scope of religious ideology and uses various ways to convey this to the reader, in this verse and the one which follows, the issue of the prohibition *(taḥrīm)* of some types of food is brought up.

During the time of Prophet Muḥammad ﷺ, some people were spreading news about several types of food which used to be permissible *(ḥalāl)* and pure *(ṭayyib)* during the Era of Ignorance *(Jāhiliyyah)*. In this verse, Allah ﷻ addressed the believers living during the time of Prophet

Muḥammad ﷺ to remind them that if they have true faith *(īmān)*, then they should be made aware that they are permitted to only eat those pure foods which He has specified, and which are recognized as such in the teachings of Islam. In addition, they must remember to show their thanks and appreciation to Allah ﷻ if they truly submit to Him and worship Him alone.

The pure and lawful foods, and other blessings are in accordance with the nature of the human being, and thus are not forbidden - they have been created by Allah ﷻ for us - so why should the believers not make use of them?!

We should also recognize that in Islam, we have a principle in Jurisprudence that everything is permissible *(ḥalāl)* unless it is deemed to be impermissible *(ḥarām)*. One of the unfortunate realities which Muslims have put themselves into is not knowing the basic principles of the Islamic rulings such that they confuse things, and consider everything to be impermissible until otherwise proven. This makes our lives quite complicated, and at the same time it means losing members of the community because they feel that the religion is so strict that it deems everything to be impermissible unless they can prove its permissibility, so it is not worth following such teachings. Such people may remain 'spiritual' but outside of the fold of Islam.

At the same time, we all face a crisis in that whatever is permissible for consumption often has impermissible things mixed into it - and when we consume such things, we risk it impacting our spiritual well-being and elevation.

It is between these two positions that a believer needs to navigate oneself in order to ensure that one does not make life overly complicated, but at the same time ensure that what one is consuming is permissible.

Keys of Guidance

- The soul and essence of self-improvement, asceticism, and God-consciousness are not in conflict with making use of the bounties which Allah ﷻ has provided for humanity.
- The proper way of giving thanks *(shukr)* to Allah ﷻ is to use what

a person has been given properly and what it was intended for. For example, if someone is gifted an expensive shirt and one says: 'thank you,' to the person who gave it to them, but then one uses it to wash their car, this would be considered as being ungrateful for that gift because they did not use it how it was meant to be used. Therefore, true thankfulness is rooted in using an item for the purpose that it was intended for.

- Giving thanks to Allah ﷻ is a sign of a Godly person, and outlines that one is practicing true Monotheism *(Tawḥīd)*. For example, if a person thinks that the sustenance which one has is due to their own hard work, or wealth management, or so on, and that Allah ﷻ is not the source of what one has earned, then that individual will not thank the Almighty at all because they feel that whatever they have received is through their own hard work.
- A true servant of Allah ﷻ does not forbid oneself from what Allah ﷻ has considered to be lawful for them.

Verse 173

إِنَّمَا حَرَّمَ عَلَيۡكُمُ ٱلۡمَيۡتَةَ وَٱلدَّمَ وَلَحۡمَ ٱلۡخِنزِيرِ وَمَآ أُهِلَّ بِهِۦ لِغَيۡرِ ٱللَّهِۖ
فَمَنِ ٱضۡطُرَّ غَيۡرَ بَاغٖ وَلَا عَادٖ فَلَآ إِثۡمَ عَلَيۡهِۚ إِنَّ ٱللَّهَ غَفُورٞ رَّحِيمٌ ١٧٣

He (Allah ﷻ) has only made unlawful *(ḥarām)* for you carrion[78] *(maytah)*, and blood, and the flesh[79] of swine, and that (an animal)

---

[78] In Islamic terminology, carrion *(maytah)* is defined as an animal whose meat is normally permissible for human consumption, however because this animal died on its own - either due to natural causes, an accident, or it was attacked and killed by another animal - it is now rendered impermissible for human consumption, and its entire carcass is deemed impure *(najis)*. This word is also used to refer to an animal which was not slaughtered according to the rules of Islam.

[79] Although in this verse, the Qur'ān seems to limit what is prohibited to the 'flesh' of swine (pig), however it is clear that this prohibition extends to anything

which is offered (slaughtered) in the name of other than Allah. Yet whoever is constrained by dire necessity to eat of them, provided one does not covet (that which is forbidden), nor transgress (the bounds of necessity), no sin shall be upon them. Surely Allah is All-Forgiving *(Ghafūr)*, All-Merciful *(Raḥīm)*.

Allah ﷻ is the Creator, and He created us and put us on Earth for a purpose. In order for humanity to achieve the ultimate purpose for which they were given life, it is a logical obligation upon Allah ﷻ that He needs to guide us to all of the elements that can take us to the ultimate purpose. At the same time, He needs to warn us about any obstacles that will be detrimental for our spiritual growth. Thus, Allah ﷻ provides us guidelines at every juncture of life, even in regards to the food and drink which we are permitted or prohibited from consuming.

Whatever we consume has a profound effect upon us - not only our physical body, but more importantly it impacts our soul in ways which we cannot even imagine. Any food or drink that we consume remains a physical part of us, as we grow muscle and fat from it, and as such it becomes a literal part of our body. This food impacts our ultimate purpose of existence, and has a deep relationship with us - even more than we can ever imagine due to the intense connection which exists between our body and soul. It is for this reason that Allah ﷻ has explained - sometimes in great depth in the verses of the Qur᾿ān - the harms of consuming

---

which comes from the pig - this includes the bones by which gelatin is made, and the fat through which lard is produced. It should be noted that in Islam, the entire body of the pig is also impure *(najis)* and this includes the skin; so Muslims must be careful when it comes to purchasing and using leather products which are made in non-Muslim countries because if they are made from either pig, or even an animal whose meat is permissible for consumption (such as a cow), however that animal was not slaughtered according to the prescribed method of Islam, then such clothing or items cannot be worn or kept with a person during the prayers; and touching them if there is any moisture on one's hands will render the hand and potentially anything touched with that hand, impure *(najis)*.

certain things.

In order to clarify the forbidden *(ḥarām)* foods and bring an end to the excuses which people were offering about what was permissible to eat and what was not, based on the ways of the pre-Islamic Era of Ignorance, in this verse Allah ﷻ directs His words to the believers. Since this verse is connected to previous verses in this chapter, most notably verse 168 in which Allah ﷻ was speaking in a more general tone, in this verse under review, He provides specific guidance.

Here, Allah ﷻ reminds the believers that He has only forbidden carcasses (animals which are not slaughtered according to the specific Islamic rules, as well as those who died on their own accord, or were killed by another animal); blood; anything from the pig; and any other animal which was slaughtered for anything or anyone other than Allah ﷻ.

If a person ever faces a situation which necessitates them to eat something forbidden in order to save one's life, then the Qur'ān makes an exception and says that if nothing else is available to eat, then as long as that individual does not exceed the limits which would enact oppression against oneself, there is no sin on them as long as one eats only that much of that food - which is normally impermissible - as is needed to save one's life.

To further make it clear that a person does not use this urgency as an excuse to go beyond the limits and indulge in the forbidden, Allah ﷻ includes two phrases:

1. Provided that a person does not desire (that which is forbidden) *(ghayru bāghin)* - meaning that one does not over-indulge and satisfy one's pleasures by eating or drinking the impermissible item.
2. They do not transgress (the bounds of necessity) *(wa la ʿādin)* - meaning that they do not exceed in eating more than that which is necessary.

Therefore, Allah ﷻ is explaining that the permission to consume something which is normally impermissible is reserved only for those who do are in dire need of eating it, yet do not enjoy eating that forbidden thing, and also they do not exceed that specific amount which is required to save themselves from death.

At the end of this verse, Allah ﷻ reminds the believers that He is All-Forgiving, and All-Merciful. The same God who has forbidden certain foods, with His own unique special brand of mercy has allowed their limited use in times of an extreme emergency.

Keys of Guidance

- Allah ﷻ places extra importance on discussing that which human beings should consume, and has repeatedly warned against eating harmful and forbidden foods. It is true that Allah ﷻ has created everything on Earth for the human being to make use of, but at the same time He has also determined (for their own benefit) that there are certain things which they are not permitted to eat and drink.
- Compulsion often changes the verdict in many Islamic rulings, therefore at times things which are normally impermissible can be made permissible at times of absolute necessity. The limits of how this works can be found in the Qur'ān or narrations from the Immaculates, and have been further explained by the jurists *(fuqahā')* based on their understanding of the verses of the Qur'ān and the *ḥadīth*.
- Islam is a comprehensive religion which is relevant for all times, all places, all people, and all circumstances. There is never a 'dead-end' in life because Allah ﷻ has given the believers guidelines in the Qur'ān, which were further elaborated upon by Prophet Muḥammad ﷺ and the Immaculate Imāms of the Ahlul Bayt ؑ that scholars use to help ease the circumstances which believers will face in their lives.

Verse 174

إِنَّ ٱلَّذِينَ يَكۡتُمُونَ مَآ أَنزَلَ ٱللَّهُ مِنَ ٱلۡكِتَٰبِ وَيَشۡتَرُونَ بِهِۦ ثَمَنٗا قَلِيلًا
أُوْلَٰٓئِكَ مَا يَأۡكُلُونَ فِي بُطُونِهِمۡ إِلَّا ٱلنَّارَ وَلَا يُكَلِّمُهُمُ ٱللَّهُ يَوۡمَ ٱلۡقِيَٰمَةِ

وَلَا يُزَكِّيهِمْ وَلَهُمْ عَذَابٌ أَلِيمٌ ﴿١٧٤﴾

Surely those who conceal the truths and commandments in the Book that Allah has sent down and sell them for a trifling price, they eat nothing but fire that goes into their stomachs, and [their actions will result in the fact that] Allah will not speak to them on the Day of Resurrection, nor will He purify them, and for them is a painful punishment.

History of Revelation

According to the unanimous opinion of the commentators of the Noble Qur'ān, this verse and the next two verses were revealed about the People of the Book (the Jews and the Christians), and more specifically related to the Jewish scholars who were living during the time of Prophet Muḥammad ﷺ who knew the attributes and signs which the Promised Prophet would have because they were mentioned in their Divinely-revealed Scriptures, and they had conveyed them to the people.

However, once Prophet Muḥammad ﷺ made his open declaration of Prophethood, and these Jewish (and other) scholars saw that people were gravitating toward him and his message, they feared that if this continued, their personal interests would be endangered and the gifts which were showered upon them, and the lavish parties which the people used to hold in their honor would end. Therefore, they resorted to their old ways of doing all that they could in order to dissuade people from accepting Prophet Muḥammad ﷺ and his message.

They began to hide the qualities and characteristics which had been mentioned in the Tawrāh that would have guided the people to accept this final Messenger.

It is in this context that Allah ﷻ revealed these verses in which He strongly condemned their actions.

Another Censure for Hiding the Truth

This verse emphasizes what was mentioned previously regarding the concealment of the truth.

Allah ﷻ states that those who conceal what He has sent down in the Books, meaning the previous Scriptures which were revealed to the People of the Book, and more notably the Jews, and sell it for a small price through the gifts that they were receiving and the lavish dinner parties which they were indulging in due to their status as religious leaders of the community, were in fact consuming fire into their stomachs.

Allah ﷻ then deals with an important spiritual punishment which they will face which is even more painful than the material punishment - and He says that on the Day of Resurrection, not only will Allah ﷻ not speak to them, but He will not even purify them, so in that state, they will be left to undergo a painful retribution. It must be noted that the reality of why Allah ﷻ speaks with this tone is that these individuals has the potential to elevate themselves in this world, however they did not take advantage of this and decided to lower themselves, thus they destroyed their capacity to listen to the advice of Allah ﷻ. As a general principle, Allah ﷻ guides us in this world through many ways and provides us with multiple opportunities. He has left the door to seek forgiveness *(tawbah)* and ask for repentance *(istighfār)* wide open for everyone. During this life is the time to maximize our fullest potential and is the world of actions - however, once our death comes and we cross over into the grave and beyond, that is the world of witnessing and experiencing the results of the actions carried out in this world.

One of the greatest Divine gifts which a person could ever be graced with in the world to come is for Allah ﷻ to 'speak' to them, and this is something which is reserved only for the people of true faith *(īmān)*. The various modes of communication which Allah ﷻ uses with us in this world are based on the ability of an individual; and some examples of these are as follows:

1. He uses the path of the innate nature *(fiṭrah)* of the human being, and the power of wisdom which we have.
2. He sends wise people to us that provide us with guidance.
3. He uses the language of the heart, or speaks to His exceptional servants through Divine inspiration *(ilhām)* which is something other than Divine revelation given to the Prophets of Allah.

4. He uses the power of revelation *(waḥī)* - a process which is reserved for Prophets ﵇ and Messengers ﵇. This can take place via at least three methods:
    a. Through a third-party, such as angel Jibrāʾīl ﵇.
    b. It can be through an inanimate object, such as a bush, in the case of Prophet Mūsā ﵇.
    c. It can be through some other form, such as by truthful dreams or a direct revelation to the heart - such as what Prophet Ibrāhīm ﵇ experienced when Allah ﷻ ordered him to go through the process of slaughtering his son, Prophet Ismāʾīl ﵇.

Keys of Guidance

- Although this verse is referring to those leaders who conceal the truth from others, it equally applies to other areas, as well as any kind of deception which can result in such consequences. When we deceive people, it is like we are mixing poison with honey. Although it may taste sweet, it is deadly. Thus, when we are dishonest in our business practices, or we take the rights of others, especially the most vulnerable people in society such as the orphans or poor, or we are engaged in bribery and other destructive practices, even though we may think that we have a made a financial profit, the food we consume from that money is being compared to consuming fire. This fire will burn us from inside, thus we have actually created our own hell.

- Love of this transient world and excessive devotion to it is a major threat to all believers, however it is especially dangerous for the religious scholars *(ʿulamāʾ)* whose responsibility is to provide authentic teachings and guidance to the common people.

- A punishment needs to fit the crime, therefore those who close the way for people to hear the word of Allah ﷻ in this temporal world will be deprived of the pleasure of hearing the word of Allah ﷻ on the Day of Judgment.

Verse 175

أُوْلَـٰٓئِكَ ٱلَّذِينَ ٱشْتَرَوُا۟ ٱلضَّلَـٰلَةَ بِٱلْهُدَىٰ وَٱلْعَذَابَ بِٱلْمَغْفِرَةِ ۚ فَمَآ أَصْبَرَهُمْ عَلَى ٱلنَّارِ ﴿١٧٥﴾

Such are the ones who have bought deviation in exchange for guidance, and punishment in exchange for forgiveness. How they persevere in their striving to reach the fire!

This verse makes the situation of this group even clearer, and confirms the outcome of their efforts to dissuade people from the truth.

Everyone loves religion as it is innate to our nature - Allah ﷻ created all human beings to be attracted to Him, and having a desire to know and follow Him.

Unfortunately, even today, there are people who conceal the truth and end up creating a community of followers who act excessively in the name of religion. This is seen in the likes of the extremist groups who operate under the guise of various religions such as the Wahhābi movement, the KKK (Ku Klux Klan), the Zionists, as well as religious fanatics and extremist Evangelical Right-Wing Christians, Hindus, Buddhists, etc.

On the opposite end of the spectrum are those who completely detach from all forms of religion. Not only that, but they have an incredible hatred toward religion and anyone who practices any faith. Such people create their own bubble of life and focus on their self-styled "spirituality" which compromises all values and truths. They promote beliefs such as: "Do what you like as it is your intention that matters most to the universe," or "Love is enough," and other such preposterous beliefs.

One reason why Allah ﷻ constantly emphasizes on using our intellect is to make sure that we are not blind followers, and that we know the truth ourselves.

In this verse, Allah ﷻ notes that this harmful transaction which they are engaged in will be of no benefit for them, and it will actually bring them harm because they have exchanged guidance for deviation, and have sold the path of righteousness for eternal torment.

In this way, they have - as a proverb best describes them: 'burnt the candle at both ends.'

At the end of this verse Allah ﷻ makes it clear by adding how they persevered in their striving to reach the fire, and thus they will also have to persevere in enduring it!

Keys of Guidance

- Concealing the truths of the religion, especially when it proves advantageous in the life of this temporal world, is one of the unfortunate sins which some individuals - as well as those who call themselves "religious scholars" - engage in. A true scholar of religion devoted to Allah ﷻ would never even think about selling the eternal bliss of the world to come for the temporary pleasures of this short life.
- Selling the religion through concealing the truths of the teachings which Allah ﷻ has sent for the guidance of humanity will entail the most severe of punishments in the world to come, and this can be understood through the phrase at the end of this verse where it says: "How they persevere in their striving to reach the fire (and enduring it)" because this expression has only been used for these kinds of individuals.

Verse 176

ذَٰلِكَ بِأَنَّ ٱللَّهَ نَزَّلَ ٱلْكِتَٰبَ بِٱلْحَقِّ ۗ وَإِنَّ ٱلَّذِينَ ٱخْتَلَفُوا۟ فِى ٱلْكِتَٰبِ لَفِى شِقَاقٍۭ بَعِيدٍ ﴿١٧٦﴾

That is so because Allah has sent down the Book with the Truth. Those who differ about the Book are surely in extreme defiance.

In this verse, Allah ﷻ summarizes what He stated so far where He talked about the threats and promises of suffering which the obstinate people will face who have been trying to conceal the truth from the people.

He makes a straightforward statement that whatever has been mentioned up until this point is factual, and that people should realize these are all candid warnings because it is Allah ﷻ who has sent down this Book, the Qurʾān, as well as all of the previous Books to the past Prophets. All of these Scriptures were revealed with the truth, containing clear signs and proofs to remove any ambiguity.

However, in order to protect their own immoral interests, there were and continue to be people who try to justify their own positions through distorting the Book of Allah ﷻ, and they endeavor to create differences within the Scripture itself.

The words of Allah ﷻ in regards to these people and their outcome is clear as He states that those who are at variance regarding the Book by believing in part of it and disbelieving in another part; or believing in one or some of the Divine Books, while disbelieving in the others - have certainly veered far away from the truth into a wide division.

Keys of Guidance

- For guidance, Allah ﷻ sent a Book and guides. We must take this guidance in totality and not choose what serves our personal interests. The moment that Islam becomes a "pick and choose" religion is where deviation begins. Therefore, as believers, we have to take the Qurʾān, Prophet Muḥammad ﷺ and the Ahlul Bayt ﷷ as a complete package for our guidance.

- The source of religious differences, and differences which exist within the various sects of one religion is not due to Allah ﷻ, the Book which He revealed, nor the Prophets ﷷ, Messengers ﷷ, or Imāms ﷷ which He deputed, but rather it is due to the inaccurate readings of the corrupt scholars, fake leaders, deviant influential people, unqualified leadership, etc., and their intentional misrepresentation of the words of Allah ﷻ.

- It is the concealment of facts which exist in the Book of Allah ﷻ, or in the authenticated teachings of the Prophet ﷺ and his righteous successors, the Imāms ﷺ, which has led and continues to lead to divisions, fractures, and misunderstandings among the people of faith.

Verse 177

لَّيْسَ ٱلْبِرَّ أَن تُوَلُّوا۟ وُجُوهَكُمْ قِبَلَ ٱلْمَشْرِقِ وَٱلْمَغْرِبِ وَلَـٰكِنَّ ٱلْبِرَّ مَنْ
ءَامَنَ بِٱللَّهِ وَٱلْيَوْمِ ٱلْـَٔاخِرِ وَٱلْمَلَـٰٓئِكَةِ وَٱلْكِتَـٰبِ وَٱلنَّبِيِّـۧنَ وَءَاتَى ٱلْمَالَ
عَلَىٰ حُبِّهِۦ ذَوِى ٱلْقُرْبَىٰ وَٱلْيَتَـٰمَىٰ وَٱلْمَسَـٰكِينَ وَٱبْنَ ٱلسَّبِيلِ وَٱلسَّآئِلِينَ
وَفِى ٱلرِّقَابِ وَأَقَامَ ٱلصَّلَوٰةَ وَءَاتَى ٱلزَّكَوٰةَ وَٱلْمُوفُونَ بِعَهْدِهِمْ إِذَا عَـٰهَدُوا۟ ۖ
وَٱلصَّـٰبِرِينَ فِى ٱلْبَأْسَآءِ وَٱلضَّرَّآءِ وَحِينَ ٱلْبَأْسِ ۗ أُو۟لَـٰٓئِكَ ٱلَّذِينَ صَدَقُوا۟ ۖ
وَأُو۟لَـٰٓئِكَ هُمُ ٱلْمُتَّقُونَ ﴿١٧٧﴾

Righteousness is not to turn your faces to the East or the West; rather, piety is [personified by] those who have faith in Allah and the Last Day, the angels, the Book, and the Prophets; and who give their wealth for the love of Him, to the relatives, the orphans, the needy, the traveler, and the beggar; and for [the freeing of] the slaves; and maintain the prayer *(ṣalāh)*, and give charity *(zakāh)*, and those who fulfill their covenants when they pledge themselves, and those who are patient in stress and distress, and in the heat of battle. They are the ones who are true [to their covenant], and it is they who are the God-conscious (those with *taqwā*).

The change of the *qiblah* caused a great deal of controversy among the Jews and the Christians, especially the Jews because they lost their greatest honor in that the Muslims were following their *qiblah* and praying in the direction of Jerusalem and thus they began to openly protest.

The Qur'ān clearly responded to them in verse 142 of Sūrah al-Baqarah where Allah ﷻ referred to them as: "The (hypocritical) fools among the people..."

This current verse was revealed and confirmed that all of this back and forth about the change in the *qiblah* is redundant because what is more important than the direction of prayer *(qiblah)* are the other issues which are the criterion that speak about the value of the human being, and these are very important things that need to be considered.

Allah ﷻ then explains some of these issues in this verse.

The Source of Righteousness

In the interpretation of the verses about the changing of the *qiblah* which we reviewed, we stated that on one hand the opponents of Islam, and on the other hand the new Muslims made a fuss about the changing of the direction of the *qiblah*.

Addressing both of these groups, this verse tells them that righteousness and piety is not only that you turn your face to the East or the West during prayers - or whatever direction Allah ﷻ determines as the focus point - meaning that all of these discussions which the People of the Book, and some of the Muslims were having in regards to the *qiblah* and its change, and all of the time which was being wasted on this point of contention was absolutely worthless.

The direction of the *qiblah* is part of the worship and ritual of the prayers, as well as many other acts of worship. Since all of the parts of worship are defined by Allah ﷻ, the true core and essence of worship is to do what Allah ﷻ asks us to do in the ways that He wants us to do them, and to display our unwavering and unquestioned commitment to those actions. If Allah ﷻ decides to change some of the parts of worship such as the direction of the *qiblah*, we are expected to obey these orders, and realize that we are still doing what He wants us to do. We must realize that the main focus is to abide by the commands of Allah ﷻ, and we must not formulate things by our own desires. When it comes to the specifics of the acts of worship which Allah ﷻ has legislated, we must look at the overall purpose, core, and essence of these points.

Allah ﷻ wants us to have a greater mindset which is that we need to have a holistic approach to our duties and responsibilities. Worship of Allah ﷻ is like a jig-saw puzzle - every act of worship, even the smaller parts which makeup that act of worship - are all individual pieces of the puzzle. We can never take one piece and act with that piece alone, presuming that it represents the whole picture. We must recognize it as being just one piece that has to be complemented with all other pieces to make it complete.

This is the message that Allah ﷻ is giving to humanity by presenting it through various different angles.

The holistic formula of Allah ﷻ, as He says in the conclusion of this verse, is that all of these guidelines are there so that human beings can gain God-consciousness *(taqwā)*; and these instructions are as follows:

1. Believing in Allah ﷻ, and the Day of Judgment, etc.
2. The worship of Allah ﷻ through the prayers *(ṣalāh),* and other acts of devotion.
3. Serving the community, and overall society of believers through things such as charity *(zakāh)* and other means.
4. Community building through fulfilling one's promises, and various acts to strengthen the bonds of fraternity.
5. Self-building through bearing difficulties with patience, and the other noble ethical traits required to strengthen the soul.

In this verse, the Qur'ān outlines the most important principles of virtue in the areas of faith *(īmān)*, morality *(akhlāq)*, and action *(ʿamal)* by introducing six main themes.

Allah ﷻ starts off by telling the Muslims living during the time of Prophet Muḥammad ﷺ especially those who were attacking the Muslims for the change in *qiblah* that virtue, and subsequently the virtuous people are those who believe in Allah ﷻ and the Day of Resurrection, and they believe in all of the angels, and the Book - this being a reference to all of the Books that Allah ﷻ sent for the guidance of humanity - especially the Qur'ān, and also belief in all of the Prophets which He appointed.

After belief in these things, the subject turns to almsgiving, self-sacrifice, and financial assistance to others. In this regard, Allah ﷻ states that the keys to righteousness are that people give away their wealth, even though they have love for it, and perhaps even a dire need of it themselves. One may ask: Who should they spend their wealth on? Allah ﷻ lists certain categories of people who should be given assistance: one's relatives, the orphans, the poor, the destitute who are stranded on a journey, the beggars, and finally the slaves.

No doubt, it is difficult to part with wealth because almost everyone loves it and what it can bring to them.

We should note that the meaning of the phrase *ḥubbihī* - out of love for it/Him can be understood and translated as either 'a person spends out of what they have despite the love of wealth,' OR 'for the sake of the love of Allah ﷻ within their heart.' In short, we can merge both loves together in trying to understand this portion of the verse in that even though a person loves wealth, and needs or desires it to maintain one's lifestyle and fulfill one's own personal requirements, however for the sake of and for the love of Allah ﷻ, they end up giving it to the needy, hoping to attain the pleasure of Allah ﷻ and a much better return from Him. Thus, for His sake, they sacrifice their love of wealth for others.

This position of the verse refers to the reality of life for most people, however we should note that although this love for wealth and what it can provide is in the hearts of many people, however to attain the pleasure of Allah ﷻ, there are some individuals who will struggle against the soul, and do their best to spend their wealth and provide to those who are in need.

The third principle from the multiple principles of *taqwā* which this verse speaks about is steadfastness in prayer.

If the prayers are performed by fulfilling all of their conditions and maintaining the limits, and completed with full sincerity *(ikhlāṣ)* and humbleness *(khuḍūʿ)*, then this can bring up a person spiritually to get closer to His Creator, and help one refrain from sins, just as Allah ﷻ says: "Recite and convey to them what is revealed to you of the Book, and establish the *ṣalāh* (in conformity with all of its conditions). Surely, the *ṣalāh* restrains from all that is indecent and shameful, and all that is evil; and the remembrance of Allah is the greatest (of all types of worship and this is not restricted to the *ṣalāh*). And Allah knows everything that you do."[80]

The fourth principle of *taqwā* mentioned in this verse is paying the prescribed purifying alms *(zakāh)*; and this refers to all of the prescribed, obligatory wealth taxes which Islam has laid down, such as *zakāh*[81], *khums*,[82] etc.

There are many people who are willing to help the poor, however they are not prepared to give their obligatory financial dues which Islam has mandated for everyone.

On the other hand, there are some Muslims who refuse to part with any of their wealth when it comes to recommended forms of charity, and they will only give the obligatory financial dues which are required of

---

[80] Qur'ān, Sūrah al-'Ankabūt (29), Verse 45:

اتْلُ مَآ أُوحِىَ إِلَيْكَ مِنَ ٱلْكِتَٰبِ وَأَقِمِ ٱلصَّلَوٰةَ إِنَّ ٱلصَّلَوٰةَ تَنْهَىٰ عَنِ ٱلْفَحْشَآءِ وَٱلْمُنكَرِ وَلَذِكْرُ ٱللَّهِ أَكْبَرُ وَٱللَّهُ يَعْلَمُ مَا تَصْنَعُونَ ۝

[81] *Zakāh* is a financial obligation in Islam where Muslims must pay a certain amount of charity or tax on nine items which is then to be spent on the poor, or for other necessities as outlined by the teachings of Islam.

These nine items are:
1. Two types of coins (gold and silver).
2. Three types of livestock (camels, cows, and sheep).
3. Four kinds of grains (wheat, barley, dates, and raisins).

The amount of *zakāh* which is payable on each item is different, and this is discussed in detail in the jurisprudential resources.

Zakāh is very important in Islam, and is a due which is an obligation to pay. In religious resources, *zakāh* has the same status as *ṣalāh* and struggle *(jihād)*, and it is one of the basic pillars of religion. This term is mentioned in 59 verses of the Qur'ān, and there are over 2,000 *ḥadīth* in regards to *zakāh*.

[82] *Khums* which literally means one-fifth is a jurisprudential term that refers to an obligatory tax in Islam which is payable on a person's annual surplus income, taking into account the required conditions detailed in the books of Islamic Jurisprudence.

Khums is one of the mandatory obligations of Islam, and is mentioned in the Qur'ān in Sūrah al-Anfāl (8), Verse 41; and there are more than 100 *ḥadīth* discussing its specifics.

them.

This verse of the Qur'ān considers a righteous person to be one who gives both - the obligatory and recommended forms of charity.

The fifth principle of *taqwā* which has been mentioned is that these people uphold and fulfill the promises which they make to others.

The true prosperity in social existence is the mutual trust which people have for one another, and it is for this reason that in the *ḥadīth* it mentions that Imām Muḥammad al-Bāqir ﵇ said: "There are three things which Allah, the Mighty and the Glorious, has not permitted anyone to forsake: returning a trust to its owner - irrespective of whether he is a good person or an evil one; fulfilling one's promises and covenants - irrespective of whether it has been made to a good person or an evil one; being good and kind toward one's parents - irrespective of whether they are good or evil."[83]

The sixth and last item in the life of a person striving to attain God-consciousness is that of self-building through bearing difficulties with patience, and working to attain the other noble ethical traits required in strengthening the soul - the most potent of which is developing the trait of perseverance *(ṣabr)* in one's life - whether this be in the face of trials, sicknesses, on the battlefield, or anywhere else that patience is needed.

At the end of this verse, as a summary and to emphasize the six outstanding attributes which people need to have, Allah ﷻ concludes by saying that those individuals who have these traits and make active use of them are the truthful ones *(ṣādiqīn)* and they have God-consciousness *(taqwā)*.

Their truthfulness is manifest from the fact that their actions are in accordance with their beliefs, and their God-weariness is evident because they practice what they preach: meaning that they fulfill their duty to Allah ﷻ, and ensure that the needy and deprived people around them - both close ones and strangers - are all taken care of to the best of their ability.

---

[83] *Biḥār al-Anwār*, Vol. 74, Pg. 56. The initial text of this tradition is as follows:

ثَلَاثٌ لَمْ يَجْعَلِ اللهُ عَزَّ وَجَلَّ لِأَحَدٍ فِيهِنَّ رُخْصَةً أَدَاءُ الْأَمَانَةِ إِلَى الْبَرِّ وَالْفَاجِرِ...

It is interesting to note that the above six salient attributes include doctrinal *(ʿaqāʾid)*, moral *(akhlāqī)*, as well as practical *(ʿamalī)* aspects.

Keys of Guidance

- We must be balanced in our vision of life and in implementing the teachings of Islam. We cannot look at the teachings of the Qurʾān, the Prophet ﷺ, and his Ahlul Bayt ؑ as individual boxes, as if they are not related to one another. Rather, we need to look at the comprehensive teachings of Islam in an all-inclusive manner. We must realize that we need all of them in our life to complete our true submission to Allah ﷻ and the religion of Islam. Some people take Islam to be like a restaurant which offers an all-you-can-eat buffet with hundreds of types of food on the table. A customer takes one's plate and proceeds to fill it with only those foods that one likes to eat, leaving aside things that are not desired. However, the teachings which Allah ﷻ has provided to humanity cannot be like this, they must be whole-heartedly accepted and followed in their totality - even those which a person may not 'like' in the initial stages, as everything on the menu of submission is meant to give a well-balanced religion, free of extremism in any form.

- In order to get to the actual nut, a person needs to crack the shell. One of the duties of the Prophets ؑ and the Heavenly Books which Allah ﷻ sent was to do just this. They were sent and deputed to change the culture and thought patterns of the people. Whereas some individuals look at religion as merely an outside shell, and the acts of worship as being the goal, the Prophets came to challenge that opinion, and show human beings that there is more to worship and obedience to Allah ﷻ than just the outward apparent aspects of submission.

- Simply knowing the concepts of religion is not sufficient, nor is it overly important; rather, what is of value is to understand the teachings of the religion and then to apply those teachings into real life.

- Being a good person does not only mean communicating with Allah

ﷻ and "praying" to Him, but along with that a "religious person" should also recognize that one must be active in the social area of life as well, communicate with other people, and try to help alleviate the social problems which fellow human beings are facing - starting with their own family members, and then the overall society.

- The purpose of alms in Islam - whether it be the obligatory dues which a believer must give, or the recommended acts of charity - is not only to satisfy the hunger of other people and provide them with the basic material needs, but rather it is also to ensure that those who are giving this money do not develop a strong affinity to wealth, thus it allows them to detach themselves from this transient world for the sake and pleasure of Allah ﷻ.
- The Qur'ān is emphatic that when it comes to financial assistance we need to start with our own family members first, and then work outside of that circle. We need to ensure that we have a good balance when it comes to financial donations - ensuring that our parents, siblings, or blood-relatives who are in financial distress are taken care of first off, and then when possible, helping others - and what better time to give than during our lifetime with our own hands, rather than waiting for after our death to have our wealth distributed by others.
- There are many people who 'claim' to have true faith, however the sphere of true believers who act on the entire contents of what the religion teaches are a very small group.

Verse 178

يَٰٓأَيُّهَا ٱلَّذِينَ ءَامَنُواْ كُتِبَ عَلَيۡكُمُ ٱلۡقِصَاصُ فِي ٱلۡقَتۡلَىۖ ٱلۡحُرُّ بِٱلۡحُرِّ وَٱلۡعَبۡدُ بِٱلۡعَبۡدِ وَٱلۡأُنثَىٰ بِٱلۡأُنثَىٰۚ فَمَنۡ عُفِيَ لَهُۥ مِنۡ أَخِيهِ شَيۡءٞ فَٱتِّبَاعُۢ بِٱلۡمَعۡرُوفِ وَأَدَآءٌ إِلَيۡهِ بِإِحۡسَٰنٖۗ ذَٰلِكَ تَخۡفِيفٞ مِّن رَّبِّكُمۡ وَرَحۡمَةٞۗ فَمَنِ ٱعۡتَدَىٰ بَعۡدَ ذَٰلِكَ فَلَهُۥ عَذَابٌ أَلِيمٞ ١٧٨

O you who believe! Prescribed for you is *qiṣāṣ* (a justice system of consequences and retribution) in cases of (deliberate, unjust) killing: a free man for a free man, a slave for a slave, a female for a female. Yet if the person (the murderer) is granted some remission by one's brother (any of the heirs of the victim), then what falls on the pardoning side is fulfilling in fairness what has been agreed upon, and the (guilty) side should make the payment kindly enough to please the other side. This is a lessening (of the laws of the penal code) from your Lord, and a mercy. Then whoever offends after that, for them is a painful punishment.

From this verse onwards, we see the phrase "prescribed for you" *(kutiba)* being used in certain instances. Allah ﷻ starts to provide us with spiritual prescriptions for goodness *(birr)* - the first one being a justice system *(qiṣāṣ)*, followed by writing the last will and testament *(waṣīyah)*, then fasting *(ṣawm)* and so on.

As the first command of what has been prescribed upon the Muslim community in the order of mention in this chapter is that of *qiṣāṣ*, we need to understand that this is not to be looked at as retribution or retaliation. Rather, since Islam presents its followers and the entire society with a complete system of life, as much as is possible to be formulated and enacted in this temporal world, *qiṣāṣ* becomes one form of societal justice which as we will see, has been implemented to ensure balance in society.

This verse has a direct connection to the previous verse which was speaking about a holistic and complete concept of goodness, and one of the areas of this was the overall human society. Thus, from this verse onwards, some of the evils of society are looked at, and how to overcome them in order to create an ideal system.

History of Revelation

The custom of the Arabs of the pre-Islamic Era of Ignorance *(Jāhiliyyah)* was that if someone from their tribe was killed, then in retaliation they would kill as many people as they could from the tribe where the killer came from. This practice went on to such an extent that they were willing to destroy an entire tribe in retaliation for the killing of one person!

It was in this context that the verse under review was revealed as a way and an order to limit the retribution in the case of an unjustified murder.

This Islamic ruling *(ḥukm)* was in fact a middle ground between two different rulings which existed at that time.

Some people considered retribution as a proper recompense, while others felt that the payment of blood-money *(diyah)*[84] was sufficient.

---

[84] The *diyah* is a 'financial sum' that should be paid to a person, or one's heir in the case of when a person is killed, or has a body part severed in an accident, or due to a physical injury.

The detailed rules of *diyah,* as well as the specific amounts that must be paid based on the type of injury are mentioned in the books of Jurisprudence.

The amount of *diyah* increases in some circumstances, such as the occurrence of a crime in the sanctuary of Mecca, or if performed in the four inviolable months which include: Rajab, Dhūl Qaʿdah, Dhūl Ḥijjah, and Muḥarram.

There is a verse in the Qur'ān which is referred to as the 'Verse of the *Diyah*' where Allah ﷻ says:

وَمَا كَانَ لِمُؤْمِنٍ أَن يَقْتُلَ مُؤْمِنًا إِلَّا خَطَـًٔا ۚ وَمَن قَتَلَ مُؤْمِنًا خَطَـًٔا فَتَحْرِيرُ رَقَبَةٍ مُّؤْمِنَةٍ وَدِيَةٌ مُّسَلَّمَةٌ إِلَىٰٓ أَهْلِهِۦٓ إِلَّآ أَن يَصَّدَّقُوا۟ ۚ فَإِن كَانَ مِن قَوْمٍ عَدُوٍّ لَّكُمْ وَهُوَ مُؤْمِنٌ فَتَحْرِيرُ رَقَبَةٍ مُّؤْمِنَةٍ ۖ وَإِن كَانَ مِن قَوْمٍۭ بَيْنَكُمْ وَبَيْنَهُم مِّيثَـٰقٌ فَدِيَةٌ مُّسَلَّمَةٌ إِلَىٰٓ أَهْلِهِۦ وَتَحْرِيرُ رَقَبَةٍ مُّؤْمِنَةٍ ۖ فَمَن لَّمْ يَجِدْ فَصِيَامُ شَهْرَيْنِ مُتَتَابِعَيْنِ تَوْبَةً مِّنَ ٱللَّهِ ۗ وَكَانَ ٱللَّهُ عَلِيمًا حَكِيمًا ﴿٩٢﴾

And never is it for a believer to kill another believer unless it is by mistake; and whoever kills a believer by mistake must set free a believing slave, and pay blood-money to his family (legal heirs), unless they forgo it as a freewill offering. If he (the victim), while himself a believer, belonged to a people hostile to you (with who there is no treaty), then (the expiation is to) set free a believing slave. If he (the victim) belonged to a (non-Muslim) people between whom and you there is a treaty, then (the expiation is to) pay blood-money to his heirs, and to set free a believing slave. But he who has no means (to make such expiation), must fast for two consecutive months

Islam imposed and regulated the laws of retribution *(qiṣāṣ)*[85] as a permissible legal recourse for the guardians of the family of the victim who was unjustly killed, but it also provided a secondary option which is the payment of "blood-money."

The late ʿAllāmah Sayyid Muḥammad Ḥusayn Ṭabāʾṭabāʾī mentions a beautiful point in relation to this verse where he says: "The heir of a murdered person who has the right to retaliation has extraordinarily been described here as the 'brother' of the murderer; this expression has been used to awaken the feeling of love and kindness in the heart of the aggrieved party, and gives a hint to him that remission and forgiveness is highly preferable in the eyes of Allah ﷻ."[86]

There is Life in the Laws of Retribution

From this verse onwards, a series of Islamic rulings *(aḥkām)* are introduced.

The first issue is in regards to the respect of life, and this ruling was put in place to invalidate the ways and customs of the Era of Ignorance *(Jāhiliyyah)*.

Addressing the believers, Allah ﷻ states that in regards to those who have been killed unjustly, these rules of retribution *(qiṣāṣ)* as defined by Islam will apply.

The word *qiṣāṣ* comes from the root *qaṣṣa* and it means 'searching for something, and following the traces which one thing left behind' and as

---

- a penance from Allah (a way of repentance); and Allah is All-Knowing (of everything including what is in your hearts), All-Wise." (Qurʾān, Sūrah an-Nisāʾ (4), Verse 92)

85 The term *qiṣāṣ* literally means 'retribution,' and it is a term used in Islamic Jurisprudence to refer to 'retaliation or retribution for intentional crimes.' There are two kinds of *qiṣāṣ*: *qiṣāṣ* for life, and *qiṣāṣ* for body parts. The ruling of *qiṣāṣ* is taken to be an essential ruling in Islam, supported by a number of Qurʾānic verses, *ḥadīth*, and the consensus of scholars. Some of the reasons for the permissibility of *qiṣāṣ* in Islam include: securing criminal justice, protecting social safety, and preventing individual acts of revenge.

86 ʿAllāmah Ṭabāʾṭabāʾī, *Al-Mizān fī Tafsīr al-Qurʾān*, Vol. 2, Pg. 324.

such, anything which would come after another thing would be referred to as *qiṣāṣ* by the Arabs. The reason for this was because if one murder happened, then another would follow as a form of retribution, thus the Arabs used this word to describe this act.

The choice of the word, retribution *(qiṣāṣ)*, indicates that the legal guardians of the victim have the right to do to the killer exactly what he/she enacted upon the innocent person who was murdered, as Allah ﷻ mentions in the Qur'ān that: "And We prescribed for them in it: A life for a life, and an eye for an eye, and a nose for a nose, and an ear for an ear, and a tooth for a tooth, and a (like) retaliation for all wounds (the exact retaliation of that which is possible). But whoever remits (the retaliation), it will be an act of expiation for them. And whoever does not judge by what Allah has sent down, then it is those who are the wrongdoers."[87]

However, we see that in describing the laws of retribution, Allah ﷻ did not stop at this sentence, and in the following portion of the verse He explicitly raises the issue of equality and says that if a free person was innocently killed, then the one upon whom retribution should be meted out will be a free person; a slave should be killed for a slave who was innocently slain; and a female should be killed for an innocent woman who was murdered.

In this regard, it is mentioned in *Tafsīr al-Mizān* that: "Before the advent of Islam and until this verse was revealed, the Arabs believed in requiting a murder with killing, but the retaliation had no defined limit. It all depended on the strength or weakness of the aggrieved party. Sometimes they killed a man for a man, and a woman for a woman - thus keeping a balance between the crime and its punishment. However, at other times they killed ten people for one person murdered, or a free man for a slave, and a chief for an ordinary man. Many times, a tribe destroyed another one in retaliation of a single man; but Islam opted for

---

[87] Qur'ān, Sūrah al-Mā'idah (5), Verse 45:

وَكَتَبْنَا عَلَيْهِمْ فِيهَآ أَنَّ ٱلنَّفْسَ بِٱلنَّفْسِ وَٱلْعَيْنَ بِٱلْعَيْنِ وَٱلْأَنفَ بِٱلْأَنفِ وَٱلْأُذُنَ بِٱلْأُذُنِ
وَٱلسِّنَّ بِٱلسِّنِّ وَٱلْجُرُوحَ قِصَاصٌ ۚ فَمَن تَصَدَّقَ بِهِۦ فَهُوَ كَفَّارَةٌ لَّهُۥ ۚ وَمَن لَّمْ يَحْكُم بِمَآ أَنزَلَ
ٱللَّهُ فَأُو۟لَـٰٓئِكَ هُمُ ٱلظَّـٰلِمُونَ ﴿٤٥﴾

a middle course between confirmation of retaliation and its negation. It prescribed retaliation, but did not make it obligatory; and it allowed remission along with the payment of blood-money. Then it laid down the foundation of justice by prescribing equality between the murderer and the murdered, telling us that: the free for the free, a slave for a slave, and a female for a female."[88]

In this verse, Allah ﷻ is mentioning just some of the possible scenarios of someone who has been killed as an example to let the believers know that there are many situations, and that each one will have its own unique ruling in terms of the *qiṣāṣ* - it may be the death penalty, blood-money, etc. Thus, we cannot make a general rule for all types of killings, however the one overlying ruling which Allah ﷻ does present and which He encourages is forgiveness and to accept the blood-money, rather than resorting to corporal punishment.

In this verse and in Islamic Law in general, we see that the retribution is at different levels based on various factors, and this is because the blood-money is different depending on who was killed. This does not mean that there is discrimination in the laws of Islam, but rather just like today when people go to court the outcome varies depending on who was killed, their position in society, etc.; thus, in Islam we see a similar concept. For example, although killing an innocent person is a crime, however if the person killed was a head of state, a judge, a police officer, or someone else who holds a level of authority, then if the accused is found guilty, they will be subject to a much stricter sentencing than if they were to kill for example, a homeless person. There is no doubt that murder is murder, and each human life is sacred, however society has determined that there has to be variations in sentencing based on the severity of the crime, and the position of the one who was killed.

Why Blood-money?

Why has the Qur'ān laid out such a comprehensive system of enacting justice in this temporal world for the crime of murder, and what is the philosophy behind the blood-money *(diyah)*?

---

[88] *Tafsīr al-Mizān,* Vol. 2, Pg. 328.

Perhaps we can point to some of the following reasons for this system:

1. In English, we have a saying which goes: "Justice must be seen to be done," and in the case of the penal code of Islam, we recognize that people need to feel that the justice system is fulfilling its role and doing its best to ensure that people know that they will be held responsible for their actions in this world. In addition, those who have lost a loved one also need to be able to see that justice is being served.
2. Being given 'blood-money' over the death of a loved one cannot bring that person back to life, however the Law-Giver, Allah ﷻ, has taken into consideration the rights of all parties involved, and recognizes that the loss of a family member has the potential to negatively impact the remaining members from a financial perspective.
3. The *diyah* does not have to be financial compensation. The judge in an Islamic-based Court of Law may determine that if the person or their family is not able to pay the amount required, then they need to repay the family through working or some other way, and as a last resort, they may go to prison for a determined period of time as a means of compensation.

In short, when it comes to a complete justice system, there are many variables at play, thus we cannot generalize anything.

In order to clarify that retribution is a **right** for the guardians of the victim, but it is not a mandatory action which must be carried out, and if they want the guardians can forgive the killer and take the blood-money, or they can simply forgive and forget and not ask for any money in return, Allah ﷻ adds that if someone was to give one's brother in religion something to appease them, then in doing so the verdict of retribution will transform into accepting blood-money rather than killing the guilty person.

In either case, people involved must follow the right path - meaning that those who are allowed to either seek retribution or accept blood-money must take into consideration the financial state of the one who is offering the blood-money, and the killer must pay this money to the family of the victim.

At the end of this verse, in order to emphasize and guide the believers to an important point, Allah ﷻ states that transgressing beyond the limits which the religion has set, regardless of who does it, carries a hefty penalty; and this ruling is an alleviating and mercy from Him, and if someone still exceeds the limits of the Islamic rulings after these rulings have come down and been made clear for the believers, then there will be a painful retribution for them.

On one hand, the just ruling of retribution and amnesty or total forgiveness *(ʿafw)* was meant to condemn the corrupt method of the Age of Ignorance in which sometimes hundreds of people were killed in retaliation for one innocent life.

On the other hand, it did not close the door to the killer being completely forgiven for their crime.

From a third angle, this ruling informs people that after forgiveness has been requested and granted, and the blood-money is paid, then no one has a right to violate this agreement and avenge the killing - unlike during the Time of Ignorance in which sometimes the guardians of the murdered one would still kill the guilty person after having accepted their pleas of pardon and having been paid the blood-money.

Philosophy of Qiṣāṣ

The philosophy and essence of *qiṣāṣ* has four main outcomes that we need to reflect upon, and they are:

1. When a person loses a loved one through murder, it is one of the hardest times in their life. Their emotions are running high, they are angry, upset, and are looking for answers - and they are seeking justice.

For that reason, the first thing Allah ﷻ says in this verse is that the grieving parties need to cool their hearts, thus let them know that there is a way to seek justice through retribution *(qiṣāṣ)*. At the first level, they are reminded that if the defendant is found guilty in a court of law, then they can potentially be put to death.

After the sense of justice has been acknowledged and communicated, and the process which has to be followed has been articulated to the plaintiff, Allah then connects further with them by reminding them that forgiveness of their brother-in-faith who made this huge mistake of killing a beloved one is better for the individual than asking for their death, so the believer is then advised to forgive the murderer.

At the next stage, if the grieving people cannot bring themselves to forgive the murderer, then Allah ﷻ suggests another route. Instead of enacting the death penalty, the grieved ones are encouraged to accept *diyah* - blood-money - to recover some of the justice.

The reason why *qiṣāṣ* has all of these variables at play - the death penalty, forgiveness, paying the blood-money - is because these situations are never simple. As can be seen in any case, there are multiple layers of complexity, and sometimes it is not easy to see who is at fault or what degree of guiltiness they bear. It is often a challenge to determine exactly what happened, or understand the circumstances which existed at that moment when a crime was perpetrated.

Therefore, the Qur'ānic and Islamic principle of *qiṣāṣ* is the true form of justice for humanity, given all of the perspectives.

Today, we see that the judicial system in many countries is extremely subjective. Many young people who committed crimes while juveniles perhaps did not fully understand the ramifications of what they were doing, or they were brought up living in harsh circumstances and did not know any better, or sometimes people have just been at the wrong place at the wrong time, thus have been sentenced to unfair or lengthy prison terms.

Qiṣāṣ is also attempting to destroy the animosity between the parties by calling them brothers of one another, and urging them to exact forgiveness which is a more holistic program than what we see today in society.

Keys of Guidance

- In the law of retribution, the principles of equality and justice must be maintained. Justice is the foundational pillar of Islam, so even in matters of the penal code it must be at the forefront of our minds - not revenge.
- Determination and compassion are both required when it comes to the laws of Islam. The commandments in this verse and the unique

way in which Allah ﷻ explains this ruling shows us that the relatives of the victim are considered as the 'brother' of the murderer, and as such the murderer, even though he may have committed the act intentionally, however one should still not exit the borders of Islam and brotherhood.

Verse 179

وَلَكُمْ فِي ٱلْقِصَاصِ حَيَوٰةٌ يَٰٓأُو۟لِى ٱلْأَلْبَٰبِ لَعَلَّكُمْ تَتَّقُونَ ﴿١٧٩﴾

There is life for you in *qiṣāṣ* (a justice system of consequences and retribution), O you who possess intellect! Perhaps you may become God-conscious.

This verse which Allah ﷻ presents to us with a meaningful phrase answers many questions on the issue of retribution *(qiṣāṣ)* where He says to the people of understanding that in this subject of retribution, there is life, so perhaps they may become God-conscious and be people who attain *taqwā*.

This verse which should be engraved in the minds of everyone as the universal declaration and slogan of Islam clearly shows that in the laws of retribution, there is no revenge - rather, it is a means of ensuring the continued life of a civil society.

On the one hand, the rules of *qiṣāṣ* guarantee the life of society because if there was no penalty of retribution for certain societal crimes, then the lives of innocent people would be in danger as the hard-hearted people would feel free to commit any crime they want. This is seen in countless countries in the world where criminals know that they will either not be caught, or if they are, they will not have to suffer the consequences for their actions.

On the other hand, the law of *qiṣāṣ* could also be a killer's lifeblood because it should control individuals from the thought of murdering innocent people because one would understand that by killing another human being, they themselves may be given the death penalty.

It is also important to note that the Qur'ān has provided a clear balance between the Judaic law of retribution and the Christian law of complete forgiveness.

For example, the law given to Prophet Mūsā ﷺ on Mount Sinai and recorded in the Old Testament noted that execution is the outcome for several offenses including: murder (but not accidental killings), striking or cursing a parent, kidnapping, adultery, incest, bestiality, sodomy, rape of a betrothed virgin, witchcraft, incorrigible delinquency, breaking the Sabbath, blasphemy, sacrificing to false gods, oppressing the weak, and other transgressions. (See Old Testament: Exodus 21, 22, 35; Leviticus 20 & 24; Deuteronomy 21-24)

On the flip side, the Christian Bible seems to say that through the Christian belief in the death of Prophet 'Isā ﷺ, something which Muslims categorically deny, his blood was a recompense for the sins which people perform.

The Qur'ān presents a middle ground of *qiṣāṣ* in which one can either forgive the murderer; an amount of money can be paid (which has its own philosophy to it); or the death penalty can be enacted, which we spoke about in the commentary of the previous verse.

To conclude, we need to confirm that the Qur'ānic laws which Allah ﷻ has instructed are there for the welfare of the entire society, and just because they do not make sense to us today or may not fit with the data coming from current research, it does not mean that the laws are outdated or ineffective. Rather, we must realize that had the rules been implemented accurately from the first day, human society would not be in the situation they find themselves in today with skyrocketing numbers of people being incarcerated for violent crimes.

Keys of Guidance

- The administration of justice guarantees the life of a society, whereas when injustice and inequality reign, that society is destined for its own death and downfall.
- Human society requires a balance between compassion and justice - compassion sees that the guilty party is forgiven, while justice sees

that a person pays the price for one's crimes. Allah ﷻ who is All-Merciful and All-Compassionate is also All-Just and the Avenger.

Verse 180

كُتِبَ عَلَيْكُمْ إِذَا حَضَرَ أَحَدَكُمُ ٱلْمَوْتُ إِن تَرَكَ خَيْرًا ٱلْوَصِيَّةُ لِلْوَٰلِدَيْنِ وَٱلْأَقْرَبِينَ بِٱلْمَعْرُوفِ ۖ حَقًّا عَلَى ٱلْمُتَّقِينَ ﴿١٨٠﴾

Prescribed for you, when death approaches any of you if one leaves behind wealth, is to make a testament (will) in favor of one's parents and near relatives according to customary good (and religiously approvable practice) - a duty upon the God-conscious ones *(al-muttaqīn).*

Previously, the discussion centered on matters of life and the issue of retribution *(qiṣāṣ).* In that verse, Allah ﷻ spoke about retribution as a system of goodness *(birr)* in society. This verse under review speaks about the second form of goodness which is limited to the family who writes a will.

In this verse and the next two verses, Allah ﷻ deals with a portion of the rulings of the last will and testament related to financial issues, and starts off the discussion by providing one universal and mandatory ruling *(ḥukm)* by saying that it has been prescribed - meaning that it has been made an obligation upon the testator[89] that when death comes, if the person is leaving behind anything good, meaning something of value, then one needs to bequeath it properly to the surviving family members as outlined by Islam. The Almighty concludes this verse by saying that this is an obligation upon those who have God-consciousness *(taqwā).*

Although according to the spirit of the law, writing a last will and testament is a highly recommended action *(mustaḥab)* in Islam, however by Allah ﷻ using the phrase "prescribed for you..." *(kutiba ʿalaykum)*

---

[89] The person making a will.

it denotes that this is a strongly recommended action that one should adhere to.[90]

It is noteworthy that instead of using the word "wealth" Allah ﷻ has chosen to use the word "goodness" - and this shows that Islam considers the wealth and capital which has been obtained through legitimate means and is used for the benefit of society as being "goodness and blessed wealth," and sought to change the opinion of those who mistakenly think that in its essence, wealth is inherently evil.

At the same time, this verse is also a subtle reference to the fact that our wealth must have been gained through legitimate means, because wealth earned through illegal or illicit channels which a person leaves behind for one's inheritors is "not good," rather it is nothing more than evil and misery for oneself.

The necessity of writing a last will and testament can be seen in the verse under review by the usage of the phrase "...according to customary good and religiously approvable practice..." *(bil maʿrūf).*

This short phrase indicates that the last will and testament must be explained in detail, and needs to take into account the amount of inheritance which is in one's estate, the specific amounts which are

---

[90] In his book: *Making an Islamic Will*, Sayyid Muhammad Rizvi states:

"Although the law (secular as well as Islamic) does not say that the making of a will is a must, but by looking at the consequences of not having a will, it is necessary - both from the legal aspect, as well from the religious aspect.

Firstly, if a person dies without a will, then the government will appoint an executor who will divide the estate among the heirs as he/she seems fit. The payment and fees of that executor for this job will come out of your estate, and the government system will take its time in getting this job done!

Secondly, from the religious point of view, your heirs may get more or less than the shares which are specified for them in Islam. Therefore, by not writing a will, you are leaving the door open for a non-Islamic authority to distribute your estate according to its own views.

Thus, not having a will is costly, as well as problematic, from both the secular as well as the Islamic points of view. Considering the consequences, I think it is an obligation *(wājib)* for a Muslim to have an Islamic will; more so when you realize that the law of the land allows you to do so.

inherited by the heirs, meaning who will get each amount, and other such issues such that if the common people would look at that will, they would consider it to be something written with common sense in mind and would not think that it was written by someone who was discriminating, or was prejudice to some family members over others, as this can lead to family strife after a person dies, and deviation from the principles of truth and justice.[91]

Keys of Guidance

- Although with the arrival of death, an individual leaves this world, however one's record of actions does not come to a complete close. Rather, a will - or lack thereof - will ensure that one's book of deeds continues to remain open with actions being written in it based on how a person formulated one's last will and testament.
- In addition to the official amount of inheritance that one's family members will receive from the estate of an individual based on the specific amounts which the teachings of Islam have laid out in detail, an individual writing a will can consider an extra share for one's parents, or other relatives - especially those who may not receive anything. One can also donate a portion of their wealth to charitable causes which will entail the person to continue to get rewards as long as that goodness remains.
- It is interesting that the Qur'ān mentions that when making the will, a person needs to keep in mind their parents while in most circumstances, the parents pass away before their children. It is possible that the reason for why this has been mentioned is because when we draft a will, we need to see the conditions and needs of everyone present while we are alive. If one leaves behind parents they are usually older, vulnerable, and in need of more support, so

[91] The rulings on how to write an Islamic will can be found in the book by Sayyid Muhammad Rizvi, *Making an Islamic Will* which is available at www.al-islam.org/making-islamic-will-sayyid-Muhammad-rizvi. (Last accessed on September 24, 2022)

a believer needs to be conscious about that. Of course if the parents both pass away before an individual does, then one can change the details in one's will accordingly.

Verse 181

فَمَنْ بَدَّلَهُۥ بَعْدَ مَا سَمِعَهُۥ فَإِنَّمَآ إِثْمُهُۥ عَلَى ٱلَّذِينَ يُبَدِّلُونَهُۥٓ ۚ إِنَّ ٱللَّهَ سَمِيعٌ عَلِيمٌ ﴿١٨١﴾

Then if anyone changes the will after hearing it (and the will is not carried out as it must be), then the sin thereof is on those who change it. Surely Allah is All-Hearing *(Samīʿ)*, All-Knowing *(ʿAlīm)*.

When a will is written in a comprehensive fashion and covers all of the areas mentioned in the previous verse and the commentary explained by the scholars, then it is said to be honorable and sacred, and any change to it after the death of an individual by anyone is forbidden.

This verse clearly states that the sin is on those who change the last will and testament after hearing it, and if they think that Allah ﷻ is not aware of their conspiracies, then they are sorely mistaken, because He confirms by mentioning two of His important traits *(Ṣifāt)* that He is All-Hearing, and All-Knowing.

This verse refers to the fact that any offenses carried out by an executor of the last will and testament will never result in any diminishment in the reward of the testator. They will receive the full reward from Allah ﷻ for fulfilling their responsibility of writing the last will and testament, and the only ones who will be guilty of a crime and sin are the executors or people who changed the specifics of the inheritance about who was to get what and how much.

Keys of Guidance

- It is not allowed for an executor or the inheritors who stand to inherit from the last will and testament to change the facts and figures - this is forbidden and considered a sin - except in the case that the author of the will had made a mistake in the division of the estate amongst one's inheritors, as will be mentioned in the next verse. There is no problem if the inheritors themselves decide to share the inheritance with one another after the amounts have been determined and distributed, but they must ensure that the specific conditions of the will are acted upon.

- Islam considers the right of ownership both in one's lifetime and also after death; therefore even after death, no one is permitted to alter the last will and testament of a deceased person.

Verse 182

فَمَنْ خَافَ مِن مُّوصٍ جَنَفًا أَوْ إِثْمًا فَأَصْلَحَ بَيْنَهُمْ فَلَآ إِثْمَ عَلَيْهِ إِنَّ ٱللَّهَ غَفُورٌ رَّحِيمٌ ﴿١٨٢﴾

But if anyone fears from the testator (that) an injustice (favoritism) or sin (was committed), and (a person) brings about a settlement between the parties (by making the necessary changes), then no sin will be upon them. Surely Allah is All-Forgiving *(Ghafūr)*, All-Merciful *(Raḥīm)*.

So far, this Islamic ruling *(ḥukm)* has been made clear that it is highly recommended, or perhaps even an obligation given the laws of a secular society that a Muslim should write one's last will and testament. It was also mentioned that any form of alteration in the last will and testament in which the amounts which people receive, or who receives how much has been classified as a major sin.

However, as we know that every law can have exceptions based on certain changes in conditions and circumstances - just like in the rules of purification before the daily prayers in which we are obligated to perform *wuḍū'*, however if we do not have water, or we are not allowed to use it for whatever reason, or it is harmful, etc., then we must perform *tayammum* instead.

This verse notes that if anyone fears - and this is a fear which is reasonable and based on concrete facts, not merely on speculation - that the testament which was done by the now deceased testator had written one's will in such a manner that one showed bias toward some heirs over others, and by not ensuring that the stringent conditions which Islam has laid down for those who are entitled to inherit, and how much each heir receives have not been met; or in addition to this, the inheritors are concerned that the executor will fall into sin by fulfilling what is written in the will because it violates the laws which Allah ﷻ has laid down; or if the executor tries to correct the inaccuracies in the will by ensuring that everyone gets their fair share based on the rulings of Islam - then there is no offence on them, and they will not be subject to the sin of changing the last will and testament, because as Allah ﷻ previously said that He is All-Hearing, and All-Knowing, He also add that He is All-Forgiving, and All-Merciful.

Therefore, this exception applies to cases where the last will and testament was not written properly, and it is only in such a circumstance that the executor has the right to change the will to ensure that everyone is given their rights according to the rules of Islam.

Of course, if the testator is still alive, and the executor or family are reviewing the will with them and they notice that it has not been written according to the Islamic guidelines, then they should advise the person that certain changes need to be made to ensure that the will is in line with the Islamic requirements. If a person dies without being able to make the changes oneself, then the executor is permitted to make the amendments to ensure that the will follows the rules of inheritance laid down by Islam.

The phrase '...an injustice...' *(janafan)* means 'deviation from the right and desired path' which may have crept into the will unknowingly by the testator; while the term '...a sin...' *(ithm)* refers to deliberate nonconformities which a person knowingly made in one's last will and testament.

We must stress on the point that if a testator did make a mistake - knowingly or unknowingly - then the heirs should work together to make peace with one another, rather than letting it escalate.

Today, we see many times that things get very ugly very quickly. Misunderstandings turn into disagreements which turn into fights that eventually end up in the secular courts of law. Such a slippery slope must be avoided at all costs, and if we abide by the Qur'ānic process in this regard, we see that Allah ﷻ is reminding us to deal with such matters peacefully and within the family, rather than airing our dirty laundry outside for others to see.

A simple three-step process would be as follows:

1. Make a will.
2. As long as it is written according to the laws of Islam and everyone has been given their rights, nothing can be changed.
3. If there are legal issues within the will and some parties who are entitled to inherit are not given what they are entitled to, then such issues must be dealt with peacefully within the family - or at most with respected family or friends being used to mediate - especially those who have no vested interest in the will.

Philosophy of the Last Will and Testament

As the Qur'ān clearly notes, there are only some relatives of the deceased who inherit from a person, and that too specific amounts,[92] while perhaps

[92] The inheritors and their inheritance percentages are covered in detail in Sūrah an-Nisā' (4), Verses 11 and 12 as follows:

يُوصِيكُمُ ٱللَّهُ فِىٓ أَوْلَـٰدِكُمْ ۖ لِلذَّكَرِ مِثْلُ حَظِّ ٱلْأُنثَيَيْنِ ۚ فَإِن كُنَّ نِسَآءً فَوْقَ ٱثْنَتَيْنِ فَلَهُنَّ ثُلُثَا
مَا تَرَكَ ۖ وَإِن كَانَتْ وَٰحِدَةً فَلَهَا ٱلنِّصْفُ ۚ وَلِأَبَوَيْهِ لِكُلِّ وَٰحِدٍ مِّنْهُمَا ٱلسُّدُسُ مِمَّا تَرَكَ إِن كَانَ
لَهُۥ وَلَدٌ ۚ فَإِن لَّمْ يَكُن لَّهُۥ وَلَدٌ وَوَرِثَهُۥٓ أَبَوَاهُ فَلِأُمِّهِ ٱلثُّلُثُ ۚ فَإِن كَانَ لَهُۥٓ إِخْوَةٌ فَلِأُمِّهِ ٱلسُّدُسُ ۚ
مِنۢ بَعْدِ وَصِيَّةٍ يُوصِى بِهَآ أَوْ دَيْنٍ ۗ ءَابَآؤُكُمْ وَأَبْنَآؤُكُمْ لَا تَدْرُونَ أَيُّهُمْ أَقْرَبُ لَكُمْ نَفْعًا ۚ
فَرِيضَةً مِّنَ ٱللَّهِ ۗ إِنَّ ٱللَّهَ كَانَ عَلِيمًا حَكِيمًا ﴿١١﴾

Allah commands you in (the matter of the division of the inheritance among) your children: for the male is the equivalent of the portion of two females. If there are more than two females (with no males), for them is two-thirds of the inheritance; and if there is only one, then the half. As for the parents (of the deceased): for each of the two is one-sixth of the inheritance, in case of his having left a child; but if he has left no children, and his parents are his only heirs, then for his mother is one-third. If he has (a surviving mother, together with or without sisters) two or more (surviving) brothers, then for his mother is one-sixth (all of these commands have to be put into effect) after deduction for any bequest he may have made (provided such bequest is in conformity with the relevant teachings of Islam), and any debt (incurred by him) (meaning that first the debt is paid, then the bequest is fulfilled, and then the inheritance is shared). Your parents and your children: you do not know which of them is nearer to you in (bringing you) benefit. This (law of inheritance) is an ordinance from Allah (that you must absolutely obey). Surely, Allah is All-Knowing (of your affairs and what benefits or harms you), All-Wise.

وَلَكُمْ نِصْفُ مَا تَرَكَ أَزْوَٰجُكُمْ إِن لَّمْ يَكُن لَّهُنَّ وَلَدٌ ۚ فَإِن كَانَ لَهُنَّ وَلَدٌ فَلَكُمُ ٱلرُّبُعُ مِمَّا تَرَكْنَ ۚ مِنۢ بَعْدِ وَصِيَّةٍ يُوصِينَ بِهَآ أَوْ دَيْنٍ ۚ وَلَهُنَّ ٱلرُّبُعُ مِمَّا تَرَكْتُمْ إِن لَّمْ يَكُن لَّكُمْ وَلَدٌ ۚ فَإِن كَانَ لَكُمْ وَلَدٌ فَلَهُنَّ ٱلثُّمُنُ مِمَّا تَرَكْتُم ۚ مِّنۢ بَعْدِ وَصِيَّةٍ تُوصُونَ بِهَآ أَوْ دَيْنٍ ۗ وَإِن كَانَ رَجُلٌ يُورَثُ كَلَٰلَةً أَوِ ٱمْرَأَةٌ وَلَهُۥٓ أَخٌ أَوْ أُخْتٌ فَلِكُلِّ وَٰحِدٍ مِّنْهُمَا ٱلسُّدُسُ ۚ فَإِن كَانُوٓا۟ أَكْثَرَ مِن ذَٰلِكَ فَهُمْ شُرَكَآءُ فِى ٱلثُّلُثِ ۚ مِنۢ بَعْدِ وَصِيَّةٍ يُوصَىٰ بِهَآ أَوْ دَيْنٍ غَيْرَ مُضَآرٍّ ۚ وَصِيَّةً مِّنَ ٱللَّهِ ۗ وَٱللَّهُ عَلِيمٌ حَلِيمٌ ﴿١٢﴾

And for you is a half of what your wives leave behind, if they have no children; but if they have a child, then you shall have one-fourth of what they leave behind - after deduction for any bequest they may have made and any debt (incurred by them). And for them is one-fourth of what you leave behind, if you have no children; but if you have a child, then they shall have one-eighth of what you leave behind - after deduction for any bequest which you may have made and any debt (incurred by you). And if a man or a woman has no heir in the direct line, but has a brother or a sister, for him or her is one-sixth; but if there are two or more, then they shall be sharers in one-third - after deduction for any bequest that may have been made or debt; neither (bequest or debt) intending harm (to the rights of the heirs in such ways as declaring fictitious debts or bequeathing more than one-third of one's estate). A commandment from Allah. Allah is All-Knowing (about all of your intentions, actions, and outcomes), All-Clement (not hasty to

it is possible that other family members and perhaps some friends or close acquaintances may be in dire need of financial assistance.

Also, in the case of some of the heirs, oftentimes the amount of inheritance which they will receive may not meet their needs. Therefore, alongside the law of inheritance, Islam places the law of "willing" - which is something specific to select individuals, and through this allows Muslims to decide on how to use one-third of their property however they want after their death.[93]

In addition, sometimes a person wants to do good deeds, but for some reason does not succeed in performing them during one's lifetime. Logic dictates that an individual should not be deprived of being able to do good deeds with what Allah ﷻ has given them, thus a person can stipulate to have them performed on one's behalf with the wealth that one leaves behind after one's death. Therefore, from the total wealth, a person is permitted to make personal use of one third as they wish, however such things must be written out in one's last will and testament.

Of course, a will is not limited to the above cases only; rather when writing one's last will and testament, a person must specify if they have any debts or things entrusted to them in detail so that after death, the rights of the people or the Divine rights which were incumbent on the now-deceased can all be fulfilled.

Within the Islamic traditions, there are many *ḥadīth* which emphasize on writing a will; for example, we read in a statement from Prophet Muḥammad ﷺ that he has been quoted as saying: "A person who dies without (having written) a will, his death is the death of ignorance (the pre-Islamic Era of *Jāhiliyyah*)."[94]

---

punish the errors of His servants).

[93] This right of distributing the one-third according to one's own wish can be only exercised if a person makes a will about it. One can do whatever they like with that one-third: give it to a family-member, a relative, a friend, donate it to a charitable cause or organization, have your remaining prayers *(ṣalāh)* or fasts *(ṣawm)* performed if you missed any, etc.

[94] *Wasā'il ash-Shīʿah*, Vol. 13, Pg. 352. The initial portion of this tradition is as follows:

Maintaining Justice in the Last Will and Testament

There are many examples in the *ḥadīth* which emphasize on not being unfair, and not harming others in the writing of the last will and testament; and when reviewing such statements from Prophet Muḥammad ﷺ and the Ahlul Bayt ؑ, we can conclude that just like the writing of a will is a good deed, encroachment of the rights of others within it is condemned and considered a major sin.

Imām Muḥammad al-Bāqir ؑ is reported to have said: "Whoever observes justice in [writing] one's will, it is as if they have given the same property in the way of Allah during one's lifetime; and whoever transgresses when [writing] one's will, the grace of Allah will be taken away from them on the Day of Resurrection."[95]

Violation, oppression, and causing harm to others in the writing of the last will and testament is when a person wills more than one-third of one's estate - which is the maximum amount that one is entitled to allot - to be spent on specific purposes after one's death, because by doing so, a person will deprive one's rightful heirs of their legitimate rights, or one will commit unfair discrimination due to the existence of unjustified love or hate which a person may have for certain family members who are entitled by the laws of Allah ﷻ to inherit from them.

Thus, to summarize:
1. A person must ensure that one writes their last will and testament.
2. Whoever is put in a position to be the executors of a will must ensure that they do not change anything in the will - as long as it is written according to the Islamic laws.
3. If changes need to be done, then they must be done peacefully and by strictly observing the Islamic laws.

Keys of Guidance

- We must ensure that we observe the correct order when it comes to

---

مَنْ مَاتَ بِغَيْرِ وَصِيَّةٍ مَاتَ مِيْتَةً جَاهِلِيَّةً...

[95] *Wasā'il ash-Shīʿah*, Vol. 13, Pg. 359. The initial portion of this tradition is as follows:

the principle of "importance" and "greater importance." Although it is crucial to write a will, and it is important to ensure that it is fully implemented after the death of an individual, it is of "greater importance" to ensure that justice is maintained, and that no conflicts or confrontations will occur among the family members after one's death. If it is found that the will contains instructions which go against the laws of Islam, and thus certain people are excluded from the inheritance that they are entitled to by Allah ﷻ, then such a will must not be followed by the executors, and they would need to do what is just even if that means going against the written statements in the will.

- Islam is a religion built on the foundation of justice and fairness. Not only is Allah ﷻ All-Just and All-Fair and this is how He deals with His creations, but He also expects humanity to deal with one another - friend or foe - with justice and equity. This point is stressed in multiple verses of the Qur'ān in which we are told that even in the case of two Muslims having a major disagreement which may lead to war and the shedding of innocent blood, a third-party needs to step in and negotiate a peace treaty between them based on justice. Allah ﷻ says: "And if two parties of believers should fight, then make peace between them (and act promptly). But if one of them aggressively encroaches the rights of the other, then fight you all against the aggressive side until they comply with Allah's decree (concerning the matter). If they comply, then make peace between them with justice and be equitable. Surely Allah loves those who act justly."[96]

مَنْ عَدَلَ فِي وَصِيَّتِهِ كَانَ كَمَنْ تَصَدَّقَ بِهَا فِي حَيَاتِهِ...

[96] Qur'ān, Sūrah al-Ḥujurāt (49), Verse 9:

وَإِن طَآئِفَتَانِ مِنَ ٱلْمُؤْمِنِينَ ٱقْتَتَلُوا۟ فَأَصْلِحُوا۟ بَيْنَهُمَا ۖ فَإِنۢ بَغَتْ إِحْدَىٰهُمَا عَلَى ٱلْأُخْرَىٰ فَقَٰتِلُوا۟ ٱلَّتِى تَبْغِى حَتَّىٰ تَفِىٓءَ إِلَىٰٓ أَمْرِ ٱللَّهِ ۚ فَإِن فَآءَتْ فَأَصْلِحُوا۟ بَيْنَهُمَا بِٱلْعَدْلِ وَأَقْسِطُوٓا۟ ۖ إِنَّ ٱللَّهَ يُحِبُّ ٱلْمُقْسِطِينَ ﴿٩﴾

Verse 183

يَـٰٓأَيُّهَا ٱلَّذِينَ ءَامَنُوا۟ كُتِبَ عَلَيْكُمُ ٱلصِّيَامُ كَمَا كُتِبَ عَلَى ٱلَّذِينَ مِن قَبْلِكُمْ لَعَلَّكُمْ تَتَّقُونَ ﴿١٨٣﴾

O you who believe! Prescribed for you is fasting *(al-ṣiyām)* as it was prescribed for those before you, so that perhaps you may attain God-consciousness *(taqwā)*.

Types and History of Fasting

In this verse, Allah ﷻ informs the Muslims that fasting is not something unique to the Qurʾānic plan of self-building, but rather even previous communities had methods of fasting in their Divinely-taught code. Some examples throughout history of others who have fasted can be found in the stories of the Prophets.

In regards to Prophet Ādam ؑ: When Prophet Muḥammad ﷺ was asked why Allah ﷻ made fasting compulsory for 30 days, he answered: "Since the fruit remained in [Prophet Ādam's] stomach for 30 days, Allah made 30 fasts incumbent upon Ādam and his progeny. However it is His grace that He allowed them to eat before dawn. Fasting was obligatory on Ādam, therefore it is compulsory for my nation as well."[97]

Prophet Nūḥ ؑ: When Prophet Nūḥ ؑ boarded the ship on the first day of the month of Rajab, he ordered all of those who were with him to fast on that day.[98]

Prophet Mūsā ؑ: When Prophet Mūsā ؑ went to the mountain to receive the Ten Commandments from Allah ﷻ after he and his community

---

97 Shaykh Ṣadūq, *ʿIllal ash-Sharāʾiʿ*, Vol. 2, Pg. 379. The initial portion of this tradition is as follows:

لِأَيِّ شَيءٍ فَرَضَ اللهُ عَزَّ وَجَلَّ الصَّوْمَ عَلَى أُمَّتِك بِالنَّهَارِ ثَلَاثِينَ يَوْمًا...

98 Naysābūrī, Abūl Qāsim ʿUbaydillāh al-, *Fadhail Shahr Rajab*, Tradition 9, Pg. 499. The initial portion of this tradition is as follows:

وَفِي رَجَبٍ حَمَلَ اللهُ تَعَالَى ذِكْرُهُ نُوحًا فِي السَّفِينَةِ فَصَامَ رَجَبًا وَأَمَرَ مَنْ مَعَهُ أَنْ يَصُومُوا...

were saved from the Pharaoh, Allah ﷻ ordered Prophet Mūsā ؑ to make his way to a specific spot and fast for 30 days at the foot of the mountain, which he did.⁹⁹

Prophet ʿĪsā ؑ told the Isrāʾīlites: "Fast for 30 days and Allah ﷻ will fulfill whatever you require." They fasted for 30 days, then told Prophet ʿĪsā ؑ: "If we work for anyone they give us food to eat. We fasted for 30 days and suffered from hunger. Now pray to Allah so that He may send us a tray full of food from the heavens." Soon the angels brought a *māʾidah* (a table spread with food from heaven) for them with seven loaves and seven fishes in it. All of them ate from it.¹⁰⁰

From these examples, we can see that fasting was not introduced at the time of Prophet Muḥammad ﷺ, but that previous Prophets ؑ and their followers also were commanded to fast. Now that we have determined that fasting is an old practice done for many generations, let us take a look at what fasting is for Muslims today.

Fast of the Month of Ramaḍān: The Source of God-Consciousness (Taqwā)

There is a natural progression in this series of verses in that Allah ﷻ continues His prescriptions of righteousness *(birr)*. It began with a discussion on retribution *(qiṣāṣ)*, followed by last will and testament *(waṣīya)*, then on fasting *(ṣawm)*.

Qiṣāṣ concerns the welfare of the entire society and community; *waṣīya* takes into consideration the family unit; and *ṣawm* is concerned with the betterment of individuals.

With the explanation of various important rulings *(aḥkām)* in Islam as seen in the previous verses of the Qurʾān, we are now introduced to

---

⁹⁹ Tafsīr of the Qurʾān attributed to Imām Ḥasan al-ʿAskarī ؑ, Pg. 248. The initial portion of this tradition is as follows:

فَلَمَّا فَرَّجَ اللهُ تَعَالَى عَنْهُمْ، أَمَرَهُ اللهُ عَزَّ وَجَلَّ أَنْ يَأْتِيَ لِلْمِيعَادِ...

¹⁰⁰ *Biḥār al-Anwār*, Vol. 14, Pg. 262, Sect. 18, Ḥadīth 5. The initial portion of this tradition is as follows:

صُومُوا ثَلَاثِينَ يَوْمًا، ثُمَّ اِسْأَلُوا اللَّهَ تَعَالَى مَا شِئْتُمْ يُعْطِيكُمُوهُ...

another ruling *(ḥukm)* which focuses on the important act of worship, and that is fasting during the month of Ramaḍān.

In introducing this action, Allah ﷻ uses the same emphatic tone which He used in previous verses by directly addressing the believers, and informing them that fasting has been prescribed for them just as it had been prescribed upon the nations which came before them.

The philosophy of this act of worship is expressed as being put into place in order to build a true human being, just like Allah ﷻ states that it is through this fasting that perhaps the believers may become God-conscious - people of *taqwā*.

Keys of Guidance

- When speaking to people, if we use respectful, pleasing words, then they will be more willing to accept our message. In this regard, there is a tradition mentioned in *Tafsīr Majmaʿ al-Bayān* which states that the pleasure of being addressed by Allah ﷻ with the phrase of: "O you who believe" is such that it makes the difficulties associated with fasting much easier to bear.[101]
- One of the tools which people can use for children, adults, and others is to let them know that even though a particular action may be difficult to perform, other communities and nations have also had to practice or perform a similar thing. When we are told that others have also been subject to related challenges, it can help make our outlook on life and a particular action easier to perform and accept.
- In certain instances in the Qurʾān, Allah ﷻ highlights the philosophy behind certain acts of worship, such as He has done for fasting in the month of Ramaḍān, because when people know the result of their work or are given the rationale behind why they are instructed to carry out tasks, they are more willing and ready to do it, and will

---

[101] *Tafsīr Majmaʿ al-Bayān*, under the commentary of this verse under review. This tradition is as follows:

لَذَّةُ مَا فِي النِّدَاءِ أَزَالَ تَعَبَ الْعِبَادَةِ وَالْعَنَاءِ.

even enjoy it.

Verse 184

أَيَّامًا مَّعْدُودَٰتٍ ۚ فَمَن كَانَ مِنكُم مَّرِيضًا أَوْ عَلَىٰ سَفَرٍ فَعِدَّةٌ مِّنْ أَيَّامٍ
أُخَرَ ۚ وَعَلَى ٱلَّذِينَ يُطِيقُونَهُۥ فِدْيَةٌ طَعَامُ مِسْكِينٍ ۖ فَمَن تَطَوَّعَ خَيْرًا فَهُوَ
خَيْرٌ لَّهُۥ ۚ وَأَن تَصُومُوا۟ خَيْرٌ لَّكُمْ ۖ إِن كُنتُمْ تَعْلَمُونَ ﴿١٨٤﴾

(Fasting is for) a fixed number of days (in the month of Ramaḍān). If any of you is (so) ill that you cannot fast, or are on a journey (of less than ten days), then (you) must fast the same number of other days (after the month of Ramaḍān). But for those who can no longer manage to fast, there is a redemption (penance - *fidyah*) which is feeding a person in destitution (for each day missed). Yet better it is for one who volunteers greater good (by giving more than what is obligatory), and then you should fast (when you are able to) is even better for you, if you only knew (the benefits and worth of fasting).

In order to lessen the weight of fasting, Allah ﷻ proceeds to list some of the rules in regards to this act of worship:

1. The period of fasting is described as a 'few days.'[102]
2. Two groups of people:
   a. One that is temporarily ill,[103]

---

[102] Based on verses of the Qur'ān and the *ḥadīth*, scholars have outlined the various rulings regarding the sighting of the new moon to start and end the month of Ramaḍān - providing the believers with a time frame for when these fasts are to be kept. The details can be found by referring to the Islamic Laws manual of the *marjaʿ taqlīd* which a person follows for their daily requirements.

[103] Those who are ill, and confident based on the opinion of their doctor and what they themselves know regarding their body and its limitations, that they will

b. A traveler[104]

cannot fast in the month of Ramaḍān, but they will need to make up the fasts that they missed in the same amount after the month of Ramaḍān; before the next month of Ramaḍān, or else in addition to the performance of fasting, there will also a penalty which must be paid.

3. Those for whom fasting is difficult, and as a result they are unable to fast at all, such as those with a chronical illness or the elderly, must pay a redemption fee by feeding the poor.[105]

---

not be able to fast during the month of Ramaḍān are not permitted to fast for that period in which they are sick. However, once they are well again, they must make up those missed fasts before the next month of Ramaḍān. Those who fail to make up the fasts before the next year (if they were able to health-wise make them up) must pay a penalty known as a *kaffārah.* The details for all of these cases are covered in the books of Jurisprudence.

[104] In Islam, in order to be deemed a "traveler," a person must meet certain specific criteria. This will also entail one to offer the daily prayers in the shortened *(qaṣr)* form, and make it impermissible for that individual to fast during the period in which one is considered to be a traveler. It should be noted that there are some instances in which a person may be on a journey far away from home, may meet the criteria for distance traveled, and even fulfill other conditions, however they do not qualify for the other criteria which Islamic jurists have laid down that would exempt one from fasting during the trip, and thus they would even have to pray their daily prayers in full. For example, a person who travels as part of their career (airline pilots, taxi drivers, businessmen who travel frequently for meetings, etc.), or those whose travels include sinful purposes would not be exempt from fasting. As the scenarios in this area are vast, readers should refer to the books of Jurisprudence of the *marjaʿ taqlīd* that they follow in order to determine their responsibility.

[105] The elderly or those who have a terminal illness who are not able to fast and know for certain that they will never be able to fast, or people dependent on medication which must be taken at certain times of the day and thus are not able to fast are exempt from this obligation, however they are required to pay *fidyah* in lieu of not being able to fast. The details of this ruling are covered in the books of Jurisprudence.

Allah ﷻ concludes this verse by saying that if a person does 'good,' then that is better for them - meaning that if they either give more in charity than what is needed, or fast when they recover - in which case even if a person had paid the redemption fee because they thought that they may not be able to fast again, but then later on they regained their health - they are encouraged to make up the fasts of the past month of Ramaḍān that they missed.[106]

If a person really knew the true benefits which are earned in this world and the next for the fasts during the month of Ramaḍān, then one

---

The word *fidyah*, literally means an exchange. In Islamic jurisprudence, there are some actions which although are not prohibited, but one should give some *fidyah* if they are done. According to the Qur'ān, one such case is not fasting for people who cannot fast due to health or other reasons - and thus it is permitted for them not to fast. This *fidyah* consists of giving about 750 grams of food, such as wheat, to a person in need. This applies to the following:

1. **Pregnant or nursing women:** a pregnant woman for whom or for whose fetus it is harmful to fast or a woman who feeds her baby and it is harmful to the baby or for the woman to fast, should pay the *fidyah* in addition to fasting at another time, that is, performing the *qaḍā'*.

Continuous sickness: if a person cannot fast because of a sickness and their illness lasts until the next Ramaḍān, then they do not have to fast at another time, that is they do not have to perform the *qaḍā'*, but they should give a *fidyah* for every day of fasting they could not perform.

2. **Old men and women:** old men and women for whom it is difficult to fast have to pay the *fidyah.*

Please refer to the books of Jurisprudence of the scholar which you follow for the specific rulings in this regard.

[106] According to Āyatullāh as-Sīstānī: "Fasting is not obligatory on someone who, due to old age, cannot fast or finds fasting excessively difficult. However, in the latter case, for each day [that one does not fast] one must give one *mudd* of food - i.e. wheat, barley, bread, or something similiar to this - to a poor person. If someone who has not fasted on account of old age is able to fast after the month of Ramaḍān, then the recommended precaution is that he should make up the fasts that a person was not able to keep." (*The Islamic Laws*, Rulings 1694 and 1695)

would ensure that they try their best to make up the fasts even if one is not legally obligated to do so.

This sentence is yet another emphasis on the philosophy of fasting, and just like all other forms of worship in Islam, fasting adds nothing to the status and glory of Allah ﷻ - rather, the advantages and rewards all return back to the individual who fulfills one's duties and obligations.

Keys of Guidance

- The rules of Islam are clearly defined; however the religion also provides valid alternatives or exemptions for each person in every situation that an individual may find oneself in. As for the case of fasting, the able-bodied people have one ruling to follow, while those who are traveling, temporarily or chronically sick, as well as the elderly, all have unique rules which are applicable to them.
- If an individual falls into a unique situation based on one's own personal circumstance, this does not mean that one will not be able to benefit from the general philosophy and spiritual benefits of the Islamic rulings. For example, a person who is (temporarily) sick or traveling is exempted from fasting during the month of Ramaḍān, however since they need to make up the missed days later on, they can still enjoy the benefits of fasting which is to attain God-consciousness.
- The Divine commandments are such that when it comes to compensations which we must offer in lieu of not being able to perform certain acts of worship, Allah ﷻ legislates the minimum amount upon everyone, but then He leaves it to each person to see one's own personal circumstances and give more if one is able to. When it comes to offering the compensation for not being able to fast in the month of Ramaḍān, Allah ﷻ states that it is an obligation to feed one hungry person, however if a person can do more than that, then this is something which is highly recommended *(mustaḥab).*

Verse 185

شَهۡرُ رَمَضَانَ ٱلَّذِيٓ أُنزِلَ فِيهِ ٱلۡقُرۡءَانُ هُدٗى لِّلنَّاسِ وَبَيِّنَٰتٖ مِّنَ
ٱلۡهُدَىٰ وَٱلۡفُرۡقَانِۚ فَمَن شَهِدَ مِنكُمُ ٱلشَّهۡرَ فَلۡيَصُمۡهُۖ وَمَن كَانَ مَرِيضًا
أَوۡ عَلَىٰ سَفَرٖ فَعِدَّةٞ مِّنۡ أَيَّامٍ أُخَرَۗ يُرِيدُ ٱللَّهُ بِكُمُ ٱلۡيُسۡرَ وَلَا يُرِيدُ بِكُمُ
ٱلۡعُسۡرَ وَلِتُكۡمِلُواْ ٱلۡعِدَّةَ وَلِتُكَبِّرُواْ ٱللَّهَ عَلَىٰ مَا هَدَىٰكُمۡ وَلَعَلَّكُمۡ
تَشۡكُرُونَ ١٨٥

The month of Ramaḍān (is the month) in which the Qurʾān was sent down as guidance for humanity, and as clear signs of Guidance *(Hudā)*, and the Criterion *(Furqān)* (between truth and falsehood). Therefore, whoever of you is present (witnesses) this month, must fast in it, and whoever (of you) is so ill that cannot fast, or is on a journey (must fast the same) number of other days. Allah desires ease for you, and He does not wish hardship for you, so that you can complete the number of days required, and exalt Allah for He has guided you, and perhaps you will give thanks (due to Him).

In the previous verse, the length of fasting, as well as some of the rulings and their philosophies were mentioned.

In this verse, Allah ﷻ brings up the following points:

1. Fasting is for a few numbers of days, and takes place in the month of Ramaḍān which is the ninth month of the lunar calendar.
2. This is the month in which the Qurʾān was revealed by Allah ﷻ to Prophet Muḥammad ﷺ.
3. The Qurʾān is introduced as a Book of Guidance for all of humanity, and it contains signs of guidance; it is also a Criterion - differentiator between right and wrong.

In order to put extra emphasis on this ruling of fasting, Allah ﷻ reiterates the verdict of fasting for those who are travelers or sick, and tells the believers living during the time of Prophet Muḥammad ﷺ and in the future that those who are 'present' during the month of Ramaḍān (or witness this great month) must fast. However, those who are sick or on a journey must not fast, and instead will wait until they are able to, and then make up the number of days which they missed during the month of Ramaḍān afterwards when they have the ability.

By repeating this ruling in the Qur'ān, Allah ﷻ wants the Muslims to understand that just as fasting is a Divinely-mandated duty for the healthy believers, leaving the fast for those who are sick or travelers is also a Divinely-mandated duty, and it is a sin to oppose this ruling. In other words, if an individual is sick and the health professionals advise not to fast and the person also feels that the fasting will be detrimental to one's health, then one is **not** permitted to fast, in fact it is actually forbidden *(ḥarām)*. In addition, a person who fits the criteria for a traveler is also **not** permitted to fast - it is impermissible.

Near the end of this verse, Allah ﷻ deals with the philosophy of the legislation of fasting and tells the believers that Allah ﷻ wants ease and comfort for the believers, and does not wish to put them through difficulty. He points out that although the act of fasting for the entire month of Ramaḍān may seem to be difficult, very strict, or restrictive in one's life, however it is for the ease and well-being of a believer - both spiritually and physically.

Allah ﷻ then adds that the objective is to complete these days - meaning that every healthy person needs to fast for one month out of a year, and it is for this reason that if someone is sick or traveling during the month of Ramaḍān, then they need to make up the number of days which they missed to complete the number of fasts that they normally would have performed.

In the final portion of this verse, Allah ﷻ states that people must exalt Allah ﷻ for He has guided humanity, and perhaps through this we may be able to give thanks to Him.

Various Outcomes of Fasting

Some of the important benefits that a person attains from fasting are that it:

1. Softens the soul;
2. Strengthens one's will-power and determination;
3. Moderates the cravings.

Despite hunger, thirst, and desire for sexual gratification, a fasting person must forgo food, water, and one's spouse, and practically prove to oneself that one is not like a wild animal who should just satisfy their needs whenever one wishes. Through fasting, a person is able to show that they can take control of the rebellious soul and control their desires. In fact, the greatest philosophy of fasting is its spiritual effect on the soul of an individual.

Fasting upgrades a human being from being a member of the animal kingdom to ascend to the angelic realms; and the portion of this verse which mentions that: "...perhaps you may gain (in your) God-consciousness" points to this reality.

We have a famous *ḥadīth* which says: "Fasting is a shield against the fire"[107] and this also points to the reality of fasting.

It has also been narrated that Prophet Muḥammad ﷺ said: "There is a door in Paradise which is called *Rayyān* and only those who fasted (in the transient world) will be permitted to enter through it."[108]

In yet another tradition it has been stated that: "When the last person enters through this door (of *Rayyān*), it will close permanently."

Societal Benefits of Fasting

Fasting also teaches a lesson in equality for the members of society.

It has been narrated from Imām Jaʿfar aṣ-Ṣādiq ؑ that Hishām ibn al-Ḥakam asked him about the reason for the legislation of fasting to which the Imām ؑ replied: "The purpose for fasting is so that the rich and the poor can become equal, because the rich do not feel the suffering of hunger, and as such they may not have mercy on the poor because the

---

[107] *Biḥār al-Anwār*, Vol. 93, Pg. 256. This tradition is as follows:

أَلصَّوْمُ جُنَّةٌ مِنَ النَّارِ.

[108] Ibid., Pg. 252. The initial portion of this tradition is as follows:

إِنَّ لِلْجَنَّةِ بَابًا يُدْعىٰ الرَّيَّانُ...

rich can provide themselves with whatever they want, whenever they want it. It is for this reason that Allah wanted there to be a level of equality among His creations, so that the rich also feel the pain of hunger and suffer the hardships, such that their hearts burn for the needy people and they can be merciful toward them."[109]

Medical Benefits of Fasting

In medicine, the miraculous outcome of fasting in the treatment of various diseases has been proven, and as we know the cause of many diseases is something as simple as excessive eating. The excess food which people eat is not absorbed by the body, thus it ends up piling up in the form of fat, or it remains in the system as a surplus of sugar, and both of these are the cause of many health problems.

The extra food which remains in the body is actually like stinking sludge fields which allow the cultivation of all types of germs and infectious diseases, so the best way to fight these diseases is to destroy these sludges through fasting.

Fasting helps to burn off the excess fat and detoxify the body from the waste which remains in it, and this act also shakes up the body to get it back to its natural state of being.

In a famous *ḥadīth*, Prophet Muhammad ﷺ has been quoted as saying: "Fast so that you can stay healthy."[110]

The Prophet ﷺ also said: "The stomach is the home of all pains, and fasting is the best medication."[111]

---

[109] *Wasā'il ash-Shī'ah*, Vol. 7, Section 1, Book of Fasting, Pg. 3. The initial portion of this tradition is as follows:

إِنَّمَا فَرَضَ اللهُ الصِّيَامَ لِيَسْتَوِيَ بِهِ الْغَنِيُّ وَالْفَقِيرُ وَذٰلِكَ أَنَّ الْغَنِيَّ لَمْ يَكُنْ...

[110] *Biḥār al-Anwār*, Vol. 93, Pg. 255. This tradition is as follows:

صُومُوا تَصِحُّوا.

[111] Ibid., Vol. 59, Pg. 260. This tradition is as follows:

أَلْمَعِدَةُ بَيْتُ كُلِّ دَاءٍ وَالْحَمْيَةُ رَأْسُ كُلِّ دَوَاءٍ.

Fasting in the Previous Nations

The current, altered version of the Tawrāh and the Injīl also point to fasting as a common practice for the Jews and Christians. In addition, other nations also practiced fasting, most notably when they were faced with periods of grief and tribulations.

The Tawrāh clearly indicates that Prophet Mūsā ﷺ fasted for 40 days.[112]

Whenever the Children of Isrā'īl wanted to repent to Allah ﷻ and seek His pleasure, they would fast.[113]

In the New Testament, there are multiple references to Prophet ʿIsā ﷺ having fasted for a period of 40 days.[114]

Therefore, if Allah ﷻ states in the Qur'ān that He prescribed fasting on the generations which came before the Muslims, then there is ample historical evidence that the past Prophets also fasted themselves and directed their followers to do the same, and passages which confirm this are still present in the books of the Jews and Christians, despite the fact that distortions have occurred in their Scriptures.

---

[112] Old Testament, Book of Exodus 34:28:

> Moses was there with the LORD 40 days and 40 nights without eating bread or drinking water. And he wrote on the tablets the words of the covenant - the Ten Commandments.

[113] In the Old Testament in the Book of Leviticus 23:27, there is a reference to the fasting which the Jews perform during the Ten Days of Repentance which are marked on the first ten days of the Hebrew month of Tishrei. This holiday season begins with Rosh Hashanah and ends with Yom Kippur - the Day of Atonement:

> Howbeit on the tenth day of this seventh month is the day of atonement; there shall be a holy convocation unto you, and ye shall afflict your souls; and ye shall bring an offering made by fire unto the LORD.

[114] New Testament, 4 Matthew 1-3:

> Then Jesus was led by the Spirit into the wilderness to be tempted by the devil. [2] After fasting 40 days and 40 nights, he was hungry. [3] The tempter came to him and said: "If you are the Son of God, tell these stones to become bread."

Choosing the Month of Ramaḍān

Seeing as how the month of Ramaḍān was selected to be the period in which fasting was made an obligation upon the Muslims, in this verse of the Qurʾān, Allah ﷻ speaks about the superiority of this month by saying that it is the time in which the Qurʾān was revealed to Prophet Muḥammad ﷺ. In reviewing the *ḥadīth*, we see that all of the Divinely-sent Books - the Tawrāh, Injīl, Zabūr, Ṣuḥuf, and the Qurʾān were sent down in the month of Ramaḍān.

In this regard, Imām Jaʿfar aṣ-Ṣādiq ؑ has been quoted as saying: "The Tawrāh was revealed on the 6th of the blessed month of Ramaḍān; the Injīl was sent down on the 12th of the month; the Zabūr came down on the 18th, while the Noble Qurʾān was revealed on the night of *al-Qadr*."[115]

Thus, the month of Ramaḍān was always a month of revelation of the great Heavenly Books, and the month of spiritual training.

The training program of fasting must also be coordinated and run parallel to the Divinely-sent Book in order for a wayfarer to be able to gain a greater and deeper awareness of the Heavenly teachings so as to cleanse a person's body and soul from the pollution of sin.

🗝 Keys of Guidance

- The philosophy of the acts of worship (the *aḥkām*) is not always obvious to us. They are multi-dimensional, and if Allah ﷻ mentions one of the reasons for why He has implemented an act of worship, then we must realize that it may not be the only reason behind that action. For example, when Allah ﷻ says that He does not want difficulty for us in worship thus we are not to fast during the month of Ramaḍān if we are traveling, this may be just one reason for a particular ruling to be given, and we must appreciate that there

---

[115] *Wasāʾil ash-Shīʿah*, Vol. 7, Section on the Rulings of the Month of Ramaḍān, Sec. 18, Ḥadīth 16. The initial portion of this tradition is as follows:

نَزَلَتْ التَّوَرَاةُ فِي سِتٍّ مَضَتْ مِنْ شَهْرِ رَمَضَانَ وَنَزَلَ الْإِنْجِيلُ فِي أَثْنَتَيْ عَشْرَةَ لَيْلَةِ...

could be many other reasons. Another reason for such a ruling as mentioned in the *ḥadīth,* is that when traveling one is away from that which is familiar. They are distanced from their normal comforts and this is challenging in itself, but it brings one closer to Allah ﷻ - just as fasting is meant to do. Thus while traveling, Allah ﷻ tests us by commanding us not to fast, and through not fasting we become closer to Allah ﷻ.

- For the period of one month when we lessen our daily meals to one a day - as we eat a lighter pre-dawn meal *(suḥūr)* and our main dinner *(ifṭār),* we feel the pains of hunger and physical weakness. If we were to share that one meal we are skipping every day - lunch - for 30 days to the poor, just imagine how Muslims could reduce world hunger and malnutrition during the blessed month of Ramaḍān! With 1.7 billion Muslims fasting 30 days in this holy month, that would equal about 51 billion meals! If an average lunch costs around $5.00, that means we would be able to contribute $255 billion into the global campaign to eradicate hunger, poverty, malnutrition, and many other societal challenges.
- There is a tradition which tells us that when we fast in the month of Ramaḍān, we should reflect on the hunger and thirst we will face on the Day of Judgment, standing in the presence of Allah ﷻ, waiting to account for our actions. In the state of fasting when we are hungry and thirsty, we must remember our purpose on Earth, and resolve to work for a better hereafter.
- The value of the month of Ramaḍān lies in the fact that the Noble Qur'ān was revealed in this month; and parallel to this, the value of a human being can also be gauged by the extent of one's connection to this sacred Book and how much this Divinely-sent Book penetrates into one's heart and soul.
- Guidance has numerous levels to it - there is an initial stage which is universal guidance which Allah ﷻ provides to all of His creations. Once a person accepts this first step in guidance, then Allah ﷻ will take that individual 'by the hand' to help them further improve, and

make their way further on the path of true felicity.

Verse 186

وَإِذَا سَأَلَكَ عِبَادِى عَنِّى فَإِنِّى قَرِيبٌ ۖ أُجِيبُ دَعْوَةَ ٱلدَّاعِ إِذَا دَعَانِ ۖ
فَلْيَسْتَجِيبُوا۟ لِى وَلْيُؤْمِنُوا۟ بِى لَعَلَّهُمْ يَرْشُدُونَ ﴿١٨٦﴾

And when My servants ask you (O Muḥammad ﷺ) about Me, then surely I am near, I answer the prayer of the suppliant when one calls upon Me. So let them respond to My call, and believe and trust in Me, so that perhaps they may be guided.

This verse is connected to the previous verses, and here this verse is included with the topic of fasting because while one is in a state of fasting, they are emotionally charged and spiritually equipped to really communicate with Allah ﷻ. It is in such an opportune time that the believer is prepared to receive the blessings from the connection which the supplication creates with one's Lord. This connection has the potential to be so strong that in such a state of spiritual receptivity, a believer may forget the hardship and weakness which can sometimes emanate from fasting.

History of Revelation

A person once asked Prophet Muḥammad ﷺ: "Is Allah so near to us that we can pray to Him in a low voice, or is He far away that we need to call upon Him with a loud tone?" To this innocent question, the above quoted verse was revealed, answering this person and the entire Muslim community that Allah ﷻ is very close to His servants.[116]

---

[116] Ḥaṣāwī, Muḥammad ibn Zayn ad-Dīn al-, *'Awālī al-Layālī*, Vol. 2, Pg. 73, Ḥadīth 218. The initial portion of this tradition is as follows:

أَنَّ سَائِلًا سَأَلَ رَسُولَ اللّٰهِ ﷺ: فَقَالَ أَ قَرِيبٌ رَبُّنَا فَنُنَاجِيَهُ أَمْ بَعِيدٌ فَنُنَادِيَهُ...

The Weapon Known as Supplication (Duʿāʾ)

One of the means of communication between the servants and Allah ﷻ is supplication *(duʿāʾ)*, and in this verse Allah ﷻ speaks directly to Prophet Muḥammad ﷺ and tells him that when His servants ask the Prophet ﷺ about Allah ﷻ, he should say to them that: He, Allah ﷻ, is very near.

When a servant engages in talking to Allah ﷻ through *duʿāʾ*, it creates one of the most intimate relationships possible between a person and one's Lord. The spiritual barriers between a servant and Allah ﷻ are torn apart, and the humble servant finds oneself in a state of complete openness to talk and connect to the Almighty Creator. This unique relationship is very powerful and can elevate a human being to pinnacles of spiritual perfection and connection with the One God.

That is why we see in the supplications from the immaculate leaders of the Ahlul Bayt ﷺ such as *Duʿāʾ Kumayl*, or the supplications composed by Imām ʿAlī as-Sajjād ﵇ compiled in the famous book, *Aṣ-Ṣaḥīfah al-Kāmilah as-Sajjādiyyah,* and many other supplications and whispered prayers that the Imāms would open their hearts to their Lord, leaving nothing unsaid or untold. They would sincerely and humbly implore their Lord, while at the same time, have full trust in His Infinite Wisdom.

Some examples of this level of profound conversation between the servant and the Master, Allah ﷻ, are found in *Duʿāʾ Kumayl* where Imām ʿAlī ﵇ is quoted as saying: "I have wronged myself, and I have been audacious in my ignorance, and I have depended upon Your ancient remembrance of me and Your favor toward me. O Allah! O my Protector! How many ugly things You have concealed! How many burdensome tribulations You have abolished! How many stumbles You have prevented! How many ordeals You have repelled! And how much beautiful praise, for which I was unworthy, You have spread abroad! O Allah, my tribulations are tremendous, and my bad state is excessive, and my good deeds are inadequate, and my fetters have tied me down, and my far-fetched hopes have held me back from my gain, and this world with its delusions, and my own soul with its offenses, and my delay have deceived me. O my Master! So I ask You by Your Might not to let my evil works and acts veil my supplication from You, and not to disgrace me through the hidden things You know of my secrets, and not to hasten me to punishment for what I have done in private: my evil acts in secrecy, and my misdeeds, and my continuous negligence, and my ignorance, and my manifold passions, and my forgetfulness."[117]

In reality, Allah ﷻ is even closer than we can ever imagine - He is actually nearer to us than we are to our own selves - and He is even closer to us than our jugular vein, as He states in the Qur'ān: "Surely, it is We Who have created the human being, and We know what suggestions one's soul makes to a person, and We are nearer to them than one's jugular vein."[118]

Going back to this current verse from Sūrah al-Baqarah, Allah ﷻ then adds that He answers the call of a person who is supplicating when one calls upon Him on the condition that the supplicant ensures that they accept and answer the invitation of Allah ﷻ, believe in Him as their One True God, and that through this they may possibly be guided to their destination and goal in life.

Interestingly, in this verse, Allah ﷻ refers to Himself in the first person a total of seven times, and in this way He establishes a crucial connection, closeness, and love for His servants by saying:

1. **My** servants (عِبَادِي);
2. About **Me** (عَنِّي);
3. Indeed **I** am near (فَإِنِّي قَرِيبٌ);
4. **I** respond (أُجِيبُ);
5. When one calls upon **Me** (دَعَانِ);
6. Let them answer **Me** (فَلْيَسْتَجِيبُواْ لِي);
7. And believe in **Me** (وَلْيُؤْمِنُواْ بِي);

Supplication is a type of worship, and display of humility and servitude to Allah ﷻ through which an individual is able to develop a further devotion

---

[117] *Du'ā' Kumayl.* The initial portion of this part of the supplication is as follows:

ظَلَمْتُ نَفْسِي وَتَجَرَّأْتُ بِجَهْلِي وَسَكَنْتُ إِلَى قَدِيمِ ذِكْرِكَ لِي وَمَنِّكَ عَلَيَّ. أَللّٰهُمَّ مَوْلايَ كَمْ مِّنْ قَبِيحٍ سَتَرْتَهُ وَكَمْ مِّنْ فَادِحٍ مِّنَ الْبَلَاءِ أَقَلْتَهُ...

[118] Qur'ān, Sūrah Qāf (50), Verse 16:

وَلَقَدْ خَلَقْنَا الْإِنْسَانَ وَنَعْلَمُ مَا تُوَسْوِسُ بِهِ نَفْسُهُ وَنَحْنُ أَقْرَبُ إِلَيْهِ مِنْ حَبْلِ الْوَرِيدِ ﴿١٦﴾

to the Almighty. Just as all acts of worship which Islam has endorsed have an aspect of spiritual training *(tarbiyah)* to them, supplicating to the Creator also has a similar effect.

Those who say that supplications are an act which seeks to interfere with the work of Allah ﷻ, and Allah ﷻ will only do that which He finds appropriate so there is no need to pray to Him and ask Him for our needs and desires - do not realize that the gifts from Allah ﷻ are divided according to merits, and the more deserving a person is, the greater the share of blessings one will be entitled to receive. This level of merit though is not static - a person can work harder to increase one's merit with Allah ﷻ, allowing them to have greater potential for their supplications to be accepted and fulfilled.

It is for this reason that Imām Jaʿfar aṣ-Ṣādiq ؑ has been quoted as saying that: "Indeed there is with Allah, the Noble and Grand, a status [each person has] which one cannot attain except through asking Him (through prayers and supplications)."[119]

Religious scholars have been quoted as saying: "When we make supplications to Allah ﷻ, we are actually connecting ourselves to the never-ending power which all of the creations in existence are also connecting themselves to."

Keys of Guidance

- Supplication *(duʿā')* is the strongest weapon that a believer has access to, as the supporting partner in this weapon is the unlimited, All-Powerful Allah ﷻ.
- Communication is usually from the Lord to His servant - as takes place when we read the Qur'ān, however *duʿā'* is a type of communication from the servant to one's Lord.
- Without a doubt, Allah ﷻ is very close to us, but we must ask ourselves how close are we to Allah ﷻ? If we see that some sort of

---

[119] *Uṣūl al-Kāfī*, Vol. 2, Pg. 466, Section on the Merits of Supplication and Encouragement Toward It, Ḥadīth 3. This tradition is as follows:

إِنَّ عِنْدَ اللهِ عَزَّ وَجَلَّ مَنْزِلَةً لاَ تُنَالُ إِلَّا بِمَسْأَلَةٍ.

His retribution is affecting us, it may be due to us having distanced ourselves from Him.

- Although Allah ﷻ knows everything, and we believe Him to be the All-Knowing *(al-ʿAlīm)*, the All-Hearing *(as-Samīʿ)*, and All-Seeing *(al-Baṣīr)*, and even before we ask Him for anything it is already known to Him, however it is still our duty to pray to Him, and ask Him for all of our needs. This not only helps us at a psychological level, but it also allows us to be able to expand our inner capacity and permit more of His blessings to encompass us.

Verse 187

أُحِلَّ لَكُمۡ لَيۡلَةَ ٱلصِّيَامِ ٱلرَّفَثُ إِلَىٰ نِسَآئِكُمۡۚ هُنَّ لِبَاسٞ لَّكُمۡ وَأَنتُمۡ
لِبَاسٞ لَّهُنَّۗ عَلِمَ ٱللَّهُ أَنَّكُمۡ كُنتُمۡ تَخۡتَانُونَ أَنفُسَكُمۡ فَتَابَ عَلَيۡكُمۡ
وَعَفَا عَنكُمۡۖ فَٱلۡـَٰٔنَ بَٰشِرُوهُنَّ وَٱبۡتَغُواْ مَا كَتَبَ ٱللَّهُ لَكُمۡۚ وَكُلُواْ وَٱشۡرَبُواْ
حَتَّىٰ يَتَبَيَّنَ لَكُمُ ٱلۡخَيۡطُ ٱلۡأَبۡيَضُ مِنَ ٱلۡخَيۡطِ ٱلۡأَسۡوَدِ مِنَ ٱلۡفَجۡرِۖ ثُمَّ أَتِمُّواْ
ٱلصِّيَامَ إِلَى ٱلَّيۡلِۚ وَلَا تُبَٰشِرُوهُنَّ وَأَنتُمۡ عَٰكِفُونَ فِي ٱلۡمَسَٰجِدِۗ تِلۡكَ حُدُودُ
ٱللَّهِ فَلَا تَقۡرَبُوهَاۗ كَذَٰلِكَ يُبَيِّنُ ٱللَّهُ ءَايَٰتِهِۦ لِلنَّاسِ لَعَلَّهُمۡ يَتَّقُونَ ١٨٧

It is lawful for you to go to your wives (engage in sexual intimacy) on the night of the fast. They are a garment (of modesty) for you and you are a garment (of modesty) for them. Allah knows and you know that you would betray yourselves and follow your desires (and engage in sexual intimacy), so He has turned to you in lenience (and protected you from possible sins). Then associate in intimacy with them (during the allowable times) and seek what Allah has ordained for you. And (you are permitted to) eat and drink until you discern the white streak of dawn against the blackness of the night; and observe the fast until the night sets in.

But do not associate in intimacy with them (your wives) during the period when you are in spiritual retreat *(iʿtikāf)* in the *masājid*. These are the bounds set by Allah, so do not draw near them. Thus does Allah make His Revelations clear to people so that perhaps they may attain God-consciousness *(taqwā)*.

History of Revelation

We understand from the *ḥadīth* that at the beginning of the revelation of the Qurʾān when fasting was made an obligation upon the believers, the Muslims were only permitted to eat or drink before going to bed at night. Thus, if someone fell asleep and woke up later on in the evening or at night, then they were not allowed to eat or drink, and they had to fast again the next day not having consumed anything.

In addition to this, in the earlier stages when fasting was first made an obligation, it was expressly forbidden for spouses to have sexual intercourse for the entire month - not even at night.

A companion of Prophet Muḥammad ﷺ named Mutʿam ibn Jubayr was a weak man but he still fasted. One day he entered his house at the time of breaking the fast *(ifṭār)*, and his wife was busy preparing food for him, however because he was so tired from his long day of work, he fell asleep. When he woke up he thought to himself: "I no longer have the right to break my fast." Thus, he went back to sleep, and the next morning while in a state of fasting, not having eaten anything the previous evening, came out to work and helped build the trench around the city of Medina, as the Muslims were on the precipice of the Battle of Aḥzāb. Busy with the work he was engaged in, he became unconscious and passed out due to extreme hunger and weakness. Prophet Muḥammad ﷺ came to see him and was deeply affected when he saw Mutʿam in this state.

In addition to this, a group of young Muslims who did not have the power to control their sexual desires had intercourse with their wives at night during the month of Ramaḍān; and they also came to see Prophet Muḥammad ﷺ to discuss the challenges that they were facing with fasting during the days, and not being able to have intimate relations even at night.

It was at this point that the verse under review was revealed to Prophet Muḥammad ﷺ allowing Muslims to eat all night (until a certain time), and have sexual intimacy with their spouses during the nighttime.

Expansion in the Rules of Fasting

When Allah ﷻ sent the Prophets - one after the other - He delivered certain rulings for specific times for those people. Although these were specific rulings with set conditions, the people who followed them in future generations either altered them, or created different interpretations as to how these rules should be followed.

However, since the Qur'ān was the last and eternal Book, the rulings it brought down needed to be appropriate for all people, and for all times.

Therefore, Allah ﷻ needed to fix the understanding of the rulings which already existed among the people, such as the commandment of fasting, and realign it to be eternal and manageable, and as the same time allowing those who follow the rules to attain God-consciousness *(taqwā)*.

Furthermore, the rulings did not come all together at one time. Rather, they came in a staggered fashion - building up gradually and over a period of time. The best way for Muslims to understand this progression in the practical rulings is to study the history of revelation of the verses of the Qur'ān as this will help them understand how the jurisprudential commandments were built.

As with any set of rules - be it obligations or prohibitions - people need to ease into the rulings slowly, gaining guidance, and clarification from the teachings which Prophet Muḥammad was delivering from Allah ﷻ. Just like a person who wants to lose weight has to start off by making incremental changes in their diet - as one will not be able to successfully lose weight if they quit everything at once - similarly, since Allah ﷻ knows the mentality of people, He too ensured their acceptance and practice of the rulings by bringing them into their daily lives gradually. As the understanding and acceptance of the people grew, Allah ﷻ sent more verses to the Prophet .

We read in the history of revelation of this verse that when the initial ruling[120] for fasting was given to the Muslims, intercourse with one's spouse was strictly forbidden during the month of Ramaḍān; and the Muslims were also not permitted to eat or drink anything after going to sleep. This can be understood as being a test for the young Muslim community, as well as a way to mentally and physically prepare them to accept the rulings of fasting.

This verse contains four rulings about fasting, and the spiritual retreat (referred to in Arabic as *iʿtikāf)*[121] in the masjid, and these include:

1. Sexual intercourse with your wives is permissible during the nights in the month of Ramaḍān.[122]

Allah ﷻ deals with the philosophy of this subject and says that your wives are a clothing for you, just like you are a clothing for them, and you are there to adorn and protect one another.

There are many functions of clothing, some of which include the following: it protects a person from various elements, and safeguards the body from anything hitting it; it covers any flaws and defects that a person may have on one's body; clothing also serves as an ornament and means of beautification; and in this portion of the verse, all three meanings are valid in relation to a husband and wife - and how they

---

[120] Muslim scholars note that fasting became obligatory for Muslims on the 28th of the month of Shaʿbān, in the second year after the migration to Medina - about 13 days after the changing of the *qiblah.*

[121] *Iʿtikāf* is a recommended worship in Islam which consists of at least three days of fasting to a maximum of ten days, all the while living in a masjid engaged in the worship of Allah ﷻ. Although there is no specific time to perform *iʿtikāf,* it is reported that Prophet Muḥammad ﷺ used to engage in this special act of worship during the last days and nights of the month of Ramaḍān. For further details on this important spiritual action, refer to the article: *Iʿtikāf: The Spiritual Retreat* written by Saleem Bhimji available on www.al-islam.org/articles/itikaf-spiritual-retreat-shaykh-saleem-bhimji. (Last accessed on September 25, 2022)

[122] Allah ﷻ uses the term 'go into' *(ra-fa-tha)* which literally means 'to speak to someone about matters of intimacy between a man and woman' and sometimes this word can literally mean 'sexual intercourse with one's spouse,' and in the verse under review, this second meaning is the one which Allah ﷻ intended.

should protect, cover, and beautify one another.

The Qur'ān then states the reason for this change in the Divine law by Allah ﷻ saying that He knows that some Muslims were being disloyal to themselves by performing actions which were forbidden, and then asking Allah ﷻ to forgive them, so He accepted their repentance and forgave them.

Further to this, in order for the Muslims to not become more infected with sins, by His Grace and Mercy, Allah ﷻ made the spiritual program of fasting easier and reduced the limitations about what cannot be done during the nighttime. In this verse, He tells the believers that they are now allowed to have sexual relationships with their spouses during the night hours of the month of Ramaḍān - permitting them to seek that which Allah ﷻ has ordained for them in their spouses.

2. Allah ﷻ then states the second commandment by telling the Muslims that they are permitted to eat and drink until the white thread of the morning is clear from the black thread of night. This is referred to in the Islamic terminology as *imsāk* (the time when a person must stop eating and drinking and begin one's fast).
3. The third ruling is then mentioned where they are told to complete the fast until night.[123]

This sentence emphasizes the prohibition of eating, drinking, sexual intercourse, and refraining from the other things mentioned in the books of Jurisprudence, during the day for those who are fasting, and it informs people about the start and end time of the fast which is from the pre-dawn time *(imsāk)* until the end of the day in the evening when the night starts *(maghrib)*.

4. Finally, in the last ruling, Allah ﷻ tells the Muslims not to engage

[123] The definition of 'night' or the time when a Muslim is permitted to break their fast is defined as the time of *Maghrib* prayer. In the evening at the time of sunset, there is a redness in the western part of the sky where the sun sets. Gradually, this redness carries over and covers the eastern part of the sky. Once this redness has passed overhead, and dissipated from the eastern part of the horizon, this marks the time of the *Maghrib* prayers, as well as the time when a Muslim can legally break their fast.

in sexual activity with one's spouse while they are performing the sacred spiritual retreat *(i'tikāf)* in the masājid.

The expression of this ruling in this fashion has been done to show that there is an exception to the previous ruling because when a person is involved in the spiritual retreat, they are obligated to fast for a minimum of three days, and during that period they are not permitted to engage in any sexual activity with their spouse - obviously during the day it is not permissible because they are fasting, but even at night since one is in a state of spiritual retreat, it is also not allowed at that time either.

At the end of this verse, speaking about the previous commandments, Allah ﷻ reminds the believers that these are all the limits *(ḥudūd)* of Allah ﷻ and one must not approach them - meaning one must not encroach upon or violate any of them.

Due to the fact that approaching a limit may lead a person to be tempted to break the laws, or it could sometimes cause an individual to cross the limits and fall into sin, Allah ﷻ has been very careful in how He worded this warning to the believers.

Indeed it is Allah ﷻ and Him alone who reveals such verses to humanity for the sole purpose that they may become righteous people - those of God-consciousness *(taqwā)*.

From Beginning to End - The Goal is Taqwā

Interestingly, in the first verse that we read about the rules of fasting, the ultimate goal was described as attaining God-consciousness.

The same phrase is mentioned in this last verse in regards to fasting where Allah ﷻ says that perhaps through fasting and following the rules and regulations which He has laid down, a believer may attain God-consciousness.

This shows that the actions contained in the month of Ramaḍān are a means to cultivate the spirit of piety, self-control, development of the inner power to avoid sins, and to realize that as human beings we have a responsibility to Allah ﷻ and are not free to do as we wish.

Keys of Guidance

- The soul and essence of this verse is the phrase that Allah ﷻ has used which states: 'It is permissible for you to go to your wives (for sexual intimacy)' shows us that Allah ﷻ has created us with certain desires, and He has also provided us with an outlet to fulfill those desires. We cannot subdue or fight our desires - however we must use the permissible means which He has given us and instructed us to use in order to satisfy our needs and requirements. The message which we must recognize is that we have to fulfill our desires in the right manner, at the right time, and this is the balance which Islam teaches us. We must not degrade ourselves to be at the level of animals who do whatever they want, whenever they want, and however they want - nor are we expected to go to the other extreme of suppressing our desires completely.

- One of the other crucial aspects of this verse is to show the importance of a strong and loving relationship with one's spouse. This verse shows us that a husband and wife are meant to **complete** one another - not **compete** with one another. Together, they will enjoy real peace and tranquility.
- A reduction and simplification of the Islamic rulings is one of the unique characteristic of Islam - both in the rulings which came in the early days of Islam which were then abrogated by Allah ﷻ, and also with respect to the rulings of Islam compared to those of Judaism and Christianity.
- Worshiping during the day, and enjoying the legitimate pleasures in the night are signs of the comprehensiveness of any religion. If a religion claims to be from the One True God, but it denies its followers the legitimate pleasures which Allah ﷻ Himself has provided for them, then one must doubt that religion. We see that during the month of Ramaḍān, the day time is to be devoted to Allah ﷻ such that even food, drink, and sexual relationships are not permissible, however during the night time these are all allowed because Allah ﷻ knows that human beings need to satiate their natural desires.

Verse 188

وَلَا تَأْكُلُوٓا۟ أَمْوَٰلَكُم بَيْنَكُم بِٱلْبَٰطِلِ وَتُدْلُوا۟ بِهَآ إِلَى ٱلْحُكَّامِ لِتَأْكُلُوا۟
فَرِيقًا مِّنْ أَمْوَٰلِ ٱلنَّاسِ بِٱلْإِثْمِ وَأَنتُمْ تَعْلَمُونَ ١٨٨

And do not consume your wealth among yourselves in false ways; nor submit it to those in authority so that you may sinfully consume a portion of other people's goods, and that too while you know.

This verse refers to an important Islamic principle which governs some economic issues, and in a way it covers some of the chapters of Islamic Jurisprudence in the field of economics.

First off, Allah ﷻ tells the believers that they are not permitted to consume another person's property in vain or unjustly.[124] This part of the verse presents a general description of any type of exploitation of someone else's belongings in an inappropriate manner, without their express permission. In addition, it also relates to all transactions which do not pursue an appropriate goal, or do not have a rational basis.

Interestingly, the placement of this verse after the verses of fasting (Verses 182-187 of this chapter) shows us a correlation which exists between these two issues. In the previous verses, Allah ﷻ spoke about the prohibition of eating and drinking solely for performing an act of worship of Allah ﷻ, while in this verse under review, the prohibition is in regards to "consuming" the property of other people through inappropriate means, and this is another type of fasting and method of taming the soul; and in fact both are considered branches of God-consciousness - the same God-consciousness which was introduced as the ultimate goal of fasting.

The term 'consume' *(ta'kulū)* mentioned in this verse has a broad definition and includes any kind of violation upon the property of others.

In the next part of this verse, Allah ﷻ points to a clear example of

---

[124] The word translated as 'false ways' *(bāṭil)* refers to 'wrecking or destroying.'

"encroaching upon the property of others in vain" which is mentioned as taking the wealth of people unjustly and squandering it.

This is something which certain people consider as their right, thinking that they have seized it by the verdict of a judge. Thus, Allah ﷻ goes on to say that believers must not take possession of the wealth of others, only to turn around and give it to those in authority so that they may sinfully consume a portion of other people's goods; and they do all of this knowingly and with full awareness that what they are doing is wrong and it is a sin.

Bribes and Kickbacks - a Major Socio-Economic Problem

One of the great calamities which has affected humankind since ancient times and continues until today with an even greater severity is the scourge of bribery. This is one of the biggest obstacles to the implementation of social justice which should normally protect the interests of the most vulnerable in society, but it ends up favoring the economic elite who actually need to be controlled by such laws.

Obviously, if the door to bribery and kickbacks is opened, then the rules which have been categorized and need to be put in place will backfire, because the strong, rich, and powerful only will have the power to pay bribes and offer kickbacks to get what they want. As a result, laws will become a toy for the rich and elite to play with, enabling them to continue their societal domination and violation of human rights and other rights. For this reason, Islam considers paying and receiving bribes and kickbacks as major sins.

Although the ugliness of bribery is known in many societies around the world, it takes a new shape today under the guise of various deceptive phrases and titles.

Rather than referring to it as a bribe, those who offer such payments and those who receive them use names such as: gifts, compliments, fee for services rendered, incentives, and other such deceptive terms.

This alteration in name can no way change its nature in any form, and as such, money or anything given and taken under such pretexts is forbidden *(ḥarām)* and illegitimate according to the balanced and fair teachings of Islam.

In Sermon 223 of *Nahj al-Balāghah*, we read a story about Ashʿath ibn Qays who brought a gift to the just court of Imām ʿAlī ؑ. Ashʿath was a man who thought that he could resort to giving the judge a "gift" and in return, he would win his court case.

One evening, Ashʿath ibn Qays came to the house of Imām ʿAlī ؑ and presented him with a container full of delicious sweets - referring to it as a gift.

Seeing this, Imām ʿAlī ؑ became very upset. In the sermon he delivered, the Commander of the Faithful, Imām ʿAlī ؑ has been quoted as saying: "An even stranger incident than this [here he is referring to something else] is that a man (Ashʿath ibn Qays) came to us in the night with a closed flask full of honey paste, but I disliked it as though it was the poisonous venom of a serpent or its vomit. I asked him (Ashʿath) whether this flask (of honey) was a reward, or charity *(zakāh)*, for these are forbidden to us, the family of the Prophet. He (Ashʿath) replied that it was neither this nor that, but rather it was just a present. I said to him: 'What is wrong with you!? Have you come to deviate me from the religion of Allah? Are you mad, or have you been overpowered by some *jinn*, or are you speaking senselessly? By Allah, even if I am given all of the domains of the seven heavens with all that exists under the skies in order that I may disobey Allah to the extent of taking even one grain of barley from an ant, I would never do it! For me your world is lighter [meaning more worthless] than a leaf in the mouth of a locust who is chewing on it. What has ʿAlī to do with bounties that will pass away and pleasures that will not last? We seek the protection of Allah from the slip of wisdom and the evils of mistakes, and from Him we seek support.'"[125]

Islam has condemned bribery in all of its forms, and as such we read in the life history of Prophet Muḥammad ﷺ that once he was informed about how one of his governors had accepted a bribe in the form of a gift. He became extremely upset and said to his companion: "What reason did

---

[125] *Nahj al-Balāghah*, Sermon 223. The initial portion of this tradition is as follows:

وَأَعْجَبُ مِنْ ذٰلِكَ طَارِقٌ طَرَقَنَا بِمَلْفُوفَةٍ فِي وِعَائِهَا، وَمَعْجُونَة شَنِئْتُهَا، كَأَنَّمَا عُجِنَتْ بِرِيقِ حَيَّةٍ أَوْ قَيْئِهَا...

you have to take something which was not your right?"

The man replied to the Prophet ﷺ saying: "What I received was a gift, O Messenger of Allah!"

The Prophet ﷺ replied to him that: "If you were to sit at home and were not appointed as the local governor to that area on my behalf, then would people have still come and given you (such) gifts?"

Prophet Muḥammad ﷺ then ordered that the gift be taken and put into the public treasury *(baytul māl)*, and he dismissed that companion from his appointed position.[126]

How beneficial it would be if Muslims took inspiration and guidance from the Noble Qur'ān, and the Immaculate leaders - Prophet Muḥammad ﷺ and the 12 Imāms, his successors from the Ahlul Bayt, rather than sacrifice their honor in this world, and their standing in the world to come due to following their desires and submitting to the worldly temptations and being engulfed in the taking of bribes.

Keys of Guidance

- Attaining any property or wealth must be carried out in the appropriate manner - such as through business, agriculture, industry, inheritance, gifts, etc.; however taking possession through falsehood by way of bribes, kickbacks, etc. does not actually lead to real ownership in the rulings of Islam.
- Islam considers people as being the owners of their property, but it does not accept the notion which some ideologies espouse that allows 'collective' ownership.
- The roots of bribery and deviated transactions are: injustice, greed, lack of a good system, poverty, lack of compensating people properly - such as police officers, or other law enforcement officials not being paid what they deserve, a dishonest culture, not having good checks and balances, etc.

---

126 *Al-Imām ʿAlī*, Vol. 1, Pp. 155-6. The initial portion of this tradition is as follows:

كَيْفَ تَأْخُذُ مَا لَيْسَ لَكَ بِحَقٍّ؟...

- Bribery and other types of economic corruption which lead to other forms of societal decay cannot be eliminated over night. The roots of resolving this issue lie in promoting and instilling God-consciousness *(taqwā)*, remembering the Day of Judgment and its accountability, and recognizing and realizing that these deviations will impact our society, our children, and ourselves.

Verse 189

يَسْـَٔلُونَكَ عَنِ ٱلْأَهِلَّةِ ۖ قُلْ هِىَ مَوَٰقِيتُ لِلنَّاسِ وَٱلْحَجِّ ۗ وَلَيْسَ ٱلْبِرُّ بِأَن تَأْتُوا۟ ٱلْبُيُوتَ مِن ظُهُورِهَا وَلَـٰكِنَّ ٱلْبِرَّ مَنِ ٱتَّقَىٰ ۗ وَأْتُوا۟ ٱلْبُيُوتَ مِنْ أَبْوَٰبِهَا ۚ وَٱتَّقُوا۟ ٱللَّهَ لَعَلَّكُمْ تُفْلِحُونَ ﴿١٨٩﴾

They ask you (O Muḥammad ﷺ) about the new moon. Say: "They are timekeeping signs for the people and (for the sake of) the pilgrimage *(Ḥajj)*." It is not piety that you come into houses from their rear; rather piety is (personified by) one who has God-consciousness *(taqwā)*, and comes into the houses from their doors, thus be conscious of Allah ﷻ so that you may prosper.

History of Revelation

A group of Jews living during the time of Prophet Muḥammad ﷺ asked him: "What is the crescent moon for and what is its use?" In response to them, this verse of the Qur'ān was revealed mentioning its material and spiritual benefits in organizing the system of life.

A group of people also came to Prophet Muḥammad ﷺ with some other questions. The Qur'ān presents these questions in the following manner: "They ask you, O Muḥammad," and one of the questions which they asked was in regards to the new crescent moon *(ahillah)*.

This phrase: "they ask you" *(yas'alūnaka)* which comes in the Qur'ān as a present/future tense verb shows us that such questions were asked to Prophet Muḥammad ﷺ not just once, but several times throughout his

Prophetic mission.

To this particular question, Allah ﷻ responds and tells Prophet Muḥammad ﷺ to inform them that the new crescent moon is there in order to be able to compute time so that people can have a calendar which runs on the cycle of nature. The new crescent moon also benefits people in charting out their lives, and allows them to determine the timings of the *Ḥajj* pilgrimage, and other necessary Islamic injunctions.

Therefore, the new crescent moon is used both in daily life, and in order to determine certain acts of worship which take place at specific times during the year. In fact, the moon is actually such a perfect natural calendar for human beings that everyone - literate and illiterate - anywhere in the world can use it.

This is one of the advantages of Islamic law in that it uses natural means, and as such its instructions are set according to these natural scales to calculate time and coordinate religious events, and the passage of time does not affect it in any way.

In the next portion of this verse, the discussion focuses on the *Ḥajj* and its calculation by the new crescent moon which Allah ﷻ mentioned at the beginning of this verse. However, in addition to pointing out that the new crescent moon aids in determining when the *Ḥajj* season will start, Allah ﷻ also points to one of the superstitious customs and traditions of the Era of Ignorance *(Jāhiliyyah)*.

In speaking about this superstitious practice which used to take place during the *Ḥajj* season, Allah ﷻ wanted to make it clear that He was forbidding people from performing this act. It was customary in the Era of Ignorance that during the *Ḥajj* period people who were wearing the special *iḥrām* clothing would not enter the house through the door. Rather, they would either enter through a window, or make another entrance at the back of the house.

Allah ﷻ clarified to them that this practice was from the Era of Ignorance, and it had nothing to do with the Islamic teachings. The Almighty also confirmed to them that this was not a good action to continue with, and instead what was righteous is that a person attains God-consciousness so that they can be successful, and people should enter houses through the front doors.

This verse has a wide meaning, and from it we can understand the connection between the beginning and the end of the verse, and that in order to do anything - whether religious or non-religious - one must enter that deed in the correct way, not in deviant or perverted ways. When it comes to acts of worship such as the pilgrimage or fasting, it must only be performed at the appointed time which is determined by the crescent moon.

The phrase which Allah ﷻ mentions: "...it is not righteousness..." *(laysa al-birr)* may refer to another subtle fact that rather than asking Prophet Muḥammad ﷺ about the teachings of the religion, their question to him in regards to the new crescent moon is just like the action of a person who goes home to his house, and rather than entering the front (and obvious main entrance) door, one goes to the back of one's house, carves a hole into the mud and bricks chiseling away at it, and makes another passage way into one's own house! Similarly, the believers were being enjoined to enter into the Islamic laws through the appropriate channels, rather than trying to carve out their own rulings for themselves. In essence, they were required to follow the rulings being given to them, which were clear and simple to follow, rather than to complicate the religion.

Various Questions of the People

In 15 verses of the Qur'ān[127] the phrase: "They ask you (Muḥammad)" *(yas'alūnaka)* has been mentioned, and this shows that the people had questions which they used to ask Prophet Muḥammad ﷺ on various issues.

Interestingly, not only did the Prophet ﷺ never get upset, but he in fact welcomed such questions with open arms and responded to them through Qur'ānic verses! From this we can deduce that:

1. Questioning is one of the rights that people have over their leaders;
2. Questions are a key to solving problems;

---

[127] See Qur'ān: 2:189, 2:215, 2:217, 2:219 (two questions are present in this verse), 2:220, 2:222, 4:153, 5:4, 7:187 (two questions are present in this verse), 8:1, 17:85, 18:83, 20:105, 33:63, 79:42.

3. Questions are windows to knowledge;
4. Questions are also the means of transmitting knowledge.

In essence, in every society, asking questions to the right people is a sign of the vibrancy of thought and awakening of the mind, and the existence of all of these questions at the time of Prophet Muḥammad ﷺ is a sign of the active minds which the people of that era had in the light of the Qur᾿ān and the noble teachings of Islam.

Keys of Guidance

- The movement of the planets and the moon is built upon a precise plan by Allah ﷻ, and the schedule which it creates can be effective in the plan of worship and order which people need in their daily lives.

- When we see that the celestial bodies which Allah ﷻ has created are all in perfect order and harmony, and are oriented to regulate the affairs of humanity, then is it not sad to see that humanity sees the order in the universe yet acts with chaos, disorder, and a feeling of a lack of accountability to anyone - especially Allah ﷻ!?

- Islam has fought against ignorant and superstitious customs, and has encouraged its followers to ask questions, but to ask the right type of questions to the right people; and those who are being asked are obligated to do their best to respond appropriately to the inquirer.

- Righteousness is not something which is developed in a vacuum or on one's own accord, rather goodness is defined by and developed by working within the framework of Divine Revelation, and the teachings and guidance of the immaculate leaders, Prophet Muḥammad ﷺ and his Ahlul Bayt عليهم السلام.

- Sometimes people have good intentions and perform actions which they think are good but in actuality they are not really good; for example, stealing something to feed the poor. Similarly, in this verse Allah ﷻ is saying that some people used to sneak into people's houses in order to help them, but perhaps they did not realize that this is not the appropriate way to help. We must be very careful to identify and consult with what is good and how it should be executed properly so that we are doing the right things.

Verse 190

وَقَٰتِلُواْ فِي سَبِيلِ ٱللَّهِ ٱلَّذِينَ يُقَٰتِلُونَكُمۡ وَلَا تَعۡتَدُوٓاْۚ إِنَّ ٱللَّهَ لَا يُحِبُّ ٱلۡمُعۡتَدِينَ ١٩٠

And defend Allah's cause (in order to exalt His Name) against those who fight against you, but do not transgress the limits. Surely Allah does not love those who transgress the limits.

History of Revelation

This was the first verse which was revealed about war against the enemies of Islam; and after its revelation Prophet Muḥammad ﷺ fought against those who came out to battle the Muslims, but he refrained from fighting against those who did not oppress the Muslims, and this policy continued until the order came from Allah ﷻ which said: "Then, when the (four) sacred months (of respite, during which fighting with those who associate partners with Allah and violate their treaties was prohibited to you) are over, then (declare war on them and) kill the polytheists wherever you find them, and seize them, and confine them, and lie in wait for them at every conceivable place..."[128]

Explanation of this Verse

In the verse under review, the Qur'ān commands the Muslims to stand up and defend themselves against those who draw their swords in opposition to the Muslims by telling them to fight (defend themselves) in the cause of Allah ﷻ.

---

128 Qur'ān, Sūrah at-Tawbah (9), Verse 5:

فَإِذَا ٱنسَلَخَ ٱلۡأَشۡهُرُ ٱلۡحُرُمُ فَٱقۡتُلُواْ ٱلۡمُشۡرِكِينَ حَيۡثُ وَجَدتُّمُوهُمۡ وَخُذُوهُمۡ وَٱحۡصُرُوهُمۡ وَٱقۡعُدُواْ لَهُمۡ كُلَّ مَرۡصَدٖ...

The interpretation of the phrase: 'for the sake of Allah' *(fī sabīlillāh)* clarifies the main purpose of wars in Islam, and states that they are never for revenge, political ambition, territorial expansion, or for gaining the spoils of war - because these goals would all affect the different aspects of a war such as: the type of war, the types of weapons used, how the prisoners of war are dealt with, and other issues. Thus, in Islam, wars and all facets of it are determined by the phrase: 'for the sake of Allah.'

The Qurʾān then advises to observe justice - even on the battlefield, and against the enemies of Islam - as Allah ﷻ tells the Muslims not to exceed the limits which Islam had laid down for military attacks because Allah ﷻ does not love those who transgress the limits.

When war is for Allah ﷻ alone and in the way of Him, then there should be no aggression or exceeding of the limits. For this reason, in wars which took place under the strict guidance of the rules of Islam - unlike the wars of our time - soldiers were advised to observe various moral principles. For example, if the enemy fighters lay down their arms, or individuals cannot fight to defend themselves, or some soldiers lose their weapons, or others do not have the ability to continue fighting such as the wounded, old men, women, and children, then they must not be attacked or abused in any way.

In addition, orchards, plants, crops, etc., must not be destroyed, and toxic substances must not be used to poison the enemy's drinking water - meaning that chemical, biological, and microbial warfare are all prohibited when it comes to how to conduct a war based on the teachings of Islam.

Keys of Guidance

- Defending a person's self, home, and country, as well as retaliating are all human rights; thus if someone disputes with a Muslim, attacks an individual or one's country, then a Muslim is justified to stand up and defend oneself.

- The purpose of war in Islam is not to take land, control the water supply, colonize another country, or seek revenge. Rather, the purpose of war in Islam should be to defend the truth by removing the corrupt elements within society and the world, and to facilitate the freeing of thoughts of humanity, and save people from the superstitions of idol worship and slavery to anything other than Allah ﷻ, and all of the baseless ideologies.

- Even in war, justice and fairness must be observed. Allah ﷻ in the Qur'ān has repeatedly instructed its followers not to carry out any form of excessiveness when it fulfills the commandments of the religion - in any and all areas of life, the limits and boundaries which Islam has laid down must be adhered to and never exceeded.
- Even when it comes to defending a person's natural right to survive and live in peace and security, Allah ﷻ must always be kept in mind. This means that even though others may launch a war against the believers, or put the general public into fear, or take away their safety, although the Muslims are within their God-given rights to defend themselves, still the sacred defense and our conscious direction must be that whatever is done is for the sake of Allah ﷻ *(fī sabīlillāh)* and not personal motivation or grudges. Therefore, even in the harshest of situations which a person would ever find themselves in, like during a war, we are told that just as Allah ﷻ is All-Compassionate *(Raḥmān)* and All-Merciful *(Raḥīm)*, we must actively remember Him and apply these attributes in our lives. Thus, if for example a situation arises when two siblings get into a dispute with one another, they should bring to memory the love and mercy which their mother has shown them in the past that will allow them to calm down and not transgress the limits.

Verse 191

وَٱقْتُلُوهُمْ حَيْثُ ثَقِفْتُمُوهُمْ وَأَخْرِجُوهُم مِّنْ حَيْثُ أَخْرَجُوكُمْ ۚ وَٱلْفِتْنَةُ
أَشَدُّ مِنَ ٱلْقَتْلِ ۚ وَلَا تُقَٰتِلُوهُمْ عِندَ ٱلْمَسْجِدِ ٱلْحَرَامِ حَتَّىٰ يُقَٰتِلُوكُمْ فِيهِ ۖ
فَإِن قَٰتَلُوكُمْ فَٱقْتُلُوهُمْ ۗ كَذَٰلِكَ جَزَآءُ ٱلْكَٰفِرِينَ ﴿١٩١﴾

And fight them (in defense) wherever you come upon them, and drive them out from where they drove you out. Corruption is worse than killing. And do not fight against them in the vicinities of the Sacred Mosque *(Masjid al-Ḥarām)* unless they fight against you there; but if they fight against you (there), then fight them - such is the recompense of the (rebellious) unbelievers.

Connection to the Previous Verse

When Prophet Muḥammad ﷺ took over Mecca in the Conquest of Mecca in the eighth year after the migration, he proceeded to give a general pardon and amnesty to all of its inhabitants. In addition, he even announced that anyone who takes refuge in the sacred precincts *(Ḥaram)* of Mecca or puts down their weapons would also be included in this general pardon. The Noble Prophet ﷺ exhibited great compassion and mercy in this event. Even those who were in the house of one the leading enemies of Islam, Abū Sufyān, were safe and secure and his house was a sanctuary.

It must be noted that this amnesty came at a time when many of these same people were responsible for the torturing and killings of countless Muslims. They were also guilty of exiling the believers and confiscating their homes and belongings which they had to leave behind. All of this and much more was carried out by these ruthless people of Mecca who had even tortured Prophet Muḥammad ﷺ and the early Muslim community of Mecca.

In this verse, Allah ﷻ is referring to some of the individuals who abused this kindness of Prophet Muḥammad ﷺ and started provoking them and creating mischief, hoping to instigate a civil war, resorting to guerilla warfare tactics by planning to launch surprise attacks to disturb the peace, and create an unrestful environment in society.

Therefore, this verse permitted the Muslims to take a stand of self-defense and allowed them to double their efforts to stand as a united body to counter this corruption *(fitnah)* before it became the cause of the downfall of the city and its inhabitants.

If this verse had not been revealed, the Muslims would have continued to bear this injustice patiently and would not have initiated to even defend themselves properly. Such a weak stance would have eventually resulted in turning the lives of everyone into chaos.

Thus, this verse completes the directives given by Allah ﷻ in the previous verse, and discusses this point more clearly addressing Prophet Muḥammad ﷺ and the Muslims who were with him at that time.

It tells the idol worshipers - those people who were not worried about executing any type of crime against humanity - that they will be fought against wherever the Muslims happen to find them.

In addition, just like the polytheists had no qualms about expelling the Muslims from their homes and city in Mecca, Allah ﷻ tells the Muslims that when they have an upper hand, they are free to expel the polytheists from their homes; and whatever the Muslims do is more than fair as an act of self-defense. Allah ﷻ then adds that distortion or corruption *(fitnah)* - in this case, idol worshiping - is worse than fighting and killing the idolaters - meaning that the rebels would use the idol worshipers as a justification to create further corruption in the society. Obviously, corruption *(fitnah)* is not limited to idol worshiping, however it is one of the results of the rooted corruption in society.

The term *fitnah* is very broad and can cover various forms of oppression, some of which include:

1. Oppressing others and taking their rights;
2. Performance of sins in which a person is said to be corrupting and oppressing themselves.

During the time of Prophet Muḥammad ﷺ, there were hidden agendas at hand which promoted and propagated corruption, and the easiest and most effective way for those powers to do so was through the guise of idol worshiping.

Even today, one of the main ways which is used to promote corruption *(fitnah)* in society is through the disguise of establishing links through two completely foreign things, for example, the promotion of LGBTQ rights is heralded through the platform of human rights and other such things.

The word *fitnah* comes from the Arabic word *fatan* and it literally means 'putting gold into fire to separate it from any impurities.' The word *fitnah* and its derivatives have been mentioned in numerous[129] occasions within the Noble Qurʾān with various meanings, however all of the usages and interpretations of this word in the Qurʾān go back to its original meaning which is 'testing something to remove the impurities from it.'

The religion of idolatry, and the various individual and social corruptions which are tied to it had become prevalent in Mecca and the surrounding areas, and it managed to pollute the safe Sanctuary *(Ḥaram)* that Allah ﷻ had established for humanity. Allah ﷻ rightfully states that the corruption of idol worship is even worse than murder and slaughter, so in this particular verse, the Almighty tells the Muslims at the time of Prophet Muḥammad ﷺ that they should not fear having their blood shed and being killed by defending themselves against idolatry and its practitioners, as the offense of polytheism and such corruption is even worse than fighting and killing.

The Qurʾān then refers to another issue and states that Muslims must always respect the sanctity of the Sacred Mosque which Allah ﷻ has established. Based on this order from Allah ﷻ, the Muslims were told that they are not permitted to fight the polytheists anywhere in the precincts of this sacred place unless the polytheists fight the Muslims there and they need to defend themselves.

Allah ﷻ then states that if the polytheists fight the Muslims in or around the Sacred Mosque, then the Muslims are well within their rights of self-defense to fight and remove them there as that is the recompense of the disbelievers because when the idol worshipers violate the sanctity of the safe sanctuary which is *Masjid al-Ḥarām*, then silence is no longer an option. They must be given a firm response so that they never abuse the sanctity of this sacred place, and they recognize the importance of respecting the safe sanctuary which Allah ﷻ has defined.

---

129 See Qurʾān: 2:102, 2:191, 2:193, 2:217, 3:7, 4:91, 4:101, 5:41, 5:49, 5:71, 6:23, 6:53, 7:27, 7:155, 8:25, 8:28, 8:39, 8:73, 9:47, 9:48, 9:49, 9:126, 10:83, 10:85, 16:110, 17:60, 17:73, 20:40, 20:85, 20:90, 20:131, 21:35, 21:111, 22:11, 22:53, 24:63, 25:20, 27:47, 29:2, 29:3, 29:10, 33:14, 37:63, 39:49, 38:24, 38:34, 44:17, 51:13, 51:14, 54:27, 57:14, 60:5, 64:15, 72:17, 74:31, 85:10.

🔑 Keys of Guidance

- There are times in which Muslims must respond to the attacks against them - however one must ensure that they do not take matters into their own hands and enact 'vigilante justice.'[130]

- Repeatedly, the sentence in this verse in regards to killing and warfare has been taken out of context by individuals who wish to use such verses of the Qur'ān unfairly against the Muslims. They do so with ill-intentions to portray the peace loving, overwhelming majority of Muslims as terrorists and killers - something which cannot be further from the truth. It is important to recognize the background and historical context behind the revelation of such verses of the Qur'ān to be able to clarify these misconceptions amongst people.

- Even today, in an era of expanded knowledge of Islam and the teachings of the Noble Qur'ān, some factions of so-called Muslims have taken this verse and others like in to suit their own agenda. They have used such verses for their own benefit, claiming that Islam must spread with war and violence - something which is completely contrary to the vision of the Qur'ān, and the teachings of Prophet Muhammad ﷺ and his successors - the Imāms of the Ahlul Bayt ؑ. This misunderstanding of key verses in the Qur'ān, and the life examples *(sīrah)* of Prophet Muhammad ﷺ is something which they have misinterpreted themselves - thus creating their own version of Islam. History of the past, and even today has shown that when other Muslims do not agree with their own personal interpretation of Islam, they are considered as having left Islam and unbelievers *(kāfir)*, which then legitimises their blood to be shed and for them to be killed. The damage which such individuals and groups have done to tarnish the reputation of Prophet Muhammad ﷺ, Islam,

---

[130] Vigilante justice often describes the actions of a single person or group of people who claim to enforce the law, but lack the legal authority to do so. However, this term can also describe a general state of disarray or lawlessness, in which competing groups of people all claim to enforce the law in a given area.

the Qurʾān, and the general Muslim community at large has been extremely detrimental.

Verse 192

فَإِنِ ٱنتَهَوْا۟ فَإِنَّ ٱللَّهَ غَفُورٌ رَّحِيمٌ ﴿١٩٢﴾

Then if they desist (in their aggressions against the people), surely Allah is All-Forgiving *(Ghafūr)*, All-Merciful *(Raḥīm)*.

Allah ﷻ always combines warnings and threats of retribution with good tidings in order to provide a balance and healthy training for the soul of the sinners.

Here, the Qurʾān opens up the way for them to return to the path of cordial relations, and the cessation of all hostilities where Allah ﷻ tells the Muslims at the time of Prophet Muḥammad ﷺ that if the rebels stop their corruption, then they will forgiven because indeed Allah is All-Forgiving, All-Merciful.

Keys of Guidance

- This verse calls for a change in one's mindset such that even in times of anger and heightened sense of emotions, one must let mercy and compassion prevail in their actions.
- There are no dead-ends in life, especially in the sight of Allah ﷻ, and as such Islam has even opened the path for the belligerent disbelievers that when they realize that what they have been doing is wrong, and they repent and come to the straight path, Allah ﷻ is All-Forgiving and All-Merciful.
- Just as we have the saying: 'forgive and forget,' Allah ﷻ also confirms this beautiful slogan, and tells us that when the disbelievers renounce the sedition which they were involved in and lay down their weapons to cease hostilities , then they should not be criticized for their past ways because Allah ﷻ has forgiven them and shown His Mercy to them.

Verse 193

وَقَٰتِلُوهُمْ حَتَّىٰ لَا تَكُونَ فِتْنَةٌ وَيَكُونَ ٱلدِّينُ لِلَّهِ ۖ فَإِنِ ٱنتَهَوْا۟ فَلَا
عُدْوَٰنَ إِلَّا عَلَى ٱلظَّٰلِمِينَ ﴿١٩٣﴾

But (if the rebels persist in causing disorder and corruption, then continue to) fight against them until there is no longer disorder and corruption, and (know that) Allah's religion (which is full of justice with compassion) will prevail. However, if they desist, then there is no hostility except upon the wrongdoers.

In this verse, the purpose of the sacred struggle *(jihād)*[131] in Islam has been explained in which Allah ﷻ begins by telling the Muslims at the time of Prophet Muḥammad ﷺ that they are permitted to fight against the rebels of Mecca until corruption ceases - although some of them used idol worshiping as an excuse to create corruption.

In the context of this verse, religion means justice, therefore Allah ﷻ is saying that this religion of Islam and its guidelines are rooted in justice and compassion, because without order, people would live in misery and

---

[131] The word *jihād* comes from an Arabic root which means 'hardship, effort, exertion in work, reaching to the conclusion of something, and ability.' The most important idiomatic meaning of this world is found in religious texts and it refers to 'a specific type of effort which is expended' - that is, struggling in the way of Allah ﷻ with one's life, property, wealth, and possessions with the aim of spreading or defending Islam.

In addition, within the religious texts, this word is often used in its literal sense, such as the term *jihād al-akbar* or 'the major struggle' which has been defined as 'the struggle of the soul in order to tame it from its temptations, lusts and desires.' In addition, some deeds have been considered as an act of *jihād* or struggle, such as enjoining good and forbidding evil, speaking truth to power, a person's attempt to revive a good custom which has been forgotten in society, taking proper care of one's spouse, earning a living through permissible means, and other such noble actions.

fear.

To this, Allah ﷻ adds that if the rebels give up their wrongdoings, then the Muslims are not permitted to harass them because it is not allowed to attack anyone except those who are persecuting the believers.

The three goals for *jihād* which are mentioned in this verse include:

1. The elimination of rebellion.
2. The eradication of polytheism as it was used by the polytheists to justify their actions.
3. Putting an end to repression.

Jihād in Islam

The powerful dictators, authoritarians, Firʿawns, Namrūds,[132] and Qārūns[133] of this Earth have always tried to disrupt the goals of the Prophets which Allah ﷻ deputed. They stand against the messages of Allah ﷻ and are never satisfied until they abolish the pure religion which Allah ﷻ has established for the betterment of humanity.

At the same time, the true believers who rely on reason, logic, and morality, must stand up against such tyrants and oppressors, and forge ahead in the path of Allah ﷻ by fighting against these aggressors and crush them.

---

[132] Namrūd ibn Kanʿan, or Nimrod as he is known by his Biblical name, was the king of Babylon at the time of Prophet Ibrāhīm ؑ. The actual name Namrūd is not mentioned in the Noble Qur'ān, however he is spoken about on two occasions (see Qur'ān, 2:258 and 21:68). He himself was an idol worshiper and this was common in his kingdom. Since the priests had foretold that a boy would be born named Ibrāhīm, and he would fight idolatry and conquer the kingdom of Namrūd, fearing this he ordered that every boy born should be killed, however Ibrāhīm ؑ survived by the will of Allah ﷻ.

[133] Qārūn ibn Yaṣhura, or Korah as he is known by his Biblical name, was among the elite of the Children of Isrā'īl. For his evil actions, the Qur'ān mentions him alongside the Pharaoh and Hāmān. He was the first among the major rebels who revolted against Prophet Mūsā ؑ, but he finally believed in him and left Egypt together with the Children of Isrā'īl. But after some time, Qārūn began to disobey the orders of Allah ﷻ which led to his punishment and eventual death.

In essence, *jihād* is a general law in the entire world and is seen in everything around us, because all living creatures are constantly fighting for their survival, standing up to those who wish to destroy them - whether this be in the plant kingdom,[134] animal kingdom, or within humanity.

In any case, one of the honors of the Muslims and the religion of Islam is that it combines religion with governance and politics, and has placed the teachings of the sacred struggle along with its religious program. Ultimately, the sacred struggle in Islam pursues certain pre-defined goals, and this is one of the aspects of Islam which separates the Muslims from all other religions - at least at the theoretical level, as practically other religious claim to be proponents of peace, non-violence, and love - but what the world has seen from them is something entirely different.

We read in the above verses that Islam permitted the sacred struggle *(jihād)* for multiple reasons - which we will review here.

1. Jihād: Used to Extinguish Rebellions

The Islamic theory of the 'pre-emptive strike' *(jihād al-ibtidāʾiyyah)* is there to grant freedom to the oppressed; however, as we will speak about later, in Shīʿah Jurisprudence this is only permissible under the direction of a Divinely-appointed immaculate leader, which in our case is the 12th successor of the Prophet, Imām al-Mahdī عجل الله تعالى فرجه الشريف. As he has knowledge given to him by Allah ﷻ, and through the blessings of the Almighty he knows what is best for humanity, so in our era he is the only one who has the

[134] Compared to the hectic rush of our bipedal world, a plant's life may appear an oasis of tranquility. But look a little closer. The voracious appetites of pests put plants under constant stress: They have to fight just to stay alive; and they do fight! Far from being passive victims, plants have evolved potent defenses: chemical compounds that serve as toxins which signal an escalating attack, and solicit help from unlikely allies. However, all of this security comes at a cost: energy and other resources that plants could otherwise use for growth and repair. So to balance the budget, plants have to be selective about how and when to deploy their chemical arsenal. (Taken from www.nautil.us/issue/31/stress/when-plants-go-to-war. Last accessed on October 1, 2022)

legal right to call for this.

Allah ﷻ has put obligations and various programs in place to ensure the freedom, prosperity, development, and well-being of all of humanity. Prophets were directly sent by Allah ﷻ and were mandated to convey the teachings which would grant humankind these and many other benefits.

If a person or a community saw these as obstacles toward what was in their own personal interests, or sought to create impediments to the invitation from Allah ﷻ, then the Prophets had every right to stop them by first using peaceful means.

If diplomatic methods did not yield the intended results, and individuals refused to allow humanity to progress and reach the goals which Allah ﷻ intended, and the Prophets were unable to remove the obstructions through peaceful means, then they were permitted by Allah ﷻ to use force to free the people from the intellectual bondage and social slavery.

It is vital to note that in the lifetime of the Noble Prophet Muḥammad ﷺ, during his 23 years of the open propagation of the final message of Allah ﷻ, there were over 80 major and minor battles that took place - and all of these were defensive battles.

The conditions which must be present, even for a Divinely-appointed leader such as a Prophet, a Messenger, or an Imām to launch an offensive war - what we refer to in today's terminology as a pre-emptive strike - are extensive and almost impossible to reach. Just as an example, the higher level books of Islamic Jurisprudence note that there must be a complete justice system in place, all of humanity needs to have complete knowledge of their actions, the proof *(ḥujjah)* of Allah ﷻ must have been completed over that society, etc.; are some of the numerous conditions which must be fulfilled before a leader can even think about an offensive war.

It is clear that in our era, such conditions are far from being fulfilled, and even if the majority of them were, the fact that we are without a Divinely-appointed leader to make the call, as Imām al-Mahdī himself is in occultation makes this invalid currently.

2. Defensive Jihād

All laws - both the celestial which are laws that come from Allah ﷻ directly, as well as terrestrial which are human-made laws - give an individual and society who have been attacked, the right to stand up and defend themselves, and to use all of the reasonable means at their disposal to preserve their existence, and this sacred struggle is referred to as the defensive *jihād*.

The wars which took place in the history of Islam such as:

1. Aḥzāb;[135]
2. Uḥud;[136]
3. Mu'ta;[137]
4. Tabūk;[138]

---

[135] The Battle of Khandaq (Battle of the Trench), which was also known as The Battle of Aḥzāb (Battle of the Confederates), took place in the fifth year of migration. It initially broke out by the stratagem of the Banū Naḍīr tribe in which the Quraysh united with all of its allies, including the polytheist Arab tribes, to eradicate Islam. The number of enemy soldiers was 10,000, while the Muslims army was made up of only 300 soldiers.

[136] The Battle of Uḥud was fought against the polytheists of Mecca in the third year after the migration. The Quraysh marched toward Medina because they wanted to avenge the losses faced in the Battle of Badr.

[137] The Battle of Mu'ta was one of the major military expeditions in the early Islamic period which took place between the Muslims and the Roman army in the eighth year after the migration.

[138] The Battle of Tabūk was the final war which Prophet Muḥammad ﷺ took part in. It occurred during the Islamic months of Rajab and Shaʿbān in the ninth year after the migration in the region of Tabūk. As Prophet Muḥammad ﷺ was heading toward Tabūk to fight the Romans, some of his companions - specifically the hypocrites - refused to join the army, while others tried to weaken the morale of the soldiers. Before the expedition, the Prophet ﷺ appointed Imām ʿAlī ؑ to be in charge of the Muslim community in Medina in his absence. After a few days, the Muslim army returned to Medina from Tabūk without any actual confrontation with Romans, however some verses of the Qur'ān were revealed about the hypocrites, exposing them and their secret intentions.

5. Ḥunayn,[139]

and some other battles fall into the category of this type of *jihād* and had a defensive aspect to them.

3. The Intellectual Attempt to Enlighten the World to Monotheism

Islam respects freedom of belief and does not allow that anyone be forced to accept religion in general, or Islam in particular. For this reason, the teachings of Islam have given communities which had Divine Scriptures revealed to them, such as the Jews and Christians, sufficient opportunity to study and reflect on the Qurʾān, and accept it as a continuation of the teachings given to the past Prophets, Mūsā ◈ and ʿIsā ◈.

However, if after being presented the facts and deliberating upon it, the followers of Judaism and Christianity refuse to accept the Qurʾān and the teachings of Prophet Muḥammad ﷺ, then they are permitted to stay on their faith traditions, and the Islamic laws would deal with them as a recognized religious minority and establish peaceful coexistence with them under special conditions that are neither complicated, nor difficult, and they are then known as the *Ahl adh-Dhimmah*.[140]

Islam has taken a hard stance against polytheism and idolatry because this is neither a religion (*dīn*), nor a creed. Rather, it is seen as a superstition, perversion from the true teachings of Monotheism, and an illogical belief. However, in the multi-cultural world in which we live today, just as Islam did 1,400 years ago, we are requried to live in peace and harmony with people of all religions, whether they be monotheistic,

---

[139] The Battle of Ḥunayn transpired after the conquest of Mecca in the eighth year after the migration, in the area of Ḥunayn between the Muslims who were the under the leadership of Prophet Muḥammad ﷺ, and the tribes of Hawāzin and Thaqīf who resided in the area of Ṭāʿif.

[140] These are non-Muslims from among the People of the Book, referring to the Jews, Christians, Zoroastrians, and Sabians who live under the protection of an Islamic government with special terms and stipulations.

polytheistic, or even the trans-polytheistic faiths. As Muslims, we need to recognize that for the most part, people follow the ideology which they were born into and that our responsibility is not to criticize their beliefs, but to educate them in regards to the One True God - Allah ﷻ, and the beauties of Monotheism as exemplified by the Qur'ān and the teachings of Prophet Muḥammad ﷺ and his Ahlul Bayt ؑ.

We cannot 'force convert' anyone to Islam, we are merely required to provide the education and 'complete the argument' *(itmām al-ḥujjah)*, and allow for the teachings to sink into a person's conscious. Ultimately, Allah ﷻ will judge us all based on His Unlimited Knowledge.

From what we have said so far, it is clear that Islam harmonized *jihād* by introducing correct principles and the logic of reason, however we know that the enemies of Islam - especially the leaders of the Christian Church of the past, and even some of the evangelical Churches of today, as well as the biased Orientalists - have distorted the facts, issued statements against the sacred struggle, and have harshly attacked this Divine law. It is as if they are afraid of the growth of true Muḥammadan Islam in the world due to its logical teachings and unique program of life which Islam provides its followers, compared to other ideologies in the world that have created a terrible, false image, and misrepresentation of Islam.

4. Jihād: Supporting the Oppressed

Protecting the oppressed against the oppressors is a vital Islamic principle that must be observed, even if it leads to a sacred struggle.

Islam does not allow for Muslims to be indifferent to the pressures which the oppressed people of the world are put under, so this *jihād* becomes one of the most valuable Islamic precepts, and this also confirms the authenticity of this religion coming from the One True God in that it is concerned about the rights of the victimized, and does not allow for them to remain in their abject state.

Keys of Guidance

- Spiritual uncleanliness must be removed before spiritual purification can take place, just like evil must be eradicated before good can be built in its place. In its goal to do away with superstitions and the irrationality of idol worship, Islam called for its gradual replacement with the teachings of Monotheism - based on knowledge, logic and understanding and not by brute force. The Qur'ān recognizes that those who have been born into or follow a polytheistsic way of life may not have ever seriously thought about what they were following, or perhaps they were not ever provided with the alternative of Monotheism *(Tawḥīd),* and as such they need to be weaned off of their polytheistic tendencies through knowledge and education. During that time period while they are on another path, and even if they decide to stay on their beliefs, Allah ﷻ expects the Muslims to live with non-Muslims of all denominations with peace and respect. The religion of Islam never allows a Muslim to encroach on the rights of other human beings simply because they do not follow their path. If and when a person is able to see that the religious system one is following is not logical, and that the One True God is other than what one perceived Him to be, can the foundation of the Divinely-revealed religion of *Tawḥīd* of Allah ﷻ be established in a person's heart.

- Allah ﷻ confirms that there is always a path back to Him, and the doors of repentance are never closed to anyone under any circumstances. Even if a stubborn enemy who worshipped idols one's entire life realizes the errors in one's way, changes course, and comes to the One True God - Allah ﷻ will forgive Him as He is the All-Forgiving, All-Merciful.

Verse 194

ٱلشَّهۡرُ ٱلۡحَرَامُ بِٱلشَّهۡرِ ٱلۡحَرَامِ وَٱلۡحُرُمَٰتُ قِصَاصٞۚ فَمَنِ ٱعۡتَدَىٰ عَلَيۡكُمۡ
فَٱعۡتَدُواْ عَلَيۡهِ بِمِثۡلِ مَا ٱعۡتَدَىٰ عَلَيۡكُمۡۚ وَٱتَّقُواْ ٱللَّهَ وَٱعۡلَمُوٓاْ أَنَّ ٱللَّهَ
مَعَ ٱلۡمُتَّقِينَ ١٩٤

A sacred month is (retributive) for another sacred month, and if the sanctity is violated, then respond with *qiṣāṣ* (a just method of retaliation). Then, should anyone aggress against you, assail them in the manner they assailed you; and have God-consciousness *(taqwā)*, and know that Allah is with the God-conscious ones (those with *taqwā*).

The polytheists of Mecca knew that fighting in the inviolable months *(ashhuru al-ḥurum)* which include: Rajab, Dhūl Qaʿdah, Dhūl Ḥijjah, and Muḥarram was not permissible in the teachings of Islam, and actually even in the pre-Islamic Era of Ignorance *(Jāhiliyyah)* wars were not allowed in these four months. However, they still intended to launch a surprise attack and fight the Muslims during these forbidden months. The polytheists may have thought that just because they wanted to disregard the reverence which these sacred months had, the Muslims would not disregard their sanctity, thus they would not put up a fight against them because they would want to uphold the sacredness of these months of ceasefire.

However, the verse in question put an end to that notion, thwarted their plans, and ordered the Muslims that if the polytheists take up arms and attack you during these sacred months, then you must stand up and defend yourselves. Therefore in this verse, Allah ﷻ says that a forbidden month is retributive against a forbidden month - meaning that if the enemies violate the respect and honor of it and attack the Muslims, then the Muslims have a God-given right to retaliate because breaking sanctities has retributions associated with it.

This is in fact a kind of retaliation *(qiṣāṣ)* which was put in place so that the polytheists would never think of abusing the sanctity of the sacred months, or the honorable land of Mecca.

The word 'inviolate values' *(ḥurumāt)* is the plural of *ḥurmah,* and it means 'something which must be protected and whose sanctity must be honored.' The reason why the Sacred Mosque in Mecca is called a *Ḥaram* is because this word means 'a place of sanctity and respect in which disregard of life' - whether it be plant life, animal life, or obviously human life - is not permissible at all. In addition to this, in Islamic law, unlawful actions and shameful deeds are referred to as impermissible or *ḥarām* because people are prohibited from performing them.

Allah ﷻ then points to a general command, and tells the Muslims living during the time of Prophet Muḥammad ﷺ that if anyone transgresses against them, then they are permitted to return the aggressions in a similar manner, however while doing so they must ensure that they always have the consciousness of Allah ﷻ, and they do not exceed the limits of retaliation and self-defense, as Allah ﷻ is only with those people who have God-consciousness - those of *taqwā*.

Modern-day Christianity likes to preach 'turn the other cheek' as the New Testament of the Bible has been quoted as saying: "You know that you have been taught: 'An eye for an eye and a tooth for a tooth.' But I tell you not to try to get even with a person who has done something to you. When someone slaps your right cheek, turn and let that person slap your other cheek. If someone sues you for your shirt, give up your coat as well. If a soldier forces you to carry his pack one mile, carry it two miles. When people ask you for something, give it to them. When they want to borrow money, lend it to them."[141] However, the progressive teachings of Islam as embodied in the Noble Qur'ān do not give such an order, because such an abnormal directive will actually provide further impetus to an aggressor.

Interestingly enough, the Christians of today do not practice this mandate properly at all, and some even go entirely against this teaching.

The teachings of the Qur'ān give everyone the right to retaliate in the same amount that they were abused, and it has stated that surrendering to an aggressor is synonymous to death, while resisting hostility is equal to life, and this is the logic of Islam. However, Islam is a religion which always encourages peace and reconciliation, thus we must remember that forgiveness is highly encouraged, and even if a person has the right to retaliate, Allah ﷻ has made the reward of forgiving much greater; and it is for this reason that we see the importance of God-consciousness *(taqwā)* emphasized in this verse.

At the end of this verse, Allah ﷻ states that He is with those who have

---

[141] New Testament, Book of Matthew 5:38-42.

God-consciousness, and this is a subtle allusion to the fact that He will never leave the believers alone, especially those with this trait of *taqwā*, and He will always be there to assist them.

Keys of Guidance

- Not all times of the year are the same; nor is every land on Earth the same. The sanctity of some places on Earth, and some months is greater than others, and as such in Islam they must be given special respect; and acts of aggression and oppression during these times - whether they be against others or one's own self - will be met with a stiffer penalty by Allah ﷻ.
- For any legal or legislative system to be fair and just, and in order to guarantee that everyone's rights are looked after, it must ensure that people who are persecuted and harassed do not fall into despair for themselves and their families, and that the system does not encourage or turn a blind eye to the aggressors and assailants. Thus, retribution of those acts of hostility need to be carried out to ensure that the rights of innocent people are upheld, however Islam makes a strict condition with its followers that they must never be excessive, and that they must observe God-cosciousness even during times of war.

Verse 195

وَأَنفِقُوا۟ فِى سَبِيلِ ٱللَّهِ وَلَا تُلْقُوا۟ بِأَيْدِيكُمْ إِلَى ٱلتَّهْلُكَةِ ۛ وَأَحْسِنُوٓا۟ ۛ إِنَّ ٱللَّهَ
يُحِبُّ ٱلْمُحْسِنِينَ ﴿١٩٥﴾

And spend in Allah's cause (out of whatever you have) and do not ruin yourselves by your own hands (by refraining from spending. Whatever you do) do it in the best way (in the awareness that Allah sees it). Surely Allah loves those who are devoted to doing good.

This verse completes the discussion in this section concerning the sacred struggle *(jihād)*, and highlights that property and wealth are required to facilitate this sacred struggle, just like it requires men with sincerity and determination to be successful. It is soldiers who determine the outcome of a war, but they cannot fight without sufficient equipment - including weapons, ammunition, means of transportation, food, medical supplies, etc.

Therefore providing the means of sacred struggle against the enemies is one of the duties mentioned in this verse, and Allah ﷻ explicitly commands the believers to give whatever they can in His way, and they should not destroy themselves with their own hands by refusing to spend in His cause.

At the end of this verse, Allah ﷻ provides a commandment to the people who engage in good deeds and tells them to continue to be righteous because Allah ﷻ loves the virtuous ones who perform acts of goodness.

Almsgiving Prevents the Destruction of Society

Although this verse was revealed in the context of the sacred struggle, at the same time it expresses a general truth which is that financial donations save societies from the poison of corruption.

When donating money, or in general helping others for the sake of Allah ﷻ is forgotten, and wealth is consolidated in the hands of a small group of people and the majority are deprived, and economic disparity appears within society, then in no time at all a huge explosion will engulf the general public.

In such a situation, the masses will rise up to protest the disproportion of wealth distribution in society, and the rich people and their wealth will figuratively and literally burn in the fire of a grass-roots led revolution.

Therefore, the relationship which exists between giving in the way of Allah ﷻ, and the downfall of the 'haves' of the society will become clear.

In fact, even before wealth provides any benefit to the deprived, it is in the best interest of the rich to ensure that they give their fair share to society in order to ensure balance and stability, and to protect what they have. In this regard, the Commander of the Faithful Imām 'Alī ؑ has been quoted as saying: "Fortify and protect your property by giving *zakāh.*"[142]

Keys of Guidance

- A strong economy is vital for any movement to have traction and in order to be able to forge ahead, and as such the sacred struggle is not possible without financial support, and people giving up some comforts and luxuries. If individuals do not use their property to defend themselves when the enemy invades, then they will suffer a humiliating defeat.
- The best form of 'insurance' in order to insure that our lives, our property, and the social well-being of the entire society remains strong is through acts of charity, and by giving to those people or causes who need the most help for the sake of Allah ﷻ.
- Charity *(infāq)* is a means to elevate one's status with Allah ﷻ to become *muḥsin.* The rank of goodness *(iḥsān)* - or becoming a person of goodness - a *muḥsin* - is higher than that of a *muttaqī* - someone with *taqwā.* The primary meaning of the word *iḥsān* is "perfection" or "excellence" which is related to the word "goodness." Thus, not only does such a person "do good," but more than this, they do it to the best possible level. This shows us that charity is one of the key means for us to move to this rank faster than through other possible ways. Therefore we understand that charity does not only affect society, but rather it also helps oneself grow personally.

Verse 196

وَأَتِمُّواْ ٱلْحَجَّ وَٱلْعُمْرَةَ لِلَّهِ ۚ فَإِنْ أُحْصِرْتُمْ فَمَا ٱسْتَيْسَرَ مِنَ ٱلْهَدْيِ ۖ وَلَا تَحْلِقُواْ رُءُوسَكُمْ حَتَّىٰ يَبْلُغَ ٱلْهَدْىُ مَحِلَّهُۥ ۚ فَمَن كَانَ مِنكُم مَّرِيضًا أَوْ بِهِۦٓ أَذًى مِّن رَّأْسِهِۦ فَفِدْيَةٌ مِّن صِيَامٍ أَوْ صَدَقَةٍ أَوْ نُسُكٍ ۚ فَإِذَآ أَمِنتُمْ فَمَن

[142] *Biḥār al-Anwār*, Vol. 78, Pg. 60, Ḥadīth 138. This tradition is as follows:

حَصِّنُوا أَمْوَالَكُمْ بِالزَّكَاةِ.

تَمَتَّعَ بِٱلْعُمْرَةِ إِلَى ٱلْحَجِّ فَمَا ٱسْتَيْسَرَ مِنَ ٱلْهَدْيِ ۚ فَمَن لَّمْ يَجِدْ فَصِيَامُ
ثَلَٰثَةِ أَيَّامٍ فِى ٱلْحَجِّ وَسَبْعَةٍ إِذَا رَجَعْتُمْ ۗ تِلْكَ عَشَرَةٌ كَامِلَةٌ ۗ ذَٰلِكَ لِمَن لَّمْ
يَكُنْ أَهْلُهُۥ حَاضِرِى ٱلْمَسْجِدِ ٱلْحَرَامِ ۚ وَٱتَّقُوا۟ ٱللَّهَ وَٱعْلَمُوٓا۟ أَنَّ ٱللَّهَ
شَدِيدُ ٱلْعِقَابِ ﴿١٩٦﴾

And complete the *Ḥajj* and the *ʿUmrah* for Allah, and if you are impeded (after you have already put on the *iḥrām*[143] - the specific clothing for the pilgrimage), then send (to Mecca) a sacrificial offering that you can afford. Do not shave your heads (to mark the end of the state of consecration for the pilgrimage) until the offering has reached its destination and is sacrificed. However, if any of you is ill (such that one is obliged to leave the state of consecration), or has an ailment of the head, then he must give a redemption *(fidyah)* by fasting, or giving alms *(ṣadaqah)*, or offering a sacrifice. When you are secure (meaning that when the pilgrimage is not impeded, or the impediment is removed), then whoever takes advantage of the *ʿUmrah* before the *Ḥajj*, must give a sacrificial offering which one can afford. Whoever cannot afford the offering, (they are required to) fast for three days during the *Ḥajj*, and for seven days when you return (home) - that is, ten days

[143] The specific attire which is required *(iḥrām)* is the first action of the rites of *Ḥajj* and *ʿUmrah,* and it starts from one of the five specific points where a person is obligated to wear it, which is referred to as the place of *miqāt.* The *iḥrām* outfit for men is two plain pieces of unstitched white cloth: one is worn around the waist *(izār),* and the other is over the shoulders *(ridāʾ).* The *iḥrām* is one of the elemental parts *(rukn)* of *Ḥajj,* and after entering the state of *iḥrām* some of the acts which are permissible in normal conditions become temporarily prohibited, and if they are performed then there is a specific atonement *(kaffārah)* for committing some of them. More details can be found in the books which discuss the pilgrimage.

in all. This is for those who do not live in the vicinity of the Sacred Mosque. Act in due reverence of Allah and be God-conscious, and know that Allah is severe in retribution.

Some Important Rules of Ḥajj

In this lengthy verse, many rulings in regards to the *Ḥajj* pilgrimage have been stated which are as follows:

1. At the beginning, Allah ﷻ provides a general command to perform *Ḥajj* and *ʿUmrah* in full, and He adds that these acts of worship are to be done in compliance with the orders of Allah ﷻ.

In fact, right at the outset of this verse, Allah ﷻ mentions the motivations for these two major acts of worship - the *Ḥajj* and *ʿUmrah* - and then advises the believers that there should be nothing but Divine motivation, a clear intention, and seeking to attain closeness to Him when performing these or other actions.

2. Allah ﷻ then speaks about those, who after having worn the *iḥrām* clothing, are not able to perform the *ʿUmrah* of the *Ḥajj* due to some obstacle such as severe illness or fear of the enemy, and tells the Muslims that if they are besieged, or certain impediments do not allow them to enter Mecca after entering into the state of *iḥrām*, then they must slaughter the animal which they had brought with them for the *Ḥajj* rites and come out of the state of *iḥrām.*
3. Allah ﷻ then points to another requirement, and informs the Muslims that they must not shave their heads - as is customarily done when men complete the *Ḥajj* - until their animal for sacrifice reaches its place and is slaughtered.
4. Allah ﷻ then goes on to mention that if one of the Muslims fall sick, or have some illness on their head or in their hair which would necessitate them to shave their hair off before completing the rites of the pilgrimage, then they have to pay an atonement *(fidyah)* which is either fasting, providing alms, or sacrificing an animal - a sheep. The word which Allah ﷻ uses in this verse '... a sacrifice...' *(nusuk)* is the plural of the word *nasika* which means 'an animal who has been slaughtered,' and this word also comes in

the meaning of general acts of worship *('ibādat)*. A person who is in this situation (of having to pay a penalty) is at liberty to choose one of the three ways mentioned above to atone for not being able to perform one's obligations.

5. Allah ﷻ then adds that when a person is safe from the sickness or the enemy, then those who are able to complete the *'Umrah* and start the *Ḥajj* - need to realize that when it comes time to slaughter an animal, they need to slaughter what is possible for them. Here, Allah ﷻ is pointing out the fact that in the *Ḥajj at-Tamattuʿ*, it is required to carry out the sacrifice of an animal, and it does not matter if the sacrifice is a camel, a cow, or a sheep, and without this an individual is not permitted to come out of the state of *iḥrām*.
6. Allah ﷻ then goes on to state the ruling *(ḥukm)* of a person who is not able to sacrifice an animal while performing *Ḥajj at-Tamattuʿ*, and He says that if a person does not have an animal to sacrifice, then one must fast for three days during the *Ḥajj* season and seven days when one returns home - a full ten day requirement. Therefore, if an animal is not found which one can slaughter, or the financial situation of a person does not allow one to afford an animal, then the compensation is ten days of fasting. The usage of the word 'in all' *(kāmilah)* points to the fact that the fasting of ten full days takes the place of slaughtering an animal which the person was not able to perform, and the visitors to the house of Allah ﷻ should not be disappointed if they could not offer an animal to sacrifice.
7. Allah ﷻ goes on to mention another ruling and says that all of this is for those people who do not reside near the Sacred Mosque. Therefore, those who are residents of the city of Mecca or its surrounding areas are not permitted to perform *Ḥajj at-Tamattuʿ*, and instead their obligation is to perform what is known as *Ḥajj al-Qirān* or *Ḥajj al-Ifrād* - the details of which are mentioned in the books of Islamic Jurisprudence.

After stating these seven rules, Allah ﷻ commands the Muslims to have consciousness of Him and know that He is swift in retribution.

The emphasis which Allah ﷻ gives at the end of this verse shows that

He is stressing to the Muslims that they ensure they do not neglect any of the details of this important act of worship in Islam, because failure to perform these actions in the prescribed way will result in the negation of the *Ḥajj* and the loss of its valuable blessings.

Importance of Ḥajj

Ḥajj is considered to be one of the most important acts of worship legislated in Islam, and it provides many personal blessings upon the individual who performs it correctly. *Ḥajj* is a ceremony which has the potential to shake the enemies of Islam to the core, and reinvigorate Muslims on a yearly basis.

Ḥajj is an act of worship which the Commander of the Faithful, Imām ʿAlī ﷺ, called the flag and vital slogan of Islam, and in his last will and testament which he noted in the final hours of his life, he is quoted to have said: "Have the consciousness of Allah (and) keep Allah in view about the matter of your Lord's House (the Kaʿbah). Do not forsake it as long as you live, because if it is abandoned then you will not be spared."[144]

Various Types of Ḥajj

Through research and taking guidance from verses of the Noble Qurʾān, the traditions of Prophet Muḥammad ﷺ, and the Imāms of the Ahlul Bayt ﷺ, the esteemed Muslim jurists have divided *Ḥajj* into three types:

1. *Ḥajj at-Tamattuʿ* is for those who live 48 miles (86 km) or more away from Mecca;
2. *Ḥajj al-Qirān* is to be performed by those who live less than the above mentioned distance from Mecca, and have an animal with them which they will offer as a sacrifice on the required day. They enter the state of *iḥrām* by reciting the *talbīyyah*[145] and by affixing

[144] *Nahj al-Balāghah,* Letter 47. This tradition is as follows:

وَاللَّهَ اللَّهَ فِي بَيْتِ رَبِّكُمْ، لاَ تُخْلُوهُ مَا بَقِيتُمْ، فَإِنَّهُ إِنْ تُرِكَ لَمْ تُنَاظَرُوا.

[145] *Talbīyyah* is one of the obligatory acts of *iḥrām* in *Ḥajj* and *ʿUmrah* and consists of some specific phrases that include the Arabic word *Labbayk* (لبّيك). By saying the *talbīyyah,* one enters the state of *iḥrām* (as this is a physical and

something around the neck of the animal to demarcate that animal as being dedicated for sacrifice;

3. *Ḥajj al-Ifrād* is performed by those who live less than this distance of 48 miles from Mecca and do not have to perform the sacrifice of an animal, however it is a condition that the pilgrim has to have the animal with them when they enter into the state of *iḥrām.*

In *Ḥajj at-Tamattu'*, a person first performs the *'Umrah;* they then exit the state of *iḥrām* - both physically and spiritually - and after a period of time when the actual *Ḥajj* season beings they once again wear the *iḥrām* and perform the *Ḥajj* rites in its special days.

When it comes to the other two types of *Ḥajj* - *Qirān* and *Ifrād*, a pilgrim must first perform the rites of *Ḥajj,* and once that is complete then one will end off with the rites of the *'Umrah* with a slight difference in these two in that in the *Ḥajj* of *Qirān*, one must bring the animal which they wish to sacrifice with them, however in the *Ḥajj* of *Ifrād*, there is no need to perform a sacrifice at all.

Keys of Guidance

- It is very important to understand that Allah ﷻ gives us general

---

spiritual state) and must refrain from those actions which are prohibited in this state. *Labbayk* in *Ḥajj* is a response to the call of Allah ﷻ, and a reminder that we all are His servants.

The word *talbīyyah* (تلبية) is derived from "l-b-y" or "l-b-b" which means 'residing and staying in a place, answering, responding affirmatively, and saying *labbayk*;' in addition, the latter also means the pure extract of something. Hence, in Arabic, the intellect is called *lubb*, and an intellectual is called *labīb*. Accordingly, the meaning of *labbayk* in response to any caller would be: 'I am sincerely here at your service,' or 'I am abiding upon your compliance.'

As a Jurisprudential term, *talbīyyah* means 'saying special phrases that include the word *labbayk* (which means responding to Allah's ﷻ call) in the *iḥrām* of *Ḥajj* and *'Umrah*.'

It is narrated that while saying the *talbīyyah*, Imām aṣ-Ṣādiq's (ع) mood would changed and his voice would tremble. Replying to the question regarding this change in his demeanor, he replied: "I am afraid that Allah rejects me and says: 'No *labbayk* and no blessing.'"

guidelines with respect to the Islamic practices such as *Ḥajj*, however, not all of the details are mentioned in the Qur'ān, thus we must refer to the experts in Islamic Jurisprudence for these. Obviously they derive the rulings based on their research into the Qur'ān and *ḥadīth* as their primary sources, trying to understand how Prophet Muḥammad ﷺ performed the acts of worship. Thus, the jurists have a weighty responsibility on their soldiers, and employ an intense and rigorous process to derive the details of worship - in this case, the rites of *Ḥajj*.

- The religious obligations which a Muslim is expected to perform must be done fully and completely - they cannot be left half way, however Allah ﷻ is All-Merciful and acknowledges that there may be times when a person is not able to complete certain actions due to unforeseen factors, therefore there are variations built into the laws so that a person can compensate for actions which one may not be able to perform due to internal factors such as a sickness, or external issues such as threats from enemies.
- *Ḥajj* has been in existence even before the coming of Prophet Muḥammad ﷺ and the religion of Islam, however due to the passage of time, it was changed and corrupted by the polytheists. Therefore, the Qur'ān emphasized to the Muslims at that time that they need to observe the changes in the laws in order to bring this great act of worship back in line with the true Abrahamic teachings.

Verse 197

ٱلْحَجُّ أَشْهُرٌ مَّعْلُومَٰتٌ ۚ فَمَن فَرَضَ فِيهِنَّ ٱلْحَجَّ فَلَا رَفَثَ وَلَا فُسُوقَ وَلَا
جِدَالَ فِى ٱلْحَجِّ ۗ وَمَا تَفْعَلُوا۟ مِنْ خَيْرٍ يَعْلَمْهُ ٱللَّهُ ۗ وَتَزَوَّدُوا۟ فَإِنَّ خَيْرَ ٱلزَّادِ
ٱلتَّقْوَىٰ ۖ وَٱتَّقُونِ يَٰٓأُو۟لِى ٱلْأَلْبَٰبِ ﴿١٩٧﴾

The *Ḥajj* is in the well-known months. Whoever undertakes the duty of *Ḥajj* in these (must know that) there is no (permissibility to engage in) sensual indulgence, nor wicked conduct, nor disputing during the *Ḥajj*. Whatever good you do, Allah knows it. Take your provisions; for surely the best provision is God-consciousness *(taqwā)*, so be God-conscious (and have the reverence of Allah ﷻ), O people of discernment!

Here, the Qur'ān continues to speak about the rules *(aḥkām)* of *Ḥajj*, and provides the believers with a set of new instructions:

1. Allah ﷻ starts off by saying that *Ḥajj* is only performed in certain known months - and here He is referring to the three months in which *'Umrah* can be performed as part of the actual *Ḥajj* ritual, and these are the months of Shawwāl, Dhūl Qa'dah, and Dhūl Ḥijjah.
2. Allah ﷻ then refers to another commandment which those who enter into the state of *iḥrām* and begin to engage in the rites of *'Umrah* and *Ḥajj* need to know, and that is while they are in this spiritual state they are not allowed to enjoy any sensual pleasures such as sexual intercourse, and the other things which must be kept away from that are detailed in the book of Islamic Jurisprudence;[146] nor are they allowed to engage in any sinful acts or take part in arguments.

The environment of *Ḥajj* must be one in which the human soul

---

[146] These include: Hunting; sexual union; kissing one's wife; touching one's wife; looking at and flirting with one's wife; masturbating; reciting the marriage formula *(nikāh)*; applying perfume; wearing sewn clothes for men; wearing antimony *(surmah)*; looking in the mirror; wearing shoes, slippers, or socks for men; expressing outrage *(fusūq)*; quarrelling; killing insects found on the body such as lice; beautifying oneself; applying oil; removing hair from the body; covering the head for men, or dipping one's body in water for both men and women; covering the face for women; sheltering in shaded places for men; doing something to intentionally make blood come out from one's body; cutting the finger or toe nails; extracting a tooth; and according to some scholars, carrying weapons. (Taken from www.sistani.org/english/book/47/2093/. Last accessed on November 30, 2022)

can be strengthened, and one is able to take from that spiritual energy, and thus a pilgrim is expected to cut oneself off from the material world as one travels to the transcendental realms.

At the same time, the connection of unity, solidarity, and fellowship must be strengthened among the Muslims during the *Ḥajj* season and anything that can upset this has been forbidden.

3. In the next stage, one of the spiritual issues of *Ḥajj* has been spoken about which is related to sincerity *(ikhlāṣ),* and Allah ﷻ states that whatever good deeds you do, be sure that Allah knows it. This statement of Allah ﷻ is something which offers the believers spiritual ecstasy to know that their good deeds are all done in the presence of Allah ﷻ. In continuation, Allah ﷻ goes on to tell the believers to prepare their spiritual baggage, and that they should know that the best thing which they can prepare themselves with and take is God-consciousness *(taqwā),* and that they (the believers) must have the reverence of Allah if they are people of intellect and understanding.

This sentence is a subtle reference to the fact that during the pilgrimage, there are many times where a believer is able to prepare and 'pack' one's spiritual provisions, so one must ensure that they do not neglect doing this - meaning that the trip is not just a physical journey from one place to another in order to carry out some rituals without any thought behind why they have been commanded to be performed. Thus, a pilgrim should try to understand what one is meant to achieve through each of the actions that they are obligated to do.

A pilgrim must realize that as one walks through the holy land, one is actually walking in a region which was the embodiment of the early history in which the scenes of the sacrifices of Prophet Ibrāhīm ﵇ and others have taken shape, and several events which are the unique manifestations of proximity to Allah ﷻ took place.

This is such a special land that those who visit it with an awakened spirit and an active spiritual heart will be able to take great benefits from it - as long as while they are on this journey they continuously fill their spiritual baggage with the immaterial gifts which they will acquire at every stage, and then they will have ample provisions to provide for their spiritual needs for the rest of their lives.

Keys of Guidance

- In Islamic spirituality, time plays a key role in the outcomes of things. We see that the Qur'ān tells the believers that the five daily prayers *(ṣalāh)* must be performed in their allotted time; the obligatory fasting is carried out during the month of Ramaḍān; the financial obligation of *khums* and *zakāh* are due at certain times every year; and *Ḥajj* is performed at a particular time as well.
- The environment in which the acts of worship which Islam has mandated, for example the *Ḥajj*, must always remain pure and clean - not only physically clean and disinfected, but more importantly spiritually pure, and that is why many actions are impermissible for a person who is in the state of *iḥrām.*

Verse 198

لَيْسَ عَلَيْكُمْ جُنَاحٌ أَن تَبْتَغُوا۟ فَضْلًا مِّن رَّبِّكُمْ ۚ فَإِذَآ أَفَضْتُم مِّنْ عَرَفَٰتٍ فَٱذْكُرُوا۟ ٱللَّهَ عِندَ ٱلْمَشْعَرِ ٱلْحَرَامِ ۖ وَٱذْكُرُوهُ كَمَا هَدَىٰكُمْ وَإِن كُنتُم مِّن قَبْلِهِۦ لَمِنَ ٱلضَّآلِّينَ ﴿١٩٨﴾

There is no blame on you (Muslims) that you should seek the bounty of your Lord (by trading during the pilgrimage). So when you press on in multitude from ʿArafāt (after you have stayed there for the required time period) then remember Allah at *Mashʿar al-Ḥarām* (also known as *Muzdalifah*); and remember Him knowing how He has guided you, for formerly you were of those who were astray.

In this verse, Allah ﷻ seeks to eliminate misconceptions which some Muslims living during the time of Prophet Muḥammad ﷺ may have engaged in, or had in mind in the matter of *Ḥajj,* so He says to them that it is not a sin for Muslims to enjoy the bounties of their Lord - referring to the economic benefits during the days of *Ḥajj*.

During the pre-Islamic Era of Ignorance *(Jāhiliyyah)* in the season of *Ḥajj*, the polytheists considered any type of transaction, trade, carrying of cargo, or even the transport of passengers for a profit as sinful, and they believed that if anyone engaged in any of these actions then their *Ḥajj* was invalidated.

The above verse was revealed to the Muslims and declared that this notion which stemmed from the Days of Ignorance was worthless and invalid, and Allah ﷻ clearly told the Muslims that there is no problem in them trading and making money during the actual *Ḥajj* itself, and even in general throughout the *Ḥajj* season.

Therefore Muslims were permitted to take advantage of any lawful *(ḥalāl)* trade, and were told that this was an act of kindness of Allah ﷻ over His servants; and they were allowed to work and make money and eat from the fruits of their labor during this special time of year.

In addition, it was understood by the early Muslims living during the time of Prophet Muḥammad ﷺ that travelling from their respective region to meet at the House of Allah ﷻ could serve to be the basis of creating a universal economic boon in the Muslim societies - both in Mecca, and when the pilgrims returned back home - having purchased goods which were being sold by Muslims from various regions.

In the continuation of this verse, Allah ﷻ then turns His attention to the rituals of the *Ḥajj* and states that when the Muslims leave ʿArafāt[147] they must ensure that they continue to remember Allah ﷻ when they reach the area known as *Mashʿar al-Ḥarām*, and that they persist in remembering Him, and recall how He guided the Muslims who at one

[147] Known as both ʿArafah or ʿArafāt, it is a region approximately 3 square miles (8 square kilometers) on the east of Mecca. The sojourn in ʿArafāt is an essential part of the *Ḥajj at-Tamattuʿ* rites. Pilgrims must stay in the desert of ʿArafāt on the ninth of Dhūl Ḥijjah. According to a *ḥadīth* from Prophet Muḥammad ﷺ, there are certain sins which are only forgiven after the stopover in ʿArafāt; in addition, Imām al-Ḥusayn ؑ recited his well-known supplication of ʿArafah *(Duʿāʾ al-ʿArafah)* in the land of ʿArafāt.

time had gone astray and deviated from the true teachings.

A Few Key Points

1. The importance of sacred places such as *ʿArafāt*, *Muzdalifah*, and *Mashʿar.*

In Islam, although every place is created by Allah ﷻ and He is the true Master over time, however there are some places and certain times where Allah ﷻ opens His Door of Mercy even wider than at other times and places. This general principle shows us that there are specific places and times which are of significant importance.

The reason they find value is due to the individuals who are involved in, or the actions that were done at those specific times and places.

These were acts of devotion done with complete sincerity, and as such Allah ﷻ accepted those actions and elevated them to a level where they become highly recommended, or even obligatory actions which all other Muslims must perform, otherwise those places and moments in history would have remained just like any other place or time - either forgotten with the passage of time, or written about in a book of history to be studied from an anthropological point of view.

This golden rule which Allah ﷻ has established in the Qurʾān holds true for us as well, and is not limited to just sacred lands such as Mecca, Medina, and beyond. In reality, our homes and our workplaces, and the time that we spend in them can become unique and endowed with special Blessings and Mercy from Allah ﷻ if we perform actions with sincerity which are accepted by Allah ﷻ. Simple actions such as helping our family, performing our tasks with true intentions, giving in charity, sacrificing our things by donating to others who are in need, and doing anything for the sake of Allah ﷻ, are all ways to elevate our homes or offices to be sacred spaces, deserving of extra Mercy from Allah ﷻ.

Since Allah ﷻ specifically mentions the land of ʿArafāt in this verse, let us take a closer look at this land and why it is so special.

At the level of the physical earth which it covers, ʿArafāt is a land just like any other land - rocky ground with some trees and shrubs growing around it. However, its significance begins with the importance of this physical space, and its recorded history which is tied to Prophet Ādam and his wife, Ḥawwāʾ - the founders of humanity.

Following their 'spiritual descent' to Earth, and after a long period of separation, they finally met at this location and proceeded to lay the foundation of the future of humankind. They recognized the greatness of Allah ﷻ, acknowledged their past slips, and turned their own fate around to raise themselves to levels of greatness with the help of Allah ﷻ.

While in ʿArafāt, when Prophet Ādam turned to Allah ﷻ after the incident of the tree,[148] Allah ﷻ gave him a choice by showing him two lofty positions: He was allowed to either stay in the previous position he had by being permitted to go back to the garden he was in; or he was allowed to stay on the Earth with all of the difficulties and tests that would entail - however he would then have the potential to reach an even higher position. Needless to say, Prophet Ādam chose the latter, and thus remained on Earth. It was his decision which he made with true sincerity *(ikhlāṣ)* and his covenant with Allah ﷻ that marked the land of ʿArafāt as a sacred place with special mercy.

2. The connection between the phrase: 'and remember Him' *(fadhkurū)*, and these locations is that the defining factor of making a time or place full of blessings is the active remembrance of Allah ﷻ *(dhikrullāh)*.

Allah ﷻ repeats this word so that we can remain connected with Him, as this is the secret to and the start and continuation of *ikhlāṣ* and sincere actions toward Him.

Keys of Guidance

- One of the goals of the Qurʾān is to fight against oversimplification of the acts of worship. There were some people who thought that religion was a one-dimensional thing, and that acts of worship were just 'rituals' to perform devoid of any meaning, philosophy, or outward benefits. They thought that the rites of the pilgrimage *(Ḥajj)* were merely acts of dry worship with no worldly benefits associated with them, and that people should not seek any material

[148] To read more about this, refer to the commentary of Verses 35 and 36 of Sūrah al-Baqarah found in the book, *The Clear Guidance*, Volume 1.

gains through the *Ḥajj*. However, Allah ﷻ rejected this idea and wanted to change the mindset of the believers.

- It is through focusing on Divine providence *(tawfīq)* which Allah ﷻ grants to His servants based on their hard work and personal reflection that a believer engages in, that one can recall their past mistakes and sins, and ask Allah ﷻ to forgive them, and this increases their love and affection for the Grace and Mercy of Allah ﷻ.

Verse 199

ثُمَّ أَفِيضُوا۟ مِنْ حَيْثُ أَفَاضَ ٱلنَّاسُ وَٱسْتَغْفِرُوا۟ ٱللَّهَ ۚ إِنَّ ٱللَّهَ غَفُورٌ رَّحِيمٌ ﴿١٩٩﴾

Then press on in multitude from where all of the (other) people press on, and implore Allah's forgiveness. Surely Allah is All-Forgiving *(Ghafūr)*, All-Merciful *(Raḥīm)*.

Continuing what was mentioned in the previous verse, Allah ﷻ tells the Muslims living during the time of Prophet Muḥammad ﷺ that they must now leave where they are in this holy land of ʿArafāt, and along with the masses of believers go toward the land of Minā.[149]

The word which has been translated as 'press on' *(afīḍhū)* comes from

---

[149] The land of Minā is located around 4 miles (7 km) northeast of *Masjid al-Ḥarām*, between the Sacred Mosque and *Muzdalifah* - also known as *Mashʿar al-Ḥarām.*

The plain of Minā is around 2 miles long and 500 meters wide, and is situated between two lines of mountains.

From the morning of *Eid al-Aḍḥā* on the 10th of Dhūl Ḥijjah until the 12th of Dhūl Ḥijjah, *Ḥajj* pilgrims need to perform some rituals in this land which include: the stoning of the pillars representing Shayṭān, sacrificing an animal, cutting some of their hair or shaving the entire head (for men), and staying these nights in Minā.

the Arabic root word of *faiḍ* which means 'flowing water.' When a large group of people begin to move from one location to another it resembles a flowing stream of water, and it could be for this reason that this word has been used here.

In the *ḥadīth* it has been mentioned that during the Period of Ignorance, the tribe of Quraysh believed many incorrect things about themselves, and even used to say that they specifically were not permitted to go to ʿArafāt during the *Ḥajj* season because they believed ʿArafāt to be outside of the physical boundaries of the sanctuary of Mecca.

It was for this reason that this verse of the Noble Qurʾān was revealed to refute this mistaken belief. Allah ﷻ also ordered the Muslims to make a stop *(wuqūf)* in ʿArafāt, then proceed to *Mashʿar al-Ḥarām,* and then to Minā.

At the end of this verse, Allah ﷻ orders the Muslims to ask Him for forgiveness, for Allah ﷻ in indeed the All-Forgiving, All-Merciful. The Muslims were thus being commanded to ask for forgiveness about their incorrect notions which were a carry-over from the Days of Ignorance and went against the spirit of the equality of *Ḥajj.*

In these verses of the Qur'ān, three places of stop *(wuqūf)* during the pilgrimage have been mentioned:

1. ʿArafāt, which is approximately 11 miles (18 km) from Mecca;
2. *Mashʿar al-Ḥarām* which is also known as *Muzdalifah,* and is around 6 miles (10 km) from Mecca;
3. Minā which is about 4 miles (7 km) from Mecca, and is the place where the sacrifice of an animal takes place, stoning of the three *jamarāt* occurs, and certain other actions happen which allow a pilgrim to come out of the *iḥrām* in order to mark the day of Eid.

First Stop in Ḥajj

The visitors to the House of Allah ﷻ in the city of Mecca embark on *Ḥajj* after performing the *ʿUmrah.*

The first step in *Ḥajj* is the stop *(wuqūf)* at ʿArafāt.

As for why this land has been named ʿArafāt may refer to the fact that this land is a suitable environment for 'knowing Allah ﷻ and recognizing His Pure Essence,' because it comes from the Arabic root of *ʿa-ra-fah* which means 'to know or to recognize.'

Truly, the spiritual attraction that a person can find upon entering this land of ʿArafāt cannot be described by any expression or word - it must be experienced in order to be understood.

Human beings who lead monotonous lives; the desert dwellers; and those who want to escape from the hustle and bustle of the material world - flee their daily surroundings and gather under the sky at ʿArafāt to breathe in the clean spiritual air, and purify themselves from the pollution of sin which they have been inhaling at home.

ʿArafāt is a land whose breeze carries the whispers of Angel Jibrāʾīl ﷺ. It is the place where the courageous chants of Prophet Ibrāhīm *al-Khalīl* ﷺ came from, and the life-giving reverberations which emanated from the voice of Prophet Muḥammad ﷺ can still be heard. In this memorable land which seems to be separated by a window to a world behind the existence in which we live, a pilgrim is not only intoxicated by the love of one's Lord, but one also joins in the chorus of all creations as they busy themselves in the praise and glorification of their Creator. People who have lived a lifetime but lost themselves to the material world are able to search for and find even more than what they were looking for - for here they are able to truly recognize themselves.

This land is ʿArafāt, and what an interesting and appropriate name it has been given!

Second Stop in Ḥajj

The second halt for a pilgrim is at a place referred to as *Mashʿar al-Ḥarām.* The word *mashʿar* comes from the Arabic root word *shuʿūr* which means 'consciousness.'

On that historical night, meaning the 10th night of Dhūl Ḥijjah when the pilgrims of the House of Allah ﷻ have concluded their training in ʿArafāt during the day, then proceed to spend the night until morning on the soft sands under the starry sky in the land which is a small example and a curtain over the major Day of Resurrection.

Wearing the pure and clean clothing of the *iḥrām* garb, a pilgrim feels the coming of new springs of thought and reflection within oneself, and clearly hears its sound within the depths of one's heart, and thus this land is known as Mashʿar - a place of consciousness.

Keys of Guidance

- The *Ḥajj* is not just "one action;" rather it is a series of things that need to be done in a specific, successive sequence - both inside of the city of Mecca and outside of it.
    1. We begin by performing what is known as *ʿUmrah at-Tamattuʿ* - and this helps us purify ourselves and make the initial connection with Allah ﷻ.
    2. Once complete, when the days of *Ḥajj* arrive, the Muslims then begin the second part of the spiritual journey which is known as *Ḥajj al-Tamattuʿ* where they leave the vicinity of *Masjid al-Ḥarām* and go eastward to ʿArafāt. In this solemn and sacred land, the goal is to know Allah ﷻ as the Sole Creator, and for us to recognize ourselves as His servants.
    3. Next, the pilgrims move westward to *Muzdalifah* which is a reminder of the Day of Judgment, and a time to reflect on our purpose of being created, and the consequences of our actions.
    4. Finally, the pilgrims make their way to Minā, the land of love and strengthening of the relationship with Allah ﷻ. It is a place where the pilgrims seek to strengthen their faith in Allah ﷻ and receive His special mercy and blessings.[150]
- As the years progressed from the time of Prophet Ibrāhīm ﵇, there were many things which were added to the *Ḥajj* rituals by the

---

[150] The *Ḥajj* is not limited to these places. Rather, the acts of worship and where they are to be done are quite dynamic and take weeks or months to learn before one makes this uplifting journey. In addition to the Jurisprudential aspect of *Ḥajj*, there is also the spiritual aspect - WHY we do these actions. Although these may not fully be understood, the Prophet ﷺ and his Ahlul Bayt ﵈ have provided us some insight and understanding in this area. For further reading into the deeper reasons of the actions that we have been commanded to perform, one can refer to *Secrets of the Hajj* authored by Āyatullāh Shaykh Ḥusayn Maẓāherī, translated into English by Saleem Bhimji, to be published soon by Al-Kisa Foundation.

polytheists and others. In order to purify this great act of worship, Allah ﷻ very clearly re-defined the rules to make sure that anything which was contradictory to the guidelines of *Ḥajj* were removed for the Muslim community, as He intended to ensure that they would perform it properly. There were other acts which were being done at the outset of Islam which did not contradict the teachings of Islam, and therefore Allah ﷻ did not reject them, and some of these practices were actually adapted into the final set of teachings of the *Ḥajj* rituals.

- In all of the actions of *Ḥajj*, people have been ordered to move together as one united nation of Muslims such that no one is left behind. However, the motif of the Qur'ān as seen in many verses is that we should never follow the majority if the mainstream are doing wrong; but in certain acts of worship, we should make it a point to perform them in congregation - things such as the obligatory daily prayers, or regular programs which Muslims hold to recite various supplications - because there is a different spiritual feeling that a person gets from performing prayers *(ṣalāh)* and reciting supplications *(duʿās)* at home alone compared to praying in a congregation.

Verse 200

فَإِذَا قَضَيْتُم مَّنَٰسِكَكُمْ فَٱذْكُرُوا۟ ٱللَّهَ كَذِكْرِكُمْ ءَابَآءَكُمْ أَوْ أَشَدَّ ذِكْرًا ۗ
فَمِنَ ٱلنَّاسِ مَن يَقُولُ رَبَّنَآ ءَاتِنَا فِى ٱلدُّنْيَا وَمَا لَهُۥ فِى ٱلْءَاخِرَةِ مِنْ
خَلَٰقٍ ﴿٢٠٠﴾

Then when you finish your rites (of *Ḥajj*), then remember Allah as you would remember your fathers, or with a more ardent remembrance. Among the people there are those who say: 'Our Lord, give us in this world,' but for such there is no share in the hereafter.

History of Revelation

In a *ḥadīth* from Imām Muḥammad al-Bāqir ﵇ we read that: "[In the pre-Islamic Era of Ignorance *(Jāhiliyyah)* when they finished the *Ḥajj* rites and had performed the sacrifice and were making their way back to Mina], they would recount the achievements of their forefathers and say, 'My father was someone who took on ther responsibility of the blood-money *(diyah)*, and he was the one that fought and killed so and so. They would also take an oath by their fathers and say, "No, I take an oath by my father! No, I take an oath by my father!"[151]

This verse was revealed and commanded them to refrain from this action which was filled with excessive bragging, wasting time, and without a purpose. They were to realize that what they were doing was creating animosity, hatred, and supremacism amongst one another - all of which is contradictory to the wisdom and philosophy of this magnificent act of worship known as *Ḥajj*. They needed to understand that they were in Mecca, performing this act of worship which was meant to purify them, and help them become true human beings.

Interpretation

This verse is a continuation of the discussions related to *Ḥajj* which were mentioned in the previous verses, and here Allah ﷻ begins by saying that when you Muslims have performed your rites *(manāsik)* of *Ḥajj*, then remember Allah ﷻ - but with an even more fervent remembrance than in the past when during the Era of Ignorance you used to remember your forefathers (more than God).

This interpretation does not mean that a person should mention both one's ancestors and Allah ﷻ, rather it means that if the Muslims felt that in the past they used to remember their forefathers because of their qualities or gifts which they may have inherited from them, then why do they not make mention of Allah ﷻ - as it is from **Him** that the

[151] *Wasā'il ash-Shī'a*, Vol. 23, Pg. 235. The Arabic text is as follows:

كَانُوا يَفْتَخِرُونَ بِآبَائِهِمْ يَقُولُونَ أَبِى الَّذِى حَمَلَ الدِّيَاتِ وَ الَّذِى قَاتَلَ كَذَا وَ كَذَا إِذَا قَامُوا بِمِنًى بَعْدَ النَّحْرِ وَ كَانُوا يَقُولُونَ أَيْضاً يَحْلِفُونَ بِآبَائِهِمْ لَا وَ أَبِى لَا وَ أَبِى

entire universe, and all of the bounties of this world emanate from? It is **only** Allah ﷻ who has all of the Attributes of Majesty *(Jalāl)* and Beauty *(Jamāl),* and is the Custodian *(Walī)* of all blessings.

When these people would mention their ancestors, it became a battle of bragging to one another and showing off which resulted in creating an aura of animosity and hatred amongst one another. Although some of the things which they mentioned about their forefathers were good traits that they had, however overall this was neither the place nor time to engage in such discussions or arguments. Rather, this was a time to reflect on Allah ﷻ and what He had blessed the people with.

Although the verse states: 'as you mention your fathers' *(ka dhikrikum)* - *'ka'* at the beginning of this phrase translates to 'as' which refers to how it is good to remember our roots and where we have attained the countless blessings from, however Allah ﷻ is guiding us and redirecting our thought pattern that when we remember our ancestors we should pray for them and ask for their forgiveness. It is permissible to remember them in certain acts of worship, such as during *Ḥajj* or other actions, and this can be seen in the supplications which are recounted in the Qur'ān where we pray for our ancestors who have preceded us in faith, however the goal is to include them in our acts of worship by asking for their forgiveness and an elevation of their status in the world to come, not merely to have a gathering which is full of boasting and negative competition.

The phrase: 'remembrance of Allah' *(fadhkuru Allah)* includes all types of remembrance *(adhkār)* of Allah ﷻ which take place during and after the rites of *Ḥajj.*

To conclude this verse, Allah ﷻ divides humanity into two categories, and says that there are some who say: "O Allah! Grant us good in this world" - but they do not ask for anything else so they will receive nothing in the hereafter.

As for the second group of people and their appeal to Allah ﷻ, that will be covered in the next verse.

Keys of Guidance

- When it comes to the remembrance of Allah ﷻ - it must be in copious amounts, but not only in terms of the quantity of remembrance for which there is no limit, but rather it must be abundant in terms of its quality as well, and the love and sincerity with which it is performed.

- We must never be shallow or presume that our supplications to Allah ﷻ are unimportant. When we find ourselves in the best times and sacred places of worship, we must make sure that we are comprehensive in our appeal to Allah ﷻ, and not only ask for the goodness of this short, temporal, and material life.
- The conclusion of this verse is that Allah ﷻ is showing us that people have two different mindsets: there are those who do everything for this short-lived, material world *(dunyā)*. This even extends to when they remember their ancestors as this is done solely for their worldly benefits. However, on the other hand, there is another group of people who perform everything in such a way that they are able to build the life of this world so that they will be successful in this world AND the hereafter. Therefore, even when they remember their ancestors, they do so with the vision that true life is in the hereafter. In addition, there is actually a third group as well who just focus on the hereafter and destroy their life in this world, but this mode of thinking and life is not at all aligned with the balanced teachings of Islam.

Verse 201

وَمِنْهُم مَّن يَقُولُ رَبَّنَآ ءَاتِنَا فِى ٱلدُّنْيَا حَسَنَةً وَفِى ٱلْـَٔاخِرَةِ حَسَنَةً وَقِنَا عَذَابَ ٱلنَّارِ ﴿٢٠١﴾

And among them there are those who say: "Our Lord, give us good in this world and good in the hereafter, and save us from the punishment of the fire."

In continuation of the previous verse which spoke about one group of people who were only concerned about this world, Allah ﷻ contrasts them with a second group who say: "Our Lord! Give us good in this world and also good in the hereafter, and protect us from the punishment of the fire."

This part of the verse refers to the desires of the people and their goals in respect to this great act of worship which is the *Ḥajj.*

There are some people who want both from the *Ḥajj* rituals - the needs of this world and also the spiritual gifts. They realize that the life of this world is merely a place for spiritual development and completion!

What is the meaning of 'goodness' *(ḥasanah)* in this verse? In a *ḥadīth* from Prophet Muḥammad ﷺ he has been reported to have said: "Whomsoever Allah gives a grateful heart, and a tongue engaged in the remembrance of the truth, and a believing spouse who helps one in the affairs of this world and the next - that person has been granted good *(ḥasanah)* in this world and the hereafter, and they will be given protection from the torment of the fire."[152]

Of course, the meaning of 'good' is general and means 'any type of goodness,' and thus it has a broader meaning which includes all of the material and spiritual gifts; so what is mentioned in the above narration is just one example of this word.

Keys of Guidance

- This temporal world *(dunyā)* is a great platform and asset to build the next world, but those who do not recognize this will end up ruining their capital and losing out on the world to come.
- It has been recommended to recite this verse daily in the prayers in the position of *qunūṭ.*[153] Not only are the believers recommended to

---

[152] *Majmaʿ al-Bayān*, Vol. 1, Pg. 298. The initial portion of this tradition is as follows:

مَنْ أُوتِيَ قَلْبًا شاكِرًا وَلِسانًا ذاكِرًا وَزَوْجَةً مُؤْمِنَةً...

[153] *Qunūt* is a recommended action in prayers *(ṣalāh)* as well as in the state of making supplication *(duʿā')* to Allah ﷻ. Literally, *qunūt* means "obeying with humility." The word *qunūt* and its derivations have been mentioned 13 times in the Qur'ān in the meanings of supplication, worship, prayer, and obedience.

'recite' this daily, but they should also remind themselves every day that they need to remain in such a mindset in which they ensure that they have a good balance of working in this world and also working for the world to come - and that they use the capital of this world properly and ensure that they invest it, metaphorically speaking, in the best possible manner to give the greatest return in the world to come.

- This world and the hereafter are not in conflict with one another - provided that a believer seeks the goodness and virtue in this world which will enable one to attain the goodness of the next life, and one acts in accordance to the teachings of Islam and the verses of the Qur'ān.

Verse 202

أُوْلَـٰٓئِكَ لَهُمْ نَصِيبٌ مِّمَّا كَسَبُواْۚ وَٱللَّهُ سَرِيعُ ٱلْحِسَابِ ﴿٢٠٢﴾

Those people will have a portion according to what they have earned; and Allah is Swift at Reckoning.

The phrase 'those people' which Allah ﷻ uses at the beginning of this verse refers to the second group of people - those who seek the good of this world and the good of the hereafter from Allah ﷻ. He is saying that those who work hard, and at the same time are continuously praying to Allah ﷻ will have a share of what they earned because Allah ﷻ is quick to reward His servants.

In fact, this verse is the opposite of the sentence which was mentioned in verse 200 when it spoke about the first group of people where it said that they will have no share in the hereafter. However, there are some

---

In *qunūt*, the person raises their hands up to their face with the palms facing upwards, and supplicates to Allah ﷻ. In most prayers, *qunūt* is performed once in the second *rak'ah* after the recitation of Sūrah al-Fātihah and the other chapter, before going into *rukū'*. It is not necessary that a certain supplication or prayer be recited in *qunūt* and as such, any recitation can be recited in any language.

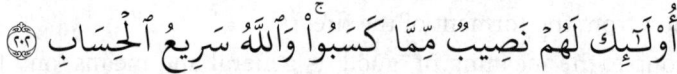

commentators of the Qur'ān who have stated that this verse refers to both groups of people.

The first group - those who only wanted the provisions of this life will get exactly what they wanted, provided that they work for it; while the second group - those who asked for the goodness of this life and the world to come will get both as long as they work for it, and continue to ask Allah ﷻ for both. This understanding can be seen in another portion of the Qur'ān where Allah ﷻ says: "Whoever wishes for only the immediate gains (of this transitory life), We readily grant thereof as much as We please to whomsoever We will. Thereafter We consign him to Hell, wherein he will burn, disgraced, and disowned. But whoever wishes the hereafter and strives for it as it should be struggled for while being a believer, then for those (who do so) their striving shall be recognized with thanks and reward (by Allah). Each do We supply - these ones, as well as those ones - from the gift of your Lord (in this world); and never has the gift of your Lord been restricted."[154]

Keys of Guidance

- On the Day of Resurrection, a person will only benefit from some of their deeds - not all of them. A person may have performed thousands, if not millions of actions in their lifetime, however if they did not have the right intention - that is seeking closeness to Allah ﷻ; or they had a double intention of wanting to please Allah ﷻ, but at the same time wanted to show and please the creations of Allah ﷻ, then the rewards for these type of action will be different.
- There can be no reward - whether it be physical or spiritual - without hard work and sincere effort. We must constantly supplicate and pray to Allah ﷻ, however at the end of the day, we need to fulfill

[154] Qur'ān. Sūrah al-Isrā' (17), Verses 18-20:

مَّن كَانَ يُرِيدُ ٱلۡعَاجِلَةَ عَجَّلۡنَا لَهُۥ فِيهَا مَا نَشَآءُ لِمَن نُّرِيدُ ثُمَّ جَعَلۡنَا لَهُۥ جَهَنَّمَ يَصۡلَىٰهَا
مَذۡمُومٗا مَّدۡحُورٗا ﴿١٨﴾ وَمَنۡ أَرَادَ ٱلۡأٓخِرَةَ وَسَعَىٰ لَهَا سَعۡيَهَا وَهُوَ مُؤۡمِنٞ فَأُوْلَٰٓئِكَ كَانَ سَعۡيُهُم
مَّشۡكُورٗا ﴿١٩﴾ كُلّٗا نُّمِدُّ هَٰٓؤُلَآءِ وَهَٰٓؤُلَآءِ مِنۡ عَطَآءِ رَبِّكَۚ وَمَا كَانَ عَطَآءُ رَبِّكَ مَحۡظُورًا ﴿٢٠﴾

our responsibilities in the life of this world.

Verse 203

وَٱذْكُرُوا۟ ٱللَّهَ فِىٓ أَيَّامٍ مَّعْدُودَٰتٍ ۚ فَمَن تَعَجَّلَ فِى يَوْمَيْنِ فَلَآ إِثْمَ عَلَيْهِ
وَمَن تَأَخَّرَ فَلَآ إِثْمَ عَلَيْهِ ۚ لِمَنِ ٱتَّقَىٰ ۗ وَٱتَّقُوا۟ ٱللَّهَ وَٱعْلَمُوٓا۟ أَنَّكُمْ إِلَيْهِ
تُحْشَرُونَ ﴿٢٠٣﴾

And remember Allah during the (three) appointed days (around *Eid al-Aḍhā*); then whoever is in haste and content with two days, there is no sin upon them; and whoever delays (continuing the rites of throwing the pebbles at the *jamarāt* on the third day also), there is no sin upon them who is careful of the bounds of God-consciousness. And have God-consciousness, and know that before Him you will be gathered.

This is the last verse in this section of Sūrah al-Baqarah which speaks about *Ḥajj,* and it seeks to break the tradition of the pre-Islamic Era of Ignorance regarding the boasting of one's ancestors.

In this verse, Allah ﷻ advises the Muslims that after the Eid celebration and the 'completion' of the pilgrimage they need to continue their remembrance of Allah ﷻ on certain days - what He refers to as the restricted days *(ayyām maʿdūdāt),* also known as *ayyām at-tashrīq* - the word *tashrīq* literally refers to 'drying something out' - and it could be that because in the early days of Islam, after the animals were sacrificed as part of the *Ḥajj* rituals, the meat would be dried and then eaten later. Another interpretation states that the word *tashrīq* comes from the word *shurūq* which means 'sunrise' because as per the Islamic rulings, the animal that is to be sacrificed is then eaten over these three days, but it is not to be slaughtered until after sunrise on the day of *Eid al-Aḍḥā.*

What is this Remembrance (Adhkār)?

In the *ḥadīth* of the Prophet ﷺ and the Ahlul Bayt , his particular remembrance has been defined as a supplication which is recited after ten specific prayers *(ṣalāh)* which start with the noon *(Ẓuhr)* prayer on the day of *Eid al-Aḍḥā,* and end with the morning *(Fajr)* prayer on the 12th day of Dhūl Ḥijjah.

After each of these ten (obligatory) prayers, the following supplication should be recited: "Allah is greater (than anything which can be used to describe Him); Allah is greater; there is no god but Allah, and Allah is greater; Allah is greater and all Praise is for Allah; Allah is greater for having guided us. Allah is greater for having sustained us with [the produce of) cattle livestock, and all Praise is for Allah for having tested us."[155]

Allah ﷻ then adds the following command and says that those who hasten and engage in the remembrance of Allah ﷻ only on two days are not guilty of committing any sin; and those who delay and engage in the remembrance of Allah ﷻ over three days are also not guilty of any sin - as long as they have the consciousness of Allah *(taqwā)* in their hearts.

This interpretation in fact, refers to the flexibility in the remembrance of Allah ﷻ between two days and three days.

It should be noted that the 10th, 11th, 12th of the month of Dhūl Ḥijjah are the three days and nights when one needs to stay in Mina after the completion of the rites at ʿArafāt and *Muzdalifah.*

---

155 The Arabic text of this prayer is as follows:

أَللّٰهُ أَكْبَرُ، أَللّٰهُ أَكْبَرُ، لَا إِلٰهَ إِلَّا اللّٰهُ وَاللّٰهُ أَكْبَرُ، أَللّٰهُ أَكْبَرُ وَلِلّٰهِ الْحَمْدُ، أَللّٰهُ أَكْبَرُ عَلَىٰ مَا هَدَانَا أَللّٰهُ أَكْبَرُ عَلَىٰ مَا رَزَقَنَا مِنْ بَهِيمَةِ الْأَنْعَامِ، وَالْحَمْدُ لِلّٰهِ عَلَىٰ مَا أَبْلَانَا.

Note: According to the jurists, the above is said after ten of the consecutive prayers, the first being after the noon *(Ẓuhr)* prayer on the day of *Eid al-Aḍḥā,* and the last one being the morning *(Fajr)* prayer on the 12th day of Dhūl Ḥijjah. However, if a person is still in Minā on the 13th of Dhūl Ḥijjah, then it is recommended that one says this supplication *(takbīrāt)* after 15 consecutive prayers, the first being the noon *(Ẓuhr)* prayer on the day of *Eid al-Aḍḥā,* and the last one being the morning *(Fajr)* prayer on the 13th day of Dhūl Ḥijjah.

In early Islamic history, there was a dispute about the number of days that the believer needed to stay in Mina to the extent that people were accusing one another of sinning if they left before a certain day. In order to respond to them and clear this issue, this verse was revealed to provide clarity and state that one needs to stay on the 11th and 12th for sure, and if a person also stayed on the 13th, then it was okay, however they needed to refrain from accusing others of doing something which they felt was wrong.

At the end of this verse, Allah ﷻ gives a general command and tells the believers that they need to have consciousness *(taqwā)* of Allah ﷻ, and know that they will all be gathered before Him. This sentence may be taken to indicate that Allah ﷻ is speaking to the *ḥujjāj* - those who have performed the *Ḥajj* rituals, and He is telling them that now that the spiritual ceremonies of the *Ḥajj* have cleansed you of your past sins, and you will return back home purified because of this pilgrimage just like when a new born child comes into this world from one's mother with no sins on their record - however you must be careful not to defile yourself by committing future sins.

Keys of Guidance

- *Ḥajj* is a means of creating and cleansing a human being in its holistic nurturing: physical, spiritual, mental, communal, and individual level. As we see in the *Ḥajj* rites, there are various actions which must be performed, and each one of these fit into a category of creating a real human being in all of the potential dimensions of excellence. A person has the potential to become a well-rounded believer with God-consciousness *(taqwā)* and righteousness after they perform the *Ḥajj* correctly. That is why when a Muslim man or woman returns from *Ḥajj*, they are referred to as '*ḥujjatullāh*' which literally means 'the proof of Allah ﷻ,' because they are now an ambassador of Allah ﷻ to the rest of society - believers and non-believers. One is often called *al-Ḥājj* which is a very lofty title, but a person must work hard to uphold that title and honor this status by living with God-consciousness.

- Simply performing virtuous actions in sanctified lands is not enough; a person must also be righteous and have God-consciousness. We see that in this verse, Allah ﷻ repeats the word *taqwā* two times in addressing the pilgrims to the House of Allah ﷻ, and that too to those in the sacred land of Minā - because the influence of Satan is everywhere even in the 'holy lands' - so imagine those who are living in secular countries which are devoid of the remembrance of Allah ﷻ and any sacred symbols such as the Kaʿbah, the Mountain of ʿArafāt, and other places? Therefore, we must try harder to connect with Allah ﷻ through our actions, families, strengthening and working within our local communities, attending the *masājid*, etc.

Verse 204

وَمِنَ ٱلنَّاسِ مَن يُعْجِبُكَ قَوْلُهُۥ فِى ٱلْحَيَوٰةِ ٱلدُّنْيَا وَيُشْهِدُ ٱللَّهَ عَلَىٰ مَا فِى
قَلْبِهِۦ وَهُوَ أَلَدُّ ٱلْخِصَامِ ﴿٢٠٤﴾

And from among the people there is one whose conversation on (the affairs of) the present, worldly life fascinates you, and they call on Allah to bear testimony about what is in their heart, yet they are the staunchest of enemies.

History of Revelation

Regarding the revelation of this and the next two verses, it has been stated that they were revealed about a man named Akhnas ibn Sharīq.

Akhnas happened to be a handsome and eloquent man who pretended to befriend Prophet Muḥammad ﷺ; he asserted that he loved the Prophet ﷺ and that he had accepted the religion of Islam.

The Prophet ﷺ had been commanded by Allah ﷻ to judge by the apparent as opposed to using 'knowledge of the unseen' *(ʿilm al-ghayb)* although he was permitted to access this with the permission of Allah ﷻ, so he treated him warmly whenever he met him. However, unbeknownst to the Muslim community, Akhnas was a hypocrite.

In one incident, he set fire to the crops of some of the Muslims and killed their cattle, and it was at this time that these three verses of the Noble Qur'ān were revealed, removing his veil of secrecy and hypocrisy from him and his actions, allowing the rest of the community to see his true nature.

Interpretation

In this verse, there is reference to a group of hypocrites, and Allah ﷻ describes them by saying that there are some people whose speech in the life of this world is such that when you listen to them, you are put into a state of wonder; and outwardly, they display such a show of piety and extreme love to you Muslims, however Allah ﷻ is aware of what is truly in their hearts as they are the most stubborn of enemies.

The word which Allah ﷻ uses to describe these hypocrites is 'staunchest or most fierce' *(aluddu)* and this means 'someone who bears a deep-seated animosity to another person;' and the word enmity *(khiṣām)* takes on the meaning of the verbal noun *(maṣdar)* and means 'enmity and hostility.'

Keys of Guidance

- In the previous verses, Allah ﷻ was talking about His remembrance and living an Islamic lifestyle; and how there were some people who were trying to weaken and damage Islam by taking advantage of the guidance of Allah ﷻ. They would constantly pretend to be active Muslims, and did their best to show others that they were living an Islamic lifestyle outwardly through their prayers, fasting, etc., however their true goal was to ruin Islam from the inside.
- Muslims need to be careful not to be deceived by the eloquent, magical words of other Muslims as it is very well possible that those individuals who come around the Muslim community pretending to be sincere devotees may actually be hypocrites in disguise.
- In most cases, the topics which the hypocrites speak about is the life of this transient world in order to influence the naïve Muslims

- very rarely does a hypocrite come around the Muslim community and speak about matters of spirituality or the hereafter.

Verse 205

وَإِذَا تَوَلَّىٰ سَعَىٰ فِي ٱلْأَرْضِ لِيُفْسِدَ فِيهَا وَيُهْلِكَ ٱلْحَرْثَ وَٱلنَّسْلَ ۗ وَٱللَّهُ لَا يُحِبُّ ٱلْفَسَادَ ﴿٢٠٥﴾

And when they leave you, they rush about in the land (in order) to provoke disorder and corruption, and to ruin the sources of life and human generations. Surely Allah does not love disorder and corruption *(fasād).*

Speaking to the Muslims at the time of Prophet Muḥammad ﷺ, Allah ﷻ tells them about such hypocrites who live in the midst of them; and the Almighty states that another sign of their inner enmity is when they, the hypocrites turn away from the Muslims - meaning when they leave the company of the believers - they cause corruption on Earth, and even destroy the agriculture and cattle. Since this is something which is very displeasing to Allah ﷻ, He confirms that He does not like disorder - and obviously as a natural outcome, He also does not like those who create disorder and corruption on the Earth.

If these people were sincere in their friendship and love for the Prophet of Islam ﷺ and his followers, then they would never have committed corruption on the Earth, nor destroyed the property of others. Their appearance is that of true friendship, but inwardly they are ruthless and stubborn enemies.

The word *ḥarth* refers to 'crops,' and *nasl* refers to 'children,' and the word *awlād* refers to 'children of both humans and non-humans.' Thus, the sentence which has been translated as: 'ruin the sources of life and human generations' means 'corruption in the society through the use of wealth and people.'

Keys of Guidance

- One of the tactics of the hypocrites is that as long as things are running smoothly and going good on one side, they want to be on that side. However, the moment that the tides change and things become hard, they flip and go to the other side.
- If and when the incompetent people come to power - whether that be in a family setting, in a community, or at the level of governance of a city, province, state, or country - they will wreak havoc and spread corruption and harm.
- The greatest danger is the destruction of the economy and culture of a nation because without either of these, the society will fall into ruin and wreak anarchy, and debauchery will rule.

Verse 206

وَإِذَا قِيلَ لَهُ ٱتَّقِ ٱللَّهَ أَخَذَتْهُ ٱلْعِزَّةُ بِٱلْإِثْمِ فَحَسْبُهُۥ جَهَنَّمُ وَلَبِئْسَ ٱلْمِهَادُ ﴿٢٠٦﴾

And when he is told: "Be fearful of your duty to Allah," vainglory seizes and thrusts him toward (greater) sin. Hell will settle the account for him, and how evil a cradle indeed that is!

In this verse, Allah ﷻ adds that when this hypocrite is told to stop his destructive actions and fear Allah ﷻ and have God-consciousness in his heart, the fire of stubbornness burns in him and leads him to sin.[156]

He does not listen to the recommendations which people are giving him, nor does he pay attention to the Divine warnings, but instead with his constant display of pride and arrogance, he continues to act contrary to the teachings of his religion.

---

[156] The original meaning of this word *'izzah* is 'honor' and its opposite is *dhillah* or 'humiliation,' however in this verse the meaning of it is 'pride and arrogance.'

Such a person can only be subdued through the fire of Hell, and therefore at the end of this verse Allah ﷻ says that the fire of Hell will be sufficient for such a person, and what a terrible place that will be!

Keys of Guidance

- The best criteria which we can use that Allah ﷻ has provided to us in the Qur'ān to assess people is that of God-consciousness *(taqwā)*. Although this is a trait of the heart, it can be seen in the words and actions of a person.
- Allah ﷻ gives people countless chances in life, and He exhausts every possible way to guide individuals before their death so as to leave no excuse for why they did not gravitate toward the Straight Path.
- The arrogant people in this world will never listen to the good advice that well-wishers give them.

Verse 207

وَمِنَ ٱلنَّاسِ مَن يَشْرِى نَفْسَهُ ٱبْتِغَآءَ مَرْضَاتِ ٱللَّهِ ۗ وَٱللَّهُ رَءُوفٌۢ بِٱلْعِبَادِ ﴿٢٠٧﴾

And (in contrast, there is) from among the people one who sells himself in seeking Allah's pleasure. And Allah is All-Affectionate *(Ra'ūf)* toward His servants.

History of Revelation

The famous commentator of the Ahl as-Sunnah, al-Thaʿlabī states: "When the Prophet of Islam ﷺ decided to migrate (from Mecca to Medina), the polytheists surrounded his house to attack him (on the night of migration), so he ordered ʿAlī to sleep in his bed and cover himself with a green cloth which was specific to the Prophet ﷺ himself.

At this time, Allah sent revelation to (the Angels) Jibrā'īl ﷺ and Mīkā'īl ﷺ saying: 'I created a brotherhood between the two of you, and made the life of one of you longer than the other. Which one of you is willing to sacrifice yourself for the other?'

Neither one of them was ready to do this, so Allah ﷻ revealed to them: 'Right now 'Alī is lying on the bed of the Prophet, ready to sacrifice his own life for him. Go to the Earth and be his guardian.'

At that point, Jibrā'īl (a) sat next to the head of 'Alī (a) and Mīkā'īl (a) sat near his feet, and Angel Jibrā'īl (a) said to him: 'Blessed are you 'Alī! It is because of you that Allah is boasting to the angels!'

It was at this time that the verse under review was revealed, and this historical night became known as *Laylat al-Mabīt* - which literally means 'the event of spending the night.'"[157]

Commentary

The connection which we need to recognize in this verse with the previous verses is that after Allah ﷻ mentioned His remembrance *(dhikr)* and living an all inclusive Islamic lifestyle, He presents one example of a hypocrite *(munāfiq)*, and now one example of a true believer who lived his life according to the principle of the active and constant remembrance of Allah ﷻ *(dhikr)*. This individual lived the ideal Islamic lifestyle, had his complete trust in Allah ﷻ at all times, and sacrificed himself for the Almighty to uphold the true teachings of the religion of Islam.

Although this verse was revealed about the migration of Prophet Muḥammad ﷺ from Mecca to Medina, and speaks about the self-sacrifice of Imām 'Alī (a), it also has a general meaning and content. In fact, the contents of this verse are the direct opposite to what was said in the previous verses about the hypocrites.

In this verse, Allah ﷻ says that from among the people there is a person who sells his life for the pleasure of Allah ﷻ, then He concludes the verse by reminding the believers that He is All-Affectionate to His servants.

The phrase which Allah ﷻ uses at the end of this verse: '...Allah is All-Affectionate toward His servants,' may indicate that although He is the same One who grants human beings life, He turns around and buys

---

[157] *Biḥār al-Anwār*, Vol. 19, Pp. 38, 39, 64, and 86; Vol. 36, Pp. 40, and 43.

back that life - and that too for the highest price which is nothing other than His pleasure!

It is noteworthy that in this verse: the seller is the person - a servant of Allah ﷻ; the buyer is Allah ﷻ; the property being sold is the life of the individual; and the price of this transaction is the satisfaction of Allah ﷻ. In other verses of the Qur'ān, we see that Allah ﷻ has mentioned the price of such transactions as being eternal Paradise and salvation from the fire of Hell.

In any case, this verse shows us one of the greatest virtues of Imām ʿAlī (ع) recorded in the Noble Qur'ān - which a majority of the Islamic sources have mentioned.

Keys of Guidance

- The greatest benefit for a person lies in one selling the best commodity - which is one's own life; and that too to the best purchaser - who is Allah ﷻ; for the best price possible - which is the satisfaction of Allah ﷻ, not the benefits of Paradise, nor to be distanced from Hell, but only to gain the pleasure of Allah ﷻ.
- Accepting danger and maybe even a loss of life, and preparing one's self for this, as long as it is done for the sake of Allah ﷻ is the best action; and even if one is not martyred in the way of Allah ﷻ in such an action, the sheer fact that one is ready and willing to sacrifice one's own life for the greater good, and solely for His pleasure is sufficient to grant a person a lofty status.

Verse 208

يَـٰٓأَيُّهَا ٱلَّذِينَ ءَامَنُوا۟ ٱدْخُلُوا۟ فِى ٱلسِّلْمِ كَآفَّةً وَلَا تَتَّبِعُوا۟ خُطُوَٰتِ ٱلشَّيْطَـٰنِ ۚ
إِنَّهُۥ لَكُمْ عَدُوٌّ مُّبِينٌ ﴿٢٠٨﴾

O you who believe! Come in full submission to Allah, all of you, and do not follow in the footsteps of Satan, for indeed he is an open enemy to you.

There is a clear connection between this verse and the previous ones as Allah ﷻ provides us with two examples.

In the previous verses, Allah ﷻ brought forth the example of the hypocrites and explained to us their nature - those who are living as 'external Muslims' only. From there, in the previous verse, Allah ﷻ then went on to explain and provide us with the great example of the true believer - one who has completely submitted to Allah ﷻ.

In this verse, Allah ﷻ is inviting the believers to true faith which is complete submission.

It is important to note that the guidance of Allah ﷻ guidance is for all and every single human being has some level of submission to the truth. Therefore in this verse, Allah ﷻ is inviting the believers to the path of complete submission.

World Peace in the Shadow of True Faith

After referring to two distinct groups in the previous verses - the corrupt hypocrites and the pure believers - Allah ﷻ now addresses those who have faith and believe in Prophet Muḥammad ﷺ and says to them that they must all come to peace and reconciliation.

The two Arabic words *silm* and *salām* both come from the same root and mean 'peace and amity,' thus the meaning of this verse is that such peace and tranquility are possible only in light of the chosen faith which is Islam.

When we reflect on the various factors of human differences such as language, race, and other things, a strong link between the hearts of humanity is necessary, and that link can only be through true faith in Allah ﷻ which is something far above all incidental differences that humanity has.

Allah ﷻ then adds, telling the believers that they must not follow the footsteps of Shayṭān, the Devil, for he is an open and clear enemy to humanity.

The word used in this verse which has been translated as 'steps' *(khuṭuwāt)* is the plural of *khuṭwah* and it literally means 'a step or stride.' This reality is once again repeated here in that deviation from peace and justice, and surrendering to the motivations which lead to enmity, war, and bloodshed that have ravaged humanity from the start all began from simple events, will grow into something much more dangerous and lead to all-out wars of nations.

The phrase: '...for indeed he is an open enemy to you,' presents us with a living and clear argument which is that the Shayṭān's enmity with the humankind is nothing hidden - from the day when Prophet Ādam ﷺ was created, the back of Iblīs broke with the enmity that he had against the first human being. Therefore, with such an open and apparent enmity how is it possible for humans to succumb to his temptations?!

Keys of Guidance

- Allah ﷻ has invited both the hypocrites - as seen in the example which He gave, as well as the believers, and is addressing them, saying that it does not matter who the person is - they are invited to come *(udkhulu)* and enter into submission. He then emphasizes by saying 'all of you' - and here we see the depth of the hope and encouragement which only Allah ﷻ can provide to His creations.
- One of Shayṭān's main tactics to try and deviate us is where he starts by getting us to take small steps in sinning. When we walk down that path of 'minor sins' and they begin to become commonplace for us, and we are not concerned about our actions anymore, then gradually he introduces us to much more grievous sins. As we were already habituated to performing the minor sins, we eventually move into the major sins and end up in a critical situation. The sad irony of the situation is that the individual eventually has no idea about how they got to such a low place in one's life. This is the meaning of the 'footsteps' *(khuṭuwāt)* of Shayṭān.
- It is impossible to enter into an environment of peace, harmony, and reconciliation unless it is under the shadow of true faith in Allah ﷻ, and following the teachings of the Qur'ān.
- The temptations which Shayṭān has at his disposal should not force a person to sit idly, because we have the ability to oppose him and live a life of righteousness; and since human beings have been given free-will by Allah ﷻ, we are also commanded and guided to disobey

the insinuations of Shayṭān.

- Shayṭān, also known as Iblīs in the Qur'ān is the enemy of peace and unity, and all of the divisive voices which stem in the community and society are the mouthpieces of this Devil, and therefore the believers must always be vigilant and alert.

Verse 209

فَإِن زَلَلۡتُم مِّنۢ بَعۡدِ مَا جَآءَتۡكُمُ ٱلۡبَيِّنَٰتُ فَٱعۡلَمُوٓاْ أَنَّ ٱللَّهَ عَزِيزٌ حَكِيمٌ ٢٠٩

Then if you stumble and fall back after the clear proofs of the truth have come to you, then know that Allah is All-Glorious *('Azīz)*, All-Wise *(Ḥakīm)*.

In this verse, Allah ﷻ warns the believers that if they slip from the path of obedience after all of the clear signs have come to them from Allah ﷻ and they end up being misled, or try to be a continuous two-faced hypocrite, then they should know that no one can escape the Justice of Allah ﷻ as no one can break Him or deceive Him.

The plan is clear, the path is well-defined, and the destination is known, so there is no way that the believers should slip and accept the evil temptations which are all around!

If someone deviates, then they have no one to blame except for themselves, and everyone must realize that Allah ﷻ, the All-Mighty and All-Wise will deal with people accordingly and justly.

Keys of Guidance

- Once again in this verse, Allah ﷻ is trying to wake us up and give us another chance to change our ways - and this is seen through the usage of the command verb: 'know!' *(fa'lamu)*.
- Those who knowingly commit wrongdoings and do not ask Allah ﷻ for forgiveness, nor do they mend their ways are basically waiting

for the punishment of Allah ﷻ.

- The penalties which Allah ﷻ has in place for the sinners are not because of Him wanting to avenge or take revenge, but rather they are based on His Wisdom because He is All-Wise.

Verse 210

هَلۡ يَنظُرُونَ إِلَّآ أَن يَأۡتِيَهُمُ ٱللَّهُ فِي ظُلَلٖ مِّنَ ٱلۡغَمَامِ وَٱلۡمَلَٰٓئِكَةُ وَقُضِيَ ٱلۡأَمۡرُۚ وَإِلَى ٱللَّهِ تُرۡجَعُ ٱلۡأُمُورُ ٢١٠

Do they await anything but that (the command of) Allah should come to them in the shades of the clouds with the angels, and the matter be decided (once and for all)? And to Allah all matters are returned.

Although this verse seems to be a complex verse of the Qur'ān, however if we pay careful attention to the words used in it, we will be able to remove the ambiguity which may seem to be there.

In this verse, Allah ﷻ is directing His speech to Prophet Muḥammad ﷺ and says to him: Do they - meaning those who follow the whispers of Shayṭān, after all of the proofs and perfect programs for life as embodied in the Qur'ān have come to them, now expect that Allah ﷻ and the angels should come to them in the shadows of the clouds, and through this give them yet another reason for them to believe - as if everything else which they have seen is not enough!? Allah ﷻ confirms that if this is what they are waiting for, then they need to realize that such a thing is impossible, and the matter be settled.

What is the meaning of '...and the matter be settled?'

This is a reference to the descent of Divine punishment on the stubborn disbelievers, and we understand this to be the meaning because the apparent reading of this verse shows that it is related to the life of this world.

At the end of this verse, Allah ﷻ says that all things will return to

Allah ﷻ - as is understood from the belief in the Day of Judgment.

The matters concerning the sending of Prophets, revelation of the Scriptures, and explanation of the truths return to Allah ﷻ just like the matter of the reckoning, and rewards and punishments all return to Him as well.

Seeing Allah ﷻ

Of course, sensory observation occurs only in the case of objects which have a shape to them and occupy space. Therefore, it does not make sense to speak about 'seeing Allah ﷻ' as He is beyond time and space. His Pure Essence is not seen with the human eye - not in this world, nor in the hereafter, and the logical proofs which have been mentioned about this are so clear that it does not require any further explanation.

Of course, witnessing Allah ﷻ with the eyes of the heart is possible both in this world and the next, and certainly in the resurrection when His Pure Nature has a stronger manifestation, this observation will be even more intense.

In this regards, we have a famous *ḥadīth* from Imām ʿAlī ؑ when a Jewish scholar asked him: "Have you seen your Lord that you worship Him?"

Imām ʿAlī ؑ answered: "Woe be on you! I do not worship a Lord whom I have not seen."

The questioner asked: "How have you seen Him?"

Imām ʿAlī ؑ replied: "The human eye cannot (physically) see Allah, but one's heart can (spiritually) perceive Allah by real belief."[158]

Keys of Guidance

- Here, Allah ﷻ wants to invoke and awaken us one more time that we need to wake up as we have sufficient proofs which He has

---

[158] *Al-Kāfī*, Vol. 1, Pg. 98, Ḥadīth 6. The initial portion of this tradition is as follows:

جَاءَ حِبْرٌ إِلَىٰ أَمِيرِ الْمُؤْمِنِينَ صَلَوَاتُ اللهِ عَلَيْهِ فَقَالَ يَا أَمِيرَ الْمُؤْمِنِينَ هَلْ رَأَيْتَ رَبَّكَ حِينَ عَبَدْتَهُ...

provided to us. We need to stop making excuses for our disbelief and hypocrisy.

- Although Allah ﷻ can do anything He Wills, however we must realize that there are certain things which are not 'possible' - and one is to see Allah ﷻ with the physical eyes. There are times when people who do not want to believe in Allah ﷻ will make up any sort of excuse to get away from believing - such as asking the Prophet of their time to allow them to see God.
- The source and return of everything is to Allah ﷻ - why do people want to see Him when they can see His presence in themselves and in the world around them.

Verse 211

سَلْ بَنِيٓ إِسْرَٰٓءِيلَ كَمْ ءَاتَيْنَٰهُم مِّنْ ءَايَةٍۭ بَيِّنَةٍۗ وَمَن يُبَدِّلْ نِعْمَةَ ٱللَّهِ مِنۢ بَعْدِ مَا جَآءَتْهُ فَإِنَّ ٱللَّهَ شَدِيدُ ٱلْعِقَابِ ﴿٢١١﴾

(O Muḥammad ﷺ) Ask the Children of Isrāʾīl how many clear proofs We gave to them, and whoever tampers with Allah's blessing after it has come to them (should know that) surely Allah is severe in retribution.

This verse provides one of the clear instances about what was mentioned in the previous verses where we read about the three groups of people: the believers, the disbelievers, and the hypocrites. We reviewed some of the details about the disbelievers who stubbornly ignored the clear verses of the Qurʾān, and the obvious proofs which had been sent by Allah ﷻ, yet they used to make excuses for why they did not accept Prophet Muḥammad ﷺ. The Children of Isrāʾīl were one clear example of such individuals.

One of the reasons why Allah ﷻ repeatedly uses the example of the Children of Isrāʾīl is because they were a community who had received many blessings from Allah ﷻ. The historical evidence shows that a group from among them misused the gifts which Allah ﷻ provided for them, and they deviated. The nature of humankind is such that even when they are being bestowed with gifts, they gravitate toward ungratefulness; thus Allah ﷻ wants the Muslims to take examples from history - in this case from the Children of Isrāʾīl - so that they do not repeat those same mistakes.

Allah ﷻ ordered Prophet Muḥammad ﷺ to go to the Children of Isrāʾīl - the Jews who were living during his time - and ask them how many clear signs Allah ﷻ gave them? However, as we see throughout the Qurʾān and in the books of history, the Jews misused the blessings, and the material and spiritual favors which had been given to them by Allah ﷻ.

Allah ﷻ then adds the following - while still speaking to the Prophet ﷺ - that whoever transforms the blessings of Allah ﷻ after they have come to them - meaning that they use the blessings of Allah ﷻ in the wrong way - will be severely punished by Allah ﷻ as He is stern in retribution. The meaning of 'transforming the blessings' is when a person uses the material and spiritual resources at one's disposal in deviant and sinful ways, rather than in the ways that Allah ﷻ expects them to be used.

The matter of altering blessings and the painful outcome which this will lead to is not limited to something which only the Children of Isrāʾīl engaged in, rather even today the industrialized world is suffering from this tribulation. Allah ﷻ has provided countless blessings, and has given the today's society numerous capabilities which have are unprecedented. However, due to people distancing themselves from the teachings which the Prophets deputed by Allah ﷻ brought, they have transformed the blessings of Allah ﷻ and expended them in the course of annihilation and eradication of their own selves!

Humanity is misusing the blessings of Allah ﷻ, and instead is creating and actively making use of the most powerful weapons of mass destruction to destroy the world, and using their material power to spread their global domination, colonization, and exploitation of the people of the world in any way possible, and have made this world an unsafe place.[159]

Keys of Guidance

- It is important for Muslims to study history - not just "Islamic history" - but even the history of previous nations to learn lessons from their accomplishments and failures. In this regard, Allah ﷻ uses the word 'ask' *(sal)* as this is a method of getting a person to deeply reflect and ponder, so that one may wake up from one's spiritual negligence and really contemplate on things.
- The blessings which Allah ﷻ gives to humanity are not provided haphazardly, but they have a responsibility attached to them and if they are not used in the way which the Bestower expects, then there will be retribution - both in this world and the world to come.

---

[159] Global military expenditure increased 75% over the past 20 years, and as of 2009 stands at around $1.7 trillion annually; and the world's military arsenals are expected to double in size by 2030, compared to 2016.

The top five military spenders in 2018 were: United States of America, China, Saudi Arabia, India, and France, which together accounted for 60% of the global military spending.

By 2030, the countries with top defense spending are expected to be: United States of America with over 1 trillion, China with $736 billion, and India with $213 billion (previously $633.6 billion, $240 billion, and $66.6 billion respectively in 2018).

In regards to global imports in 2012-16, the Middle East accounted for 29%. Saudi Arabia was the world's second largest arms importer after India, with an increase of 212%; Qatar's imports grew 245%; and the majority of the other states in the region also increased arms imports in 2012-16 compared to 2007-11. Some Middle Eastern countries, including Egypt, Saudi Arabia, and the United Arab Emirates, are buying their weapons from different suppliers to diversify their dependence on other countries, especially the United States. (Extracted from the European Commission Website in the World Military Expenditure and Weapons Trade article found at: ec.europa.eu/knowledge4policy/foresight/topic/changing-security-paradigm/world-military-expenditure_en. (Last accessed on October 6, 2022)

Verse 212

زُيِّنَ لِلَّذِينَ كَفَرُواْ ٱلْحَيَوٰةُ ٱلدُّنْيَا وَيَسْخَرُونَ مِنَ ٱلَّذِينَ ءَامَنُواْ وَٱلَّذِينَ ٱتَّقَوْاْ فَوْقَهُمْ يَوْمَ ٱلْقِيَٰمَةِ ۗ وَٱللَّهُ يَرْزُقُ مَن يَشَآءُ بِغَيْرِ حِسَابٍ ﴿٢١٢﴾

The present, worldly life has been beautified for those who are ungrateful (for Allah's blessings), and they mock those who believe (because they do not attach much importance to this worldly life). But those who are God-conscious (those with *taqwā*) will be above them on the Day of Resurrection; and Allah provides to whomsoever He wills without measure.

History of Revelation

Ibn ʿAbbās, the famous commentator says: "This verse was revealed about the aristocratic minority and some leaders of the Quraysh who were very well-off, but they mocked a group of steadfast believers who were materially poor. These rich upper class people would say to the poor: 'If the [person whom you claim is the] Prophet of Islam had any character, and if he was truly sent by Allah, then the nobles and elders (of the Quraysh and other tribes) would have followed him.' It is because of this that the above verse was revealed, responding to their baseless claims."[160]

The Beautification of this Temporal World

The most effective way to influence a person is through changing their thought pattern and understanding. It is for this reason that today, billions of dollars are spent by companies to create awareness of their products - and a 30 second commercial on the American Super Bowl football game can cost upwards of $5 million! They have realized that the media is a powerful tool which can influence society to think differently, act in a specific way, and even alter their spending habits.

---

[160] *Majmaʿ al-Bayān*, Vol. 2, Pg. 62, under the commentary of this verse.

The same tactics are used by politicians and nation-states to promote their agendas, and try to influence public opinion. This is not only something which we see today in an era of mass media and communication, but even in the early periods of human history, there were always attempts to influence the minds of the masses.

However, what the consumer-driven society which is running rampant around the world today has put into place is nothing more than a pumped-up version of the tactics employed by Shayṭān - as Allah ﷻ clearly states in the Qur'ān in multiple instances, including in the verse under review.

Since the dawn of humanity, Shayṭān promised that he would do all that he can to divert this new creation (the human being) from the path of Allah ﷻ, and entice men and women to follow him and his deviant ways.

In order to succeed, Shayṭān needs to attract people to his path, and make them forget their perpetual life in the world to come. Shayṭān does this by keeping a person busy in the trivial pursuit of this temporal, worldly life. He uses the same blessings which Allah ﷻ has created that were meant to make life manageable here and which humanity is supposed to use to build a better world to come, and exploits those blessings for his own nefarious goals.

In effect, Shayṭān makes this world appear attractive, appealing, and something which must be coveted - as if it has intrinsic value to it. However, he knew that he would be able to misguide some of humanity, but that there would always be others who would not fall for his weak plots. Nonetheless, he does all that he can to corrupt humankind.

In explaining the plan of Shayṭān, the Qur'ān employs the term 'has been beautified' *(zuyyina)* which comes from the Arabic word *zayn* that means 'beauty, embellishment, or adornment.'

This phrase has been used numerous times in the Noble Qur'ān in various ways. Sometimes, it is used for material things, such as where Allah ﷻ says: "And, indeed, We have beautified the lowest heaven (the sky of the world) with lamps (stars), and made (out of) them missiles to drive away the devils..."[161]

It is also used for spiritual purposes, where Allah ﷻ says: "...but Allah has endeared to you the faith, and made it beautiful to your hearts, and He has made unbelief, transgression, and rebellion hateful to you..."[162]

Lastly, it is used when speaking about the thoughts and imagination of human beings where the Qur'ān states: "And Shayṭān made their (evil) deeds seem appealing to them..."[163]

Another term which is used in this verse under review that is often repeated in the Qur'ān is 'the life of this world' *(ḥayāt ad-dunyā).*

The word life *(ḥayāt)* is normally used as the opposite of death *(mamāt),* and the general definition of life is 'where a person has movement and the use of one's five senses, and is able to proceed in one's existence on Earth.'

Although Allah ﷻ is the **only** truly Living Being, He gives a portion of 'life' and 'existence' to His creations at various levels.

One example of 'life' mentioned in the Qur'ān is the plant kingdom, as Allah ﷻ says: "He brings forth the living out of the dead, and brings the dead out of the living, and revives the earth after its death..."[164]

The Qur'ān also speaks about the life which Allah ﷻ gave in a unique episode in the famous story of Prophet Ibrāhīm ؑ and his attempts to better understand with full certainty, the Power of Allah ﷻ to give life to the dead, where the Qur'ān says: "...He (Allah) said: 'Then take four

---

[161] Qur'ān, Sūrah al-Mulk (67), Verse 5:

وَلَقَدْ زَيَّنَّا ٱلسَّمَآءَ ٱلدُّنْيَا بِمَصَٰبِيحَ وَجَعَلْنَٰهَا رُجُومًا لِّلشَّيَٰطِينِ...

[162] Ibid., Sūrah al-Hujurāt (49), Verse 7:

...وَلَٰكِنَّ ٱللَّهَ حَبَّبَ إِلَيْكُمُ ٱلْإِيمَٰنَ وَزَيَّنَهُۥ فِى قُلُوبِكُمْ وَكَرَّهَ إِلَيْكُمُ ٱلْكُفْرَ وَٱلْفُسُوقَ وَٱلْعِصْيَانَ...

[163] Ibid., Sūrah al-Anfāl (8), Verse 48:

وَإِذْ زَيَّنَ لَهُمُ ٱلشَّيْطَٰنُ أَعْمَٰلَهُمْ...

[164] Ibid, Sūrah ar-Rum (30), Verse 19:

يُخْرِجُ ٱلْحَىَّ مِنَ ٱلْمَيِّتِ وَيُخْرِجُ ٱلْمَيِّتَ مِنَ ٱلْحَيِّ وَيُحْيِ ٱلْأَرْضَ بَعْدَ مَوْتِهَا...

birds (of different kinds), and tame them to yourself (to know them fully). Then (cut them into pieces and mix the pieces with each other and) put on every one of the hills a piece from them, then summon them, and they will come to you flying (being brought back to life and recreated)...'"[165]

Allah ﷻ also provides life to human beings as He notes in the Qur'ān: "And it is He Who has given you life, then He causes you to die, then He will bring you to life again. However, humankind is ever ungrateful."[166]

In addition, the Qur'ān speaks about a spiritual life which some people have based on their righteous actions in the life of this world: "Whoever does good, righteous deeds, whether male or female, and is a believer, most certainly We will make him (or her) live a good life..."[167]

Lastly, Allah ﷻ gives us a final indication that there is a life which He bestowed upon people in the world to come where He states: "And this present, worldly life is nothing but a pastime and play, but indeed the abode of the hereafter is the (eternal) life, if they only knew."[168]

Going back to the verse under discussion, the meaning of life is this worldly life, and the relative worth and importance that it has as it relates to this temporal life.

However, the warning which is implied in this verse is that Shayṭān will try his best to twist the blessings which Allah ﷻ has provided to humanity that are meant to get closer to Him and pave the roads to prosperity in the world to come, by trying to negatively influence and

---

[165] Qur'ān, Sūrah al-Baqarah (2), Verse 260:

...قَالَ فَخُذْ أَرْبَعَةً مِّنَ ٱلطَّيْرِ فَصُرْهُنَّ إِلَيْكَ ثُمَّ ٱجْعَلْ عَلَىٰ كُلِّ جَبَلٍ مِّنْهُنَّ جُزْءًا ثُمَّ ٱدْعُهُنَّ يَأْتِينَكَ سَعْيًا ۚ وَٱعْلَمْ أَنَّ ٱللَّهَ عَزِيزٌ حَكِيمٌ ﴿٢٦٠﴾

[166] Ibid., Sūrah al-Ḥajj (22), Verse 66:

وَهُوَ ٱلَّذِىٓ أَحْيَاكُمْ ثُمَّ يُمِيتُكُمْ ثُمَّ يُحْيِيكُمْ ۗ إِنَّ ٱلْإِنسَٰنَ لَكَفُورٌ ﴿٦٦﴾

[167] Ibid., Sūrah an-Naḥl (16), Verse 97:

مَنْ عَمِلَ صَٰلِحًا مِّن ذَكَرٍ أَوْ أُنثَىٰ وَهُوَ مُؤْمِنٌ فَلَنُحْيِيَنَّهُۥ حَيَوٰةً طَيِّبَةً...

[168] Ibid, Sūrah al-ʿAnkabut (29), Verse 64:

وَمَا هَٰذِهِ ٱلْحَيَوٰةُ ٱلدُّنْيَآ إِلَّا لَهْوٌ وَلَعِبٌ ۚ وَإِنَّ ٱلدَّارَ ٱلْءَاخِرَةَ لَهِىَ ٱلْحَيَوَانُ ۚ لَوْ كَانُوا۟ يَعْلَمُونَ ﴿٦٤﴾

deceive humankind. His goal is to use the same material blessings which Allah ﷻ has given, but he will try to keep people so busy with their pursuit of the life of this world, that it will take them away from the true purpose of everything which Allah ﷻ has created in this world and its real usage.

Rather than people seeing wealth as a way to feed the needy and shelter the homeless, Shayṭān will make wealth seem appealing to us such that we use it to purchase expensive mansions; eat lavish meals and spend at high-end restaurants; buy the latest cars; purchase high-ticketed clothing and accessories, etc. The goal of Shayṭān will be to engage in this form of mental machinations with people to get them to see the blessings of Allah ﷻ in the light of how they can benefit from them in this life, instead of how humanity can use His gifts to create a more enjoyable life in the hereafter.

In essence, rather than becoming servants of the One who created everything (Allah ﷻ), Shayṭān wants us to become a servant of the things which Allah created. Therefore, the important phrase which the Qur'ān uses in this verse, and in many other places about the 'life of this world'[169] is something that we must be aware of and actively ensure that we are not pursuing.

Therefore, once again, Allah ﷻ draws our attention to the fact that we must be cautious of Shayṭān and be aware of our surroundings. It cannot be said that Allah ﷻ created us, then just left us to the evil whisperings of Shayṭān. No! He has not only told us that Shayṭān is our clear and open enemy, but at the same time, He has also pointed us to his sinister tactics.

What has clearly been condemned in the teachings of Islam is when a person attaches oneself to the temporal, illusory aspects of this world and all that is within it - regarding it as being the goal of life, rather than a means to the goal - which is to reach Allah ﷻ. Otherwise, we know that everything on earth has been created by Allah ﷻ for humanity to use - the land, water, food, animals, minerals, natural resources, etc. - are

[169] This phrase is mentioned in the Qur'ān in the following instances: 2:86, 2:212, 6:32, 10:24, 11:15, 13:26, 20:131, 28:60, 31:33, 40:39, 42:36, 43:35, 45:35, 46:20, 53:29, 87:16-17.

all signs of Allah ﷻ and among His abundant blessings for humankind, and He has made them beautiful and beneficial, as He mentions in the Qur'ān: "It is He who created for you all that which is on the earth..."[170]

Our responsibility is to recognize the benefactor of all goodness, namely Allah ﷻ, and ensure that we use whatever He gives us from this world in the right ways to get closer to Him in this world, and to attain the goal of a high status in the world to come.

We must try our best to ensure that we do not fall prey to Shayṭān and his demonic tricks in which he will do everything that he can to beautify the life of this temporal realm, making us think that this world is the end all and be all.

Once we can recognize that wealth, children, power, status, etc. are all from Allah ﷻ and that just as easily as He can provide them, He can also take them away; and that when He gives anything to us, He expects us to use those things in the appropriate ways, we will be on the path to living 'the pure life' that He wants us to live.

Commentary

Although this verse has a direct history of revelation relating to a specific incident which occurred during the time of Prophet Muḥammad ﷺ, this does not prevent us from extracting a universal rule, or to consider that this verse actually compliments the previous verse which was about the Jewish community at the time of Prophet Muḥammad ﷺ.

Thus, this verse tells us that the life of this transient world has been made appealing to the disbelievers, and due to their pride and arrogance they mock the believers; but on the Day of Judgment, the righteous will be above them and will have the upper hand.

The reason for the believers to have the upper hand is because on the plains of Resurrection the truth will be made manifest for everyone to see and it will take on its true form, and as such the believers are the ones who will be in the highest ranks - even though in this temporal

---

[170] Qur'ān, Sūrah al-Baqarah (2), Verse 29:

هُوَ ٱلَّذِى خَلَقَ لَكُم مَّا فِى ٱلْأَرْضِ جَمِيعًا...

world they may have been looked down upon as being low and despised. This verse ends by stating that Allah ﷻ gives to whomsoever He wants without any measure or limit.

These are in fact good tidings and words of comfort for the destitute believers - that even though today they sometimes suffer silently - this verse is a stern warning to the arrogant, unbelieving, rich, stuck-up people who trample upon the rights of the subjugated.

The granting of unlimited provisions by Allah ﷻ to the people of true faith means that the actions of goodness which the believers perform can never reach to the intensity of His immense rewards. Rather, the gifts of Allah ﷻ are actually in accordance with His Grace *(Luṭf)*, and we know that His Grace and Mercy have no limits.

Keys of Guidance

- Allah uses the term 'above their heads' *(fawqahum)* as a reference to God-consciousness *(taqwā)*. What we are required to understand from this term is that this spiritual state must act like a shade above our heads, providing us with continuous guidance. God-consciousness must become an active and integral part of the mindset of a believer, as they live their lives knowing that there is a Day of Accountability that shadows over them, providing them with comfort and ease.

- By the Qur'ān using the term 'those who are ungrateful' *(kafarū)*, it is not speaking about a non-believer who is normally identified as a *kāfir* in the traditional understanding as may be in the minds of some people. Rather, in this instance, the verb is pointing to those who engage in *kufrān an-neʿmah* - 'denying or rejecting the blessings of Allah ﷻ' even after all of the proofs of His existence and His blessings have been made evident to them.

- To camouflage or obscure the blessings which Allah ﷻ has given to a person, or be ungrateful for His gifts will lead a person to disbelieve in Him. When it comes to the glitter of the life of this temporal world, those who do not believe in Allah ﷻ will be attracted and allured by it because they do not accept the life of the next world with its never-ending bounties; however in the eyes of the true believers, the allure of this temporal world is trivial.

- It is through the systems of materialism and secularism that causes people to humiliate and ridicule others; for a true believer in Allah ﷻ will never make fun of those who are not as well off as Allah ﷻ has allowed them to be - rather they will try and do their best to help the less fortunate in society however they can.
- When Allah ﷻ speaks about giving to some people 'without measure' - this is a sign of His Grace - it does not mean that Allah ﷻ cannot account for it, or that He does not give to people based on His Infinite Wisdom - even His 'unlimited gifts' are based on wisdom *(ḥikmah).*

Verse 213

كَانَ ٱلنَّاسُ أُمَّةً وَٰحِدَةً فَبَعَثَ ٱللَّهُ ٱلنَّبِيِّـۧنَ مُبَشِّرِينَ وَمُنذِرِينَ وَأَنزَلَ
مَعَهُمُ ٱلْكِتَٰبَ بِٱلْحَقِّ لِيَحْكُمَ بَيْنَ ٱلنَّاسِ فِيمَا ٱخْتَلَفُواْ فِيهِ ۚ وَمَا
ٱخْتَلَفَ فِيهِ إِلَّا ٱلَّذِينَ أُوتُوهُ مِنۢ بَعْدِ مَا جَآءَتْهُمُ ٱلْبَيِّنَٰتُ بَغْيًۢا بَيْنَهُمْ ۖ
فَهَدَى ٱللَّهُ ٱلَّذِينَ ءَامَنُواْ لِمَا ٱخْتَلَفُواْ فِيهِ مِنَ ٱلْحَقِّ بِإِذْنِهِۦ ۗ وَٱللَّهُ يَهْدِى
مَن يَشَآءُ إِلَىٰ صِرَٰطٍ مُّسْتَقِيمٍ ﴿٢١٣﴾

Humankind was (in the beginning) one community (following one way of life), Allah sent Prophets as bearers of glad tidings and warners, and He sent down with them (the Prophets) the Book with the truth so that it might judge between the people concerning that which they were differing; and only those who were given it differed concerning it, after the most manifest truths came to them, because of envious rivalry and insolence among themselves. Allah has guided by His permission those who have believed (in the Book and the Prophets, and those who now believe in the Qur'ān and

Prophet Muḥammad ﷺ) to the truth about that on which they were differing; and Allah guides whomsoever He Wills to the Straight Path.

After articulating the status of the true believers, hypocrites, and non-believers in the previous verses, at this point a fundamental and comprehensive discussion about the origin of religion, the different stages of its evolution based on human needs, and the goals which it sought to establish is covered by Allah ﷻ.

1. **One Nation with Basic Needs and Requirements:** The Almighty begins by saying that in the beginning of life on Earth, people were one community and Allah ﷻ created us with innate nature *(fitrah)* along with our desires. We know the nature of these two is that there are clashes between them. Although there were disagreements, it was not like today where we have more areas that conflict can arise in between us because human life and society which developed with the first few generations of human beings on Earth was simple.
2. **Societal Evolution and Communal Advancement:** As the population steadily increased, human life and the societies which they were living in began to evolve, and they started to take on a more distinct social configuration. Since the human being was created for societal evolution, this development and communal advancement could only take place in the nucleus of a vibrant society, and this marked the second stage of human life.
3. **The Beginnings of Religious Guidance:** However, at the time of the emergence of this maturing society, differences and conflicts began to rise within the population, both in terms of theoretical differences in areas of faith and belief, and also at a practical level in terms of working around one another, and the determination of rights and freedoms of everyone and of each distinct group within their developing societies. It was at this point in human development that humanity yearned for laws and teachings to come from Allah ﷻ which would take shape through the deputing

of His chosen Prophets that would provide a code of conduct and Divine guidance to aide in the progression of people, and put an end to the diverse disagreements that were emerging in the various aspects of their lives, and this marked the third stage of human life and development.

4. **The Need for Divine Laws and Ordinances:** Meanwhile as it states in the Noble Qurʾān, it was at this point that Allah appointed Prophets with two main responsibilities:

    1) to act as *mubashshirīn* - bearers of glad tidings of prosperity in return for faith and righteousness.

    2) to be *mundhirīn* - warn people about the consequences of straying away from the teachings that Allah was sending to deal with the differences which people were having with one another, and any transgressions they were engaged in against one another; and this was the fourth stage of their societal progress and advancement.

5. **Laying Down the Divine Laws through Prophets:** Moving on, with people going into conflict and Allah responding to their need for order in society, the Almighty sent them Prophets, and these men of Allah reminded the people about their origin and how they have all come from One Source - Allah - and that their end and eventual resurrection will bring everyone back to the presence of Allah. People are reminded that in the next world, they will find the rewards and punishments of their deeds, and by providing such basic guidance to people, they were now equipped to accept the rules and regulations from Allah.

    Therefore, at this juncture Allah says that along with sending Prophets, He also sent with them a Book of Divine teachings and laws which calls to the truth *(ḥaqq),* to be used to mediate among the people in whatever they may differ about. Thus, believing in the Prophets sent by Allah, adhering to their teachings and the Scriptures which Allah provided to humanity through the Prophets, allows for the proverbial fires of conflict to be extinguished; and this marks the fifth stage of human development.

6. **An Intense Need for Further Divinely-Sent Guidance:** This

gradual development, coupled with tranquility which the Prophets and the teachings brought to human society continued for some time, however little by little, the evil temptations and roaring waves of self-interest and ego began to penetrate the people. Therefore, the verse under review goes on to state that people of true faith - those who had disagreements, however through Allah sending Prophets and providing them with a Book of guidance - these true believers did not disagree anymore, nor did they have arguments with one another because they fully submitted to the guidance. It was only those people in society who received the Book and clear signs, but due to their deviation from the truth - let their self-interest and egos get the best of them - and this led them to revert to their old ways of arguments amongst one another, and thus they engaged in oppression and aggression against each other - the same thing which the Prophets, Messengers, and Books were sent to resolve; and this heralded in the sixth stage of human development on Earth.

7. **The Need to Mediate between Truth and Falsehood:** At this point we see that humanity divided into two groups: the first one were the true believers who fully submitted to the truth, and who constantly referred to the Divinely-sent Scriptures and teachings of the Prophets which Allah sent to them when any new differences arose to bring about a peaceful resolution. They regularly returned to the right path for guidance, and this is what Allah alludes to in the next portion of this verse in which He says that in this way, through providing this continuous stream of direction, Allah guided those who believed in the truth about what was disputed, by His command.

   However, there was still a second group of people, who although they too had received the same Book and the same Prophets from Allah, however for their own personal reasons they did not use the Divinely-sent guidance to bring them back on track. The Qur'ān confirms that this group of disbelievers who refused to submit to the teachings of Allah, and let their pride and arrogance reign supreme, remained in error and dissension; and this marks the seventh stage of the natural progression of humanity.

At the end of this verse, the Noble Qur'ān states that it is Allah ﷻ alone who guides whomsoever He wills to the Straight Path. This portion of the verse points out that Divine guidance, the Will of Allah ﷻ coupled with His Wisdom *(Ḥikmah)* is necessary and is free from any form of prejudice; and that all people who have pure intentions and the spirit of submission to the truth within them are included in His guidance.

Keys of Guidance

- Secular, human-made laws are not able to resolve disputes because every individual and group will always pursue their own desires and wants. For this reason, disputes which arise in society must be resolved through Divine law, and the Immaculate judgment of the Prophets عليهم السلام which Allah ﷻ has sent for the guidance of humanity. A law that is free from distortion and error, and an immaculate judge who does not follow the resolved desires of one's soul is what is needed for true peace on Earth.
- One of the goals of all of the Prophets عليهم السلام which Allah ﷻ sent for the guidance of humanity was to remove all forms of disunity and animosity through their impartial mediation.
- There will always be differences of opinion among the believers, and it is through the light of the guardianship of Allah ﷻ and the teachings which He provides to His representatives on Earth - the Prophets عليهم السلام, Messengers عليهم السلام, and Imāms عليهم السلام - that people are able to bring about peace and reconciliation.

Verse 214

أَمْ حَسِبْتُمْ أَن تَدْخُلُوا۟ ٱلْجَنَّةَ وَلَمَّا يَأْتِكُم مَّثَلُ ٱلَّذِينَ خَلَوْا۟ مِن قَبْلِكُم ۖ
مَّسَّتْهُمُ ٱلْبَأْسَآءُ وَٱلضَّرَّآءُ وَزُلْزِلُوا۟ حَتَّىٰ يَقُولَ ٱلرَّسُولُ وَٱلَّذِينَ ءَامَنُوا۟ مَعَهُۥ
مَتَىٰ نَصْرُ ٱللَّهِ ۗ أَلَآ إِنَّ نَصْرَ ٱللَّهِ قَرِيبٌ ﴿٢١٤﴾

(Given the history of humankind in this world) Do you think that you (the Muslims) will enter Paradise while there has not yet come upon you the like of what came upon those who passed away before you? They were visited by such adversities and hardships and were so shaken (by various life events) such that the Messenger and those who believed in him nearly cried out: "When will the assistance of Allah come?" Be aware, the help of Allah is surely near!

History of Revelation

Some commentators of the Noble Qur'ān state that in the Battle of the Confederates *(al-Aḥzāb)* when fear overcame the Muslims and they were being besieged, this verse was revealed inviting them to patience *(ṣabr)* and perseverance *(istiqāmah),* with the promise of Divine assistance and victory for them.

Commentary

From this verse, we can conclude that some believers thought that the main basis to enter Paradise was merely through expressing faith in Allah ﷻ without putting forth any efforts in this life. However, the Qur'ān speaks out against this misconception and asks the believers that do they really think that they can simply enter Paradise without having to go through any trials like those which happened with the people of the past?

Allah ﷻ reminds the believers that the people of the past were afflicted with so many troubles and sorrows, and they became upset that Prophet Muḥammad ﷺ and those who believed with him would say: So when will the help of Allah come?

Of course, neither Prophet Muḥammad ﷺ, nor his followers would have ever uttered such a statement in a voice of complaint to Allah ﷻ, rather they stated this as a request and anticipation from Allah ﷻ; and as they exercised their utmost perseverance in the face of the difficult events and resorted to Divine benevolence, they were told to be ready because the help of Allah ﷻ was approaching!

In fact, this verse refers to one of the Divine tradition *(Sunnatullāh)* which exists at all times and is applicable to all nations, and cautions the believers to remember that if they wish to be successful and achieve the blessings of Paradise, then they must face difficulties and sacrifices in this life because it is through such tests that will allow them to develop and progress in their submission to Allah ﷻ.

Keys of Guidance

- Those believers who are wanting to go to heaven, but think that just because they have faith they will not go through suffering or be tested in various aspects of their lives are very much mistaken because the Divine tradition *(Sunnatullāh)* as described in various places of the Qur'ān mentions that a person cannot claim to be a believer and not go through challenges in life.
- We must always be prepared in life to face whatever comes our way - the Divine tests can be to such a level that they may even astonish and make the Prophets ؑ anxious.
- When it comes to hardships, the Prophets ؑ, and in general even leaders of a society should never be separate from the believers. Human beings are all being tested by Allah ﷻ at different levels and for different purposes, and this includes the Prophets ؑ, the Messengers ؑ, and the 12 Imāms ؑ which Allah ﷻ deputed - everyone must face hardships in the life of this temporal world.

Verse 215

يَسْـَٔلُونَكَ مَاذَا يُنفِقُونَ ۖ قُلْ مَآ أَنفَقْتُم مِّنْ خَيْرٍ فَلِلْوَٰلِدَيْنِ وَٱلْأَقْرَبِينَ
وَٱلْيَتَـٰمَىٰ وَٱلْمَسَـٰكِينِ وَٱبْنِ ٱلسَّبِيلِ ۗ وَمَا تَفْعَلُوا۟ مِنْ خَيْرٍ فَإِنَّ ٱللَّهَ بِهِۦ
عَلِيمٌ ﴿٢١٥﴾

They ask you (O Muḥammad ﷺ) what they should spend (in

charity). Say (to the believers): "Whatever you spend on goodness (your wealth) is for (your) parents and the near relatives, and the (needy) orphans, the destitute, and the wayfarer. And whatever good you do, surely Allah has full knowledge of it *('Alīm).*"

History of Revelation

ʿAmrū ibn Jamūḥ was an extremely affluent old man who once asked Prophet Muḥammad ﷺ: "From what (of my wealth) should I give alms *(ṣadaqah)* and to whom should I give it to?" This verse was revealed to provide him with the answer that he was looking for.[171]

The Reality of Infāq

The source of *infāq (na-fa-qa)* comes from an Arabic word which means: 'reduction, doing away with, spending, hiding something, or covering something.' It is from this same root that we get the word *munāfiq* - hypocrite - as they are known 'to cover over their true nature of disbelief under the guise of faith *(īmān).*'

Practicing *infāq* is one of the most important ethical qualities in Islam which has been mentioned repeatedly in the Qur'ān and the *ḥadīth.*

From the technical point of view as it relates to the verse under review, *infāq* refers 'to giving one's wealth or anything which a person has - such as one's time, talents, and abilities - in the service of Allah ﷻ to be used for those people who are in need, for the betterment of society, or toward the promotion and advancement of the faith of Islam.'

The Qur'ān uses the word *infāq* and its derivatives over 70 times in various ways. Sometimes it is used in a general meaning such as 'to give or assist others,' while at other times, it is used for specific instances, such as in the following examples:

1. Giving *ṣadaqah.*
2. Giving *zakāh.*
3. Gifting things to others.
4. Struggling *(jihād)* with one's wealth.

[171] *Majmaʿ al-Bayān,* Vol. 1, Pg. 309, under the commentary of this verse.

5. Offering an interest-free loan *(qarḍ al-ḥasana)* to Allah ﷻ - but in actuality, it refers to giving assistance to needy believers.
6. Giving food to those who are in need.
7. Giving one's wealth - generally speaking - not a specific amount or under a 'defined cause.'
8. Paying a penalty *(kaffārah)* for breaking a religious law.

Engaging in *infāq* in the way of Allah ﷻ has numerous benefits and is not limited to merely alleviating the needs of an individual who is being helped, nor does it only help the society through lifting people out of the dire straits they find themselves in. Rather, the rewards of *infāq* are both material and spiritual; they affect the life of this temporal world, and its benefits will extend into the world to come as well - especially for the individual who is practicing *infāq* by following all of its conditions.

In order to better understand *infāq* and its various dimensions so that we can fully benefit from it, we present the following review of some important aspects of this unique opportunity which Allah ﷻ has given us to be conduits of care and concern.

The Benefits of Infāq

As with all obligations *(wājibāt)* and recommendations *(mustaḥabbāt)* in Islam, there are worldly and other-worldly benefits attached to them.

The Qur'ān and *ḥadīth* point to some of them, however there are definitely many others which are simply not conveyed to us. In any case, when Allah ﷻ encourages us to do something or refrain from something, there is a reason for it - and the most important reason is that we are the servants and He is the Master, so He has a right to legislate laws for us to follow.

The following are some of the benefits of *infāq* as enumerated in the verses of the Noble Qur'ān:

1. **Spiritual Purification of the Soul:** When carried out correctly, *infāq* can cleanse the soul of an individual from the build-up of sins which carry a negative effect upon a person, such as excessive love for this temporal world, materialism, and miserliness. For example, the Qur'ān says: "(O Muḥammad) Take alms (prescribed or voluntary) from their wealth so that you may thereby purify

them, and cause them to grow (in purity and sincerity), and pray for them. Indeed your prayer is a source of comfort for them; and Allah is All-Hearing, All-Knowing."[172]

2. **Spiritual Tranquility:** Another benefit of *infāq* is that its by-product is spiritual comfort, meaning that there will be no fear or grief for the individual in this world and the next, as Allah ﷻ tells us in the Qur'ān: "Those who spend their wealth (in Allah's way) by night and by day, secretly and in public, their reward is with their Lord; and no fear will there be concerning them, nor will they grieve."[173]
3. **Replenishment and Increase in Wealth:** Contrary to popular belief, when a person 'gives' in charity, they are not reducing their net-worth, rather through Divine Blessings, they are actually adding to it. In this regard, Allah ﷻ makes a promise in the Qur'ān when He tells Prophet Muḥammad ﷺ to tell his community the following: "Say: 'Surely my Lord extends provision for whom He wills of His servants, and restricts it (for whom He wills). But whatever you spend (in the way of Allah ﷻ), He will compensate for it; and He is the Best Provider *(Khayr ar-Rāziqīn)*."[174]
4. **Increased Proximity to Allah ﷻ:** Spending on others - and in general, any act of *infāq* in His way, permits an individual to get spiritually-closer to Allah ﷻ, as mentioned in the Qur'ān: "And from

[172] Qur'ān, Sūrah at-Tawbah (9), Verse 103:

خُذْ مِنْ أَمْوَٰلِهِمْ صَدَقَةً تُطَهِّرُهُمْ وَتُزَكِّيهِم بِهَا وَصَلِّ عَلَيْهِمْ إِنَّ صَلَوٰتَكَ سَكَنٌ لَّهُمْ وَٱللَّهُ سَمِيعٌ عَلِيمٌ ﴿١٠٣﴾

[173] Ibid., Sūrah al-Baqarah (2), Verse 274:

ٱلَّذِينَ يُنفِقُونَ أَمْوَٰلَهُم بِٱلَّيْلِ وَٱلنَّهَارِ سِرًّا وَعَلَانِيَةً فَلَهُمْ أَجْرُهُمْ عِندَ رَبِّهِمْ وَلَا خَوْفٌ عَلَيْهِمْ وَلَا هُمْ يَحْزَنُونَ ﴿٢٧٤﴾

[174] Ibid., Sūrah Saba (34), Verse 39:

قُلْ إِنَّ رَبِّي يَبْسُطُ ٱلرِّزْقَ لِمَن يَشَآءُ مِنْ عِبَادِهِۦ وَيَقْدِرُ لَهُۥ وَمَآ أَنفَقْتُم مِّن شَيْءٍ فَهُوَ يُخْلِفُهُۥ وَهُوَ خَيْرُ ٱلرَّٰزِقِينَ ﴿٣٩﴾

among the bedouin Arabs there are some who believe in Allah and the Last Day, and consider what they spend as a means of drawing closer to Allah, and of the Messenger's praying (to Allah for them). Indeed, it is a means of nearness for them (to Allah). Allah will admit them into His Mercy. Surely, Allah is All-Forgiving *(Ghafūr)*, All-Merciful *(Raḥīm)*."[175]

5. **Safety and Stability of Society:** An important social outcome of *infāq* lies in the fact that it significantly contributes to the safety and stability of society as is alluded to in the Qur'ān: "So spend in the way of Allah (out of whatever you have) and do not ruin (yourselves) by your own hands (by refraining from spending). And do good; surely Allah loves those who are devoted to doing good."[176]
6. In regards to the meaning of this verse, the commentators of the Qur'ān have noted that by not spending on others and helping out the less fortunate in society, weakens the Muslim community - ultimately exhausting the entire society, and potentially causing instability in the region.
7. **Special Mercy and Forgiveness from Allah ﷻ:** Engaging in *infāq* in the way of Allah ﷻ is one of those actions which attracts the special Mercy of Allah ﷻ, as well as the forgiveness of one's sins, as Allah ﷻ told the Children of Isrā'īl, and as an extension all true believers that: "And indeed, Allah took a solemn pledge from the Children of Isrā'īl and raised up from among them 12 leaders (and representatives). And Allah said: 'Surely I am with you if you establish the prayer, and pay the alms, and believe in

---

[175] Qur'ān, Sūrah at-Tawbah (9), Verse 99:

وَمِنَ ٱلْأَعْرَابِ مَن يُؤْمِنُ بِٱللَّهِ وَٱلْيَوْمِ ٱلْآخِرِ وَيَتَّخِذُ مَا يُنفِقُ قُرُبَٰتٍ عِندَ ٱللَّهِ وَصَلَوَٰتِ ٱلرَّسُولِ ۚ أَلَآ إِنَّهَا قُرْبَةٌ لَّهُمْ ۚ سَيُدْخِلُهُمُ ٱللَّهُ فِى رَحْمَتِهِۦٓ ۗ إِنَّ ٱللَّهَ غَفُورٌ رَّحِيمٌ ﴿٩٩﴾

[176] Ibid., Sūrah al-Baqarah (2), Verse 195:

وَأَنفِقُوا۟ فِى سَبِيلِ ٱللَّهِ وَلَا تُلْقُوا۟ بِأَيْدِيكُمْ إِلَى ٱلتَّهْلُكَةِ ۛ وَأَحْسِنُوٓا۟ ۛ إِنَّ ٱللَّهَ يُحِبُّ ٱلْمُحْسِنِينَ ﴿١٩٥﴾

(all of) My Messengers, and honor and support them, and lend Allah a good loan (by spending out of your wealth in the way of Allah), I will surely remove from you your evil deeds, and admit you into gardens beneath which rivers flow. But whoever among you disbelieves after that and is ungrateful has surely strayed from the right, even way."[177]

8. **Great Reward in the World to Come and a Good Outcome:** Engaging in *infāq* - whether through one's wealth, talents, abilities, or any other thing which a person can help others with - regardless of the amount - is never hidden from Allah ﷻ. As Muslims, we believe that the true rewards will be waiting for the individual to collect in the next life as the Qur'ān validates: "Nor do they spend any amount (for the sake of Allah), small or big, nor do they cross a valley (while traveling in the cause of Allah), but it is recorded for them (in their account) so that Allah may reward them for the best of what they were doing."[178]

The Conditions for the Acceptance of Infāq

Although there are specific conditions which govern each form of obligatory *infāq* such as *khums*, *kaffārah*, etc., however there are also some general guidelines which must be followed in order to fully benefit from the rewards of charity:

1. ***Islam and Īmān***: An individual must have complete faith in Allah

---

[177] Qur'ān, Sūrah al-Mā'idah (5), Verse 12:

وَلَقَدْ أَخَذَ ٱللَّهُ مِيثَٰقَ بَنِىٓ إِسْرَٰٓءِيلَ وَبَعَثْنَا مِنْهُمُ ٱثْنَىْ عَشَرَ نَقِيبًا ۖ وَقَالَ ٱللَّهُ إِنِّى مَعَكُمْ ۖ
لَئِنْ أَقَمْتُمُ ٱلصَّلَوٰةَ وَءَاتَيْتُمُ ٱلزَّكَوٰةَ وَءَامَنتُم بِرُسُلِى وَعَزَّرْتُمُوهُمْ وَأَقْرَضْتُمُ ٱللَّهَ قَرْضًا حَسَنًا
لَّأُكَفِّرَنَّ عَنكُمْ سَيِّـَٔاتِكُمْ وَلَأُدْخِلَنَّكُمْ جَنَّٰتٍ تَجْرِى مِن تَحْتِهَا ٱلْأَنْهَٰرُ ۚ فَمَن كَفَرَ
بَعْدَ ذَٰلِكَ مِنكُمْ فَقَدْ ضَلَّ سَوَآءَ ٱلسَّبِيلِ ﴿١٢﴾

[178] Ibid., Sūrah at-Tawbah (9), Verse 121:

وَلَا يُنفِقُونَ نَفَقَةً صَغِيرَةً وَلَا كَبِيرَةً وَلَا يَقْطَعُونَ وَادِيًا إِلَّا كُتِبَ لَهُمْ لِيَجْزِيَهُمُ ٱللَّهُ أَحْسَنَ
مَا كَانُوا۟ يَعْمَلُونَ ﴿١٢١﴾

ﷻ and the teachings of the faith - most importantly, belief in and follow the teachings of the representatives of Allah ﷻ available to them. In our era, this is none other than Prophet Muḥammad ﷺ and his 12 successors - the Imāms of the Ahlul Bayt ﷺ. In this regard, the Qur'ān states: "Believe in Allah and His Messenger, and spend (in the way of Allah ﷻ) out of all that He has entrusted to you - those among you who believe and spend, for them there is a great reward."[179]

2. Those who are identified as hypocrites and non-believers who openly reject the One True God will be deprived of the benefits of *infāq*, as the Qur'ān states: "Say: 'Whether you give willingly or unwillingly, (pretending that you give in the cause of Allah ﷻ), never will it be accepted (by Allah ﷻ) from you. Surely, you are a transgressing people. And nothing hinders their offerings being accepted from them except that they disbelieve in Allah and His Messenger, and whenever they come to the prayer they do so with reluctance, and they do not offer contributions except unwillingly (to do so).'"[180]
3. **Intention of Seeking Proximity to Allah ﷻ:** It is not enough to only engage in *infāq* - rather, it must be done with the intention of seeking the pleasure of Allah ﷻ and wanting to attain proximity to Him through the performance of those actions which He has guided the believers toward, as the Qur'ān says: "...whereas whatever you give in charity seeking the approval and good pleasure of Allah *(Wajhullāh)* - for those there will be increase (of recompense)

---

[179] Qur'ān, Sūrah al-Ḥadīd (57), Verse 7:

ءَامِنُواْ بِٱللَّهِ وَرَسُولِهِۦ وَأَنفِقُواْ مِمَّا جَعَلَكُم مُّسۡتَخۡلَفِينَ فِيهِۖ فَٱلَّذِينَ ءَامَنُواْ مِنكُمۡ وَأَنفَقُواْ
لَهُمۡ أَجۡرٞ كَبِيرٞ ٧

[180] Ibid., Sūrah at-Tawbah (9), Verses 53-54:

قُلۡ أَنفِقُواْ طَوۡعًا أَوۡ كَرۡهٗا لَّن يُتَقَبَّلَ مِنكُمۡ إِنَّكُمۡ كُنتُمۡ قَوۡمٗا فَٰسِقِينَ٥٣وَمَا مَنَعَهُمۡ أَن
تُقۡبَلَ مِنۡهُمۡ نَفَقَٰتُهُمۡ إِلَّآ أَنَّهُمۡ كَفَرُواْ بِٱللَّهِ وَبِرَسُولِهِۦ وَلَا يَأۡتُونَ ٱلصَّلَوٰةَ إِلَّا وَهُمۡ كُسَالَىٰ
وَلَا يُنفِقُونَ إِلَّا وَهُمۡ كَٰرِهُونَ ٥٤

multiplied."[181]

4. **Not Placing an Obligation upon the Recipient:** Another extremely important criteria for determining the rewards of a person who engages in *infāq* for the sake of Allah ﷻ is that one must never place the recipient in an uncomfortable position or humiliate them after having helped them, as the Qurʾān says: "Those who spend their wealth in the way of Allah, and then do not follow up what they have spent with putting (the receiver) under obligation and taunting, their reward is with their Lord, and they will have no fear, nor will they grieve. A kind word and forgiveness are better than charity followed by hurt. And Allah is Self-Sufficient *(Ghanī)*, All-Clement *(Ḥalīm)*. O you who believe! Do not invalidate your almsgiving by putting (the receiver) under an obligation and taunting - like a person who spends one's wealth to show off to people and be praised by them, and believes not in Allah and the Last Day. The parable of their spending is that of a smooth rock on which there is soil; a heavy rain falls upon it and leaves it barren. They have no power (control) over what they have earned. And Allah does not guide such disbelieving people."[182]
5. ***Infāq* from the Permissibly-Earned *(Ḥalāl)*:** It goes without saying that *infāq* which a person gives must be from permissibly-earned wealth, and the proceeds from illicit *(ḥarām)* earnings such

---

[181] Qurʾān, Sūrah ar-Rūm (30), Verse 39:

...وَمَآ ءَاتَيۡتُم مِّن زَكَوٰةٖ تُرِيدُونَ وَجۡهَ ٱللَّهِ فَأُوْلَٰٓئِكَ هُمُ ٱلۡمُضۡعِفُونَ ٣٩

[182] Ibid., Sūrah al-Baqarah (2), Verses 262-264:

ٱلَّذِينَ يُنفِقُونَ أَمۡوَٰلَهُمۡ فِي سَبِيلِ ٱللَّهِ ثُمَّ لَا يُتۡبِعُونَ مَآ أَنفَقُواْ مَنّٗا وَلَآ أَذٗى لَّهُمۡ أَجۡرُهُمۡ
عِندَ رَبِّهِمۡ وَلَا خَوۡفٌ عَلَيۡهِمۡ وَلَا هُمۡ يَحۡزَنُونَ ٢٦٢ قَوۡلٞ مَّعۡرُوفٞ وَمَغۡفِرَةٌ خَيۡرٞ مِّن صَدَقَةٖ
يَتۡبَعُهَآ أَذٗىۗ وَٱللَّهُ غَنِيٌّ حَلِيمٞ ٢٦٣ يَٰٓأَيُّهَا ٱلَّذِينَ ءَامَنُواْ لَا تُبۡطِلُواْ صَدَقَٰتِكُم بِٱلۡمَنِّ وَٱلۡأَذَىٰ
كَٱلَّذِي يُنفِقُ مَالَهُۥ رِئَآءَ ٱلنَّاسِ وَلَا يُؤۡمِنُ بِٱللَّهِ وَٱلۡيَوۡمِ ٱلۡأٓخِرِۖ فَمَثَلُهُۥ كَمَثَلِ صَفۡوَانٍ عَلَيۡهِ
تُرَابٞ فَأَصَابَهُۥ وَابِلٞ فَتَرَكَهُۥ صَلۡدٗاۖ لَّا يَقۡدِرُونَ عَلَىٰ شَيۡءٖ مِّمَّا كَسَبُواْۗ وَٱللَّهُ لَا يَهۡدِي ٱلۡقَوۡمَ
ٱلۡكَٰفِرِينَ ٢٦٤

as gambling, or business income from impermissible sales such as alcohol, drugs, and other such things will not earn an individual the rewards that one desires. In addition to this, we must ensure that we put in an honest day at work, and if we are required to work for example, eight hours, we must not short-change the company and work anything less. In this regard, the Qur'ān says: "O you who believe! Spend (in the cause of Allah and for the needy) out of the pure, wholesome things you have earned, and from what We have produced for you from the earth..."[183]

6. ***Infāq* from that which a Person Loves:** When we give anything to others, we need to give that which we ourselves love, and not suffice with left-overs, or that which is worthless. The Qur'ān is clear in this area and tells us: "Never will you attain goodness (and virtue) until you spend from that which you love. And whatever you spend, surely Allah has full knowledge of it."[184]
7. ***Infāq* based on Moderation:** Allah ﷻ does not expect a person to give away everything that one has to the needy, nor does He want to see people be so stingy that they do not give anything; thus in the Qur'ān, the picture of balance is painted where Allah ﷻ says: "And those who, when they spend (both for their own and other's needs), are neither wasteful, nor extremely miserly, but (are aware that) there is a (balanced) median between those (two extremes)."[185]
8. ***Infāq* in Secrecy:** Although *infāq* in the way of Allah ﷻ can be done in the open - and sometimes this is the only way that it is possible to carry it out - however there is something to be said about *infāq* which is done in secret such that no one else knows

---

[183] Qur'ān, Sūrah al-Baqarah (2), Verse 267:

يَـٰٓأَيُّهَا ٱلَّذِينَ ءَامَنُوٓاْ أَنفِقُواْ مِن طَيِّبَـٰتِ مَا كَسَبْتُمْ وَمِمَّآ أَخْرَجْنَا لَكُم مِّنَ ٱلْأَرْضِ...

[184] Ibid., Sūrah Āl ʿImrān (3), Verse 92:

لَن تَنَالُواْ ٱلْبِرَّ حَتَّىٰ تُنفِقُواْ مِمَّا تُحِبُّونَ ۚ وَمَا تُنفِقُواْ مِن شَىْءٍ فَإِنَّ ٱللَّهَ بِهِۦ عَلِيمٌ ﴿٩٢﴾

[185] Ibid., Sūrah al-Furqān (25), Verse 67:

وَٱلَّذِينَ إِذَآ أَنفَقُواْ لَمْ يُسْرِفُواْ وَلَمْ يَقْتُرُواْ وَكَانَ بَيْنَ ذَٰلِكَ قَوَامًا ﴿٦٧﴾

about it - not even the recipient. Such assistance actually holds a greater reward with Allah ﷻ, as the Qur'ān alludes to: "Those who spend their wealth (in the way of Allah) by night and by day, secretly and in public, their reward is with their Lord, and they will have no fear, nor will they grieve."[186]

Further to this, Allah ﷻ also mentions that: "If you dispense your alms openly, it is well, but if you conceal it and give it to the poor (in secret), then this is better for you; and He (Allah) will (make it an atonement to) remove some of your evil deeds. And Allah is fully aware of all that you do."[187]

This shows us the gradations of *infāq* in the sight of Allah ﷻ, and that giving in secret, without anyone knowing about it, has been given preference in the sight of Allah ﷻ.

9. ***Infāq* during Times of Ease and Difficulty:** Engaging in *infāq* when a person is wealthy and has all of the comforts and does not "need" the excess wealth that one has saved in their bank accounts is relatively easy. However, the challenge comes when there is a clear and present urgency in society, and a person who is in financial challenges oneself stretches out one's hand to support a certain cause or give to someone in dire need.

Arguably, the rewards from Allah ﷻ are greater at this level as an individual is more concerned about others and their welfare than oneself, as the Qur'ān beautifully articulates: "And hasten to forgiveness from your Lord, and to a garden as spacious as the heavens and the earth, prepared for the God-conscious. They spend (out of what Allah has provided for them) both in ease and hardship,

---

[186] Qur'ān, Sūrah al-Baqarah (2), Verse 274:

ٱلَّذِينَ يُنفِقُونَ أَمْوَٰلَهُم بِٱلَّيْلِ وَٱلنَّهَارِ سِرًّا وَعَلَانِيَةً فَلَهُمْ أَجْرُهُمْ عِندَ رَبِّهِمْ وَلَا خَوْفٌ عَلَيْهِمْ وَلَا هُمْ يَحْزَنُونَ ﴿٢٧٤﴾

[187] Ibid., Verse 271:

إِن تُبْدُوا۟ ٱلصَّدَقَٰتِ فَنِعِمَّا هِىَ ۖ وَإِن تُخْفُوهَا وَتُؤْتُوهَا ٱلْفُقَرَآءَ فَهُوَ خَيْرٌ لَّكُمْ ۚ وَيُكَفِّرُ عَنكُم مِّن سَيِّـَٔاتِكُمْ ۗ وَٱللَّهُ بِمَا تَعْمَلُونَ خَبِيرٌ ﴿٢٧١﴾

and they restrain their anger (even when they are provoked and able to retaliate), and pardon people (for their offenses). And Allah loves (such) people who are the doers of good"[188]

This concept is further emphasized in the Qur'ān where it shows us that people are not the same when it comes to *infāq* in the way of Allah ﷻ: "And why do you not spend in the cause of Allah when to Allah belongs the inheritance of the heavens and the earth. Not equal among you are those who spend before the victory comes and fight (for the sake of Allah, and those who do not) - they are greater in rank than those who spend after the victory comes and fight later. However, to all Allah has promised what is the best. And Allah is fully aware of all that you do."[189]

The Ranking of Recipients for Infāq

Although we would like to help everyone who needs assistance, we recognize that our time, efforts, and wealth are limited, so we must prioritize our giving.

The Qur'ān clearly lays down recommendations in terms of the ranking of recipients for *infāq*, and the order which it puts down may be surprising for some people:

1. **Immediate Family Members:** The old English adage that 'charity begins at home' is especially true when it comes to *infāq*. We have no moral standing if we are helping others while our own

---

[188] Qur'ān, Sūrah Āl 'Imrān (3), Verses 133-134:

وَسَارِعُوٓاْ إِلَىٰ مَغۡفِرَةٖ مِّن رَّبِّكُمۡ وَجَنَّةٍ عَرۡضُهَا ٱلسَّمَٰوَٰتُ وَٱلۡأَرۡضُ أُعِدَّتۡ لِلۡمُتَّقِينَ ١٣٣
ٱلَّذِينَ يُنفِقُونَ فِي ٱلسَّرَّآءِ وَٱلضَّرَّآءِ وَٱلۡكَٰظِمِينَ ٱلۡغَيۡظَ وَٱلۡعَافِينَ عَنِ ٱلنَّاسِۗ وَٱللَّهُ يُحِبُّ
ٱلۡمُحۡسِنِينَ ١٣٤

[189] Ibid., Sūrah al-Ḥadīd (57), Verse 10:

وَمَا لَكُمۡ أَلَّا تُنفِقُواْ فِي سَبِيلِ ٱللَّهِ وَلِلَّهِ مِيرَٰثُ ٱلسَّمَٰوَٰتِ وَٱلۡأَرۡضِۚ لَا يَسۡتَوِي مِنكُم مَّنۡ
أَنفَقَ مِن قَبۡلِ ٱلۡفَتۡحِ وَقَٰتَلَۚ أُوْلَٰٓئِكَ أَعۡظَمُ دَرَجَةٗ مِّنَ ٱلَّذِينَ أَنفَقُواْ مِنۢ بَعۡدُ وَقَٰتَلُواْۚ وَكُلّٗا
وَعَدَ ٱللَّهُ ٱلۡحُسۡنَىٰۚ وَٱللَّهُ بِمَا تَعۡمَلُونَ خَبِيرٞ ١٠

family members are suffering. In fact, according to some *ḥadīth*, a person who gives charity to outsiders while one's own relatives are struggling to make ends meet are deprived of the benefits of such giving. The Qur'ān tells us that people would come to Prophet Muḥammad ﷺ and ask him for guidance about *infāq*, and he would respond by revelation from Allah ﷻ: "They ask you (O Muḥammad) what they should spend (to provide sustenance for the needy). Say: 'Whatever good (from your wealth) you spend is for (your) parents and the near relatives, and the (needy) orphans, and the destitute, and the wayfarer. And whatever good you do, surely Allah has full knowledge of it.'"[190]

2. **The Orphans:** Once the parents and siblings have been taken care of, we can then think about helping others - in this case, the next group are the orphans. The verse quoted above, as well as many other verses contained in the Qur'ān show us that after parents and relatives, the next group which deserve our care and assistance are the orphans - those who have lost their father, mother, or both parents, and have not yet reached the age of maturity.
3. **The *Faqīr* and the *Miskīn*:** In Islamic terminology, there are two terms used to describe someone who is 'poor' - *faqīr* and *miskīn*. Scholars have debated whether they are one and the same, or are they different? One interpretation tells us that: the *faqīr* is a person who is financially deficient, even though they may be engaged in business or have a job, but still find it difficult to not only make ends meet, but are not able to provide the extra comforts or luxuries which others enjoy. In any case, such a person hardly ever asks anyone for help, preferring to live under the radar and not actively asking others for assistance. A *miskīn* on the other hand is an individual whose needs are more severe, and is not able to work or find a job, and for this reason they actively seek assistance - they

---

[190] Qur'ān, Sūrah al-Baqarah (2), Verse 215:

يَسْـَٔلُونَكَ مَاذَا يُنفِقُونَ ۖ قُلْ مَآ أَنفَقْتُم مِّنْ خَيْرٍ فَلِلْوَٰلِدَيْنِ وَٱلْأَقْرَبِينَ وَٱلْيَتَـٰمَىٰ وَٱلْمَسَـٰكِينِ
وَٱبْنِ ٱلسَّبِيلِ ۗ وَمَا تَفْعَلُوا۟ مِنْ خَيْرٍ فَإِنَّ ٱللَّهَ بِهِۦ عَلِيمٌ ﴿٢١٥﴾

have almost nothing, and are getting by on meager living.

4. **Dedicated to Working for Islam:** In any case, these two groups become the next category of people who are eligible for *infāq* in the way of Allah ﷻ. The Qur'ān addresses this group and says: "That (which you spend) is for the poor who have dedicated themselves to the cause of Allah (and are in distressed circumstances). They are unable to travel around the lands (to render service in the cause of Allah and earn their livelihood). Those who are unaware (of their circumstances) suppose they are self-sufficient because of their dignified bearing (and shame of wanting to ask others for assistance), but you will know them by their appearance - they do not beg of people persistently (or even at all). And whatever good you spend, surely Allah has full knowledge of it."[191]
5. **Stranded Travelers:** Those individuals who are on a journey and have lost the means to continue their trip and return home again are also eligible for *infāq* in the way of Allah ﷻ, and are referred to in the verse previously quoted about one's family and parents - in that verse they are called 'wayfarers.' They may have wealth in their homes, however as they are now stranded, helping them is a good act which will be rewarded by Allah ﷻ in this world and the world to come.
6. **Those who Migrate in the Way of Allah ﷻ:** Another category of those whom we need to assist with *infāq* are those who have made migration in the way of Allah ﷻ - leaving their homes and everything behind them, seeking a "better life," but at a current point in time, they are not in a position to support themselves and their families. The Qur'ān paints us the picture of the Muslims who left Mecca to migrate to Medina and their intense needs. In an extremely poignant manner, the Qur'ān shows us how

---

[191] Qur'ān, Sūrah al-Baqarah (2), Verse 273:

لِلْفُقَرَآءِ ٱلَّذِينَ أُحْصِرُوا۟ فِى سَبِيلِ ٱللَّهِ لَا يَسْتَطِيعُونَ ضَرْبًا فِى ٱلْأَرْضِ يَحْسَبُهُمُ ٱلْجَاهِلُ أَغْنِيَآءَ مِنَ ٱلتَّعَفُّفِ تَعْرِفُهُم بِسِيمَٰهُمْ لَا يَسْـَٔلُونَ ٱلنَّاسَ إِلْحَافًا ۗ وَمَا تُنفِقُوا۟ مِنْ خَيْرٍ فَإِنَّ ٱللَّهَ بِهِۦ عَلِيمٌ ﴿٢٧٣﴾

the inhabitants of Medina gave all that they could to help their brothers and sisters in faith settle in their new homes: "And those who had settled (in Medina), and (adopted) the faith before them. They love those who emigrated to them (for the sake of Allah), and in their hearts did not begrudge what they had been given, and (indeed) they preferred them over themselves, even though they themselves were living in abject poverty. Whoever is guarded against the stinginess of one's own soul - those are the ones who will be successful."[192]

7. **Those who Ask:** There are many times that we are approached by people on the street, or sometimes online for financial assistance, or help in other ways. Although we need to be careful about who we just send money to - especially with the growing number of online scams - when we are walking down the street and a person asks for food or some type of assistance, if we have the ability to help them, then we should give a helping hand. If we feel uncomfortable giving cash, we can take them to a local coffee shop or restaurant and buy them a healthy meal which will help them until someone else can provide for them. In this regard, the Qur'ān clearly states that: "And as for the person who asks, do not repel them."[193] We should understand that Allah ﷻ will reward us for our sincerity and intention, and even if the recipient of our help was not worthy of it, they will be accountable for that, but we will still reap the benefits of our actions.
8. **Freeing the Slaves:** Although slavery as it was practiced 14 centuries ago may not exist in that form today, however we still

---

[192] Qur'ān, Sūrah al-Ḥashr (59), Verse 9:

وَٱلَّذِينَ تَبَوَّءُو ٱلدَّارَ وَٱلْإِيمَٰنَ مِن قَبْلِهِمْ يُحِبُّونَ مَنْ هَاجَرَ إِلَيْهِمْ وَلَا يَجِدُونَ فِى صُدُورِهِمْ حَاجَةً مِّمَّآ أُوتُوا۟ وَيُؤْثِرُونَ عَلَىٰٓ أَنفُسِهِمْ وَلَوْ كَانَ بِهِمْ خَصَاصَةٌ ۚ وَمَن يُوقَ شُحَّ نَفْسِهِۦ فَأُو۟لَٰٓئِكَ هُمُ ٱلْمُفْلِحُونَ ﴿٩﴾

[193] Ibid., Sūrah aḍ-Ḍuḥā (93), Verse 10:

وَأَمَّا ٱلسَّآئِلَ فَلَا تَنْهَرْ ﴿١٠﴾

have cases of economic slavery rampant around the world - men and women working in sweatshops in developing parts of world for pennies or dollars a day. The Qur'ān acknowledges that slavery to some extent will always exist, and that it is impossible to do away with it altogether, but it did introduce laws to limit and eventually eradicate this phenomenon. Thus, it stresses on the fact that one way to spend in the way of Allah ﷻ through *infāq* is to free the slaves, where He says in the Qur'ān: "And let those who cannot find (the means) to marry keep themselves chaste until Allah grants them sufficiency out of His bounty. And if any of those whom your right hands possess desire to enter into a contract with you to purchase their freedom, then make this contract with them if you know that they are honest (and able to earn without begging, and be good, free citizens). Help them out from the wealth of Allah which He has granted you. And do not compel your slave-girls to prostitution in order to seek the (fleeting) benefits of the life of this world while they desire to remain chaste. And if anyone compels them to prostitution, then indeed Allah will be All-Forgiving, All-Merciful to them after they are subjected to such compulsion."[194]

9. ***Jihād* (Struggling) in the Way of Allah ﷻ:** The next major category where the Qur'ān expects the believers to spend their wealth, talents, and abilities in His way by engaging in *infāq* is through the sacred struggle *(jihād)*. This struggle can take place in many ways and is not limited to a military maneuver, although that is one example of *jihād* when it is needed and the Prophet ﷺ or his directly appointed representatives - one of the 12 Imāms عليهم السلام - calls for it. In this area of *infāq*, the Qur'ān states: "(O believers)

[194] Qur'ān, Sūrah an-Nūr (24), Verse 33:

وَلْيَسْتَعْفِفِ ٱلَّذِينَ لَا يَجِدُونَ نِكَاحًا حَتَّىٰ يُغْنِيَهُمُ ٱللَّهُ مِن فَضْلِهِۦ ۗ وَٱلَّذِينَ يَبْتَغُونَ
ٱلْكِتَٰبَ مِمَّا مَلَكَتْ أَيْمَٰنُكُمْ فَكَاتِبُوهُمْ إِنْ عَلِمْتُمْ فِيهِمْ خَيْرًا ۖ وَءَاتُوهُم مِّن مَّالِ ٱللَّهِ
ٱلَّذِىٓ ءَاتَىٰكُمْ ۚ وَلَا تُكْرِهُوا۟ فَتَيَٰتِكُمْ عَلَى ٱلْبِغَآءِ إِنْ أَرَدْنَ تَحَصُّنًا لِّتَبْتَغُوا۟ عَرَضَ ٱلْحَيَوٰةِ
ٱلدُّنْيَا ۚ وَمَن يُكْرِههُّنَّ فَإِنَّ ٱللَّهَ مِنۢ بَعْدِ إِكْرَٰهِهِنَّ غَفُورٌ رَّحِيمٌ ٣٣

And prepare against them whatever you can of force and horses assigned (for war), that thereby you may dismay the enemies of Allah and your enemies and others besides them, of whom (and the nature of whose enmity) you may be unaware, (but) Allah is aware of them (and of the nature of their enmity). And whatever you spend in the way of Allah will be repaid to you in full, and you will not be wronged."[195]

10. **Winning Over the Hearts of the Non-Believers:** Another category of *infāq* in the way of Allah ﷻ is to try and win over the hearts of the non-believers toward Islam. The Qur'ān most eloquently lays down those entitled to charity in this regard by saying: "The prescribed alms (the *zakāh*) are meant only for the poor, and the destitute, and those in charge of collecting (and administering) them (the *zakāh*), and those whose hearts are to be won over (for Islam), and to free those in bondage (slavery and captivity), and to help those over-burdened with debt, and in the cause of Allah, and for the wayfarer (in need of help). This is an ordinance from Allah; and Allah is All-Knowing *('Alīm)*, All-Wise *(Ḥakīm)*."[196]

Although not an official category of those who we should give our *infāq* to, students of the Islamic studies and scholars who are active in the field of education and propagation are often forgotten when it comes to providing assistance to various classes in society.

In summarizing one of the lectures of a well-known scholar of numerous sciences of the Muslim world, the late Āyatullāh Ḥasan Zādeh

---

[195] Qur'ān, Sūrah al-Anfāl (8), Verse 60:

وَأَعِدُّوا۟ لَهُم مَّا ٱسْتَطَعْتُم مِّن قُوَّةٍ وَمِن رِّبَاطِ ٱلْخَيْلِ تُرْهِبُونَ بِهِۦ عَدُوَّ ٱللَّهِ وَعَدُوَّكُمْ
وَءَاخَرِينَ مِن دُونِهِمْ لَا تَعْلَمُونَهُمُ ٱللَّهُ يَعْلَمُهُمْ ۚ وَمَا تُنفِقُوا۟ مِن شَىْءٍ فِى سَبِيلِ ٱللَّهِ يُوَفَّ
إِلَيْكُمْ وَأَنتُمْ لَا تُظْلَمُونَ ﴿٦٠﴾

[196] Ibid., Sūrah at-Tawbah (9), Verse 60:

إِنَّمَا ٱلصَّدَقَٰتُ لِلْفُقَرَآءِ وَٱلْمَسَٰكِينِ وَٱلْعَٰمِلِينَ عَلَيْهَا وَٱلْمُؤَلَّفَةِ قُلُوبُهُمْ وَفِى ٱلرِّقَابِ
وَٱلْغَٰرِمِينَ وَفِى سَبِيلِ ٱللَّهِ وَٱبْنِ ٱلسَّبِيلِ ۖ فَرِيضَةً مِّنَ ٱللَّهِ ۗ وَٱللَّهُ عَلِيمٌ حَكِيمٌ ﴿٦٠﴾

Āmulī, made a wise and beautiful point. In discussing those who are worthy of receiving financial assistance, he would say that there is no wisdom in giving such aid - the recommended *(mustaḥab)* contributions to a student of Islamic studies.

The rationale behind his statement was that the Muslim society and each local community needs to see the students of Islamic knowledge and the local scholars as pillars of the society and individuals who are providing an essential service. He went on to state that for this reason, the scholars allow the usage of *khums* to support a student of Islamic studies, or for educational purposes, so that they do not have to be dependent upon recommended acts of charity and giving - what wisdom from one of the great intellectuals of our tradition.

Thus, just as we have doctors that take care of our physical health when we require medical attention, religious scholars are there for our spiritual health and guidance - and we need to ensure that we have appropriate infrastructure that supports this work.

Thus, *infāq* is a comprehensive program which Islam created and sought to instill into the hearts of believers, and has not limited it to one or two ways.

It also brought about rules on how it is to be practiced, when it should be given, and for what purposes - clearly showing us that the Qur'ān has not left out anything when it comes to the spiritual and material progress of an individual and the community on a whole.

Commentary

Many verses of the Noble Qur'ān speak about charity and giving in the way of Allah ﷻ, and because of this the companions of Prophet Muḥammad ﷺ would ask him about the details of this deed. Thus, in this verse under discussion, Allah ﷻ starts it off by saying that people come and ask you: O Muḥammad ﷺ who should they spend on?

Allah ﷻ tells His Prophet ﷺ what to answer to the people when they ask him such a question, and states that whatever good and useful material or spiritual wealth you spend, it should be for:

1. Your parents;
2. Your relatives;

3. The needy orphans;
4. The poor;
5. Finally, the helpless.

We must keep in mind that by Allah ﷻ mentioning these five groups of people who are deserving of charity, He is merely presenting an example of who we should spend our money on, but we must not limit it to them only - there are definitely other people or causes which exist that may also need our financial support, or other types of assistance which are not listed in this verse, but are nonetheless worthy causes to sponsor.

At the end of this verse, the Qur'ān states that whatever good a person does, Allah ﷻ knows it, so basically He is saying that you do not have to go out and show people your work, or publicize your acts of charity. In fact, it is much better for you to hide your alms or good deeds in order to increase the sincerity of your actions because if you are truly looking for the reward from Allah ﷻ, then He is the One who knows everything, and He is the One in whose hands lies the true rewards for anything and everything that a person does.

Allah ﷻ uses a unique phrase in this verse where He says that '... whatever good you do...' and this can be interpreted quite widely, and includes all good deeds: be it wealth or services, material or spiritual.

Lastly, the expression 'good' also shows us that wealth in itself is not inherently evil; rather it can be one of the best means of goodness and acquiring rewards from Allah ﷻ - provided that it is used correctly.

Keys of Guidance

- A concern which many people often have is that they feel they must be recognized for their generosity in charity, however in this passage, Allah ﷻ shows us through a very clear message that what is most important is that **He** will recognize us and reward us - even if people do not realize what we have done. Even if our name is not put on a plaque, or our name is not announced in a gathering to acknowledge donors, or we do not get the accolades and recognition for our contributions, be rest assured that Allah ﷻ knows everything, and He will reward us amply for all of our actions.

- When studying the lawful recipients of charity, we see that two of the five categories fall within our own family, emphasizing that we must start with them and ensure that they are financially secure before looking to help others. Most of the time when we think of charity, we think about giving to others, however we need to engage in a massive paradigm shift in our thinking and re-align our understanding of Islam by studying the Qur'ān and the Prophetic examples and first look at home, then venture outside once our immediate family members are taken care of. We should also realize that charity is not limited to financial assistance but that it also includes other types of support.

- Wealth in itself is not evil, and those who claim that money is wicked have not recognized the true Islamic teachings, since the Qur'ān teaches us that as long as we use our wealth in the correct ways which Allah ﷻ has laid down for us through the guidance of the Qur'ān, Prophet Muḥammad ﷺ, and his immaculate family ؑ, we can safeguard our place in Paradise due to spending our money in the correct manner.

- Righteous deeds are never lost - whether they are done overtly or covertly. Those people who give to others outside of the public limelight will receive their rewards from Allah ﷻ as He is All-Knowing; and it is very well possible that their rewards will be greater than those individuals who give to the needy but promote or advertise their acts of charity - but even in those instances, their true intentions are only known to Allah ﷻ.

- There are times when we are encouraged to give in charity in secret and to ensure that others are not aware of our giving; however, there are times in which we are recommended to give our wealth openly as this will act as an encouragement to others to also support valuable causes.

- There are three places in the Islamic teachings where it is both permissible and good to give charity in the open:
    - Obligatory charity such as *khums* and *zakāh*.

- Charity for general purposes that will benefit society - such as the construction of a hospital or a park.
- Charity for foundational and educational purposes.

The reason why in these instances, charity should be given in the open is to act as an encouragement for others to also donate - as such projects will benefit all of society.

However, there are other times when we should not give charity in the open, two of which include:

1. When we give to a person or a family member, and this is related to both *wājib* or *mustaḥab* charity, as Islam wants to ensure that we preserve the dignity of other individuals.
2. If it will cause a person to brag about what they have done, or instill any kind of arrogance.

Verse 216

كُتِبَ عَلَيْكُمُ ٱلْقِتَالُ وَهُوَ كُرْهٌ لَّكُمْ ۖ وَعَسَىٰٓ أَن تَكْرَهُوا۟ شَيْـًٔا وَهُوَ خَيْرٌ لَّكُمْ ۖ وَعَسَىٰٓ أَن تُحِبُّوا۟ شَيْـًٔا وَهُوَ شَرٌّ لَّكُمْ ۗ وَٱللَّهُ يَعْلَمُ وَأَنتُمْ لَا تَعْلَمُونَ ﴿٢١٦﴾

Prescribed for you is fighting, though it is disliked by you. It may well be that you dislike a thing but it is good for you, and it may well be that you like a thing but it is bad for you. And Allah knows, and you do not know.

Connection to Previous Verses

Previously in Sūrah al-Baqarah, in Verse 177, Allah ﷻ spoke about what goodness *(birr)* was and provided humanity with a series of spiritual prescriptions which were the following:

1. He started by saying that He has prescribed *qiṣāṣ* - a comprehensive and complete social justice system for this world which humanity

needs to live by in order to maintain balance and stability in society.

2. The second prescription was the need for Muslims to write a last will and testament, and that they must ensure that they do not dispute with one another after the death of a loved one. Allah ﷻ went on to remind the Muslims that they must have a solid plan in place to deal with issues of inheritance.
3. The third prescription was in regards to fasting *(ṣiyām),* and the pilgrimage to Mecca *(Ḥajj).*

Through multiple verses of the Qur'ān, Allah ﷻ explains these two important pillars of the faith - namely fasting, and the pilgrimage to Mecca - their philosophy, and in general the philosophy of acts of worship.

Interestingly, when Allah ﷻ speaks about *Ḥajj,* in the same breath He also speaks about warfare and its conditions. This may have been done because during the period of revelation of these verses, the Muslims had peacefully taken over the city of Mecca and had complete control over that city. However, there was a group of people seeking to spread corruption. They wanted to create animosity within the society, spread mischief, and stoke the flames of war by taking advantage of the kindness and mercy of the Noble Prophet Muḥammad ﷺ.

In the verse under review, Allah ﷻ presents the growing Muslim community with their fourth prescription, helping them to further understand what goodness *(birr)* truly is.

However, when reading this verse, one may be confused as to how is fighting *(qitāl)* goodness? What is the connection between these two?

In order to establish goodness within society, there needs to be a firmly-set system of justice which can then lead to peace in society. For justice to be established and flourish, one must first remove evil within society. Without doubt, there are many ways to do this - and in certain circumstances, as this verse of the Qur'ān shows - physical force may be required.

No one denies the essential need of the use of extreme measures of force in unique circumstances when diplomacy and negotiations fail, and one party is aggressing against innocent people. Since Islam is a religion of reality and one which governs every aspect of human existence, it too does not deny the need to resort to force when required.

Given that throughout history, and even today, some people misuse the legitimacy of war, the teachings of the Qur'ān and the practical examples about how to carry oneself in wartimes as seen in the life of Prophet Muḥammad ﷺ laid down a complete code of conduct, and said that as a last resort warfare is permissible in order to restore justice. Further, the Islamic teachings laid down strict conditions for how to engage with the enemy in different circumstances.

Thus, it can be said that Islam provided humanity with a complete, holistic picture of how to use force, when to use it, and under what strict conditions.

Commentary

The previous verse focused on the subject of giving one's property or talents to those in need, while this verse focuses on giving one's life up in the way of Allah ﷻ - and really, both are required and run parallel to one another.

Allah ﷻ reminds us that fighting in His way has been decreed for the Muslims, although it is something which may be objectionable for the believers. The interpretation of the word 'prescribed' *(kutiba)* refers to the 'certainty of this Divine command;' while the word 'disliked' *(kurha)* carries the passive participle meaning, and refers to war being repulsive, detestable, and unpleasant - even if it is against the enemy and in the way of Allah ﷻ. Indeed, this is something which is natural for human beings: that they do not like to go to war, and have to kill others, and they recognize that war results in the loss of property and innocent lives, as well as injuries and hardships. For those people who love to taste martyrdom in the way of truth, and those who are at a high level of knowledge in regards to the true teachings of Islam and its injunctions regarding war, for them struggling against the belligerent enemies of the truth is a sweet drink that they run after like a thirsty person runs after something to drink, and without a doubt, such people are certainly exceptional.

From here, a fundamental principle which governs the legislative *(takwīnī)* and developmental *(tashrīʿī)* law of Allah ﷻ is mentioned in which He says that although fighting in the way of Allah ﷻ is good, however it is possible that you may not like something while it is good for you; Allah ﷻ then mentions that contrary to this, it is also possible that putting aside the act of going to war, and seeking your own personal comfort and health may be something that you like, however it is not good for you.

At the end of the verse, the Noble Qur'ān concludes by stating that it is only Allah ﷻ who truly knows the reality of this scenario, whereas we the believers with our limited knowledge, do not recognize the reality of the situation.

In His decisive tone, Allah ﷻ, the Lord of the Worlds, states that human beings should not try and govern over their affairs in matters related to their destiny, because their knowledge is limited and insignificant in every aspect - their knowledge is like a drop of water in the vast ocean of the unknown. Due to this, the believers must never oppose the Divine commandments *(aḥkām)*, and need to recognize that if Allah ﷻ has legislated actions such as the sacred struggle *(jihād)*, fasting *(ṣawm)*, pilgrimage to Mecca *(Ḥajj)*, etc., then these are all obligations *(wājibāt)* which will benefit only them.

Paying attention to this fact cultivates a spirit of discipline and submission to the Divine laws within a believer, and allows the understanding and vision of an individual to transcend beyond the limited environments which one can only perceive, and connects a person to the Infinite, which is Allah ﷻ and His All-Encompassing Knowledge.

Keys of Guidance

- When some Muslims or so-called Muslims misuse the legitimacy of war, and disregard the explicit instructions which the Qur'ān and Prophet Muḥammad ﷺ taught in this regard, this is when some ignorant and ill-intentioned people outside of the fold of Islam are given the opportunity to say that the Qur'ān is a textbook of war, that Prophet Muḥammad ﷺ cannot be a real Prophet of God as he taught violence, and that the ideology of Islam is aggressive which is incompatible with modern day society. Despite the fact that Allah ﷻ provides a comprehensive set of instructions on warfare, some "Muslims" choose to ignore the Islamic teachings and do as they please - thinking that the ends justify the means. This is why it is very important to understand these topics after researching, investigating, and weighing all of the evidence, and not simply cherry-picking to form one's opinions.

- The criterion for good and bad in the life of a believer is not ease and hardship, nor is it personal whims and desires, but rather the criterion which one must always use is to understand the bigger picture and reflect on the overall good of society; an individual must never let one's own personal prejudice taint out understandings.
- War is not something which is inherently good or bad for it depends on the motivations and goals that one is seeking in them, and as such when the sacred struggle is for the sake of Allah ﷻ and to ensure that the goals which Allah ﷻ wants are upheld through the sacred struggle, then war becomes something which is good for a believer.
- As believers, we must be ready to submit to the orders of Allah ﷻ at all times because whatever He commands and forbids is based on His Infinite Knowledge - and although we may not know the reasons why He has legislated or forbidden certain actions, we must submit ourselves to His will, for He is the All-Knowing.

Verse 217

يَسْأَلُونَكَ عَنِ ٱلشَّهْرِ ٱلْحَرَامِ قِتَالٍ فِيهِ ۖ قُلْ قِتَالٌ فِيهِ كَبِيرٌ ۖ وَصَدٌّ عَن
سَبِيلِ ٱللَّهِ وَكُفْرٌۢ بِهِۦ وَٱلْمَسْجِدِ ٱلْحَرَامِ وَإِخْرَاجُ أَهْلِهِۦ مِنْهُ أَكْبَرُ عِندَ
ٱللَّهِ ۚ وَٱلْفِتْنَةُ أَكْبَرُ مِنَ ٱلْقَتْلِ ۗ وَلَا يَزَالُونَ يُقَٰتِلُونَكُمْ حَتَّىٰ يَرُدُّوكُمْ عَن
دِينِكُمْ إِنِ ٱسْتَطَٰعُوا۟ ۚ وَمَن يَرْتَدِدْ مِنكُمْ عَن دِينِهِۦ فَيَمُتْ وَهُوَ كَافِرٌ
فَأُو۟لَٰٓئِكَ حَبِطَتْ أَعْمَٰلُهُمْ فِى ٱلدُّنْيَا وَٱلْءَاخِرَةِ ۖ وَأُو۟لَٰٓئِكَ أَصْحَٰبُ ٱلنَّارِ ۖ

هُمۡ فِيهَا خَٰلِدُونَ ﴿٢١٧﴾

They ask you (Muḥammad ﷺ) about the sacred month *(shahr al-ḥarām)* and fighting in it. Say (to them O Muḥammad ﷺ): "Fighting in it is a grave sin; however barring people from the way of Allah, disbelief in Him, denying entry into the Sacred Mosque *(Masjid al-Ḥarām)*, and to drive out its inhabitants are far more severe and more sinful in the sight of Allah than fighting (during the sacred month); and disorder (rooted in rebellion to Allah ﷻ and recognizing no laws) is even graver and more sinful than killing. And they will not cease fighting against you until they turn you from your religion, if they can. Whoever of you turns away from one's religion and dies an unbeliever - those are they whose works have been wasted in both this world and the hereafter, and those are the companions of the fire; they will abide therein forever.

History of Revelation

It has been mentioned that this verse was revealed in regards to the *sarriyah*[197] of ʿAbdullāh ibn Jaḥsh.

Before the Battle of Badr[198] while still in the city of Medina, Prophet Muḥammad ﷺ gave ʿAbdullāh ibn Jaḥsh a letter, ordering him to only open the letter after two days of traveling, and to act according to what was written in it. He and his eight travel companions who were from the inhabitants of Mecca (the *muhājirīn*) did as he was told, and read

[197] A *sariyyah* was a kind of battle in which Prophet Muḥammad ﷺ sent a group of people led by one of his companions - however he himself did not participate in it - such battles are also referred to in the Islamic literature as *baʿth.* Muslim historians have noted that the number of *sariyyah* which took place in the 23 years of the Prophetic life of the final Messenger ﷺ was anywhere from 35 to 48.

[198] The Battle of Badr was the first and most important battle which took place between the Muslims and the polytheists of Quraysh. It took place on the 17th of the month of Ramaḍān in the 2nd year after the migration.

the following statement from Prophet Muḥammad ﷺ: "After you have opened this letter, go to Nakhla (a region between Mecca and Ṭā'if) and scope out the situation with the Quraysh who are there, then return back and report what you witnessed."

ʿAbdullāh and his travel companions went on their way and when they reached Nakhla, they came across a caravan of three people from Quraysh which included a man named ʿAmrū ibn Ḥaḍramī.

ʿAbdullāh and those with him killed ʿAmrū ibn Ḥaḍramī, and brought the two remaining people of the caravan to Prophet Muḥammad ﷺ. Upon speaking to ʿAbdullāh and being judged on what had transpired, the Prophet ﷺ said to them: "I did not order you to fight as it was the forbidden months."

The two polytheists who had been captured and were now in the presence of Prophet Muḥammad ﷺ began to mock him because they felt that he had permitted his followers to engage in war and bloodshed during the forbidden months.

It was at this time that the above verse was revealed.

ʿAbdullāh ibn Jaḥsh and his companions told Prophet Muḥammad ﷺ that that they acted in this way as they were seeking the rewards which were guaranteed for those who engage in the sacred struggle, and they asked the Prophet ﷺ if they would have the rewards of those who struggled in the way of Allah ﷻ *(mujāhidīn)* to which the reply came to them in the form of verse 218 of Sūrah al-Baqarah in which Allah ﷻ says: "Surely those who believe, and who emigrate and strive in the cause of Allah - they are the ones who may hope for the mercy of Allah. And Allah is All-Forgiving, All-Merciful."[199]

Commentary

This verse seeks to answer some of the questions about the sacred struggle and its exceptions.

[199] Qur'ān, Sūrah al-Baqarah (2), Verse 218:

إِنَّ ٱلَّذِينَ ءَامَنُواْ وَٱلَّذِينَ هَاجَرُواْ وَجَٰهَدُواْ فِي سَبِيلِ ٱللَّهِ أُوْلَٰٓئِكَ يَرۡجُونَ رَحۡمَتَ ٱللَّهِۚ وَٱللَّهُ غَفُورٞ رَّحِيمٞ ٢١٨

Allah ﷻ begins by saying that they ask you, Prophet Muḥammad ﷺ, about engaging in war during the sacred month *(shahr al-ḥarām)* and immediately Allah ﷻ gives the Prophet ﷺ the response which he must convey to the community - both the believers and the disbelievers - that according to the teachings of Islam, fighting and engaging in any kind of war during the sacred months is a major sin.

Through this short phrase, Prophet Muḥammad ﷺ was showing that he firmly adheres to the tradition which existed since ancient times and was in place since the previous Prophets among the Arabs regarding the prohibition of fighting in the forbidden months of Rajab, Dhūl Qaʿdah, Dhūl Ḥijjah, and Muḥarram.

Allah ﷻ goes on to say that people should not think that this law does not have any exceptions to it whatsoever. We can never allow a corrupt person or a deviating group to commit acts of aggression, belligerence, or sin under the umbrella of this law.

It is true that upholding the law of the impermissibility of fighting during the sacred month is important, however what is even more important in the sight of Allah ﷻ is to ensure that people do not prevent others from His path - meaning that no one should stop other people from learning about the natural inclination which is the religion of Islam, and to accept the religion of truth. Therefore during these times even, fighting is permissible in order to ensure that people are not encouraged to disbelieve in Allah ﷻ; and engaging in war is allowed to safeguard the Sacred Mosque *(Masjid al-Ḥarām)* such that no one disrespects it or has the audacity to expels its inhabitants.

Allah ﷻ then states that creating mischief and an unfavorable environment which encourages people to disbelieve in Him, or even prevent them from believing in Allah ﷻ is an even greater crime than killing, because killing someone is considered a crime against the human body, however preventing people from truly knowing Allah ﷻ and being able to accept Him and follow His teachings is a crime against the human soul and a crime against the faith.

Allah ﷻ then mentions that the Muslims must ensure they are not influenced by the deviant propaganda of the polytheists who are constantly fighting against the Muslims, trying to turn them away from their religion, and will not stop at anything short of making them leave their faith in Islam. Therefore, the Muslims are ordered to stand firm against them and not pay attention to their statements in regards to their supposed respect for the sacred month, or any other such things which may arise in the future.

From here, Allah ﷻ then provides a firm warning to the Muslims that if any of them are thinking about leaving Islam, neglecting the Qur'ān, or not following Prophet Muḥammad ﷺ, and going back to their old ways, then if they do so and die in a state of disbelief, all of the good deeds which they had accumulated will be wasted in this world, and in the hereafter they will be in Hell, abiding therein forever.

Indeed, what punishment is more severe than finding out that all of one's good deeds have become destroyed with nothing left to show for them - neither in this world, nor in the next world which is even more crucial.

Keys of Guidance

- In this verse, Allah ﷻ divides sins into four circumstances:
    1. Time: The sacred months.
    2. Place: The Sacred Mosque.
    3. Individual/Family: Expelling the inhabitants of the Masjid and its precincts.
    4. Society: Creating mischief. Without doubt, sin is bad in all circumstances, especially when it comes to bloodshed - in which case it is a much more severe sin. However, Allah ﷻ wants to emphasize that there are some times and situations that we need to be even more careful. He also wants Muslims to know that there are certain places in which the performance of sins is more grievous than at other places; and lastly, that sins performed against some people are even more heinous than when performed against others.
- The determination of the gravity of sins is in the hands of Allah

ﷺ, and it is for this reason that although Muslim theologians and scholars of ethics divide the sins into two categories: major and minor, however at the same time, they tell us that do not look at the 'size of the sin' that you are performing, rather look at the 'One whom you are sinning against.'

- As believers, we must know the aspirations, goals, and efforts of our enemy so that we are able to counter them, and protect ourselves, our communities, and our future generations from them.
- The enemies of Islam are continuously lying in ambush, and not only do they desire - but they are actively encouraging the Muslims to leave the religion of Islam - and they will not be content with anything less than this. They do not seek only a temporary victory against the Muslim community, rather they want to destroy the very culture and teachings of Islam, and even continue to do so in this path until today through various means.

Verse 218

إِنَّ ٱلَّذِينَ ءَامَنُوا۟ وَٱلَّذِينَ هَاجَرُوا۟ وَجَٰهَدُوا۟ فِى سَبِيلِ ٱللَّهِ أُو۟لَٰٓئِكَ يَرْجُونَ رَحْمَتَ ٱللَّهِ ۚ وَٱللَّهُ غَفُورٌ رَّحِيمٌ ﴿٢١٨﴾

Surely those who believe, and who fled (to escape persecution or left for a meaningful purpose) and strive in the cause of Allah - they are the ones who deserve to hope for the Mercy of Allah; and Allah is All-Forgiving *(Ghafūr)*, All-Merciful *(Raḥīm)*.

History of Revelation

Commentators of the Noble Qur'ān have stated that the content of this verse is in continuation of the previous verse, and that there was a believer who had emigrated and was engaged in the sacred struggle, however he confused the new moon of Rajab, thinking that it was the month of Jumādā al-Ākhirah and had engaged in fighting. Since he had made a mistake, he was consoled that he should not feel upset because his error would be forgiven by Allah ﷻ as he had not intended to sin.

Thus in this verse, Allah ﷻ points to another group of believers and tells us that those who believed, emigrated, and fought in the cause of Allah ﷻ, and hope for His Mercy will find that He is the All-Forgiving, All-Merciful.

In the light of these three great deeds: faith *(īmān)*, migration *(hijrah)*, and sacred struggle *(jihād)*, if the true believers make unintentional mistakes, then they will be subject to Divine blessings and forgiveness.

As these three terms play an important role in the life of a believer, we need to understand them at a deeper level:

1. ***Īmān***: Allah ﷻ emphasizes that true faith *(īmān)* is not merely lip-service or claiming to follow the religion. Rather, it is a complete package or a robust way of life which a Muslim must embrace. Once "belief" enters the heart, it must mature and develop into becoming an active component of an individual's life and everything that one says and does. Therefore, a faithful person should be ready to act upon one's *īmān* through fulfilling all of their responsibilities to Allah ﷻ and society.
2. ***Hijrah***: Leaving a region and moving to another place is sometimes required - but this must be carried out solely for a meaningful purpose. What is the definition of a meaningful purpose? Simply put, it can be one of the following: an individual is forced to leave due to persecution, or a person determines that one must move on to find better opportunities for their education, career, better living conditions, etc. However such a move must be done with the mindset that a person is not sacrificing the practice of one's faith, and that by moving to another city, province, state, or country, that move will actually allow them to better practice their faith and make them become better believers.
3. ***Jihād* that comes with *Hijrah***: *Jihād* means 'to make a concerted effort and struggle in life' and naturally, this is something which comes with migration. When a person is living in one's home town and is in one's comfort zone, they automatically know what to expect. However, once someone is taken out of that realm, they need to struggle and work even harder; and they must plan their

life, especially if they want to maintain and strengthen their faith and that of their family and future generations.

Keys of Guidance

- Having hope in the Grace *(Luṭf)* and Mercy *(Raḥmah)* of Allah ﷻ requires a person to have faith in Him, and all that He has ordered one who claims belief to accept; and it may also entail a person to emigrate - not only a physical migration, but sometimes even a spiritual migration is required if one cannot physically move from one place to another; and to struggle in whatever way is possible and required - be it with one's wealth or life.
- We should always anticipate the Grace of Allah ﷻ and look forward to Him judging us by His Mercy, not His justice. We must continue to perform those deeds which Islam has outlined as being good, however we should recognize that there is always a possibility that we may slip, or destroy all of the hard work which we have done in our lifetime, or that for some other reason our actions may not be accepted at face value.
- When Muslims came to North America, Europe, and other regions of the secular world, they did so for many reasons - most notably they were looking for better opportunities for themselves and their children. Unfortunately, many of these immigrants did not have long-term plans in place to ensure the safeguarding of their faith and their future generations. They simply thought that the location they were moving to offered more benefits than their homeland. Higher religious education of their next generations was given little to no importance. Gradually, when they saw the state of affairs of their children and the fact that they were slowly leaving Islam and either embracing another religion or gravitating toward atheism, they scrambled to haphazardly create plans and chart out a vision for the future. In this way, many have had to play catch up with respect to the preservation of their Muslim identity for the next generations. This experience has shown that our centers and schools - and more importantly, those who are leading them - must be visionaries with

holistic plans in place for any future migrations to preserve both our religious identity and our worldly objectives.

Verse 219

يَسْأَلُونَكَ عَنِ ٱلْخَمْرِ وَٱلْمَيْسِرِ ۖ قُلْ فِيهِمَآ إِثْمٌ كَبِيرٌ وَمَنَٰفِعُ لِلنَّاسِ وَإِثْمُهُمَآ أَكْبَرُ مِن نَّفْعِهِمَا ۗ وَيَسْـَٔلُونَكَ مَاذَا يُنفِقُونَ قُلِ ٱلْعَفْوَ ۗ كَذَٰلِكَ يُبَيِّنُ ٱللَّهُ لَكُمُ ٱلْءَايَٰتِ لَعَلَّكُمْ تَتَفَكَّرُونَ ﴿٢١٩﴾

They ask you (O Muḥammad ﷺ) about intoxicants and games of chance (like gambling). Say: 'There is a great sin in both of them, and some profits for the people, but their sinfulness outweighs their profit.' And they ask you as to what they should spend. Say: 'All that is surplus.' Thus does Allah clarify His signs for you that perhaps you may reflect.

History of Revelation

Regarding the revelation of this verse, commentators of the Noble Qur'ān have stated that a group of companions of Prophet Muḥammad ﷺ came to see him and asked him to explain the ruling of indulging in alcohol and gambling - as these two things were known to destroy the intellect and wipe out one's wealth, and in response to their query, Allah ﷻ revealed this verse.[200]

Connection to the Previous Verses

In the previous verses, Allah ﷻ provided the believers with a complete mindset shift, and reminded the Muslims that those who have faith must struggle, and when needed they will have to migrate, however in such circumstances, they should expect the infinite Mercy of Allah ﷻ to be showered upon them.

---

200 *Mustadrak al-Wasā'il*, Vol. 17, Pg. 83, Ḥadīth 20,813.

Although the introductory phrase which is seen in this verse has been used a handful of times previously in this chapter, from this verse onwards, we will be exposed to many more verses which begin with the phrase: 'They ask you (O Muḥammad)' *(yas'alūnaka)*. Through such verses, we will see that the people around Prophet Muḥammad ﷺ were asking him questions on a wide variety of topics, and since Islam is built on thinking and we are not expected to just follow blindly, Allah ﷻ would provide the Noble Prophet with responses to convey to the people.

These verses which begin with this phrase: 'They ask you (O Muḥammad)' were introduced to help give guidance to the new and developing Muslim community of migrants, responding to the challenges which they were facing and were going to face in life.

Although these gems of guidance are meant for everyone, it is when people leave their hometown and migrate to a different land and face new challenges that they start questioning everything around them, and feel the need for increased guidance to deal with their unique situations.

In the case of the verse under review, people asked Prophet Muḥammad ﷺ about three things: intoxicants, gambling, and giving in charity *(infāq)* in the way of Allah ﷻ - a strange combination of topics to include in one verse, however through our review, we will be able to better understand why Allah ﷻ grouped these three together.

The three components of this verse under review include:

1. ***Khamr*** - all types of intoxicants - whether they are liquids such as beer, wine, and all other types of liquor; or whether they are solids such as marijuana, hashish, and other narcotics - basically, anything which can intoxicate a person to any level.
2. ***Maysir*** - all types of games of chance - those which were prevalent in the time of the early Muslim community, or the modern forms which are practiced today such as lottery tickets, games played in the physical or virtual casinos, etc.
3. ***Infāq*** - all types of charity which are given to the needy - which we previously discussed in the commentary of verse 215 of Sūrah al-Baqarah.

So how do we understand the first two questions which the early Muslims asked Prophet Muḥammad ﷺ, especially in the context of migration?

As we know, when a person faces challenges in life, they look for ways to comfort themselves, and try to cope with the difficulties which they encounter. Unfortunately, some people choose the wrong things to turn to or rely upon, and think that drinking alcohol or using drugs will solve the problems - or at least numb the pain which they are facing in life. Such things may make a person feel good for the short term, however they have devastating effects on the long-term.[201]

---

[201] Experts offer many theories why people drink (intoxicants), however one of the most commonly-stated reasons is personal-effect motives.Personal reasons (or personal-effect motives) is one reason why people drink. This is an overarching category that includes drinking to cope with, escape, avoid, or control negative emotions. Drinking for these reasons is a form of negative reinforcement. Examples of personal-effect motives for drinking (alcohol) include:

Drinking to cope with a divorce or break-up: Divorce or a break-up can be emotionally difficult and alcohol may seem like a way to cope with these types of losses. Many people who have been through a divorce or break-up tend to drink more frequently, drink larger quantities of alcohol, and/or drink alone. Nevertheless, drinking as an attempt to deal with your problems is not the answer. In fact, research has shown that those who drink in order to manage their emotions are at a greater risk of developing serious alcohol problems. Therefore, it is important to find healthy and appropriate ways to support yourself. You can do this by spending time with friends and family, keeping busy and having fun, finding healthy ways to cope (for example: writing in a journal), exercising regularly, eating healthily, and getting enough sleep.

Drinking to suppress feelings of depression, loneliness, or inadequacy: Feelings of depression, loneliness, and anxiety are all reasons why people drink alcohol. Research has found that there is a strong link between intoxication and suicide among men. For women who are feeling depressed, however, it is the consumption of alcohol, rather than intoxication which is linked to suicide ideation. Alcohol consumption can also lead you to be more impulsive, which can worsen depression symptoms. Instead of drinking as a way to cope with loneliness or depression, why not try other methods such as: calling your parents or family members; taking up a new hobby you've been meaning to take on; or talking with friends and loved ones about how you're feeling? (Extracted from:https://leveluplakeworth.com/reasons-why-people-drink-alcohol/ - Last accessed on January 20, 2022)

When a person finds that they are still down and thinks that there is no way to get out of the situation which they find themselves in, they may go toward what the society of today refers to as 'games of chance.' They may use these for one of two reasons: at one level, they may use them as merely forms of pleasure and entertainment - just as some people play video games or watch TV, some individuals use gambling to get their minds off of their problems; at other times, they may gamble as they feel that if they were lucky enough to win the jackpot, their easily-gotten earnings would solve their problems. However in gambling, the rush and euphoria which one feels is temporary and even worse if they end up losing large sums of money.[202]

As both of these are dead-ends which offer no long-term solution to

---

[202] On the 'Problem Gambling Resource Network' website they state that:

Some common reasons why people gamble are:

1. To Win Money: There is an opportunity to come out "ahead of the game." The gambler sees the possibility of entertainment at no cost and with the potential profit. The dream of the "big win" is a motivation. Financial difficulties can encourage people to gamble in the hope of winning money.

2. For Recreation: The shared experience with other gamblers, the language specific to the game of choice, and the sense of belonging to a distinct group of individuals are all factors that contribute to the social aspect of gambling.

3. To Support Charity: For some gamblers, the opportunity to be entertained while supporting a worthy cause is an incentive to participate.

4. To Escape Problems: Gambling may be an escape from problems, depression, or negative feelings. Some people gamble out of boredom and loneliness.

5. Mood Alteration: Gambling in its benign form provides stimulation and excitement. The action and excitement of gambling can be used as a form of escapism. Gamblers may experience a "high" while playing, similar to the high brought about by drugs or alcohol. This emotional experience, combined with "feeling lucky" or the belief that it is "their turn" to win, can create in some individuals a desire and a need to gamble.

(Extracted from http://www.problemgamblingalberta.ca. Last accessed on January 20, 2022)

the individual who is going through tribulations in life, Allah ﷻ reminds the believers that the one tool He has given us which is guaranteed to get us through any difficulty and weather any storm is that of *jihād* - the sacred struggle, and the endeavor to work hard and fight through the difficulties - never giving into the temptations and the possible "easy fix" of intoxicants, gambling, and other vices which are available, but are nothing more than worthless pursuits.

The third component of this verse is where Allah ﷻ advises us to be vigilant of inequality, and the various gaps in society by making sure that we are observing *infāq*.

Commentary

This verse begins with a question which the companions asked Prophet Muḥammad ﷺ about two things which were common in the pre-Islamic Era of Ignorance *(Jāhiliyyah)*: intoxicants[203] and gambling.[204]

Within the Islamic legal system *(sharīʿah)*, the word *khamr* refers to any intoxicating liquid, although in Arabic just like in English, there is a unique word for each type of intoxicating drink such as: beer, vodka, whisky, etc., but Islamically they are all grouped under the term of intoxicating beverages.

The word *maysir* which is translated as 'gambling' comes from the Arabic root of *yusr* which means 'easy and trouble-free,' and as such the Arabs used this word to describe what we call in English as gambling as it is considered to be an easy way to attain wealth.

From this point, Allah ﷻ responds to the questions of the companions of Prophet Muḥammad ﷺ, and tells him to say that both of these

---

[203] According to contemporary jurists *(marājiʿ taqlīd)*, intoxicants are not limited to only liquids such as beer, wine, etc.; also included are narcotics such as marijuana, cocaine, etc. For more information on the status of such substances, please refer to the rulings of any of the contemporary Shīʿah jurists.

[204] Gambling is any type of game in which the parties bet on some money or property to be paid to the winner. In Islamic Jurisprudence, gambling is forbidden, and it is also forbidden to play with any instruments of gambling, regardless of whether it involves betting or not.

- intoxicants and gambling - are grave sins, and there is great loss in them; although there are some material benefits for people, however their dangers far outweigh their benefits.[205] Thus, after careful research and analysis of the pros and cons of intoxicants and gambling, any sane person would come to the conclusion that the harms which are associated with these two evils are far greater than any benefits which they may deliver to an individual or society.

It should be noted that the prohibition of intoxicants took place gradually, as Islam recognized that these were things which people were habituated to indulging in, and to have to quit or leave them abruptly would have been quite difficult. Thus, we see that the injunction barring the use of alcohol took place over four verses, and the verses of the Qur'ān in relation to this were revealed over time:

1. During the first stage, Allah ﷻ said: "And there are (among the produce that Allah brings forth as nourishment for you on the revived earth) the fruits of the date-palm, and grapes: you derive

[205] In an article published by the Mayo Clinic entitled: *Alcohol use: Weighing risks and benefits*, the author states: "Understanding the risks and any possible health benefits of alcohol often seems confusing; that's understandable, because the evidence for moderate alcohol use in healthy adults isn't certain. Researchers know surprisingly little about the risks or benefits of moderate alcohol use in healthy adults. Almost all studies of lifestyle, including diet, exercise, caffeine, and alcohol, rely on patient recall and truthful reporting of one's habits over many years. These studies may indicate that two things may be associated with one another, but not necessarily that one causes the other. It may be that adults who are in good health engage in more social activities and enjoy moderate amounts of alcohol, but that the alcohol has nothing to do with making them healthier.

Any potential benefits of alcohol are relatively small and may not apply to all individuals. In fact, the latest dietary guidelines make it clear that no one should begin drinking alcohol or drink more often on the basis of potential health benefits. For many people, the possible benefits don't outweigh the risks and avoiding alcohol is the best course." (Found on www.mayoclinic.org/healthy-lifestyle/nutrition-and-healthy-eating/in-depth/alcohol/art-20044551. (Last accessed on October 7, 2022)

from them intoxicants and good, wholesome nourishment. Surely in this there is a sign for people who reason and understand."[206]

2. Next, Allah ﷻ told the Muslims: "They ask you (Muḥammad ﷺ) about intoxicants and games of chance. Say (to them): 'In both of these there is great evil, although some use for people, but their evil is greater than their usefulness...'"[207]
3. At the third stage, Allah ﷻ stated: "O you who believe! Do not approach prayer *(ṣalāh)* while you are in (any sort of) a state of drunkenness until you know what you are saying..."[208]
4. Eventually, the final verse which outright prohibited any use of intoxicants was revealed to Prophet Muḥammad ﷺ to convey to the Muslims that: "O you who believe! Intoxicants, games of chance, sacrifices to (anything serving the function of) idols (and at places consecrated for offerings to other than Allah), and (the pagan practice of) divination by arrows (and similar practices) are a loathsome evil of Satan's doing; so turn wholly away from it so that you may prosper (in both worlds)."[209]

The second question which people asked Prophet Muḥammad ﷺ as mentioned in this verse was about almsgiving, and the Qur'ān quotes

---

[206] Qur'ān, Sūrah an-Naḥl (16), Verse 67:

وَمِن ثَمَرَٰتِ ٱلنَّخِيلِ وَٱلْأَعْنَٰبِ تَتَّخِذُونَ مِنْهُ سَكَرًا وَرِزْقًا حَسَنًا ۗ إِنَّ فِى ذَٰلِكَ لَءَايَةً لِّقَوْمٍ
يَعْقِلُونَ ﴿٦٧﴾

[207] Ibid., Sūrah al-Baqarah (2), Verse 219:

يَسْـَٔلُونَكَ عَنِ ٱلْخَمْرِ وَٱلْمَيْسِرِ ۖ قُلْ فِيهِمَآ إِثْمٌ كَبِيرٌ وَمَنَٰفِعُ لِلنَّاسِ وَإِثْمُهُمَآ أَكْبَرُ مِن
نَّفْعِهِمَا...

[208] Ibid., Sūrah an-Nisā' (4), Verse 43:

يَٰٓأَيُّهَا ٱلَّذِينَ ءَامَنُوا۟ لَا تَقْرَبُوا۟ ٱلصَّلَوٰةَ وَأَنتُمْ سُكَٰرَىٰ حَتَّىٰ تَعْلَمُوا۟ مَا تَقُولُونَ...

[209] Ibid., Sūrah al-Mā'idah (5), Verse 90:

يَٰٓأَيُّهَا ٱلَّذِينَ ءَامَنُوٓا۟ إِنَّمَا ٱلْخَمْرُ وَٱلْمَيْسِرُ وَٱلْأَنصَابُ وَٱلْأَزْلَٰمُ رِجْسٌ مِّنْ عَمَلِ ٱلشَّيْطَٰنِ
فَٱجْتَنِبُوهُ لَعَلَّكُمْ تُفْلِحُونَ ﴿٩٠﴾

them as saying: The people ask you, O Muḥammad ﷺ, as to what they should spend in charity *(infāq)* to others. Allah ﷻ responds and tells the Prophet ﷺ to tell the believers that whatever excess they have should be spent on those who are in need.

Spending in Charity for Others (Infāq)

What is the essence of *infāq*?

Simply put, *infāq* is to build a bridge and narrow the distance between humanity in various aspects of life - the most common and popular being the financial inequality. However, it can also include providing education, enhancing skill sets, promoting spirituality, and engaging in and supporting the emotional and social well-being of others, etc.

When it comes to *infāq* we have two extreme concepts:

Some people believe that *infāq* is only relevant and applicable from what is 'left over' after a person spends as much as they can on themselves and their family, living in complete comfort and in the lap of luxury. Even then, people who fall into this way of thinking believe that *infāq* is just a vehicle to make themselves happy that they are contributing to the welfare of others and doing "their part." They may even feel that their contribution should only be limited to those things which are left over which they have no need for - second-hand goods, or things which they have no use for as they have upgraded things in their life.

The other extreme of *infāq* is where a person only takes care of their basic, immediate needs, and then gives everything excess they have to others - even at the price of sacrificing the comfort and betterment of the lives of their immediate family members. Some people give in charity in the thousands, however when it comes to their own family, they will not even allow them to have the basics which are common in society! Some may even try to cite the example of Prophet Muḥammad ﷺ or the Ahlul Bayt ﷺ and their level of generosity and simple living to show that just like they gave everything they had to the needy, this is the norm and they must do the same thing to follow in their example! However, obviously such people have misunderstood the historical examples and have interpreted them to suit their own narrow understanding of Islam.

If we go back to the essence of *infāq* which is to lessen the gap between humanity, then we would realize that after a person has met one's own needs of life and that of their families, then they should give to others to help elevate their community.

We know that every single person has something which they can contribute to society - and it does not always have to be money - it can be one's time, talents, contacts, etc.; and in the same vein, all of us are in need of something - and again, it does not necessarily have to be money.

So what is the balance when it comes to *infāq*?

Every individual must look at one's own circumstances, conditions, the society one lives in, their duties and responsibilities, and their potentials.

There is no doubt that Islam encourages *infāq*, however we must be strategic and know our responsibilities and priorities when engaging in the act of helping other people.

The word *'afw* which has been translated as 'left over' has multiple meanings, some of which include:

1. To destroy the effect of something.
2. The median or average of something.
3. The extra amount of something.
4. The best part of wealth or property.

It is also possible that in this verse, its meaning may be 'forgiveness or pardoning the mistakes of others.' If we take this as the intended meaning, then the interpretation of this verse would be: Say to them, O Muḥammad - the best almsgiving, even better than materially helping others is for you to forgive and overlook the mistakes of people.

Keeping in mind the social climate that existed in pre-Islamic Arabia, which was the place of revelation of the Noble Qur'ān, and that the Era of Ignorance which had existed for centuries and permeated into the minds of the inhabitants in the cities of Mecca and Medina, we know that these were people who for the most part, were engulfed in the highest levels of enmity, resentment, and a lack of empathy for others.

Perhaps the Arabs who had these traits, and other negative ethical qualities were sincerely asking about almsgiving and helping the needy, however the Qur'ān responded to them in this way, and rather than telling them what material goods they should contribute to the needy, it advised them that what is needed even greater by them is something which is far more important - and that is the quality of forgiveness of others.

Such a response is actually rooted in the styles of eloquence and rhetoric in which a speaker hears the question of an individual, however does not respond directly to it, and instead deals with something much more important that the audience truly needs to hear in their lives.

At the end of this verse, Allah ﷻ states that He makes clear His verses *(āyāt)* to the believers so that perhaps they may listen and reflect on His words.

Keys of Guidance

- Intoxicants of any type, as well as gambling - in any shape or form that it takes, whether it be in a casino or online - are all causes of corruption of the body and soul, and lead to negligence of Allah ﷻ and everything that is good. Therefore, they have been discussed side by side[210] in the Noble Qur'ān.

---

[210] See Qur'ān, Sūrah al-Baqarah (2), Verse 219:

يَسْـَٔلُونَكَ عَنِ ٱلْخَمْرِ وَٱلْمَيْسِرِ ۖ قُلْ فِيهِمَآ إِثْمٌ كَبِيرٌ وَمَنَٰفِعُ لِلنَّاسِ وَإِثْمُهُمَآ أَكْبَرُ مِن
نَّفْعِهِمَا ۗ وَيَسْـَٔلُونَكَ مَاذَا يُنفِقُونَ قُلِ ٱلْعَفْوَ ۗ كَذَٰلِكَ يُبَيِّنُ ٱللَّهُ لَكُمُ ٱلْءَايَٰتِ لَعَلَّكُمْ
تَتَفَكَّرُونَ ﴿٢١٩﴾

"They ask you about intoxicating drinks and games of chance. Say: 'In both there is great evil, though some use for people, but their evil is greater than their usefulness.' They also ask you what they should spend (in Allah's cause and for the needy). Say: 'What is left over (after you have spent on your dependent's needs).' Thus does Allah make clear to you His Revelations, that perhaps you may reflect."

See Qur'ān, Sūrah al-Mā'idah (5), Verses 90-91:

يَٰٓأَيُّهَا ٱلَّذِينَ ءَامَنُوٓا۟ إِنَّمَا ٱلْخَمْرُ وَٱلْمَيْسِرُ وَٱلْأَنصَابُ وَٱلْأَزْلَٰمُ رِجْسٌ مِّنْ عَمَلِ ٱلشَّيْطَٰنِ
فَٱجْتَنِبُوهُ لَعَلَّكُمْ تُفْلِحُونَ ﴿٩٠﴾ إِنَّمَا يُرِيدُ ٱلشَّيْطَٰنُ أَن يُوقِعَ بَيْنَكُمُ ٱلْعَدَٰوَةَ وَٱلْبَغْضَآءَ فِى
ٱلْخَمْرِ وَٱلْمَيْسِرِ وَيَصُدَّكُمْ عَن ذِكْرِ ٱللَّهِ وَعَنِ ٱلصَّلَوٰةِ ۖ فَهَلْ أَنتُم مُّنتَهُونَ ﴿٩١﴾

"O you who believe! Intoxicants, games of chance, sacrifices to (anything

- As human beings, we are obligated by our intellect and the teachings of our Creator to safeguard both our mind and our soul by banning all types of intoxicants - whether they be alcohol or drugs - so that we are able to protect our power of intellect and reason; and by banning all types of gambling, we safeguard our inner peace of mind, as well as our economic well-being.
- When dealing with other people and their practices which go against the teachings of Islam and the Noble Qur'ān, we must ensure that we are always reasonable. We need to recognize that although these are bad actions in others, there may be some good deeds that they perform as well, and perhaps when it comes to people who take intoxicants or gamble, they have not been able to truly understand that the harms of these outweigh the benefits. When we come across such situations with those who do not have the same level of conviction and belief as us, we should raise these issues with them in such a way that will get them to think and reflect on what they are doing.
- The rules which Allah ﷻ lays down are based on benefits and harms - however, we must also realize that they are not necessarily related solely to the life of this temporal world, thus we must also keep in mind the life of the world to come which is forever.
- It is also very important to note that Allah ﷻ provides us with guidance to facilitate a balanced approach in life. As such, we must keep in mind that we are not talking about absolute good or absolute evil. Most of the time, the problem is when good and evil are mixed together, and that is where Allah ﷻ gives us the

---

serving the function of) idols (and at places consecrated for offerings to other than Allah), and (the pagan practice of) divination by arrows (and similar practices) are a loathsome evil of Satan's doing; so turn wholly away from it so that you may prosper (in both worlds). Satan only seeks to provoke enmity and hatred among you by means of intoxicants and games of chance, and to bar you from the remembrance of Allah and from prayer. So then, will you abstain?"

best yardstick to distinguish between truth from falsehood so that we do not get trapped into what seems to be the truth, however it is only falsehood decorated to look right and beneficial. That is how intoxicants are marketed and promoted in the world - they are never shown on commercials as being harmful to one's health, relationships, or life in general. Consumers are not told about the high risk of cancer associated with drinking - even in "moderation." Very rarely if ever, do alcohol commercials show a person driving their car at high speed - killing others and potentially themselves. Rather, all commercials show people enjoying life, having a good time, and living the moment. Alcohol consumption is equated to having personal and societal benefits and a good way to end the week and spend time with family and friends. The truth is that they may have some benefits for certain people, however gradually they end up destroying the person, their family life, and all of society in general.

Verse 220

فِي ٱلدُّنْيَا وَٱلْـَٔاخِرَةِ ۗ وَيَسْـَٔلُونَكَ عَنِ ٱلْيَتَـٰمَىٰ ۖ قُلْ إِصْلَاحٌ لَّهُمْ خَيْرٌ ۖ وَإِن تُخَالِطُوهُمْ فَإِخْوَٰنُكُمْ ۚ وَٱللَّهُ يَعْلَمُ ٱلْمُفْسِدَ مِنَ ٱلْمُصْلِحِ ۚ وَلَوْ شَآءَ ٱللَّهُ لَأَعْنَتَكُمْ ۚ إِنَّ ٱللَّهَ عَزِيزٌ حَكِيمٌ ﴿٢٢٠﴾

In this world and the hereafter (with all of the truths related to both). And they ask you (O Muhammad ﷺ) about (how they should act in regards to the) orphans. Say (to them): "The best thing to do is that which is best for them. If you intermix (your expenses) with theirs, (there is no harm in that) for they are your comrades. Allah knows well who causes disorder and corruption from the one who reconciles. Had Allah willed, He would have imposed on you exacting conditions. Indeed Allah is All-Glorious *('Azīz)*, All-Wise *(Ḥakīm)*."

History of Revelation

After the revelation of verses in which it was noted that it was forbidden to encroach upon or make personal use of the property of the orphans,[211] there were Muslims who had previously taken orphans into their own houses and were taking care of them, but they began to distance themselves from the guardianship of these children, and some people even removed them from their homes, or created such a toxic environment for the orphans that was far worse than merely evicting them.

With this situation at play, it made things extremely difficult for both the guardians of the orphans, as well as the orphans themselves, so it was because of this that the Muslims came to Prophet Muḥammad ﷺ and posed some questions to him about how they should deal with these orphans who were in their care, and in response the above verse of the Noble Qur'ān was revealed.

Commentary

In this verse, the central point of reflection has been expressed by Allah

---

[211] This has been mentioned in two places in the Qur'ān, Sūrah al-Isrā' (17), Verse 34:

وَلَا تَقۡرَبُواْ مَالَ ٱلۡيَتِيمِ إِلَّا بِٱلَّتِي هِيَ أَحۡسَنُ حَتَّىٰ يَبۡلُغَ أَشُدَّهُۥۚ وَأَوۡفُواْ بِٱلۡعَهۡدِۖ إِنَّ ٱلۡعَهۡدَ كَانَ
مَسۡـُٔولٗا ٣٤

And do not approach the property of an orphan except in the best way (such as to improve and increase it) until he/she comes of age and is strong; and fulfill the covenant: the covenant is surely subject to questioning (on the Day of Judgment and you will be held accountable for your covenant).

See also Qur'ān, Sūrah an-Nisā' (4), Verse 10:

إِنَّ ٱلَّذِينَ يَأۡكُلُونَ أَمۡوَٰلَ ٱلۡيَتَٰمَىٰ ظُلۡمًا إِنَّمَا يَأۡكُلُونَ فِي بُطُونِهِمۡ نَارٗاۖ وَسَيَصۡلَوۡنَ
سَعِيرٗا ١٠

Surely those who consume the property of orphans wrongfully, certainly they consume fire into their bellies; and soon they will be roasting in a blaze (the likes of which you have never seen before, and the degree of whose intensity no one knows except Allah).

ﷻ with Him initially saying that as Muslims you need to think about the life of this world, and also the life of the hereafter.

In reality, although a human being has been commanded to **submit** to Allah ﷻ and His Prophets, at the same time one is also obliged to **obey** the commands of Allah ﷻ and His Prophets through **reflecting** on what one is ordered to do, and not simply "blindly" following. In other words, although the rules stem from Allah ﷻ and are conveyed through Prophet Muḥammad ﷺ, still a true believer must seek to understand the secrets of the Divine commandments, and by understanding them a person will then be in a better position to apply them in one's life.

Allah ﷻ then mentions the third question that the believers at the time of Prophet Muḥammad ﷺ asked him, and He says that they ask you O Muḥammad ﷺ about the orphans who need support. The response that Allah ﷻ provides to His Prophet ﷺ which he is then obliged to convey to the community is that rather than doing nothing to help them for fear of doing wrong to them, try and set their affairs right for their own good, for surely that is the best path that anyone can take.

Allah ﷻ is telling the people that if you have orphans in your custody, then live your life as you normally do, but at the same time allow them to live with you in such a way that they are able to blend in with your family so that they recognize that you are their brothers or sisters in faith.

Through such wordings, the Qur'ān is advising the Muslims that it is not right to shun the responsibility of caring for orphans after they have brought them into their homes, and provided for them - so how can they abandon them now? Allah ﷻ then adds that He recognizes those people who corrupt from those who reform - in other words, Allah ﷻ is aware of everyone's intentions and recognizes those who intend to misuse the property of the orphans and mix it with their own personal property in order to squander the orphan's property under the guise of being true, sincere sympathizers of their cause.

At the end of this verse, Allah ﷻ speaking to the Muslims states that had He willed, He would have made you suffer by ordering you that at the same time of your obligation to guard the orphans, you must also completely separate your property from their property and not allow any of it to mix with yours - however, Allah ﷻ will not do that because that would be extremely difficult for those who want to extend a helping hand to the parent-less children, and that He, Allah is All-Mighty, All-Wise.[212]

Keys of Guidance

- Allah ﷻ begins this verse by providing the readers with the bigger picture of this temporal world and the world to come, and as such He tells us that we must not have tunnel vision in this world when we deal with the issues of life, hardships, orphans, etc. Every action cannot be justified merely in the realm of this world, and that is why Allah ﷻ mentions the phrase: 'this world and the world to come,' in the same breath. In essence, Allah ﷻ is providing the tools to create a positive mindset and to make us recognize that we cannot confine ourselves to the life of this world - from birth to death; rather there is another life which will be forever.
- When it comes to orphans, Allah ﷻ uses the term 'reconciliation' or *iṣlāḥ*. The deeper meaning of this word is that it relates to reconciliation of their damage from all different angles: physical, emotional, financial, social, etc. In essence, we need to create a holistic program as it relates to our relationship with the orphans and what they need to mature into upright citizens, given that they have been brought up without the direct love of their parents. The damage which is caused by losing the heads of the family is very serious, and for this reason Allah ﷻ reminds the believers that the orphans of our community are like our own brothers and sisters and we must treat them as we do our own family.
- The eternal struggle on Earth is between those who seek to deviate, create confusion, and cause corruption in society - the *mufsid*; while

[212] The word translated into English as 'imposed on you' *(a'natakum)* comes from the Arabic root of *'anat* and its original meaning was 'halt when needing to do something that is dangerous;' but according to some scholars of the Arabic language, it means 'any time of difficulty that a person needs to make one's way through.'

those on the other end of the spectrum are those striving to bring about positive reforms and clean up the evils which have been left to run rampant - they are the *muṣlīḥ*. Allah ﷻ warns us that the orphans are vulnerable, and as they do not have parents or other family caregivers, we must not take advantage of them and their situation. We must not seek to exploit them and take their rights; rather, we need to ensure that we are doing what is best for them and their future. Today, we see many children that have lost their mother or father, or both, and although some stay on the straight path, unfortunately many of them go into a life of crime, get recruited into gangs, and end up on the wrong path.

- We should study and deeply reflect on the life of this world and the hereafter, and try to understand these planes of existence, and what they have to offer to the true believers.
- Anything which we can do to improve the situation of the orphans in society will be beneficial for them. Allah ﷻ uses the term that we must 'set their affairs right,' and this can include assisting them financially - either directly or through providing assistance to the orphanages around the world; but it can also relate to educational assistance by which we may provide them with an opportunity to gain life skills, or training in areas of life in order to allow them to excel and find a career path; or it may even be giving them the proper religious training which they lack due to not having parents, so that they can remain on the path of Islam.

Verse 221

وَلَا تَنكِحُوا۟ ٱلْمُشْرِكَـٰتِ حَتَّىٰ يُؤْمِنَّ ۚ وَلَأَمَةٌ مُّؤْمِنَةٌ خَيْرٌ مِّن مُّشْرِكَةٍ وَلَوْ أَعْجَبَتْكُمْ ۗ وَلَا تُنكِحُوا۟ ٱلْمُشْرِكِينَ حَتَّىٰ يُؤْمِنُوا۟ ۚ وَلَعَبْدٌ مُّؤْمِنٌ خَيْرٌ مِّن مُّشْرِكٍ وَلَوْ أَعْجَبَكُمْ ۗ أُو۟لَـٰٓئِكَ يَدْعُونَ إِلَى ٱلنَّارِ ۖ وَٱللَّهُ يَدْعُوٓا۟ إِلَى ٱلْجَنَّةِ وَٱلْمَغْفِرَةِ بِإِذْنِهِۦ ۖ وَيُبَيِّنُ ءَايَـٰتِهِۦ لِلنَّاسِ لَعَلَّهُمْ يَتَذَكَّرُونَ ﴿٢٢١﴾

And (O Muslim men) do not marry polytheist women until they (the women) believe (in the One True God). A believing slave-girl is better than a (free) woman who associates partners with Allah, even though she pleases and attracts you (with her beauty, wealth, status, or family). Nor marry (your believing women) to men who associate partners with Allah until they (those men) believe (in the One True God and in Islam). A believing male slave is better than a (free) man who associates partners with Allah, even though he pleases and attracts you. Those (the polytheists) call to the fire, while Allah calls to Paradise and forgiveness (of your sins) by His permission. He makes clear His revelations for people that they may reflect and be mindful (of their duty to Allah).

History of Revelation

A person named Murthad was commissioned by Prophet Muḥammad ﷺ to travel from the city of Medina to the city of Mecca as there was a group of Muslims there who needed safe transport to Medina. Murthad followed the orders of the Noble Prophet ﷺ and made his way to the blessed city of Mecca, and while he was there he met a beautiful woman named ʿAnāq, who knew him from the pre-Islamic Era of Ignorance. Just as she used to do in the past, she invited him to engage in sexual relationships out of the bounds of wedlock, however since Murthad was now a Muslim and this was not permitted, he turned down her request, so she asked him to marry her. Murthad told her that he would have to consult with Prophet Muḥammad ﷺ and seek his permission.

Once he completed the task which the Prophet ﷺ had asked him to do, he returned to Medina and went to see Prophet Muḥammad ﷺ and told him about what had happened with ʿAnāq. In response to his query if he could marry her or not, the verse under review was revealed which informed him and the rest of the believers that the polytheistic women are not worthy of marrying Muslim men, nor are the polytheistic men permitted to marry Muslim women.[213]

Commentary

According to the history of revelation, this verse was revealed to answer questions about the marriage of a Muslim to an idol worshipper, and Allah ﷻ clearly tells the Muslims - both men and women of the community - that they are not permitted to marry idolaters until they leave polytheism, and accept the religion of Islam and the message of the Qur'ān.

In order to further solidify this belief in the hearts and minds of the Muslim community, Allah ﷻ presents a comparison and tells the Muslim men that it is better for them to marry a believing slave-girl over a polytheist free woman - even though the beauty, wealth, or social status of the free woman may be unimaginable.

Therefore, this verse sought to ingrain in the psyche of the Muslim men that the purpose of marriage is not limited to the fulfillment of sexual desires. Rather, a wife is the life partner of her husband, as well as an educator and nurturer for the children, and she forms half of a man's persona. Thus, how can polytheism and its ominous consequences be accepted to attain outward beauty and some wealth?

Allah ﷻ then deals with another part of this ruling and turns His attention toward the women and states that the Muslim men must not oblige the unmarried, Muslim women in the society to marry polytheist men until those men leave their ways, and believe in the One True God and convert to the religion of Islam. Therefore, if an unmarried woman cannot find a free Muslim man to marry, then she should marry a man who is a believing male slave, who will be better as a spouse than a free idolatrous man even if the wealth, beauty, and social status of the free polytheist man is something which may be desirable.

At the end of this verse, Allah ﷻ presents the substantiation for why He sent down this Divine decree and that was in order to stop people from conjuring up presumptions about why such forms of marriage were not permitted; and He says that the polytheists - men or women

---

213 *Tafsīr Majmaʿ al-Bayān*, under the commentary of this verse.

- invite others to the fire of Hell due to their lack of belief in Allah ﷻ and adherence to the teachings which Allah ﷻ sent for the guidance of humanity, while Allah ﷻ invites to Paradise and His forgiveness. In addition, at the end of this verse, Allah ﷻ includes that He makes clear His revelations *(āyāt)* to the people so that perhaps they may reflect on this in their own personal lives.

Some commentators of the Qur'ān have presented a subtle point in relation to this verse, and have said that this verse along with 21 other verses of the Qur'ān which follow this (Sūrah al-Baqarah, Verses 222-242) explain the rulings *(aḥkām)* related to forming a family and its various dimensions.

In these 22 verses, 12 rulings have been stated:

1. The ruling *(ḥukm)* and impermissibility of marriage with the polytheists;
2. The prohibition of engaging in sexual relationships with one's wife during her time of menstruation;
3. The ruling of making an oath which is presented as an introduction to the oath known in the Qur'ān as *īlā'* - a type of oath which a man makes in which he swears that he will not have sexual relations with his wife;
4. The ruling about the oath known as *'īlā'* and its subsequent divorce;
5. Observing the legal waiting time period *('iddah)* after a divorce, before a woman can lawfully marry again;
6. The number of divorces permissible between a husband and his wife;
7. Retaining one's spouse in kindness or divorcing her in goodness;
8. The rulings on breastfeeding children;
9. The waiting period *('iddah)* for a woman whose husband has died;
10. Courting a woman before her waiting period ends;
11. Giving the entire wedding gift (known as *mahr, ṣidāq, ṣaduqāt, or farīḍah* in the Qur'ān) if a divorce takes place before the marriage is consummated;
12. The ruling of giving a woman a gift for the performance of a temporary, time-fixed, contractual marriage *(mut'ah);* or a divorced woman if her husband passes away, or she asks for a divorce.

These rulings are mixed with moral *(akhlāqī)* reminders and phrases which as we will see, show that the issue of forming a family is a form of worship of Allah ﷻ and should be carried out with thought and deliberation without blindly jumping into it.

Keys of Guidance

- As mentioned above, the key purpose of marriage is to shape the future of one's life and coming generations, and as such the consequences of marriage are far greater than merely this world and the couple; rather they affect multiple generations to come and impact the outcome in the next world.
- Marriage is the creation of a lifestyle, and when the two parties have different faiths or foundations, it will affect the entire life from where they go for vacation, what they define as fun, what their priorities in life will be, etc. Therefore it is very important that both parties are on the same page from the point of view of their faith if they wish to have a successful life and a prosperous hereafter. When Islam advises its followers that they are not to marry outside of the faith of Islam, it is due to the practical effects that it will have in one's daily life and the imbalance which it may cause.
- Compatibility as it relates to a man and woman who are looking for marriage is very important; and this compatibility is built upon three fundamental things:

    1. Faith *(īmān)* and God-consciousness *(taqwā).*
    2. Morals and etiquette *(akhlāq).*
    3. External factors, such as: age, height, race, education, etc.

    Therefore, we must note that faith and character is just as important if not more than the external factors.
- In choosing a spouse, faith of the individual is the most important characteristic that must be kept in the forefront of the mind. As the spouse plays a tremendous role in the nurturing of any children to come out of the marriage, it is of the utmost importance to select a righteous partner.

- When a man or woman is looking for a life partner, one must not be deceived or enchanted by the beauty, wealth, or social status of that other individual. The primary criteria must be the faith of the potential spouse.

Verse 222

وَيَسْأَلُونَكَ عَنِ ٱلْمَحِيضِ ۖ قُلْ هُوَ أَذًى فَٱعْتَزِلُوا۟ ٱلنِّسَآءَ فِى ٱلْمَحِيضِ ۖ وَلَا
تَقْرَبُوهُنَّ حَتَّىٰ يَطْهُرْنَ ۖ فَإِذَا تَطَهَّرْنَ فَأْتُوهُنَّ مِنْ حَيْثُ أَمَرَكُمُ ٱللَّهُ ۚ إِنَّ
ٱللَّهَ يُحِبُّ ٱلتَّوَّٰبِينَ وَيُحِبُّ ٱلْمُتَطَهِّرِينَ ﴿٢٢٢﴾

They also ask you (O Muḥammad ﷺ) about (the injunctions concerning) menstruation. Say (to the believers): "It is a state of discomfort (and ritual impurity), so keep away from them (by not engaging in sexual relations) during their menstruation and do not approach them (for sexual intercourse) until they are cleansed (of the menstrual blood). When they are cleansed, then (you can) go to them as Allah has commanded you (according to the urge which He has placed in your nature and within the terms that He has enjoined upon you). Surely Allah loves those who turn to Him in (sincere) repentance (of past sins and errors), and He loves those who cleanse themselves.

History of Revelation

Women's menstruation[214] is anywhere between a minimum of three days

---

[214] The menstrual cycle is the monthly series of changes that a woman's body goes through in preparation for the possibility of pregnancy. Each month, one of the ovaries releases an egg - a process which is called ovulation. At the same time, hormonal changes prepare the uterus for pregnancy. If ovulation takes place and the egg is not fertilized, then the lining of the uterus sheds this blood through the vagina; and this is a menstrual period.

and a maximum of ten days each month according to the Islamic teachings, and that is the blood which comes from a woman's uterus with its special characteristics that are mentioned in the books of Jurisprudence *(Fiqh)*.[215] In that state, a woman is referred to as a *ḥā'iḍ,* and the blood which she sees is referred to as the blood of *ḥayḍ*.

Some Jews state that according to the Judaic law, it is absolutely forbidden *(ḥarām)* for men to associate in any way with women while they are in their monthly period - even so much as eating at the same table or staying in the same room as them.[216]

In contrast to the Jewish opinion, the Christians say that there is no difference between the state of menstruation of women and non-menstruation, and as such all kinds of interaction with one's wife, even

---

[215] The specifics rules in regards to the menstrual cycle and the requirements which a Muslim woman must follow are mentioned in detail in the books of Islamic Jurisprudence.

[216] In the Old Testament, in the Book of Leviticus 15:19-27, it states:

> [19] And if a woman has an issue and her issue from her flesh be blood, she will be put apart seven days; and whosoever touches her will be unclean until the evening. [20] And everything that she lies upon in her separation will be unclean; everything also that she sits upon will be unclean. [21] And whosoever touches her bed will wash his clothes and bathe himself in water, and be unclean until the evening. [22] And whosoever touches anything that she sat upon will wash his clothes and bathe himself in water, and be unclean until the evening. [23] And if it be on her bed or on anything whereon she sits, when he touches it, he shall be unclean until the evening. [24] And if any man lie with her at all and her monthly discharge be upon him, he shall be unclean seven days; and all the bed whereon he lies shall be unclean. [25] And if a woman have an issue of her blood many days out of the time of her separation, or if it run beyond the time of her separation, all the days of the issue of her uncleanness will be as the days of her separation; she will be unclean. [26] Every bed whereon she lies all the days of her issue will be unto her as the bed of her separation; and whatsoever she sits upon will be unclean, as the uncleanness of her separation. [27] And whosoever touches those things shall be unclean, and shall wash his clothes and bathe himself in water, and be unclean until the evening.

sexual intercourse with them is permissible.[217]

The Arab pagans were more or less accustomed to the Jewish temperament, and although they did not follow the Jewish law of the Old Testament they still interacted with menstruating women by referring to the Jewish law. It was this difference and extreme views which were being taught and practiced that resulted in some Muslims coming to Prophet Muḥammad ﷺ and asking him about this issue, and the response of the Prophet ﷺ through the revelation which Allah ﷻ gave him, is seen in this verse under review.

We encounter yet another question asked of Prophet Muḥammad ﷺ about women's menstruation in this verse where Allah ﷻ replies that they ask you (Muḥammad ﷺ) about menstruation, so say to them that during this time, the woman is in a state of discomfort and ritual impurity, and it is for this reason that a man must not engage in sexual intercourse with his wife until she has finished the monthly cycle.

Allah ﷻ states that sexual intercourse is not permitted during this short time frame because in addition to it being prohibited in the teachings of Islam, it is also detrimental according to some modern research medicine, and some of the outcomes of it include the possibility of male and female infertility; it can become the breeding ground for sexually transmitted diseases; as well as inflammation of the female genitals, and the entry of contaminated blood into the male genitalia. For this reason, scholars have stated that a man and woman should not have sexual intercourse during the monthly cycle.[218]

---

217 The Christians of today are not under the Old Testament ceremonial law, and as such the Levitical ceremonial laws do not apply to them. There is no biblical reason why a married couple cannot have sex during the wife's menstrual cycle.

218 In his book, *Marriage and Morals in Islam*, Sayyid Muhammad Rizvi states: "According to the *sharīʿah*, the duration of the monthly period is between three to ten days. If the bleeding is less than three days, it is not menstruation; if it is for more than ten days, then it is menstruation for the first ten days and then it is counted as *istiḥāḍa*, irregular bleeding, during which sex is permitted. The prohibition of sex during the period is limited strictly to sexual intercourse; other intimate contact (with the exception of the vagina and anus) is allowed.

Allah ﷻ then mentions to the Muslims that once their wives are finished their monthly cycle and they have taken the religiously defined bath *(ghusl)*,[219] they have become cleansed and then you can go to them as Allah ﷻ has commanded you according to the urge which He has placed in your nature and within the terms that He has enjoined upon you. Allah ﷻ concludes this directive by saying that He loves those who turn to Him in sincere repentance for their past sins and errors, and He loves those who purify themselves.

According to some commentators of the Noble Qur'ān, the phrase 'when they are cleansed' *(yaṭhurna)* refers to when a woman is finished her menstrual blood; however a majority of commentators of the Qur'ān have taken the phrase 'so then when they are cleansed' *(faidhā taṭahharna)* to refer to a woman who has now become purified after having performed the specific *ghusl* once her menstrual cycle has ended.

In summary, according to the first sentence, after purifying oneself from the menstrual blood, sexual intercourse is permissible even if the woman has not performed the required *ghusl,* but according to the second sentence, it is not permissible to engage in sexual relationships until the *ghusl* has been taken. A person should check the ruling of the religious authority they follow to confirm their religious responsibility.

Keys of Guidance

- One of the core messages of this verse is that Allah ﷻ creates

---

However, it is better not to play with her body between the navel and the knees. If a person who is engaged in sexual intercourse with his wife discovers that her period has begun, then he must immediately withdraw from her..." (Taken from www.al-islam.org/marriage-and-morals-islam-sayyid-muhammad-rizvi/chapter-three-islamic-sexual-morality-2-its#sex-forbidden-any-time-marriage. Last accessed on October 7, 2022)

[219] The term *ghusl* is used in Islamic Jurisprudence and it refers to the Islamic ritual bath of the whole body from the head to the feet in accordance with the qualifications made by the Divine Legislator. This form of bathing is performed in a particular manner with the intention *(niyyah)* of performing the ceremonial bath to follow the orders of Allah ﷻ.

everything for a purpose and this includes women. They too have been created for the Divine purpose of reaching perfection. Women are also the manifestation of nurturers on this Earth, and therefore they need to have the tools to bear and nurture the next generation. The consequences of this is that they will be in different states, and one of those states is their monthly menstrual cycle. This state is not shameful, nor bad, in fact it is something which Allah ﷻ gave to them due to its need. However, just as Allah ﷻ is the One who gave women this certain aspect in their lives, He also explains the religious verdicts of how they should lead their lives when they are in this state.

- The state of menstruation *(ḥayḍ)* is actually a time of immense mercy from Allah ﷻ for the women. In this time, she is able to relax a bit, and as there are physical changes taking place, this becomes an opportune time to reflect on her relationship with Allah ﷻ which she may not have at other times.
- In many cultures, there are some misunderstandings about certain things during the time when a woman is in her monthly cycle, and most of these are untruths and perhaps based on superstitions handed down from generation to generation. For example, some people think that a woman cannot recite Qurʾān or *duʿās* if she is in her monthly period. In fact, during this time frame, Islam has recommended that women can and should still in engage in the worship of Allah ﷻ through performing *wuḍūʾ*, sitting on the prayer mat facing *qiblah*, and engaging in supplications *(duʿās)*, recitations *(adhkār)*, glorifications *(tasbīḥāt)*, and other such acts of worship - other than *ṣalāh* - in order to keep the spiritual connection with Allah ﷻ alive and active.[220]
- In the religion of Islam, there is no such thing as being shy when

[220] There are certain actions which a woman in menstruation cannot perform, such as touching the Arabic script of the Noble Qur'ān, going into a Masjid, and certain other things. Readers can refer to the detailed books of Islamic Jurisprudence for further information.

it comes to asking questions about the religion. There are no taboo topics that Islam is wary of, and so as long as the questioner frames the enquiry correctly and asks the right person, one should not be afraid of asking whatever is on one's mind.

- Islam is a comprehensive religion, therefore it provides its followers with rulings for all aspects of life - including intimacy between husband and wife. In addition to the verses of the Qur'ān which speak generally about this God-given desire, there are countless *ḥadīth* from Prophet Muḥammad ﷺ and the 12 Imāms ؑ which go into details about this issue.

Verse 223

نِسَآؤُكُمْ حَرْثٌ لَّكُمْ فَأْتُوا۟ حَرْثَكُمْ أَنَّىٰ شِئْتُمْ ۖ وَقَدِّمُوا۟ لِأَنفُسِكُمْ ۚ
وَٱتَّقُوا۟ ٱللَّهَ وَٱعْلَمُوٓا۟ أَنَّكُم مُّلَـٰقُوهُ ۗ وَبَشِّرِ ٱلْمُؤْمِنِينَ ﴿٢٢٣﴾

Your women (wives) are like a tilth for you (where you plant a seed to obtain produce - children), so come to your tilth as you wish, and send ahead for your souls. Have God-consciousness, and know that you will meet Him; and give glad tidings to the believers.

In this verse, Allah ﷻ points to one of the ultimate goals of sexual relations between a husband and his wife, and as such the Qur'ān begins by saying that your wives are the place of you sowing your seed, therefore the couple is given a sort of freedom to engage in sexual relations whenever they want to - except during the times when it is impermissible.

Here women are likened to the ground which a farmer uses to plant one's crops.

The late ʿAllāmah Ṭabāʾṭabāʾī mentions a point in his commentary, *al-Mizān*, in which he states that: "The meaning of this verse is as follows: Women are to humanity as tillage is to an individual. Agricultural land is needed to preserve the seed and produce food, so that the human race may continue to exist. Likewise, women are needed for the continuity of humanity. According to the system created by Allah ﷻ, a woman's womb is the place where a child is made, and develops from a microscopic sperm to a human being. Since the original place of sperm is in the body of a man, He created between a man and a woman love, compassion, and an attraction which incites a man to seek a woman. The creative purpose of this mutual attraction is to pave the way for the continuity of the human race, so there was no reason why it should be confined to one place and not another, or one time and not another, as long as it helped in achieving that goal, and does not hinder any other obligatory work."[221]

This analogy which Allah ﷻ provides in the Noble Qur'ān may shock some as to why Islam describes half of the human race - the women - with such words, however it should be understood that through it Allah ﷻ wants to provide us with a very subtle point.

In fact, the Qur'ān wants to show and prove the necessity of the presence of women in human society, and stress on the fact that women are not merely a tool for men to fulfill their sexual desires, but rather women are much greater than that because they are a means of the preservation of humanity on Earth. Therefore, the wording which Allah ﷻ uses in this verse is actually a warning to those who view women merely as a toy or a plaything to satisfy men's desires.

Allah ﷻ continues and tells the believers that they should ensure that a husband and wife make time for one another in order to develop a healthy sexual relationship, which will by the permission of Allah ﷻ, facilitate the bringing of children into this world, as He says: "To Allah belongs the sovereignty of the heavens and the earth. He creates whatever He wills. He grants to whom He wills females (daughters), and grants to whom He wills males (sons). Or He combines them both males and females (sons and daughters granted to whom He wills); and He leaves barren whom He wills. Surely He is All-Knowing, All-Powerful."[222]

---

[221] *Tafsīr al-Mizān*, Vol. 2, Pg. 279.

[222] Qur'ān, Sūrah ash-Shūrā (42), Verses 49-50:

لِّلَّهِ مُلْكُ ٱلسَّمَٰوَٰتِ وَٱلْأَرْضِ ۚ يَخْلُقُ مَا يَشَآءُ ۚ يَهَبُ لِمَن يَشَآءُ إِنَٰثًا وَيَهَبُ لِمَن يَشَآءُ ٱلذُّكُورَ ﴿٤٩﴾ أَوْ يُزَوِّجُهُمْ ذُكْرَانًا وَإِنَٰثًا ۖ وَيَجْعَلُ مَن يَشَآءُ عَقِيمًا ۚ إِنَّهُۥ عَلِيمٌ قَدِيرٌ ﴿٥٠﴾

However, it does not end with the conception of children because parents must then ensure that they work hard to raise righteous offspring, and through them send some good ahead for themselves.

Therefore, this union between a husband and wife should be used to bring children into this world who are then raised according to the correct teachings so that they can be a spiritual reserve for parents in the future, and more importantly on the Day of Resurrection.

This portion of the verse is actually warning people that when it comes to choosing a spouse, they must follow the principles which are laid down by the Qur'ān, and the *ḥadīth* of Prophet Muḥammad ﷺ and his Ahlul Bayt ؑ which have been explained by the scholars of Islam. If adhered to, then there is a better chance that all of the efforts of parents will lead them to the upbringing of righteous children, and a worthy nation of believers for the next generation.

At the end of this verse, Allah ﷻ once again commands the believers to observe God-consciousness *(taqwā)* and have the awe and reverence of Allah ﷻ, and know that we will all meet Him on the Day of Judgment. He also reminds people that as recipients of the Noble Qur'ān, the Prophet ﷺ should give good tidings to the believers - the good news of Divine mercy, felicity, and salvation in the shadow of piety.

Keys of Guidance

- Just as good seeds and good soil play an important role in crop production and a better harvest, so too a righteous man and a righteous woman - as husband and wife, and then father and mother - play a vital role in the moral and spiritual upbringing of a healthy child, and this will play a key role in the survival of the next generation.
- In the Islamic teachings, a woman is neither a commodity that can be bought or sold, nor is she is a source of spiritual darkness or temptress toward the 'original sin;' rather, Islam outlines that a woman is the founder of civilization, and a patron in human history, and she is a sender of gifts for the hereafter.
- Islam has given direction in all areas of life, and even when it

comes to the desires of the body, the Islamic teachings have laid down limits, and thus sexual interaction with one's spouse must be controlled and directed through God-consciousness.

Verse 224

وَلَا تَجْعَلُوا۟ ٱللَّهَ عُرْضَةً لِّأَيْمَٰنِكُمْ أَن تَبَرُّوا۟ وَتَتَّقُوا۟ وَتُصْلِحُوا۟ بَيْنَ ٱلنَّاسِ ۗ وَٱللَّهُ سَمِيعٌ عَلِيمٌ ﴿٢٢٤﴾

And do not (in striving to keep your oaths) make Allah a hindrance by your oaths to doing greater good, acting from piety, and making peace among people; and Allah is All-Hearing *(Samīʿ)*, All-Knowing *(ʿAlīm)*.

History of Revelation

There was a dispute between the son-in-law and daughter of one of the companions of Prophet Muḥammad ﷺ named ʿAbdullāh ibn Rawāḥa, so ʿAbdullāh vowed to Allah ﷻ that in order for their dispute to be sorted out he would not interfere - although his influence could have resolved the matter, and changed things for the better since his family wanted his involvement. This verse was revealed to the Prophet ﷺ which directed him to tell ʿAbdullāh specifically, but the entire Muslim community in general that such oaths were not allowed and baseless.

Commentary

This verse and the next verse in Sūrah al-Baqarah deal with people abusing an oath *(qasam)*, and are considered as a prelude to the discussion of the upcoming verses which speak about a specific type of oath known as *īlāʾ* in which a man swears by the name of Allah ﷻ that he will not have any sexual relations with his wife.

The purpose of an oath is to prove a person's point, and through one's oath, an individual makes Allah ﷻ a witness to one's own honesty.

In Islam, those who take oaths are divided into five categories:

1. There are those who habitually take oaths and are frequently heard saying: “I swear by Allah that I went there,” or “I swear by Allah that I did so and so,” etc. This type of oath holds no weight.
2. Those who make oaths just to prove their point even if they do not have the requisite knowledge, or scope of the situation; or they even take an oath to prove that they are lying. This type of oath is made out of ignorance, lack of knowledge, not knowing the complete picture, generalizing, or outright lying. For example, a person sees another individual walking out of a store and sees them putting something in their pocket, so they swear upon Allah ﷻ that the individual stole that thing.
3. There are those who take an oath by Allah ﷻ out of fear or desperation. For example, they are about to be punished for doing something wrong and they take an oath that they will never do that act again; or a person who has a store and they swear by Allah ﷻ to their customers that the product which they are selling is top quality when they know for a fact that it is not.
4. Those who take an oath to stop a habit or reach a certain goal, however the oath that they take is unrealistic. For example, they ask Allah ﷻ for something good and promise that if they get it they will fast for three years, or they will perform hundreds of prayers, or things like that. Although they have a good intention, it is completely unrealistic, and most likely something which will be impossible to fulfill.
5. Lastly, those who make an oath by Allah ﷻ to not get involved in a particular situation around them because of either difficulty, fear of their reputation being tarnished, or due to the hassle involved in a situation.

In the verse under review, Allah ﷻ is talking about all of these types of oaths, but most specifically the fifth category.

When used properly, an oath can be a tool of goodness; however when it is misused, it becomes one of the major obstacles to prosperity and spiritual proximity to Allah ﷻ.

There are many times in the Qur'ān where Allah ﷻ takes an oath; and in Islamic history, we see the Ahlul Bayt ؑ doing so as well, and these are generally done to guide us toward the right path or awaken us to the truth.

Keys of Guidance

- Although it is permissible to take an oath by the name of Allah ﷻ when it is absolutely necessary, however we must ensure that we do not do so if it means we are placing an obstacle in our way to do good deeds, or help humankind or society.
- In every stage of our lives, we must realize that not only does Allah ﷻ hear the words which we say, but even more than that, He knows that which remains unspoken, and what runs through our hearts; therefore, everything we say and even everything we think will be taken to account for by Allah ﷻ.

Verse 225

لَّا يُؤَاخِذُكُمُ ٱللَّهُ بِٱللَّغْوِ فِىٓ أَيْمَٰنِكُمْ وَلَٰكِن يُؤَاخِذُكُم بِمَا كَسَبَتْ
قُلُوبُكُمْ ۗ وَٱللَّهُ غَفُورٌ حَلِيمٌ ﴿٢٢٥﴾

Allah does not take you to task for a slip in your oaths, but He takes you to task for what your hearts have earned (through intention); and Allah is All-Forgiving *(Ghafūr)*, All-Forbearing *(Ḥalīm)*.

In order to complete the point that oaths should never hinder the performance of good deeds, in this verse Allah ﷻ goes on to say that He will not rebuke you Muslims for oaths which you inadvertently make, but He will rebuke you for what your hearts have earned - meaning the oaths which a person intentionally and knowingly makes that one cannot or will not be able to fulfill. However, at the end of the day, the Muslims must realize that even still, Allah is All-Forgiving and All-Forbearing.

In this verse, Allah ﷻ mentions two types of oaths:

1. Vain and worthless oaths[223] which are ineffective and must be ignored, and whose disregarding of them will have no atonement or compensation because they should not have been made in the first place;
2. Oaths taken by a person's own free-will which according to the Qur'ān originate in the spiritual heart. This oath is valid and must be adhered to, and if one opposes it, then it is both sinful and necessitates a penalty *(kaffārah)*.

Keys of Guidance

- A person's responsibility and accountability before Allah ﷻ depends on the active choices which one makes. Allah ﷻ will forgive the slips and misdeeds which an individual makes in unusual circumstances, and this is one of the manifestations of the Divine Wisdom *(Ḥikmah)* and Forgiveness *(Maghfirah)* in that He overlooks the unintentional shortcomings which people involve themselves in.

Verse 226

لِّلَّذِينَ يُؤْلُونَ مِن نِّسَآئِهِمْ تَرَبُّصُ أَرْبَعَةِ أَشْهُرٍ ۖ فَإِن فَآءُو فَإِنَّ ٱللَّهَ غَفُورٌ رَّحِيمٌ ٢٢٦

For those who vow (sexual) abstinence from their wives (due to following ignorant traditions of their ancestors, or due to fighting and enmity) they have four months time (to decide how they will resolve the situation). Then, if they go back on their vow (before the end of these four months), then surely Allah is All-Forgiving *(Ghafūr)*, All-Merciful *(Raḥīm)*.

---

[223] The meaning of the word *laghw* which has been translated in this verse as 'slip' refers to 'any action or speech which does not have an intended goal or aim, or emanates without self-determination or self-control.'

In the pre-Islamic Age of Ignorance *(Jāhiliyyah)*, women had no value or status in Arab society, therefore men devised ugly methods to separate themselves from their wives, or put emotional strain upon them, one of which is referred to in the books of history as the oath of *īlā'*.[224]

Whenever a husband got mad and wanted to display his hatred for his wife, he would take the 'oath of *īlā'*' that he will not have any sexual relations with her, and in this inhumane way put his wife in a dilemma due to multiple reasons, not only due to refusing to have intimacy with her.

This oath carried other implications because a husband was not officially divorcing his wife such that she could be free to move on with her life and marry someone else who would take care and look after her; nor was he willing to live a respectable life with her such that she could live in peace and tranquility with her spouse. Of course, taking the oath of *īlā'* did not have any ramifications on the man himself, as normally they would have multiple wives.

The aim of this verse under review was to fight against this immoral tradition which existed in pre-Islamic Arabian society, and had remained as a valid practice during the early Islamic period within the society.

The Qur'ān wanted to combat against this practice by first saying that those men who practice this oath of *īlā'* against their wives must resolve the situation within four months. These four months were prescribed as a timeline for a man who took such an oath, to clarify with his spouse on whether he wants to continue to live with her, or if he wants a complete divorce. Through this verse, Allah ﷻ wanted men to know that this was an incorrect vow to begin with, therefore there was no *kaffārah* required to be offered.

However, oaths in general, if they meet all of the conditions, but then they are broken, there is a penalty to pay.

This four month period which the Qur'ān spoke about was put in place to give the individual time to think, reflect, and seek out professional

---

[224] The word *īlā'* comes from the Arabic root of *ulū* and it means 'to show strength and to take a decision;' and since making an oath is a form of these two things, it is for this reason that this word was coined for this type of oath.

counseling to make a final decision. If before the four month period ended, the man returned to his wife, then the situation would be automatically resolved.

Surely Allah ﷻ would forgive a man in this matter, just like He promised to forgive a man who needs to break his oath, although a believer is still obligated to pay the atonement for breaking one's oath - if all the conditions are met which we will speak about later - and the oath still remains as is.

Īlā' has a Unique Ruling

In the previous verses, we reviewed vows and oaths which a person takes that Islam considers to be null and void. There, we stated that if someone takes an oath to do something or refrain from something impermissible, then that oath is automatically invalidated and there is no problem in 'breaking' that oath. This is because such an oath is not recognized by Islam to begin with as being a valid oath. However, in certain circumstances, a penalty still had to be paid. This is seen in Islam as a form of a punishment for stubborn men to get them to stop resorting to their cowardly ways of trampling upon the rights of women and to ensure that they do not repeat their cruel ways.

Islam and the Western World

In the West and based on their ill-conceived traditions, there is also something similar to *īlā'*, which the system refers to as Legal Separation.[225]

At one time in human history, divorce was not possible for Christians, so after the French Revolution one of the ways that was approved as a means of separation between a husband and a wife who no longer wanted to live together was a physical separation. In this agreement, a man and woman were temporarily separated and lived in different houses, and none of the financial or emotional requirements of marriage

[225] A "separation" is when a couple decides to live apart from each other because the relationship has broken down. The couple may have been married, or they may not have been married, but they were living together like a married couple in a common-law relationship, but now they are separated.

were applicable to either party. However, neither could that husband take another wife, nor could that woman marry another man - and this duration of separation could last up to three years, after which they had to come back together again.[226]

The Western world allowed for such a separation to continue for up to three years, but if we look at the rules of Islam, it does not give its followers the right to leave such an important matter hanging for such a long period of time, and orders a man to make his intentions clear within four months, and if he does not obey the rules of the Qur'ān, then a just Islamic government can put pressure on him to finalize his status with his wife - and either divorce her, or make up and live together again -

---

[226] In an article entitled *Divorce and Women in France*, the author writes: "Divorce first became legal in France on September 20, 1792. It was abolished in 1816, and despite divorce bills presented by legislators in the 1830s and in 1848, it was only re-established in 1884 under the Third Republic. Throughout this period, France's political climate shaped its divorce laws; divorce was regarded as republican, and even a revolutionary institution throughout the nineteenth century.

The divorce law of September 20, 1792, was indeed a revolutionary departure from what had come before. Under the ancient regime marriage was indissoluble; after 1792, couples could divorce quickly and easily ... So that unilateral divorce would not be used carelessly, a waiting period of six months was imposed ... With the return of the monarchy to France in 1816, divorce was abolished entirely. Under Louis XVII, Roman Catholicism became once again the state religion, and in accordance with its doctrine, judicial separation became the only option for unhappy couples.

The revolution of 1848 brought a new attempt to reinstate divorce in France ... In May of that year several members of the Executive Commission deposed, in the name of the government, a divorce bill to be considered by the constituent assembly. Adolphe Crémieux, the minister of justice, along with Arago, Lamartine, Marie, and Garnier-Pagès, proposed that the law of May 8, 1816 be rescinded, and that the Napoleonic law, title VI of the civil code, be brought back into force. They offered only two modifications: any judicial separation could be converted into a divorce after three years, and a spouse convicted of adultery would be prohibited from filing for divorce." (Extracted from the article found at www.ohio.edu/chastain/dh/divorce.htm. Last accessed on October 9, 2022)

allowing the woman to go on with life.

Divine Attributes at the End of Each Verse

It is noteworthy that many verses of the Noble Qur'ān conclude with Allah ﷻ mentioning some of His Attributes. Those attributes are always directly related to the contents of the verse which they are contained in, and they are not arbitrarily put there for some rhyming construct of the verse.

For example, in the verses under discussion, when talking about the oath of *īlā'* and a man's decision to break this sinful oath which he took, the verse ends with the phrase that Allah ﷻ is All-Forgiving, and All-Merciful. This should indicate to the reader that as long as a person follows the rules which Allah ﷻ has laid down, then He will forgive one's sins.

When it comes to discussing the issue of divorce, Allah ﷻ ends the verse with His two characteristics of being All-Hearing, and All-Knowing - meaning that Allah ﷻ hears your words and is aware of the motive for divorce and separation, and He will judge you accordingly because He knows everything.

Keys of Guidance

- It is very important to note that when it comes to restoring the rights of the oppressed, we need to take a holistic and balanced approach. In today's society, sometimes things are looked at from a lens of extreme misproportions, or from a purely emotional aspect; in other cases, they are driven by a specific agenda. When such ways of restorative justice are used which are devoid of logic and revelation, they tend to make matters worse, and instead of standing for the rights of another person they will be sidetracked, and all such efforts will end up being counter productive - a clear example of this is that women's rights are not equal to feminism, and when the two are confused together women will not end up getting their God-given rights.
- When problems occur in a marriage, which is a natural consequence

of two people living so close to one another, it may sometimes be necessary to separate for a while, but it is important to take this reconciliation period seriously and seek out proper guidance. During such a sensitive time in a relationship, the couple must ensure that they do not let their emotions govern the situation. In addition, they must not rely on non-experts, or even so-called experts who do not understand the situation holistically. For example, there are times when a couple may face major challenges in their marriage, and they go to an 'expert' to get advice, but that person may not be rooted in the cultural or religious sensitivities which govern the lives of the couple, thus they will not be able to fully comprehend the situation, nor provide a viable solution. They may understand the textbook solutions to deal with such situations, however it may be solely through the lens of Western or secular standards, or other types of understandings which differ drastically from a religious worldview or even the cultural nuances.

- Islam has always been an avid and active supporter of the oppressed, and as can be seen when studying history, women have unfortunately been at the brunt of the abuse of men throughout human history - not only in the pre-Islamic Era of Ignorance, but even around the world in the so-called enlightened European and Western countries up until now. However, the Qur'ān and Islam has repeatedly supported them and stood up for their rights, even though Western governments still have to debate the rights of women even until recent times.

- One of the duties of the Prophets, and as an extension the true scholars of faith who seek to protect the message of the Qur'ān is to fight against any and all superstitions, and ignorant traditions so as to ensure that they have no place in the Muslim society because they have the potential to take away the rights which have been granted to people by Allah ﷻ.

- Instead of inviting or encouraging divorce, Islam seeks to advise reconciliation and reunification of the family unit by facilitating a mediation period between a husband and a wife; and the option that they can return back to married life as long as the disputes are settled is also there, and there is no harm for either person, and they can attain the forgiveness and mercy of Allah ﷻ. However at the same time, Allah ﷻ recognizes that there are times when a husband and wife may not be able to resolve their disputes, and that it is better for them to separate in kindness, and go their own ways in respect of one another; and by following the laws which Islam has laid down they can obtain a simple divorce if the need arises.

Verse 227

وَإِنْ عَزَمُوا۟ ٱلطَّلَٰقَ فَإِنَّ ٱللَّهَ سَمِيعٌ عَلِيمٌ ﴿٢٢٧﴾

But if they resolve on divorce, then (know that) Allah is All-Hearing *(Samīʿ)*, All-Knowing *(ʿAlīm)*.

In continuation of the previous verse which spoke about the incorrect oath of *īlāʾ* which Islam came to eradicate, Allah ﷻ states that if a husband and wife decide that after the separation period they want to go through with a divorce, then they should realize that Allah is All-Hearing, and All-Knowing - He knows if they truly tried their best to reconcile, however for whatever reasons the marriage cannot continue, so they are now free to divorce on amicable terms.

If the man does not abide by one of these two ways - meaning that he neither returns to a healthy married life with his wife, nor does he allow her to leave through the process of divorce, then it is here that a Muslim Jurist *(Ḥākim ash-Sharʿ)*[227] has the right to intervene, and if required even imprison the man or exert other forms of pressure upon him to force him to make a decision so that his wife is not left hanging in life.

---

[227] The *Ḥākim ash-Sharʿ* is a person in charge of developing and administering the Jurisprudential rulings in society. The main *sharīʿah* rulers are Prophet Muḥammad ﷺ and the 12 Imāms ؑ who were given this position by Allah ﷻ. But both during their time and also in their absence, there are individuals who take on this role according to the teachings of Islam.

After the four month period ends, this man will be given another opportunity to decide what he wants to do - either go back to married life with her in kindness, or divorce her - in either case, he needs to free her from her state of uncertainty, and if he still does not want to follow this and make things difficult for his wife, then a Muslim Jurist can pass a verdict, and if need be he can pronounce the divorce by the powers vested in the position that he holds.

Keys of Guidance

- The religion of Islam accepts divorce, with all of the bitterness and ugliness which it carries, however it does not accept that a man leaves his wife without any kind of direction about where her life stands.
- It is very important to understand that Allah ﷻ connects divorce *(ṭalāq)* with Him being the All-Seeing and the All-Knowing. This is mentioned because marital life is full of secrets which both parties share with one another in the period of their joint life - whether it be personal secrets, assets, children, etc. - they have a lot of things that have happened between them. Unfortunately when divorce happens, it is almost impossible to separate everything because everything is mixed together so tightly. Therefore what happens is that:
- Sometimes, people take advantage of their circumstances, and at the same time prey on the weakness of the other party, and some individuals may even use their position of power, wealth, etc. to put the other person in a difficult situation.
    1. Oftentimes, allegations are made and accusations are created, and things can get very ugly; and at times, people may even accuse the other party of completely false charges just to get the person in trouble with the law.
    2. Many times, a person may not have the evidence to prove their innocence or the injustices carried out against them. Over all, such times are extremely difficult situations and as such, Allah

ﷻ reminds us that He Sees everything and He Knows all things, so we must act with God-consciousness every step of the way, and keep our full trust in Him alone. Ultimately, at the end of the day, each one of us will be judged by the One True God on the Day of Judgment - even if we escape the secular justice system here in this world due to its limitations.

- Many times, people who are going through divorce proceedings need to endure lengthy court battles which usually entail spending money on lawyers and other legal expenses; they expend a considerable amount of energy and drain their emotions; they end up accusing one another; and to make matters even worse, they often resort to revealing each other's secrets. At the end of it all, perhaps one of the parties may get a little bit extra - materialistic speaking - however they have lost out so much more on the spiritual and emotional aspects. The damage which they have both gone through, not to mention the families and possibly also the children, is usually a lot more than what was gained. Therefore, it is best to resolve the situation amicably with a trustworthy, God-conscious, and believing mediator, while keeping in mind that both parties need to be self-sacrificing and flexible during this entire situation.
- It is very important to recognize that the two main points which are normally argued about in any divorce case are in regards to money and children. Unfortunately, both are usually jeopardized and damaged when a lengthy, ugly legal battle takes place. In addition to other types of damages - such as to one's reputation, the emotional harm, and other detrimental effects; there are long term and everlasting consequences that will be felt on everyone - most significantly young children if they were involved. When a husband and wife are busy in such situations, they are sometimes oblivious to the state of the children, as they are so caught up in their own personal agendas and what they can get out of the divorce.

Verse 228

وَٱلْمُطَلَّقَٰتُ يَتَرَبَّصْنَ بِأَنفُسِهِنَّ ثَلَٰثَةَ قُرُوٓءٍ ۚ وَلَا يَحِلُّ لَهُنَّ أَن يَكْتُمْنَ مَا
خَلَقَ ٱللَّهُ فِىٓ أَرْحَامِهِنَّ إِن كُنَّ يُؤْمِنَّ بِٱللَّهِ وَٱلْيَوْمِ ٱلْءَاخِرِ ۚ وَبُعُولَتُهُنَّ أَحَقُّ
بِرَدِّهِنَّ فِى ذَٰلِكَ إِنْ أَرَادُوٓا۟ إِصْلَٰحًا ۚ وَلَهُنَّ مِثْلُ ٱلَّذِى عَلَيْهِنَّ بِٱلْمَعْرُوفِ ۚ
وَلِلرِّجَالِ عَلَيْهِنَّ دَرَجَةٌ ۗ وَٱللَّهُ عَزِيزٌ حَكِيمٌ ﴿٢٢٨﴾

And the divorced women shall undergo, without remarrying (another man), a waiting-period of three monthly [menstrual] cycles: and it is not lawful for them to conceal what Allah may have created in their wombs (a pregnancy), if they believe in Allah and the Last Day. And during this period (of three months), their husbands are fully entitled to take them back (as their wife), if they desire reconciliation; but in accordance with justice, the rights of the wives [with regard to their husbands] are equal to the [husbands'] rights with regard to them, although men have been given the responsibility to manage the situation properly (especially during this sensitive time of pregnancy). And Allah is All-Glorious *(ʿAzīz)*, All-Wise *(Ḥakīm)*.

In the previous verse, the discussion centered around divorce, while in this verse some of its specific rulings are covered; and five important points are mentioned here:

1. The first point that Allah ﷻ mentions is in regards to the 'waiting period' after a divorce, what is known as the *ʿiddah* about which Allah ﷻ says that a divorced woman must wait for three full periods of menstruation, and the subsequent time between each menstrual cycle when they are free from the blood of their monthly period.

   The word which Allah ﷻ uses in this verse 'courses or cycles' *(qurūʾ)* means 'the days in which a woman does not see the menstrual blood.' Since divorce must take place when a woman is **not** in her menstrual cycle and her husband has **not** had sexual intercourse with her, this time of her being free from the menstrual cycle is considered as the first 'course.' As soon as the third cycle of having her monthly menstrual blood is finished, this is the completion of the waiting period after which she is now allowed to get married again.

It should be noted that when it comes to the beginning and end of the *ʿiddah* period which is something which a woman herself will know and others may not even be aware of this, it has been left up to the woman to confirm when her three menstrual cycles have transpired so that the divorce can be finalized. In this regard, only her statement will be accepted - meaning that there are no other witnesses even required to confirm this.

In this regards, there is a *ḥadīth* in which Imām Jaʿfar aṣ-Ṣādiq ﷷ has stated the following in regards to the interpretation of this verse where he says: "Allah has allowed women to bear witness to three things [without the need of anyone else to assist in bearing witness with her] and these are: menstruation, the time that when she is free from the menstrual blood [before seeing it again], and pregnancy."[228]

2. The second commandment states that if a woman truly believes in Allah ﷻ and the Last Day, then it is not lawful for her to conceal what Allah ﷻ has created in the womb, in other words if she is pregnant she must inform her husband about that as it is his child as well.
3. The third ruling which we can extract from this verse is that a husband has the right to annul a divorce during the time of the *ʿiddah* if he has pronounced the revocable[229] divorce, as Allah ﷻ

---

[228] *Wasāʾil ash-Shīʿah*, Vol. 22, Pg. 222, Ḥadīth 28,440. This tradition is as follows:

قَدْ فَوَّضَ اللّٰهُ إِلَىٰ النِّسَاءِ ثَلَاثَةَ أَشْيَاءَ: اَلْحَيْضَ وَالطُّهْرَ وَالْحَمْلَ.

[229] According to the Jurists, divorce in Islam is of two types, one is revocable in which a husband and a wife can get back together without the need of a new

says that during the waiting period, a husband has the right to take his wife back in marriage without pronouncing a new marriage contract, if they desire a settlement.

In fact, when the wife is in the *ʿiddah* of a revocable divorce, the husband can resume married life again with her without any formalities, meaning they do not have to renew their marriage vows; and this can merely be done by him saying anything or doing anything which would show his intent to return back to married life with his wife.

4. Allah ﷻ then states the fourth commandment where He says that according to customary good and religiously approvable practice, women have rights similar to those that men have, however men in respect of their heavier duty and responsibility have a degree above the women but they must never abuse that.

Therefore, just as husbands have rights which their wives are obligated to uphold toward them, so too wives have rights which their husbands have to uphold and maintain in respect of their spouses as well.

Due to the wide-ranging differences that exist between the physical and mental abilities of men and women, the management

---

marriage contract; and the second kind is irrevocable in which the couple would need a new marriage contract if they wanted to become husband and wife again. Based on this, there are different 'types' of divorce in Islam:

1. A standard divorce: Revocable.
2. The divorce of a girl who has not yet completed nine lunar years: Irrevocable.
3. The divorce of a postmenopausal woman: Irrevocable.
4. The divorce of a woman who did not consummate the marriage: Irrevocable.
5. The "third" divorce: Irrevocable.
6. The *khulaʿ* divorce: Irrevocable.
7. The *mubārāt* divorce: Irrevocable.
8. The divorce given by a fully qualified Jurist *(Ḥākim ash-Sharʿ)* to a woman whose husband is neither prepared to pay her living expenses, nor divorce her: Irrevocable.

of the household is entrusted to the husband, and his assistant is his wife. This difference does not translate into spiritual stations and degrees of proximity to Allah ﷻ, or levels of knowledge, or ranking with Him ﷻ due to their piety - as it is very well possible that a wife may be far more spiritually and intellectually advanced than her husband.

The word which has been translated in this verse as 'customary good' *(ma'rūf)* which means a noble, reasonable, and logical act, has been is repeated a total of 12 times[230] in this collection of verses in order to warn husbands and wives that they must never abuse the rights of each other; and they must respect one another as this will strengthen their marital bond, and assist them both in gaining the satisfaction of Allah ﷻ.

5. At the end of this verse we read that Allah is All-Mighty, All-Wise.

   This last portion points out that Divine Wisdom and Planning requires that everyone in society performs the duties which have been assigned to them by the laws of the Almighty Creator which are in harmony with the structure of the physical body and immaterial soul.

   The Wisdom of Allah ﷻ dictates that the duties which have been entrusted to women strike a balance with the certain rights which men have been granted, so as to strike an equilibrium between the duties and rights of everyone in society.

Keys of Guidance

- In Islam, divorce is not simple and straightforward - it has many angles to it that must be taken into consideration. In addition to the conditions that are widely known such as: two just witnesses being present as the divorce is being verbally pronounced; a woman not

---

[230] This word *(ma'rūf)* can be seen in the following verses in this sūrah:

Verse	Arabic Text
2:228	...وَلَهُنَّ مِثْلُ الَّذِى عَلَيْهِنَّ بِالْمَعْرُوفِ...

being pregnant or in her menstrual cycles and other requirements, there are holistic factors to take into consideration as well. While the husband's responsibility for the duration of the marriage was to uphold what the Quran terms, *qāyumiyyah*, that is, the needs of his wife in all aspects of life: emotional, social, financial, spiritual, and psychosocial, the wife's responsibility was to take create a home from a house: to nurture and care for the members of this home. Therefore, many times we see women put their opportunities to further their career and make money on hold while working within the home. Islam recognizes these sacrifices which the wife is making and tells the woman that she can actually charge for the time spent working in the home. Therefore, many scholars recommend that when a couple are going through the proceedings of getting divorced, they need to have an arbitration process by which among the many things which they discuss and agree upon,

2:231	الطَّلَاقُ مَرَّتَانِ فَإِمْسَاكٌ **بِمَعْرُوفٍ** أَوْ تَسْرِيحٌ بِإِحْسَانٍ...
2:231	...فَأَمْسِكُوهُنَّ **بِمَعْرُوفٍ**...
2:232	...أَوْ سَرِّحُوهُنَّ **بِمَعْرُوفٍ**...
2:233	...فَلَا تَعْضُلُوهُنَّ أَنْ يَنْكِحْنَ أَزْوَاجَهُنَّ إِذَا تَرَاضَوْا بَيْنَهُمْ **بِالْمَعْرُوفِ**...
2:233	...وَعَلَى الْمَوْلُودِ لَهُ رِزْقُهُنَّ وَكِسْوَتُهُنَّ **بِالْمَعْرُوفِ**...
2:233	...فَلَا جُنَاحَ عَلَيْكُمْ إِذَا سَلَّمْتُمْ مَا آتَيْتُمْ **بِالْمَعْرُوفِ**...
2:234	...فَلَا جُنَاحَ عَلَيْكُمْ فِيمَا فَعَلْنَ فِي أَنْفُسِهِنَّ **بِالْمَعْرُوفِ**...
2:235	وَلَٰكِنْ لَا تُوَاعِدُوهُنَّ سِرًّا إِلَّا أَنْ تَقُولُوا قَوْلًا **مَعْرُوفًا**
2:236	...وَمَتِّعُوهُنَّ عَلَى الْمُوسِعِ قَدَرُهُ وَعَلَى الْمُقْتِرِ قَدَرُهُ مَتَاعًا **بِالْمَعْرُوفِ**...
2:240	...فَإِنْ خَرَجْنَ فَلَا جُنَاحَ عَلَيْكُمْ فِي مَا فَعَلْنَ فِي أَنْفُسِهِنَّ مِنْ **مَعْرُوفٍ**...
2:241	...وَلِلْمُطَلَّقَاتِ مَتَاعٌ **بِالْمَعْرُوفِ** حَقًّا عَلَى الْمُتَّقِينَ...

there is a discussion in which the finances are divided in such a way that allows both parties to have a new start in life and be successful in the next stage of their life.

- With responsibilities come rights - whoever takes on a responsibility also has rights which they must adhere to. For example, parents have responsibilities toward their children, and therefore they also have rights over their child; similarly children have responsibilities toward their parents, but they also have rights over them.
- Men have no right to abuse the power or authority which Allah ﷻ has granted to them within the scope of a family - they must realize that although Allah ﷻ has given them a level of 'authority' within the family, Allah ﷻ has the True Power and Authority over every creation.

Verse 229

ٱلطَّلَٰقُ مَرَّتَانِۖ فَإِمۡسَاكُۢ بِمَعۡرُوفٍ أَوۡ تَسۡرِيحُۢ بِإِحۡسَٰنٖۗ وَلَا يَحِلُّ لَكُمۡ
أَن تَأۡخُذُواْ مِمَّآ ءَاتَيۡتُمُوهُنَّ شَيۡـًٔا إِلَّآ أَن يَخَافَآ أَلَّا يُقِيمَا حُدُودَ ٱللَّهِۖ
فَإِنۡ خِفۡتُمۡ أَلَّا يُقِيمَا حُدُودَ ٱللَّهِ فَلَا جُنَاحَ عَلَيۡهِمَا فِيمَا ٱفۡتَدَتۡ بِهِۦۗ
تِلۡكَ حُدُودُ ٱللَّهِ فَلَا تَعۡتَدُوهَاۚ وَمَن يَتَعَدَّ حُدُودَ ٱللَّهِ فَأُوْلَٰٓئِكَ هُمُ
ٱلظَّٰلِمُونَ ٢٢٩

Divorce is (to be) pronounced twice. Then (at the end of each pronouncement) the husband should either retain (his wife without offending her honor and) in a fair manner, or release (her) kindly and in a manner fairer and pleasing (to her). (In the event of divorce) it is not lawful for you (the husband) to take back anything that you gave them (as a wedding gift, or gifts on other occasions), unless both of you fear that they might not be able to keep within the bounds set by Allah (in terms of the divorce). If you fear that they (the husband and wife) might not be able to keep within the bounds set by Allah (and may deviate into unlawful acts particularly because of the wife's disgust with the husband), then there is no blame on them (the couple) that the wife might pay some compensation to be released from the marriage ties. Those are the limits set by Allah, therefore do not exceed them; and whoever exceeds the limits set by Allah, they are the wrongdoers.

History of Revelation

A woman came to see one of the wives of Prophet Muḥammad ﷺ and complained to her that her husband was constantly divorcing her, then returning back to her, and this was causing her undue stress, since during the pre-Islamic Era of Ignorance, a man had the right to divorce and remarry his wife as many times as he wished, and there was no limit to it; and up until this point in time, Islam had not yet abolished this practice.

When this complaint reached Prophet Muḥammad ﷺ, this verse was revealed to him in which Allah ﷻ limited the number of times that a man can divorce his wife to three.[231]

Commentary

In the previous verse, we arrived at the conclusion that the rule of *ʿiddah* was put in place with specific conditions, and that within the time frame of the waiting period, it was possible for a husband and wife to get back together as a married couple with ease in order to ensure that no complications hindered the stability of the family.

However, some new Muslims during the time of Prophet Muḥammad ﷺ continued to follow the customs of the pre-Islamic Age of Ignorance and began to abuse the rules of divorce; and in order to place the wife under stress, a husband would divorce his wife, and before the *ʿiddah* period finished, he would reverse the divorce, return back to her, and aggravate the situation even further.

---

[231] *Tafsīr Majmaʿ al-Bayān*, Vol. 1 and 2, Pg. 329, see the history of revelation of this verse.

This verse of the Noble Qur'ān was revealed which aimed at preventing this ugly and cowardly practice, as Allah ﷻ says when He starts this verse that divorce has recourse, and a direct return to married life without a new marriage contract is only allowed two times.

These two divorces must be verbally pronounced at two separate instances and cannot be done in one sitting, although it is common to see this in some Muslim communities in which a man will simply say: "I divorce you, I divorce you," but this is not a valid divorce. According to the Islamic Jurisprudence based on the teachings of the Ahlul Bayt ؑ, the *Ja'farī Fiqh*, various conditions must be in place for a valid divorce, and one of them is that between the two verbalizations of "I divorce you" there has to be the observance of an entire period of *'iddah*.[232]

In the next portion of this verse, Allah ﷻ confirms that any time a divorce is pronounced with all of the conditions being fully met, the husband must take proper care of his wife and reconcile, or leave her in goodness.

Thus, when the first two divorces take place, if after each one they reconcile and go back to being a couple and live with one another in

---

[232] In addition to this, there are other rules that must be observed which include:
1. A man who divorces his wife must be of the age of legal responsibility *(bāligh)* and sane *('āqil)*.
2. A man must divorce his wife out of his own volition *(ikhtiyār)*, and if he has been compelled to divorce his wife, then that divorce is invalid *(bāṭil)*.
3. Furthermore, he must have an intention *(qaṣd)* to divorce his wife; therefore, if for example, a person says the divorce formula *(ṣīghah)* jokingly or while intoxicated, then it is not valid.
4. At the time of divorce, the wife must not be in a state of menstruation *(ḥayḍ)* or post childbirth/lochia *(nifās)*.
5. The man must not have had sexual intercourse with her in the period that she was clear from *ḥayḍ* and *nifās*.
6. The divorce formula must be said in correct Arabic, and it must employ the word *ṭāliq* (divorced).
7. Furthermore, two just *('ādil)* men must hear the pronunciation of the divorce formula.

For further details, please see the detailed books of Islamic Jurisprudence.

peace and harmony, then they can continue on with their married life. However, if they continue to go back to the brink of divorce, and eventually the husband pronounces the divorce with his wife for the third time, then they are **not** allowed to return back to married life - except if the conditions which will be mentioned in the next verse are fulfilled.

It should be noted that the meaning of 'separation with benevolence' means that a husband must fulfill the rights of his wife, and therefore while they are separated, he is not permitted to say inappropriate words behind her back (which is always impermissible, however during tense times one may feel rejected and want to tell others about the conduct and character of his wife), also he should not make people feel pessimistic toward her, and he must not deprive her of the possibility of remarrying someone else in the event that the two of them end up divorcing.[233]

Therefore, just like taking care of one's wife must be accompanied by the trait of goodness, so too separation with her must be accompanied by benevolence and kindness; and thus in the next portion of this verse, we see that Allah ﷻ says that at the end of each pronouncement of divorce, a husband should either retain his wife without offending her honor and in a fair manner, or release her in gentleness and in a manner that is pleasant for her.

Allah ﷻ then goes on to state in the continuation of this lengthy verse that in the event of divorce it is not lawful for a husband to take back anything what was given to his wife as a wedding gift, or gifts on other occasions, unless both fear that they might not be able to keep within the bounds set by Allah ﷻ.

Therefore, during this separation period, the husband is not permitted to take back what he had given to his wife as the dowry *(mahr)* when

---

[233] In addition to the moral conduct which a husband must maintain in regards to his wife, scholars also state that he is obligated by law to continue to provide for all of his wife's needs during the waiting-period, and these include: her food, clothing, and shelter, and they must be provided in accordance with his wife's social status; thus, during the *'iddah*, a husband is not permitted to evict his wife from the house that she is staying in.

they got married, and this is just one example of separation based on benevolence.

Some commentators of the Qur'ān feel that the meaning of this sentence is much broader than just the *mahr,* and have said that it means that the husband is not allowed to take anything back which he gave his wife during their time of being married.

Thereafter, a reference to the divorce known as the *khulaʿ* is given in which Allah ﷻ says that this is the only instance in which it is not a problem for the husband to take back what he had given to his wife as a marriage gift. In this form of divorce, a wife herself initiates the divorce process because she does not want to continue living with her husband and wants him to divorce her with the irrevocable divorce. In this case, the husband and wife are concerned that if they continue their married life, they might not be able to keep within the limits set by Allah ﷻ, so in such a case, a woman can return her marriage gift or something mutually agreed upon in order for the divorce to be finalized.

From this point, Allah ﷻ goes on to say that if a husband and wife are afraid that they will not be able to observe the Divine limits *(ḥudūdullāh),* then there is no hindrance if the woman pays an amount to acquire an irrevocable divorce. In the other instances of divorce, the process is initiated by a husband, while in the *khulaʿ* the basis for the separation is the wife, and as such she must compensate for the divorce which she wants to initiate as she wants to terminate the marriage, whereas her husband may want to continue to live with her. In this scenario, it only makes sense that she should give back the *mahr* to allow her husband to divorce her, and using that *mahr* that is returned, he can marry someone else and start a new life with her.

At the end of this verse, in referring to all of the rulings of divorce which have been stated, Allah ﷻ says that these are the limits of Allah ﷻ and the believers must not exceed them, and if they do then they are unjust and among the wrongdoers.

Types of Divorce in Islam

Divorce is a kind of *īqāʿ* - a one sided disposition - which unlike marriage, it is a unilateral action done by the man.

Within the jurisprudence of Islam, there are two kinds of divorce: *rijʿī* (revocable) and *bāʾin* (irrevocable).

In the revocable or returnable divorce, the husband can return to his wife during the waiting period *(ʿiddah)* without making a new marriage contract. However, in the irrevocable divorce, the husband cannot return back to his wife unless a new marriage contract is performed.

Islam has legislated a number of different forms of divorce based on the unique circumstances that each couple may find themselves in, and these can be divided into the following three types:[234]

1. **Standard divorce:** The man initiates the divorce, however this form is a returnable (revocable) divorce in which the husband can return to his wife and live together without a new marriage contract if they so choose.
2. ***Khulaʿ* divorce:** The woman initiates the divorce, however this form is a non-revocable divorce. If the couple wish to get back together again, they must re-do the marriage contract.
3. ***Mubārāt* divorce:** This irrevocable divorce is one in which due to mutual reasons between a husband and wife, they both resolve to separate from one another.

Keys of Guidance

- When it comes to our relationships with other people - whether it be our friends, or more importantly our spouse, we must be extremely careful before we make a decision to sever the ties. We should always allow a cool-down period to enable us to think about the decisions we want to make, as there could be a possibility that misunderstandings may have occurred which led to an impasse.
- The beautiful teachings of the Qurʾān show us that even in the most sensitive of times such as during a divorce, the following etiquettes must be observed:

[234] The Jurisprudential rulings behind each of these forms of divorce are complex and vary amongst the scholars. It is best to check the legal rulings of the scholar you follow in regards to this.

   - The spouses are not allowed to harass, abuse, or in any way hurt each other - neither through their actions nor their words;
   - Due to the bitterness of separation, a couple should compensate one another with the sweetness of kindness and respect;
   - Divorce must not be a cause of resentment, violence, or revenge; and if it is an absolute necessity, then kindness and benevolence must take precedence over bad etiquettes.
- The rules and regulations which are within the teachings of Islam are not separate from morality and the principles of decency, rather they go hand in hand with one another.
- When it comes to divorce, Islam has stressed on the fact that a husband and wife should involve others in the mediation process before they jump to the conclusion of divorce, because many times they may make such decisions based on emotions and anger, whereas when others are allowed to sit and discuss the situation with them, they may be able to diffuse the tense circumstances and allow the couple to see things more clearly.

Verse 230

فَإِن طَلَّقَهَا فَلَا تَحِلُّ لَهُۥ مِنۢ بَعۡدُ حَتَّىٰ تَنكِحَ زَوۡجًا غَيۡرَهُۥۗ فَإِن طَلَّقَهَا
فَلَا جُنَاحَ عَلَيۡهِمَآ أَن يَتَرَاجَعَآ إِن ظَنَّآ أَن يُقِيمَا حُدُودَ ٱللَّهِۗ وَتِلۡكَ
حُدُودُ ٱللَّهِ يُبَيِّنُهَا لِقَوۡمٖ يَعۡلَمُونَ ٢٣٠

If he (a husband) divorces her (his wife for a third time), then she will no longer be lawful for him unless she marries another man (of her own volition and consummates the marriage). (If she and her new husband do not get along well and) if he divorces her (after consummation of the marriage), then there is no blame on them (the woman and her first husband if they both want) to return to each other, if they think that they can keep within the limits set by Allah. These are the boundaries set by Allah; He makes them clear for a people who know (the wisdom and benefit in the bounds prescribed for them by their Creator).

History of Revelation

It is narrated in a *ḥadīth* that a woman came to meet Prophet Muḥammad ﷺ and said to him that she had married her cousin Rafāʿah. She went on to say that he divorced her three times, and after that she went and married another man named ʿAbdur Raḥmān ibn Zubayr, and after some time they too got divorced. She asked the Prophet ﷺ if she was now permitted to get back together with her first husband and marry him again?

Prophet Muḥammad ﷺ replied to her saying that she cannot remarry her first ex-husband unless she had consummated the marriage with her new second husband (and observed the *ʿiddah*), then only can she remarry the first man who was her previous husband. It was at this time that the verse under review was revealed to the Prophet ﷺ.[235]

Commentary

The commentary of the previous verse contained a lengthy discussion about the performance of two divorces, and this verse provides a commentary in regards to that previous ruling, because here Allah ﷻ says that if a husband divorces his wife for the third time, then she will no longer be lawful for him unless she marries another man of her own volition and consummates that marriage. If she and her new husband do not get along and they decide to divorce, then once she observes the required waiting period, then (and only then) can she remarry her first husband if they want to return back to one another, and if they think that they can keep within the limits set by Allah *(ḥudūdullāh).*

At the end of this verse, Allah ﷻ reminds the believers that these are the boundaries set by Allah; He makes them clear for people who know

---

[235] *Tafsīr Majmaʿ al-Bayān*, Vol. 1 and 2, Pg. 330, under the commentary of this verse.

and have wisdom, and understand that there is benefit in the restrictions which have been prescribed for them by their Creator.

Keys of Guidance

- The Islamic rulings *(aḥkām)* of Allah ﷻ are of two types:
    1. One is between us and Allah ﷻ - referred to as *ḥaqqullāh.*
    2. The second is between us and other people - what is referred to as *ḥaqqun nās.*

    Often the rulings between us and Allah ﷻ, such as praying, fasting, etc., have very precise details and conditions. Thus, we see that for the prayers, we have numerous rulings to learn and follow such as: prayer direction, time of prayer, conditions of the prayer, etc. Without knowing and following all of these rules, a person's prayers have the potential to be rejected by Allah ﷻ.

    Although Allah ﷻ is very kind and forgiving about the rights which exist between us and Him, however when it comes to the rights of people, Allah ﷻ has a much more strict code which He expects us to follow - and divorce is one of those rights between people which has multiple factors which need to be taken into account.

    As it relates to divorce, we have mentioned some of the rulings as extracted from the verses of the Noble Qur'ān, however the bulk of the rulings in regards to divorce are found in the *ḥadīth* of Prophet Muḥammad ﷺ and his successors, the 12 Imāms عليهم السلام, and are spoken about in detail in the comprehensive books of Islamic Jurisprudence.

    Unfortunately, some take the rules of Islam out of context, like those Muslims who simply say the word *ṭalāq* without the intention of divorcing their wife; or those who perform a divorce out of anger. Such people think that by merely saying the word *ṭalāq* or performing the divorce in a state of rage, a husband has actually divorced his wife, however they fail to realize that since divorce is such a serious issue, Allah ﷻ has laid down very strict and specific rules which must be put into place before a divorce can be valid.

Many times, to fix a 'mistake' which a husband may perform by divorcing his wife out of anger, or as a 'joke,' one will go in search of other rulings and take them out of context, forcing his wife to marry someone else, and then expecting that new husband to consummate the marriage, divorce his new wife just so the previous husband can once again marry his wife!

Truly this is why we see that in this and other verses, Allah ﷻ very clearly and articulately repeatedly provides us with a bigger picture and frame-work, and continuously advises us to be God-conscious, and extremely careful when it comes to learning and following the religious verdicts.

- Men must not abuse their authority within the scope of marriage, and need to realize that the power of divorce that they have been given is limited by the rules laid down by Allah ﷻ.
- Muslims should realize that Divine limits are not only in regards to acts of worship such as prayers *(ṣalāh)*, charity *(zakāh)*, pilgrimage *(Ḥajj)*, and the sacred struggle *(jihād)* - but rather, the rules also extend to family life, and the relationship between a husband and wife.

Verse 231

وَإِذَا طَلَّقْتُمُ ٱلنِّسَآءَ فَبَلَغْنَ أَجَلَهُنَّ فَأَمْسِكُوهُنَّ بِمَعْرُوفٍ أَوْ سَرِّحُوهُنَّ
بِمَعْرُوفٍ ۚ وَلَا تُمْسِكُوهُنَّ ضِرَارًا لِّتَعْتَدُوا۟ ۚ وَمَن يَفْعَلْ ذَٰلِكَ فَقَدْ ظَلَمَ
نَفْسَهُۥ ۚ وَلَا تَتَّخِذُوٓا۟ ءَايَٰتِ ٱللَّهِ هُزُوًا ۚ وَٱذْكُرُوا۟ نِعْمَتَ ٱللَّهِ عَلَيْكُمْ وَمَآ
أَنزَلَ عَلَيْكُم مِّنَ ٱلْكِتَٰبِ وَٱلْحِكْمَةِ يَعِظُكُم بِهِۦ ۚ وَٱتَّقُوا۟ ٱللَّهَ وَٱعْلَمُوٓا۟
أَنَّ ٱللَّهَ بِكُلِّ شَىْءٍ عَلِيمٌ ﴿٢٣١﴾

And when you divorce women and they reach the end of their

waiting term, then either retain them honorably or release them honorably, and do not retain them maliciously in order that you may transgress. Whoever does that, has surely wronged himself. Do not take Allah's revelations for a mockery and remember Allah's favor on you and what He has sent down on you of the Book and the Wisdom wherewith He exhorts you (to guidance). Keep away from disobedience to Allah in due reverence for Him and piety *(taqwā)*, and know that Allah has full knowledge of everything.

Further Controls in Divorce

In a follow-up to the previous verses, this verse also refers to other limits which are placed on divorce in order to ensure that a woman's rights are not overlooked.

Allah ﷻ states that when a man divorces his wife and she reaches the final days of her waiting period *(ʿiddah)*, this is the last chance for the couple to either reconcile and live together peacefully, or finalize the divorce and separate from one another respectfully - in other words, either make a sincere decision to continue married life, or separate ethically.

The Qurʾān then stresses on another point to further emphasize the issue by referring to the exact opposite of what was just stated, and Allah ﷻ says that a man must never stay married to his wife simply to harm or abuse her.

This sentence is the interpretation of the word 'in a fair manner' *(maʿrūf)*. During the Age of Ignorance, men would sometimes divorce their wives and then return to them before the waiting period ended simply to exert marital revenge. Thus, by employing strong language, Allah ﷻ is warning men that they must never think of doing this to their spouse, and they need to follow the beautiful teachings of Islam even when it comes to divorce, and He further stresses on this by saying that whoever does this has wronged his own self.

Allah ﷻ then provides a general warning to all believers that they must not take the signs *(āyāt)* of Allah ﷻ as a mockery by misusing the

Divine law.

In general, this verse refers to those who act contrary to religious teachings and try to pull the wool over the eyes of the religion and manipulate the apparent reading of the Word of Allah ﷻ. When a man gets married, then divorces his wife, and before the *ʿiddah* period is completed, he again returns to his wife with the intention of seeking revenge and to harass her, the Qurʾān considers this an act of mockery of the Divine revelations; and a true believer is one who does not play with the Divine revelations by ignoring the spirit of the commandments from Allah ﷻ, thinking that they need to only rely on the dry, soulless outward form of rulings because the sin of doing this is extremely severe, and there is a painful punishment waiting for the man who acts like this.

Allah ﷻ reminds the Muslims to consider the blessings which He has sent down, including the Heavenly Book (the Qurʾān), and the knowledge He sends down to the believers, and that through all of this He seeks to admonish the Muslims so that they may be careful of their duty to Allah ﷻ, recognizing that He is Aware of everything. This portion of the verse warns men that they must not abuse their position, and they must realize that Allah ﷻ is aware of even their inner intentions.

The phrase: 'Allah's favor' *(niʿmatullāhī)* has a broad meaning which incorporates all of the Divine blessings including the blessings of love and affection which Allah creates between spouses.

Keys of Guidance

- Divorce must always be looked at as a last resort, and even as the final option the consequences which it brings will be everlasting, especially if children are involved - that is why Allah ﷻ emphasizes that it must be carried out amicably with the fear of Allah ﷻ in mind. A couple must look at the long term consequences and effects, and not simply base their decision to divorce on emotions. The husband and wife must ensure that they do not burn all of their bridges by hating and hurting each other for some perceived short-term benefits.
- In order to improve marital relations, every couple should read,

reflect, and implement the guidance of the Qur'ān; and everyone needs to ensure that they base their lives around God-consciousness.

Verse 232

وَإِذَا طَلَّقْتُمُ ٱلنِّسَآءَ فَبَلَغْنَ أَجَلَهُنَّ فَلَا تَعْضُلُوهُنَّ أَن يَنكِحْنَ أَزْوَٰجَهُنَّ
إِذَا تَرَٰضَوْا۟ بَيْنَهُم بِٱلْمَعْرُوفِ ۗ ذَٰلِكَ يُوعَظُ بِهِۦ مَن كَانَ مِنكُمْ يُؤْمِنُ بِٱللَّهِ
وَٱلْيَوْمِ ٱلْءَاخِرِ ۗ ذَٰلِكُمْ أَزْكَىٰ لَكُمْ وَأَطْهَرُ ۚ وَٱللَّهُ يَعْلَمُ وَأَنتُمْ لَا تَعْلَمُونَ ﴿٢٣٢﴾

And when you divorce women and they reach the end of their waiting period, (then the judges and the guardians of either party) should not prohibit them from marrying their (former) husbands, (or the former husbands should not prohibit them) from marrying other men when they honorably reach mutual consent. This is an admonition to whoever among you truly believes in Allah and the Last Day; that is a virtuous way for you and purer; and Allah knows, and you do not know.

History of Revelation

One of the companions of Prophet Muḥammad ﷺ named Maʿqil ibn Yasār had a sister named Jamlāʾ who was divorced from her husband, ʿĀsim ibn ʿUday. After the marriage ended, and the waiting period came to a conclusion, she wanted to remarry her ex-husband; however her brother Maʿqil, prevented her from doing so. This verse was revealed and forbade him from opposing such a marriage.[236]

Another Cultural Chain Imprisoning Women

In the Era of Ignorance, women were chained to the cultural tradition of having their lives governed by men, and they were forced to adjust their lives according to the desires of such authoritarians in their lives.

---

[236] *Majmaʿ al-Bayān*, Vol. 1, Pg. 332.

The level of involvement and influence of men over women even extended to their choice of a spouse such that not only were the wishes of the woman given no importance in terms of who they could marry, but if she married someone with the permission of her guardian and then divorced him, if she later wanted to remarry him, then this was only possible if the male relatives of her family granted her permission.

In those days, it was common that after separation a couple would want to return to their married life again, however they were prevented from doing so due to the erroneous ideas that the men of the family had for such a reunification.

The Qur'ān condemned this and told the Muslim community at the time of Prophet Muḥammad ﷺ and beyond that when you (addressing the men) divorce your wife and they complete their waiting period, the men of the family are not allowed to prevent them from reuniting or remarrying their former spouse if they are in agreement with one another.

We understand from this verse that those women - who are referred to in Arabic as *thayyibah* - meaning 'those who were married at least once and had their marriage consummated' do not need their guardian's consent to get remarried, and even if the guardians oppose a marriage, it has no impact on the legality of their marriage.

In continuation, Allah ﷻ once again provides admonition and says that this command is one that those who have faith in Allah ﷻ and the Last Day will keep in mind and act according to.

To conclude this verse, the Qur'ān adds yet another layer of emphasis and says that this command is more effective for the family to grow spiritually and help morally cleanse a couple and the extended family, and that Allah ﷻ knows best (why such rules have been put in place by Him for us), while we the human beings, do not know (the wisdom of His rulings, but are still obligated to follow them).

These rulings have been expressed by Allah ﷻ in our favor, yet the only people who will truly understand and make the best use of this are those who have true faith in their origin *(mabdā')* and return *(maʿād)*, and are able to control their desires.

Keys of Guidance

- In some cases, after separation and proceeding with the actual divorce, a man and woman may come to a realization that the decision to separate was incorrect, so Allah ﷻ in His Infinite Knowledge has a path open for them to remarry one another if they both desire. Alternatively, if they want to marry someone else, one of the barriers that may stop them from this could be a family member who does not want them to remarry, however the Qur'ān clearly says that they should realize that others cannot be an obstacle for them to get married again.
- One key thing which we see in society is that most often, divorces end up with both parties carrying around emotional baggage. Unfortunately, this prevents individuals from moving forward in life, and this is not healthy. In some circumstances, one of the spouses may become an obstacle for the other, not allowing them to move forward through the usage of emotional blackmail, bullying, bad mouthing, etc.
- It is not acceptable to label divorced people as being bad people, or to think that they are not able to maintain a relationship. We can never know the entire story of the parties involved, and perhaps the couple were just not suitable for one another. Whatever the situation may be, it is not our place to judge or label others.
- Just because a husband and wife separate and eventually divorce one another it does not mean that they should live a life of pessimism. It may be that after divorce, they will find time to reflect on their past and the happy moments which they shared with each other, and regret the divorce and decide to get back together again.
- In order to maintain a healthy society, divorced men and women should not remain unmarried.

Verse 233

وَٱلْوَٰلِدَٰتُ يُرْضِعْنَ أَوْلَٰدَهُنَّ حَوْلَيْنِ كَامِلَيْنِ ۖ لِمَنْ أَرَادَ أَن يُتِمَّ ٱلرَّضَاعَةَ ۚ
وَعَلَى ٱلْمَوْلُودِ لَهُۥ رِزْقُهُنَّ وَكِسْوَتُهُنَّ بِٱلْمَعْرُوفِ ۚ لَا تُكَلَّفُ نَفْسٌ إِلَّا
وُسْعَهَا ۚ لَا تُضَآرَّ وَٰلِدَةٌۢ بِوَلَدِهَا وَلَا مَوْلُودٌ لَّهُۥ بِوَلَدِهِۦ ۚ وَعَلَى ٱلْوَارِثِ مِثْلُ
ذَٰلِكَ ۗ فَإِنْ أَرَادَا فِصَالًا عَن تَرَاضٍ مِّنْهُمَا وَتَشَاوُرٍ فَلَا جُنَاحَ عَلَيْهِمَا ۗ
وَإِنْ أَرَدتُّمْ أَن تَسْتَرْضِعُوٓا۟ أَوْلَٰدَكُمْ فَلَا جُنَاحَ عَلَيْكُمْ إِذَا سَلَّمْتُم مَّآ
ءَاتَيْتُم بِٱلْمَعْرُوفِ ۗ وَٱتَّقُوا۟ ٱللَّهَ وَٱعْلَمُوٓا۟ أَنَّ ٱللَّهَ بِمَا تَعْمَلُونَ بَصِيرٌ ﴿٢٣٣﴾

And the mothers should breastfeed their children for two complete (lunar) years, if the fathers wish that the period (of breastfeeding) be completed. It is incumbent upon him who fathered the child to provide the mothers (during this period) with their required sustenance and clothing according to customary good. But (keep in mind that) no soul is obligated (to act) except to its capacity; thus a mother should not be made to suffer because of her child, nor the one who fathered the child because of his child. The same duty (toward the suckling mother) rests upon the father's parents (if he has passed away). If the couple desires by mutual consent and consultation to wean the child (before the completion of the breastfeeding period of two years), then there is no blame on them. And if you desire to seek a wet-nurse for your children (who will suckle them), then there is no blame on you, provided you pay her what is due from you according to customary good. Keep away from the disobedience to Allah and act within the bounds of piety, and know that whatever you do, surely Allah sees it.

Seven Directives for Breastfeeding

This verse, which is a continuation of the discussions related to issues of marriage and family life focuses on the important issue of "breastfeeding" *(riḍāʿa),* and discusses seven important points in relation to this:

1. Mothers should breastfeed their children - whether boy or girl - for two complete lunar[237] years after birth.

   Although the guardianship of minor children is entrusted to the father, a mother is encouraged to breastfeed the child for the first two years of its infancy, thus she is in charge of taking care of her child during this period; so at this time, the so-called "right of custody" belongs solely to the mother. This is a mutual right for both the child who should be nourished by its mother, and the emotional rights of a mother toward her baby.

   The word Allah ﷻ uses in this verse: 'mothers' *(wālidāt)* is the plural of 'mother' *(wālidah),* however in Arabic, mother is also expressed by the word *umm* which has a broader meaning and sometimes refers to a mother or grandmother; and it can also mean the root or source of something.

   It is also important to note that rather than using the word *ab* for father, Allah ﷻ uses the word *wālid* which means father as well. However, since *ab* can also refer to an uncle, father-in-law, or even a teacher, a specific word has been used which is exclusive for father, as was used in the case of mother.

2. The second portion of this verse states that this verdict about two years of breastfeeding is for that woman who wants to complete the period of feeding - something which Islam has highly

---

[237] The calendar which the Muslims use, which is based on the lunar cycle, consists of 12 months in a year of 354 or 355 days. The determination of the start and end of each lunar month is based on, for the most part, localized sightings of the moon - however various scholars have offered their own rulings in these regards. Although Islam allows its followers to use their own domestic calendar for day to day life, when it comes to many religious requirements, such as fasting in the month of Ramaḍān, or performing the *Ḥajj,* and other events, it requires its followers to adhere to the lunar calendar.

recommended.

This means that the period of breastfeeding does not necessarily have to be two complete years; but it is limited to a maximum of two years for the one who wants to complete the term of breastfeeding, and a mother has the right to adjust this period based on her overall condition and health if need be.

3. The mother's living expenses, for example her food, clothing, and shelter needs must be covered by the baby's father during the period of breastfeeding so that the mother can suckle her infant with ease and no worries - and this obligation is extended for the father of the child to provide for the mother even if they are divorced.

   By Allah ﷻ using the word 'customary good' *(maʿrūf)*, this shows that the father must provide the mother of his child with whatever she requires in terms of food and clothing which are normal and appropriate for her status, and he must not be miserly, nor overly extravagant in these regards. To further explain this point, Allah ﷻ says that no one is obligated to exceed their ability - therefore, every father has a duty to provide his wife or the mother of his child to the best of his ability.

4. Allah ﷻ then conveys another important ruling that neither the mother - because of a dispute with the father of the child, nor the father - due to a strained relationship with the mother, have a right to harm the child.

   Men must not violate the right of custody and care which a mother has been given by taking away a child from her during the infancy as this would be detrimental to the child; and at the same time, a mother must not relinquish the right of a child and refuse to breastfeed, nor deprive the father the right to see his child, if they are separated or divorced.

5. Allah ﷻ then deals with another ruling which is that if the father passes away during the period when a mother is breastfeeding their child, it states that the parents of the father (that is, the grandparents of the orphan child) must continue to provide for the mother during the time that she is breastfeeding, just as the father

was required to do.

6. In continuation, the weaning of a child is discussed and the Qur'ān states that this is up to the parents to discuss and decide. Although in the previous sentence, the specific time of two years was set for the maximum time of breastfeeding, however depending on the physical and mental condition of a mother and mutual agreement, the parents can agree to stop suckling at any time before the two year period comes to an end. Allah ﷻ states that if a mother and father consult each other and agree to wean off the baby sooner, then there is no blame on either one of them.[238]
7. Sometimes a mother may not want to breastfeed her baby, or she may waive her custody of the child, or something may come up in her life that does not allow her to continue breastfeeding, so in the last part of the rulings in this verse, Allah ﷻ advises the father and mother that in this case, they need to come up with a solution. The Almighty notes that if it is either an inability to breastfeed, or an outright refusal of the mother arises, however they want their child to be naturally fed for the formative first few months of life, then they can outsource the suckling to a wet-nurse,[239] and there

---

[238] Scholars of Islam provide further guidance on this area as follows:

1. **Āyatullāh Sayyid Sīstānī:** It is recommended to breastfeed a child for twenty-one complete months, and it is not befitting to breastfeed a child for more than two lunar years.
2. **Āyatullāh Sayyid Khāmeneī:** As much as possible, it is recommended *(mustaḥab)* to breastfeed the child for two complete lunar years.

Many other *marājiʿ taqlīd* differ on the actual period with some opting for 21 months, while others have a ruling on breastfeeding for 24 months. Readers should refer to the Islamic Laws manual of the scholar they follow (do *taqlīd* to) for further guidance.

[239] A wet-nurse is a woman who breastfeeds and cares for another person's baby. Wet-nurses can be employed if a mother dies, or if she is unable to, or elects not to nurse the baby herself. Wet-nursed children may be known as "milk-siblings" and in some cultures the families are linked by a special relationship of milk kinship. Mothers who nurse each other's babies are engaging in a reciprocal act known as cross-nursing or co-nursing.

is no problem for them to find the appropriate individual provided that the mother's rights are maintained.

Some commentators of the Qur'ān have interpreted this portion of the verse to mean that a father and mother must ensure that they keep in consideration the rights of a wet-nurse, and ensure that they compensate her financially according to what is the norm and custom in the society at that time.

At the end of this verse, Allah ﷻ warns everyone and tells them to have God-consciousness and know that Allah ﷻ sees everything that we do, in case a conflict between a man and woman reaches a level that revives the spirit of revenge in them or endangers the fate of each other, or deprives their child of his/her rights; therefore before any of this transpires, all of them should know that Allah ﷻ is always watching over everyone's deeds.

Keys of Guidance

- In order to create and maintain a healthy balance in life, Allah ﷻ wants to ensure that each of the parents fulfill their responsibilities. When it comes to their children and all of the duties that upbringing them entails, neither party is allowed to run away from their obligations.
- Allah ﷻ mentions time and time again that we cannot go above and beyond the capacity which we have within us - and that He

---

According to the Islamic rulings, it is recommended that a wet-nurse who is chosen to breastfeed a child be Muslim, sane *(ʿāqilah)*, and possess admirable physical, mental, and moral qualities. It is not befitting to choose a wet-nurse who is a disbeliever *(kāfirah)*, feeble-minded, aged, or bad looking. It is also disapproved to choose a wet-nurse of illegitimate birth, or whose milk is the result of a child who was born out of fornication.

If a male child is breastfed by a wet-nurse, and the specific conditions which are mentioned in the Islamic Laws manuals are followed, then that child will be the *maḥram* (close family member) of the woman who breastfed him, as well as the wet-nurse's biological children. Further details of these specific laws can be found in the appropriate books of Islamic Jurisprudence.

would never task us to do something which we do not have the ability to perform. Thus, Allah ﷻ brings the necessity of having God-consciousness *(taqwā)* as it relates to how a husband and wife interact, with regards to their children, and that we need to have a good mindset with respect to our duties toward Allah ﷻ and others.

- Islam is a complete and comprehensive religion, thus it even lays out a plan for proper breastfeeding, and the rules related to it.
- Financial and material rights must be provided to either a mother who is breastfeeding her child, or to a wet-nurse who has taken on this task; however Allah ﷻ has left the amount to be paid open as it will depend on the era and country in which this is carried out as this will fluctuate, thus all He says is that it must be based on 'customary good' *(maʿrūf)* or whatever is usually provided, and that it should be to the extent of the ability of the father.

Verse 234

وَٱلَّذِينَ يُتَوَفَّوْنَ مِنكُمْ وَيَذَرُونَ أَزْوَٰجًا يَتَرَبَّصْنَ بِأَنفُسِهِنَّ أَرْبَعَةَ أَشْهُرٍ
وَعَشْرًا ۖ فَإِذَا بَلَغْنَ أَجَلَهُنَّ فَلَا جُنَاحَ عَلَيْكُمْ فِيمَا فَعَلْنَ فِىٓ أَنفُسِهِنَّ
بِٱلْمَعْرُوفِ ۗ وَٱللَّهُ بِمَا تَعْمَلُونَ خَبِيرٌ ﴿٢٣٤﴾

And those (husbands) among you who die, leaving behind their wives - they (the wives) shall keep themselves in waiting for four months and ten days, (as the *ʿiddah* period during which they must refrain from marrying anyone, and from self-adornment). When they (the women) have reached the end of the waiting term, and they want to marry a suitable individual, then you have no right to intervene. And Allah is fully aware of all that you do.

Irrational Attitudes toward Women

One of the challenges which women have had throughout history is trying to get married again after the death of their husbands.

We as human beings have been created to want to live in a family setting, even after the death of a spouse. As such, throughout history, this issue has been tackled in many ways by various groups through their own customs and traditions. Although certain customs may be good, however there are times when they go to such an extreme that they can often leave a widow at a dead end, and what we term as cultural captivity, and these same customs and norms of a society may end up committing the most heinous acts of injustice against a woman.

For example, in some cultures it is normal that after the death of a husband, the wife is lit on fire and has to die a painful death, or she is killed and buried alongside her husband.[240]

---

[240] This practice is seen in Hindu culture and is described as the following: "Sati (also called suttee) is the practice among some Hindu communities by which a recently widowed woman either voluntarily or by use of force or coercion commits suicide as a result of her husband's death. The best known form of sati is when a woman burns to death on her husband's funeral pyre. However other forms of sati exist, including being buried alive with the husband's corpse and by drowning.

Historically, the practice of sati was to be found among many castes and at every social level, chosen by or for both uneducated and the highest ranking women of the times. The common deciding factor was often ownership of wealth or property, since all possessions of the widow devolved to the husband's family upon her death.

In a country that shunned widows, sati was considered the highest expression of wifely devotion to a dead husband. It was deemed an act of peerless piety and was said to purge her of all her sins, release her from the cycle of birth and rebirth, and ensure salvation for her dead husband and the seven generations that followed her.

Due to the fact that its proponents lauded it as the required conduct of righteous women, it was not considered to be suicide, which is otherwise banned or discouraged by Hindu scripture.

Sati also carried romantic associations which some were at apparent pains to amplify. In this regard, Stein states: "The widow on her way to the pyre was the object (for once) of all public attention ... Endowed with the gift of prophecy and

Some women were permanently barred from ever being able to remarry, and others were isolated from the rest of the community.

In some tribes, women were required to spend time by the grave of their husbands under a filthy black tent, in dirty clothes, not permitted to apply make-up or wear any kind of jewelry, and not even wash themselves, and they had to spend days and nights at the gravesite.

This verse of the Qur'ān commanded to negate all types of such superstitions and the subsequent crimes against women, and allowed widows to marry after observing the stipulated waiting period. It instructed the women to ensure that they preserve the sanctity and privacy of their past marriage(s), and that whatever had gone on between the woman and her husband should not be divulged to anyone - especially the new husband.

Allah ﷻ states in this verse that a woman whose husband has died must wait for four months and ten days as a waiting period *('iddah)* before she is permitted to get married again. When a woman reaches the end of this waiting term, then there is no sin upon her to marry a suitable man of her choice.

---

the power to cure and bless, she was immolated amid great fanfare, with great veneration." Only if she was virtuous and pious would she be worthy of being sacrificed; consequently being burned, or being seen as a failed wife were often her only choices.

Indeed, the very reference to a widow from the point at which she decided to become a "Sati" (Chaste One) removed any further personal reference to her as an individual and elevated her to a remote and untouchable context.

It is little wonder that women growing up in a culture in which they were so little valued as individuals considered it the only way for a good wife to behave.

The alternative, anyway, was not appealing.

After the death of a husband, a Hindu widow was expected to live the life of an aesthetic, renouncing all social activities, shaving her head, eating only boiled rice, and sleeping on thin coarse matting.

To many, death may have been preferable, especially for those who were still girls themselves when their husbands died." (Extracted and summarized from www.kashgar.com.au/blogs/history/the-practice-of-sati-widow-burning - Last accessed on October 12, 2020)

Sometimes the parents or relatives of a woman may seek to interfere in her life, or look at their own interests in an upcoming marriage of hers, therefore at the end of this verse, Allah ﷻ warns everyone and says that He is All-Knowing in relation to what people do, and everyone will receive rewards or punishments according to their actions in this world.

According to *ḥadīth* from the 12 Imāms of the Ahlul Bayt ؈, we can conclude that a woman who has lost her husband and is now a widow is obligated to maintain a form of mourning during the period of her *ʿiddah* such that she is not permitted to wear any type of make-up or dress up extravagantly, and she should spend the four months and ten days in a simple and modest way. She is however allowed to go out for necessities such as doctor's appointments, groceries, for a walk, to visit family, etc.

It is worth noting that the Islamic rulings on *ʿiddah* for a widow stipulate that even if there is no possibility of a woman being pregnant, she must still observe the full required period of *ʿiddah.*

Keys of Guidance

- At the death of her husband, a wife is obligated to observe the required waiting period before she moves on with her life, or returns to a sense of normalcy, whether or not she intends to remarry.
- Neither the family of a woman, nor her husband's family have any right to interfere in her private life, or whom she chooses to marry after the death of her spouse.

Verse 235

وَلَا جُنَاحَ عَلَيْكُمْ فِيمَا عَرَّضْتُم بِهِۦ مِنْ خِطْبَةِ ٱلنِّسَآءِ أَوْ أَكْنَنتُمْ
فِىٓ أَنفُسِكُمْ ۚ عَلِمَ ٱللَّهُ أَنَّكُمْ سَتَذْكُرُونَهُنَّ وَلَٰكِن لَّا تُوَاعِدُوهُنَّ سِرًّا
إِلَّآ أَن تَقُولُوا۟ قَوْلًا مَّعْرُوفًا ۚ وَلَا تَعْزِمُوا۟ عُقْدَةَ ٱلنِّكَاحِ حَتَّىٰ يَبْلُغَ ٱلْكِتَٰبُ
أَجَلَهُۥ ۚ وَٱعْلَمُوٓا۟ أَنَّ ٱللَّهَ يَعْلَمُ مَا فِىٓ أَنفُسِكُمْ فَٱحْذَرُوهُ ۚ وَٱعْلَمُوٓا۟ أَنَّ ٱللَّهَ
غَفُورٌ حَلِيمٌ ﴿٢٣٥﴾

And there is no blame on you that (during this waiting period) you indicate a marriage proposal to such women, or keep it hidden in yourselves. Allah knows that you will think of them (with such proposals in mind), but do not make any secret engagement with them, except that you speak it properly in decent words. Do not resolve the marriage ties until the ordained term *(ʿiddah)* has come to its end. And know that Allah knows what is in your hearts, so be careful about Him; and know that Allah is All-Forgiving *(Ghafūr)*, All-Forbearing *(Ḥalīm)*.

In line with the discussion about the *ʿiddah* that a woman must observe with the passing away of her husband (whom she was married to), in this verse another ruling in relation to the woman (who is going through her waiting period) has been mentioned.

Allah ﷻ says that it is not a sin for a man to let a woman whose husband has passed away know that he wants to marry her after the *ʿiddah* has finished, or that he intends this in his heart without openly saying it to the woman while she is in her *ʿiddah*. Indeed Allah ﷻ knows that a man thinking about that woman and such thoughts about marriage are natural, however Allah ﷻ reminds the man that he is not permitted to conduct a marriage, in private or in the open with the woman during her waiting period; so Allah ﷻ confirms that the man is permitted to convey his intent to marry her in decent words, but then has to wait until the time arrives when he can actually marry her.

Allah ﷻ wants to reiterate our natural *fiṭrah* of helping others and the sense of responsibility which we must feel toward our brothers and sisters in society, especially those who are vulnerable.

When a woman loses her husband, she may face financial and emotional difficulties and may need support and assistance in raising her children, etc. As it is commonly seen, many men do not want to take on this responsibility. In fact some men may end up taking advantage of these women for their personal desires, especially since they may find the widow as an easy target due to the emotional state she finds herself in.

It is at this juncture that Allah ﷻ says to the man that if you are thinking of having relations with a widow, then you need to take on the responsibility of marrying her, taking care of her, and being a righteous husband toward her - in short, be God-conscious (have *taqwā)* and do not take advantage of the situation.

Allah ﷻ continues and states that even in such a case, a man and woman are not permitted to move ahead with the marriage until the waiting period of the woman comes to an end.

According to the Islamic rulings, if a man was to enter into marriage with a woman who is still in her *ʿiddah* period, but they did not know that they cannot do this, that marriage is null and void; and if they entered into marriage knowing that such a marriage was invalid, then that woman would actually become forbidden *(ḥarām)* for him forever and they can never marry each other.

At the end of this verse, Allah ﷻ says that everyone must know that Allah ﷻ knows what is in their hearts, and the believers must ensure that they do not do anything which goes against His rulings; and at the same time He reminds us that we should also keep in mind that Allah ﷻ is All-Forgiving, All-Forbearing.

Keys of Guidance

- Islam is a religion of the innate human nature, and since human beings are innately inclined to get married, it is for this reason that Islam recognizes and acknowledges this need, and confirms that a once a woman finishes her *ʿiddah*, discussions can be finalized, and a new marriage can take place to fulfill this human need of emotional support and physical intimacy.

- We must always pay close attention to certain things such as time and circumstances in all areas of life - even when it comes to proposing to someone for marriage. Courting a woman in specific times may not be permissible so one needs to be cognizant of these issues.

Verse 236

لَّا جُنَاحَ عَلَيْكُمْ إِن طَلَّقْتُمُ ٱلنِّسَآءَ مَا لَمْ تَمَسُّوهُنَّ أَوْ تَفْرِضُوا۟ لَهُنَّ فَرِيضَةً ۚ وَمَتِّعُوهُنَّ عَلَى ٱلْمُوسِعِ قَدَرُهُۥ وَعَلَى ٱلْمُقْتِرِ قَدَرُهُۥ مَتَٰعًۢا بِٱلْمَعْرُوفِ ۖ حَقًّا عَلَى ٱلْمُحْسِنِينَ ﴿٢٣٦﴾

There is no sin upon you if you divorce women while you have not yet touched them (consummated the marriage) or settled a dowry for them. Yet, provide for them - the well-off person according to his own capacity, and the one who is limited in his financial resources according to his capacity - with a sustenance that is honorable, an obligation upon the virtuous ones.

Following the rulings on divorce, a series of other directives are mentioned in this and the next verse, the first of which states that there is no sin on a man if he divorces his wife either before consummating the marriage (before sexual intercourse), or for some reason before they have determined the marriage gift *(mahr)* which a man is obligated to give to the woman.

Of course, if the man or couple realize after the marriage vows *(ʿaqd)* but before consummation of the marriage that they will not be able to live together for whatever reason, then it would be better for them to separate from one another and divorce before beginning married life together, because if they decide to do so later on in the marriage, then it will be more difficult for both parties.

Allah ﷻ then presents another ruling in this regard and says that the husband must make some provisions for his wife by providing her with a suitable wedding gift - and this ruling is conveyed in the Arabic phrase *'wa mattiʿuhunna.'*

However, in providing this gift to the woman, the financial means of the husband must be taken into account, and that is why in the continuation of this verse, Allah ﷻ says that the man who has financial ability should give to his wife according to his means, and the one who is not so well to do should give her a gift according to his own ability and what is suitable; and this is something which is an obligation upon the doers of good *(al-muḥsinīn)*.

It is interesting to note that the Noble Qur'ān defines the gift which a man is obligated by the religion to give to his wife as "property" *(matāʿ)*, and this word is often used to refer to a non-cash gift because money itself is not considered as a "gift" - at least not directly; meaning that a person can use money to purchase something as a gift, however money in itself is not considered as "property" *(matāʿ)*, and it is for this reason that the Qur'ān has defined the gift as a commodity, and not just an amount of currency which a man gives to his wife.

By Allah ﷻ using such a phrase, it actually shows us that this has a unique psychological impact on the woman as it is very common that when a gift is given, it is something which can be used immediately such as food, clothing, or other such things; and regardless of the price of the commodity, even if it is inexpensive, it leaves a lasting impression on the souls of the person who it is gifted to. Even if a wife was to sell the gift that she received and get cash for it, that physical money would not have the same psychological effect on her as a tangible gift has.

In the *ḥadīth* that have reached us in this regards, we often see that the Imāms of the Ahlul Bayt ﷺ would mention specific examples of gifts that are good to give to women, such as: clothing, specific types of food, or agricultural land.

Keys of Guidance

- We must maintain modesty and chastity in all aspects of our life, even in our speech - as we see that in this verse, rather than Allah ﷻ being blunt and saying that if a man and woman have divorced before having sexual intercourse, He speaks about this natural act by saying: "before they have touched one another." Thus, we too need to be careful of how we talk about such delicate issues.

- Men must be ready to compensate their wives for the bitterness which a divorce entails by giving them appropriate gifts - not because they are trying to buy them off, or that money can make the hurt go away, but Allah ﷻ shows that even though the couple never got close to one another so as to consummate the marriage, still divorce is a type of stress on the woman so she should be compensated adequately.

- A man's duty toward his family is to ensure that he provides their needs to the best of his ability; and similarly his wife and children should not place any undue stress or tension upon him to provide more than he is able to; but at the same time, he should ensure that he is working as hard as he can to fulfill his responsibilities. We must remember that Allah ﷻ wants both parties to act responsibly, and deal with each other fairly and in an amicable manner.

Verse 237

وَإِن طَلَّقْتُمُوهُنَّ مِن قَبْلِ أَن تَمَسُّوهُنَّ وَقَدْ فَرَضْتُمْ لَهُنَّ فَرِيضَةً فَنِصْفُ مَا فَرَضْتُمْ إِلَّآ أَن يَعْفُونَ أَوْ يَعْفُوَا۟ ٱلَّذِى بِيَدِهِۦ عُقْدَةُ ٱلنِّكَاحِ ۚ وَأَن تَعْفُوٓا۟ أَقْرَبُ لِلتَّقْوَىٰ ۚ وَلَا تَنسَوُا۟ ٱلْفَضْلَ بَيْنَكُمْ ۚ إِنَّ ٱللَّهَ بِمَا تَعْمَلُونَ بَصِيرٌ ﴿٢٣٧﴾

And if you divorce them before you touch them (consummate the marriage), and you have already settled a dowry for them, then (give them) half of what you had agreed upon, unless they forgo it, or someone in whose hand is the marriage tie forgoes it. And to forgo it is nearer to God-consciousness *(taqwā)*; so do not forget graciousness among yourselves. Surely Allah sees whatever you do.

This verse speaks about those women who agreed to get married to a man and had already determined the marriage gift *(mahr)*, however they end up separating before consummating the marriage, and Allah

ﷻ says that if this occurs then the man is obligated to give his wife half of what they had agreed upon as the marriage gift. This is the legal ruling in Islamic Jurisprudence, and it gives a woman the right to receive half of the wedding gift from her husband even if they divorce before consummating the marriage.

Allah ﷻ then goes on to speak about the moral and emotional aspects, and states that this ruling must be followed unless a woman agrees to absolve the man of her right to the wedding gift, or in the case that a woman is not in a mental capacity to make the determination, then the person who was involved in the marriage preparation - the legal guardian of the woman - can waive this amount that was to be paid to the wife.

In the next sentence, Allah ﷻ states that if a woman forgives the payment of the entire wedding gift and does not expect the man to pay any of it to her, then this is an act which is closer to God-consciousness.

Allah ﷻ goes on to say that as a community of believers who are striving to please Allah ﷻ, Muslims should never forget the art of forgiveness and spreading good deeds among one another because He sees what everyone does.

The phrase: "...it is nearer to God-consciousness..." expresses the duty of the husband toward the woman whom he is divorcing. It states that if a man had given the entire wedding gift to his wife and then divorced her, he should not take anything back from it; and if a man had not yet given the wedding gift to his wife and they divorce, then he should give the entire amount that he promised to his wife - although he would be entitled to receive half of it back from her.

The Qur'ān then mentions that a man should overlook it and let her keep the entire amount, as the woman in this situation would tend to face social or emotional trauma.

Undoubtedly, her husband's giving of the marriage gift will partially heal any hurt that she may feel, and although she may not want to keep any of it due to the feelings of what had happened in their marriage and perhaps not wanting to be reminded of her ex-husband, the Qur'ān presents this as a universal ruling which, without doubt, has a great wisdom to it - even if we are not able to appreciate it today. This is not to say that money or things can buy happiness, or heal the hurt which a bride may feel, however it is just one less thing for the woman to worry about while the divorce proceedings are going on.

The tone of this verse emphasizes on the basic principle of 'customary good and religiously approvable practice' *(ma'rūf)* in these matters, and stresses on the point that even in separation and an eventual divorce, such times should not be associated with contention and provoking the spirit of revenge. Rather, in this sensitive time, a man and woman should continue to display the common Islamic courtesies of magnanimity and forgiveness.

Keys of Guidance

- Being understanding and compassionate is something which both the husband and wife need to inculcate in their lives. When it comes to the wedding gift, although the husband is obligated to give half of what was agreed upon if a divorce happens before the consummation of the marriage, however compassion dictates that he should give her the entire *mahr;* while compassion on the side of the woman is that even if she gets the whole wedding gift from the husband, she relinquishes half of it and gives that back to him.
- Once again, it is important to note that in this verse, just as it was clear in the previous verses that Allah ﷻ wants both parties to act responsibly and deal with each other in a fair and amicable manner. In some cases, the couple may have decided on a large wedding gift *(mahr),* however they then come to the realization that the man honestly cannot provide that to his wife. Or, he may be able to give it to her, however it will leave him in a very difficult situation, and thus it may be unfair for him to give this amount to her. It is at this juncture that the concept of compassion and mercy comes in, and Allah ﷻ encourages the wife to forgive the amount in its entirety, or that she simply takes as much as she needs. On the other hand, when Allah ﷻ says to the man that he must give his wife a gift, or at least give her half of the agreed upon *mahr* or more, He does so because He wants the man to recognize that he needs to take on his responsibility and ensure that his wife has stability and does

not face economic hardships after they separate. The separation itself may cause her emotional distress as she deals with rumors in society and other such things, so at least her financial well-being can be taken care of in this period as she works to get herself on her own two feet. It is at those times that such moderate wedding gifts can help her sustain herself for a few months, as an insignificant gift would not suit that purpose.

Verse 238

حَـٰفِظُوا۟ عَلَى ٱلصَّلَوَٰتِ وَٱلصَّلَوٰةِ ٱلْوُسْطَىٰ وَقُومُوا۟ لِلَّهِ قَـٰنِتِينَ ﴿٢٣٨﴾

Be protective (even during times of difficulties) about the prescribed prayers *(ṣalawāt)*, and (especially) the middle prayer, and stand in the presence of Allah in humbleness (utmost devotion and obedience).

History of Revelation

Some of the hypocrites used the warm weather of the Arabian Peninsula as an excuse to try and divide the Muslims by not attending the congregational *(jamāʿah)* prayers - complaining that it was way too hot to join the prayers. Obviously this was just an excuse they had, while their true plan was to divide the Muslims and to get them to stop attending the congregational prayers.

When the numbers of participants in the congregational prayers began to dwindle and Prophet Muḥammad ﷺ found out about the plots of the hypocrites, he became upset and threatened these people with a harsh penalty for refusing to take part in such an important act of worship.

With such a harsh spiritual decline taking place in the city of Medina, this verse under review was revealed emphasizing the importance of the daily prayers in congregation, with extra special emphasis placed on the middle prayer.[241]

Connection to the Previous Verse

It is critical for us to understand that our lives will not always be smooth, predictable, or within our control; and unexpected things will come up, and we will definitely have to deal with various challenges from time to time. Therefore, Allah ﷻ wants to remind us that even though circumstances of life will change, we must constantly be connected to Him ﷻ. Although the historical revelation of this verse seems like a completely different topic, however when we spend some time to reflect on these two verses, we see that Allah ﷻ placed them in between the verses in regards to two areas of major family crises - divorce and death. Thus, Allah ﷻ wants us to recognize and be reminded that the way to make it through the hardships and difficult times of life is by having a solid connection to Him all of the time.

Importance of Ṣalāh, Especially the Middle Prayer

Ṣalāh is the one of the most effective means to establish a strong relationship between a person and Allah ﷻ, and therefore there is a great deal of emphasis on this act of worship within the verses of the Noble Qur'ān.

In the verse under discussion, Allah ﷻ states that the believers must be diligent in performing all of their five daily prayers, but they need to be extra vigilant when it comes to the middle *(wusṭā)* prayer - that accordingly to most commentators is the *Ẓuhr* prayer - and they must rise up in obedience and humility when standing for all of their prayers in the presence of Allah ﷻ. In other words, the Creator is telling the Muslims living during the time of Prophet Muḥammad ﷺ and beyond that they must not let the heat or cold, or the troubles of the world, or issues of wealth or health, or their spouse and children keep them away or distract them from this very important act of worship.

---

241 *Majmaʿ al-Bayān*, Vol. 1, Pg. 342, & Vol. 2, Pg. 126; *Ad-Durr al-Manthūr*, Vol. 1, Pg. 301; *Biḥār al-Anwār*, Vol. 79, Pg. 279; *Tafsīr al-Qurṭubī*, Vol. 3, Pg. 208; *Tafsīr Baḥr al-Muḥīṭ*, Vol. 2, Pg. 512.

The meaning of "middle prayer" *(ṣalāt al-wusṭā)* is the noon *(Ẓuhr)* prayer and the emphasis on this prayer - as was mentioned in the history of revelation - was because with the hot summer days of the Arabian Peninsula, or due to being extremely busy in the middle of the day with business and trade, the Muslims paid less attention to this prayer, compared to the other daily prayers, therefore Allah ﷻ had to remind the Muslims about the importance of this particular prayer.

Keys of Guidance

- Technically speaking, every *ṣalāh* can be a 'middle one' *(wustā)* from one perspective or another because in the 24 hour cycle of a day, the five daily prayers are scattered throughout this period. Thus, from one angle, any prayer can be a 'middle prayer.' For example, if we consider that in Islam the new day begins at sunset, then the *Maghrib ṣalāh* would the first one, making *Fajr* the 'middle prayer.' With this interpretation, we need to ensure that every prayer is protected, and that we must be vigilant because this emphasis on the 'middle prayer' could relate to any of the daily prayers.
- The *Ẓuhr* prayer is sometimes the easiest to miss as it comes right in the middle of the day - whether a person is at work, school, or at home getting things done around the house. It happens to come right in the middle of everyone's busy routine and schedule in the afternoon. Therefore, someone who is able to protect and be vigilant of their *Ẓuhr* prayers is more likely to be vigilant of their other prayers as well.
- We have a principle in Islamic teachings in which actions are referred to as being either important *(ahamm)*, or being at an even higher level of importance *(muhimm)*. For example, it is an obligation *(wājib)* to recite our prayers (*ṣalāh)* in the time period which Allah ﷻ has allocated for every particular prayer. Performing the prayer at the beginning of its time *(awwal al-waqt)* has great merit *(faḍīlah)* and is accompanied by immeasurable rewards; however it may be the case that sometimes, another responsibility that is more urgent happens at exactly the same time as the most meritorious or prime

time for the *ṣalāh*. What should a person do in this case? Does one say that the *ṣalāh* is more important and disregard the other urgent matter? It is here that a wise believer will recognize that although *ṣalāh* in its initial time is one of the best actions, however the other action, such as consoling a crying baby, or in matters which may be of life and death, these are also crucial responsibilities which at that time would take precedence. Thus, a believer would be well within the regulations prescribed by Allah ﷻ to slightly delay one's prayer - ensuring that one still performs it within the allocated time - in order to tend to the other necessities.

- Upholding the daily prayers is required for all five prayers - not just one or two of them - and this is a requirement for every Muslim during one's entire lifetime.
- Performing the prayers correctly requires a person to have some qualities such as careful attention, cheerfulness, humility, sincerity, and a love and desire to want to pray to Allah ﷻ; as well as knowledge of the prayers and all of its conditions.

Verse 239

فَإِنْ خِفْتُمْ فَرِجَالًا أَوْ رُكْبَانًا ۖ فَإِذَآ أَمِنتُمْ فَٱذْكُرُوا۟ ٱللَّهَ كَمَا عَلَّمَكُم مَّا لَمْ تَكُونُوا۟ تَعْلَمُونَ ﴿٢٣٩﴾

If you are exposed to danger (and you cannot pray normally because of different circumstances, then pray) afoot or mounted (on an animal or in any other manner possible). Then when you are safe (or can pray normally) secure, mention Allah (and establish the prayer) as He has taught you what you did not know.

In this verse, Allah ﷻ emphasizes that in the most difficult circumstances, even in something as stressful as being on the battlefield, *ṣalāh* must not be forgotten. Of course, in such situations, many of the conditions such as facing the *qiblah* and performing the actions such as *rukūʿ* and *sujūd* in their normal fashion are waved, so they take on another form.

Allah ﷻ tells the Muslims living during the time of Prophet Muḥammad ﷺ and beyond that if they are afraid due to a war which they are engaged in, or there is any other type of danger around the Muslims, then they are permitted to perform the *ṣalāh* on foot or while on their horse, camel, or any other animal, and they can even perform the *rukūʿ* and *sujūd* through gestures rather than the traditional form of performing these actions.

Protecting the integrity and sacredness of the *ṣalāh* is not only in times of safety, but a person must safeguard the sanctity of the *ṣalāh* at all times; and the prayers must be performed in such a way that the bond between the servants and the Creator of Existence remains strong.

Allah ﷻ then goes on to say that when the believers regain their security, they must remember Allah ﷻ - meaning that they are now obligated to perform their prayers in the normal fashion, just as Allah ﷻ taught us things which we did not previously know.

It is clear that we must thank Him for all of the Divinely-taught guidance such as being instructed on how to perform our prayers to Him in times of ease and safety, as well as in times of fear; and we must act according to that guidance.

Keys of Guidance

- Prayers can never be completely dropped - they must be performed regardless of the situation - however, they may take on a different form based on certain circumstances.
- Oftentimes people do not know some things, but they can gain knowledge about those things by seeking it out from the appropriate sources; however there are some things which the human being does not know, cannot know, and will never know without the direct aid of revelation *(waḥī)* from Allah ﷻ.
- The circumstances that may come up in the life of a believer are many which would cause them to have to pray in a fashion which they are not normally accustomed to. Some examples would be if a person is sick or has a physical challenge which necessitates them to pray while sitting or lying down on their bed. In addition, a

person may be on a plane or a train, and will reach their destination after the time of prayers has completed, and as such they would be required to perform their *ṣalāh* in that mode of transportation in a way that may not resemble the 'standard' way of praying. Allah x has given such exceptions because He recognizes that people may find themselves in unique circumstances, but at the same time He wants to ensure that believers never break their connection with Him.[242]

Verse 240

وَٱلَّذِينَ يُتَوَفَّوْنَ مِنكُمْ وَيَذَرُونَ أَزْوَٰجًا وَصِيَّةً لِّأَزْوَٰجِهِم مَّتَٰعًا إِلَى ٱلْحَوْلِ غَيْرَ إِخْرَاجٍ ۚ فَإِنْ خَرَجْنَ فَلَا جُنَاحَ عَلَيْكُمْ فِى مَا فَعَلْنَ فِىٓ أَنفُسِهِنَّ مِن مَّعْرُوفٍ ۗ وَٱللَّهُ عَزِيزٌ حَكِيمٌ ﴿٢٤٠﴾

And those of you who (are about to) die leaving behind wives, they should write a will and leave one year's worth of provision so that they are taken care of, and do not drive them out of their home. If they themselves leave (of their own accord), then there is no blame on you for what they may do of the lawful deeds by themselves. And Allah is All-Mighty *('Azīz)*, All-Wise *(Ḥakīm)*.

Connection with the Previous Verses

After reviewing the previous two verses that spoke about *ṣalāh* which is having a constant connection to Him, and always ensuring that we have our complete trust and reliance *(tawakkul)* in Him, Allah ﷻ continues this theme of verses and goes back to the issue of family crises and the

---

[242] For details on how to pray in various modes of transportation, while sick, etc., please refer to the Islamic Laws Manual of the *marjaʿ taqlīd* that you follow to see the complete conditions and method about prayers in these types of circumstances.

bitter realities of life. Thus we see that once again, the Qur'ān addresses matters pertaining to marriage and divorce.

One aspect of complete reliance on Allah ﷻ *(tawakkul)* is to ensure that we have fulfilled all of our obligations and prepared for what may come in the future. As we go through in life, we need to always be thinking ahead and planning for what may come. Therefore, Islam has encouraged us to have savings for those times when we will need them. Saving money and investing it for the future - whether it be for the educational needs of our children; to have a downpayment on a property, to start a business, or for a person to be able to provide for one's spouse and children in the event of their death is another need we have to adhere to.

In the book, *Mafātīḥ al-Ḥayāt* there is an event which is mentioned in regards to Salmān al-Muḥammadī (al-Fārisī) which states that he would always have one years worth of cash savings kept aside. The actual story relates to the time of Imām Jaʿfar aṣ-Ṣādiq ؑ in which he had an encounter with a man named Sufyān al-Thawrī - an individual who claimed to have distanced himself from the material allure of this temporal world. The Imām actually reprimanded Sufyān and those who have such an attitude that a true believer will use the blessings which Allah ﷻ has provided to them, however they will not go to excess in either way - neither be too miserly, nor extravagant.

Imām Jaʿfar aṣ-Ṣādiq ؑ then went on to quote from the episode that transpired at the time of Prophet Muḥammad ﷺ when some of his companions began to go to excesses in regards to their connection of the material pleasures. The Prophet ﷺ then gave them the example of who they should follow in piety - Salmān al-Muḥammadī. The Prophet ﷺ would go on to tell these companions that when Salmān received his yearly stipends from the public treasury of the Muslim state, he would keep aside money to cover at least one year of his expenses - just in case something happened to him and he was not able to provide for himself or his family.

In commenting on this, Imām Jaʿfar aṣ-Ṣādiq ؑ went on to say that some of the companions began to taunt Salmān and question his religiosity and said to him: "You who claim to have piety yet you are saving for the future? You do not know if you will live or die tomorrow!"

In his response, Salmān calmly replied to them: "Just as quickly as you suppose that I may die tomorrow, why do you not have the same level of confidence that I may live to see another day? O ignorant ones! Do you not know that if a person does not have a minimal amount of savings put aside to maintain his life such that his mind is not at ease, he will be under constant stress and will not have focus in life. However, if he has some savings put aside, then he will be able to make his way through life - tranquil (and with peace of mind)."[243]

Thus, we must appreciate that although no one knows when they will die and it is possible that one's spouse or children may pass away before the other spouse that had been saving, this does not go against the notion of preparing oneself for the future - obviously within limits and rationally. One may ask: How much should a person save? The individual must determine this themselves based on their own personal circumstances and what they project would be sufficient to help their family. There is no doubt that it is almost impossible to save "enough" for one's family, unless one is a millionaire, but whatever little can be saved will hopefully serve to assist the family in their times of need.

In this verse, Allah ﷻ starts off by saying that as for those men who are made aware that they are about to die, and will leave their wives behind must make a note in their last will and testament that for the period of one year, the expenses of their wife will be provided for them, as long as they do not "leave their husband's house" - meaning that they do not remarry within that time period. If a woman decides to get married after the death of her husband, obviously after her waiting period has ended, then she will not be entitled to receive this financial assistance for one year from the deceased husband (as now she will have her new husband to provide for her). However, Allah ﷻ says that there is no blame on you (the husband), if she (the wife), does what is best for her and works to set her future life in order.

At the end of this verse, it is almost as if Allah ﷻ is addressing the

---

[243] *Al-Kāfī*, Vol. 5, Pp. 65-68. The initial portion of this tradition is as follows:

...فَأَمَّا سَلْمَانُ فَكَانَ إِذَا أَخَذَ عَطَاهُ رَفَعَ مِنْهُ قُوتَهُ لِسَنَتِهِ حَتَّى يَحْضُرَ عَطَاؤُهُ مِنْ قَابِلٍ...

women, and wanting to comfort them so that they do not worry about their future, He says that He is able to open another way for them after the loss of their husband, and if a calamity befalls them, then there must have been wisdom in it because Allah ﷻ is All-Mighty, All-Wise.

There should be no ambiguity that based on Verse 234 of Sūrah al-Baqarah, the *ʿiddah* period of a woman after the death of her husband is four months and ten days, and the husband is obligated to provide for her expenses for the period of one entire year, so this means that he should ensure that he has savings, or in the case of some countries in the world, has a sufficient life insurance policy. This is so that a woman can have more stability in her life as she deals with the emotions and difficulties of becoming a widow and having lost her husband.

Keys of Guidance

- It is very important to understand that we need to have a good balance and strategy in the allocation of our wealth - both in our lifetime and after our death - based on the needs and circumstances of the people around us. Although wealth, and really any material items can never make up the pain of losing a loved one, however in this time of grief, if some of the material needs of a grieving person are taken care of, then they can have some level of comfort, and also use the time to mourn the loss, and reflect on other things. We see that in the situation in which a husband dies and leaves behind a wife and perhaps children as well, if there is no clearly written will, then oftentimes conflicts can emerge among the inheritors. Therefore, in addition to the emotional pain of losing a loved one, an internal battle may also take place - making things even more difficult for everyone involved. Knowing the nature of humanity, and as a form of guidance, Allah ﷻ instructs everyone to ensure that a comprehensive will is written to ensure that arguments and disagreements do not ensue after the death of anyone.
- We all need to ensure that when it comes to our responsibilities toward those whom we are connected with - such as our family members - we maintain the ties with balance. It is important that the

husband looks at the circumstances of the family members around him and acts logically, rather than based on pure emotion or other motivating factors. Today, we see many people act emotionally and leave everything they have to one person, or resort to an uncalculated or improper division of wealth. However, we must be strategic, and understand the needs of the individuals that we are responsible for, and act accordingly.

- After death, everyone must follow the guidelines of the laws of inheritance laid out by the Qur'ān, however we see the beauty of the religion of Islam in that it allows a person - during one's lifetime - to allocate how they want to distribute up to one-third of the total sum of their estate after their passing away, once all of the required expenses have been taken care of and covered. In addition, people are permitted to spend their wealth in whichever way they desire while they are alive - either on family members, for charitable causes, or on other legitimate things.
- Men are obligated to bequeath a part of their property to their wives, and as the Qur'ān shows, a spouse has priority over all others, and this is evident when a person studies the Islamic rulings in regards to writing a will, and the percentage of inheritance which a spouse is entitled to receive. Although the spouse will receive less if they have children, and there is a logical reason for this which will be discussed in more detail when we look at Sūrah an-Nisā' (4), Verses 11,12, and 176. Nonetheless, everyone is entitled to their rightful share as determined by the rules of Islam.

Verse 241

وَلِلْمُطَلَّقَٰتِ مَتَٰعٌۢ بِٱلْمَعْرُوفِ ۖ حَقًّا عَلَى ٱلْمُتَّقِينَ ﴿٢٤١﴾

For the divorced women, there shall be a provision, in accordance with honorable norms - an obligation on the God-conscious ones.

In this verse, Allah ﷻ deals with yet another ruling in regards to divorce, and states that for those women who have been divorced, the husband is obligated to provide them with a suitable gift if he considers himself to be one of the God-conscious, pious individuals; obviously this relates to those women who are divorced and are in their waiting period (ʿiddah).

Although the apparent reading of this verse seems to indicate that it includes all divorced women, however according to Verse 236 of Sūrah al-Baqarah in which Allah ﷻ says: "There is no blame on you (men) if you divorce women (with whom you made a marriage contract) while you have not yet touched them (consummated the marriage), nor appointed any marriage gift for them. Yet, make some provision for them, the affluent according to his means, and the straitened according to his means - a provision according to customary good and religiously approvable practice, as a duty upon those devoted to doing good (aware that Allah is seeing them)"[244] - this ruling is limited to women who got married, however no marriage gift *(mahr)* was agreed upon at the time of marriage, and subsequently the couple divorced before consummating the marriage.

According to the *ḥadīth* narrated from the 12 Immaculate Imāms of the Ahlul Bayt ؑ, this gift should be given to a woman after the end of her ʿiddah which signals the complete separation from her husband - but not in the case of the ʿiddah of a revocable divorce - in other words, this is a parting gift, not one through which the woman can return to married life with that husband.

🗝 Keys of Guidance

- The Qurʾān shows us that when it comes to dealing with anyone in society, even one's wife with whom a man is in the process of divorcing, everyone must observe *taqwā* and be God-conscious.

---

[244] Qurʾān, Sūrah al-Baqarah (2), Verse 236:

لَّا جُنَاحَ عَلَيْكُمْ إِن طَلَّقْتُمُ ٱلنِّسَآءَ مَا لَمْ تَمَسُّوهُنَّ أَوْ تَفْرِضُوا۟ لَهُنَّ فَرِيضَةً ۚ وَمَتِّعُوهُنَّ عَلَى ٱلْمُوسِعِ قَدَرُهُۥ وَعَلَى ٱلْمُقْتِرِ قَدَرُهُۥ مَتَـٰعًۢا بِٱلْمَعْرُوفِ ۖ حَقًّا عَلَى ٱلْمُحْسِنِينَ ﴿٢٣٦﴾

Verse 242

كَذَٰلِكَ يُبَيِّنُ ٱللَّهُ لَكُمْ ءَايَٰتِهِۦ لَعَلَّكُمْ تَعْقِلُونَ ﴿٢٤٢﴾

Thus does Allah clarify His signs to you so that perhaps you may exercise your reason (wisdom).

In this last verse about divorce and family crises, Allah ﷻ states that He has provided all of this guidance in these verses so that He can explain His revelations to you, the Muslims, that perhaps you may think and use wisdom when dealing with such sensitive issues in life.

The meaning of thinking and reasoning is that such reflection must be the origin of the movement toward action because thinking alone will not yield any results in one's life - a person must think and then act accordingly.

Keys of Guidance

- When it comes to Divine commandments and instructions for the guidance of humanity, we must first think about them, and then work to implement them so that we are able to understand their benefits which will also aid us in being able to put them into practice.

Verse 243

أَلَمْ تَرَ إِلَى ٱلَّذِينَ خَرَجُوا۟ مِن دِيَٰرِهِمْ وَهُمْ أُلُوفٌ حَذَرَ ٱلْمَوْتِ فَقَالَ لَهُمُ
ٱللَّهُ مُوتُوا۟ ثُمَّ أَحْيَٰهُمْ ۚ إِنَّ ٱللَّهَ لَذُو فَضْلٍ عَلَى ٱلنَّاسِ وَلَٰكِنَّ أَكْثَرَ
ٱلنَّاسِ لَا يَشْكُرُونَ ﴿٢٤٣﴾

Have you not regarded those who left their homes in thousands, apprehensive of death, whereupon Allah said to them: 'Die,' then He revived them? Indeed Allah is gracious to humankind, but most people do not give thanks.

History of Revelation

In one of the cities of the Levant Region (also known as Shām), a plague broke out and countless people were dying. In the meantime, many people left that region with the hope that they might escape the clutches of death. After escaping, they felt a sense of relief and thought that they were in control of their own destiny - independent of Allah ﷻ - thus they became arrogant and ignored the Divine Will and turned a blind eye to the natural factors which can result in one's death. Due to this, Allah ﷻ destroyed them in the same desert with the same disease which they fled from.[245]

Some *ḥadīth* mention that the disease which inflicted these unnamed people was a punishment from Allah ﷻ. Their leader asked them to prepare for an impending military conflict, and that they would have to leave the city to fight a battle, however by using false pretext that the plague was ravaging the region where they were being ordered to go and fight, they refused to proceed forth. Thus, the Lord afflicted them with what they had feared, and what they used as an excuse to flee from their responsibility.

The plague began to spread among the people so they fled their homes to try and run away from that plague, however they ended up perishing in the desert.

Some time passed after their death, and Ḥizqīl[246] - one of the Prophets from the Children of Isrāʾīl - asked Allah ﷻ to resurrect all of those who had died, and Allah ﷻ answered his prayer and brought them all back to life.

Connection with the Previous Verses

After the discussion on family crises which was seen in the previous verses, Allah ﷻ wants to remind us that this world is full of various

---

[245] *Tafsīr aṭ-Ṭibyān*, Vol. 2, Pg. 282.

[246] He is also known in the Qurʾān as Dhūl Kifl, and his Biblical name is Ezekiel.

challenges, and the only way to get through such episodes in our lives is to fulfill our responsibilities, and in order to do this we need to have a solid plan in place, and always observe God-consciousness *(taqwā)* in everything.

Commentary

This verse presents to us the story of a fascinating event which took place with one of the previous communities where Allah ﷻ starts out by posing a rhetorical question: Have you not seen or heard about those people - who were in the thousands - who fled their homes for the fear of death, under the false pretense that due to the plague which was ravaging their region, they could not and would not take part in an impending war.

Without mentioning the details, Allah ﷻ then points to their fate and says that He commanded them all to: "Die!" They died from the same disease that they used as an excuse to run away from the battle. However, sometime later on, the specifics of which are not identified in the Qur'ān, Allah ﷻ gave them all life again and raised them from the dead, and made the story of their lives a lesson for future generations.

By Allah ﷻ using the command form of the verb and saying 'die' *(mūtū)*, we understand that this is not simply Him "speaking" and saying the word, but rather this is considered as a Divine Command *(Amr al-Takwīnī)* of Allah ﷻ as He rules over the entire world of creation. Allah ﷻ provided the causes of their death, and they all perished swiftly. This is like what is mentioned in the Qur'ān where Allah ﷻ says: "When He wills a thing to be, He but says to it "Be!" and it is."[247]

The phrase used in this verse: "...then He (Allah) revived them (back to life)..." refers to the resurrection of these people whom He had made to die, which transpired as an answer to the prayer of Prophet Ḥizqīl.[248] Since their return to life was clearly a Divine blessing - both for themselves,

---

[247] Qur'ān, Sūrah Yāsīn (36), Verse 82:

إِنَّمَآ أَمْرُهُۥٓ إِذَآ أَرَادَ شَيْـًٔا أَن يَقُولَ لَهُۥ كُن فَيَكُونُ ﴿٨٢﴾

[248] According to some *ḥadīth*, Ḥizqīl was the third Prophet to succeed Prophet Mūsā ﷺ from the Children of Isrā'īl.

and also for those who would see this and learn a lesson from it - at the end of the verse Allah ﷻ says that indeed He is All-Gracious to His servants, however most people still do not even give thanks to Him.

When it comes to giving thanks to Allah ﷻ, we must realize that this verse of the Qur᾽ān not only refers to this group of people, but since all human beings are subject to the favors, blessings, and bounties of Allah ﷻ, every single person is indebted to Him and needs to acknowledge and thank Him.

It is due to this verse that the famous Shīʿah scholar, the late Shaykh aṣ-Ṣadūq رحمه الله discusses the return to life in this world *(rajʿat)* before the Day of Judgment and argues that: "One of our (Shīʿah) beliefs is that of the return - meaning a group of people will return to life in this world before the end of the world transpires."

This verse can also be used as supporting evidence for the resurrection of the dead before the Day of Judgment.

Keys of Guidance

- We must be vigilant as it relates to our responsibilities and cannot not run away from them. In today's culture, we see that it has become common to evade or delay in fulfilling one's responsibilities, whereas Islam teaches that it is through recognizing and upholding our duties in life that our faith and spiritual characteristics can grow and mature.
- A constant thread of the Qur᾽ān which is also seen in this verse is that as human beings, we must look at history and learn from it, and thus what is important in this analysis is to study the factors of the rise and fall of nations, but the names and places are irrelevant.
- Victories and defeats; death and life; resurrection, etc. are all examples of the Divine grace over humanity - if only we think and reflect on them.

Verse 244

وَقَٰتِلُوا۟ فِى سَبِيلِ ٱللَّهِ وَٱعْلَمُوٓا۟ أَنَّ ٱللَّهَ سَمِيعٌ عَلِيمٌ ﴿٢٤٤﴾

And fight in the way of Allah, and know that Allah is All-Hearing *(Samiʿ)*, All-Knowing *(ʿAlīm)*.

From this point on in Sūrah al-Baqarah, some verses regarding sacred struggle *(jihād)* begin, and there is a story about a past nation. By paying attention to their outcome which was mentioned in the previous verse, the relationship between these verses concerning *jihād* and the previous verse becomes clear.

Allah ﷻ begins this verse and the overall theme by telling the Muslims living during the time of Prophet Muḥammad ﷺ and beyond that they must fight in the way of Allah ﷻ, and realize that He is All-Hearing, All-Knowing: He hears the words of everyone, and is even aware of their inner intentions with respect to the sacred struggle and everything else.

Keys of Guidance

- Struggle and efforts are only valuable when they are done for Allah ﷻ and in the way of Allah ﷻ. In Islam, the sacred struggle is not for revenge, seeking power, or exploitation - it is only done to elevate the word of Allah ﷻ and to ensure that justice is established.
- When the need arises for Muslims to join efforts in the sacred struggle under a just government which is led directly by Prophet Muḥammad ﷺ, or one of his 12 successors, the Imāms of the Ahlul Bayt عليهم السلام or someone whom they directly appoint, then the believers are not permitted to put up excuses. In such a situation, the believers have an obligation to fulfill and they must follow the orders given to them, recognizing that Allah ﷻ knows the intentions of everyone, and He will judge accordingly.

Verse 245

مَّن ذَا ٱلَّذِى يُقْرِضُ ٱللَّهَ قَرْضًا حَسَنًا فَيُضَٰعِفَهُۥ لَهُۥٓ أَضْعَافًا كَثِيرَةً ۚ وَٱللَّهُ
يَقْبِضُ وَيَبْصُۜطُ وَإِلَيْهِ تُرْجَعُونَ ﴿٢٤٥﴾

Who is the one that (by giving their wealth, talents, time, life, etc. for Allah's cause) lends to Allah a handsome loan that He will return after multiplying it for them manifold? Allah confines (your means of livelihood), and He expands it; and (in either case) to Him you will be returned.

History of Revelation

It is narrated that one day, Prophet Muḥammad ﷺ said: "Whoever gives alms *(ṣadaqah)* will have twice as much (given to them in reward) in Paradise."

One of the companions of the Prophet ﷺ named Abū ad-Daḥdāḥ al-Anṣārī said: "O Messenger of Allah, I have two gardens, if I give one of them as alms, will I have twice as much in Paradise?"

The Prophet ﷺ replied: "Yes."

So from the two gardens which he owned, Abū ad-Daḥdāḥ al-Anṣārī handed over the better one as charity, and put it in the ownership of Prophet Muḥammad ﷺ for him to do whatever he pleased with it, and it was at that time this verse was revealed, and the charity which he gave increased his blessings in the life of this world two times over - and this is the meaning of 'multiplying it manifold.'[249]

Connection with the Previous Verses

In the previous verses, there was a discussion in regards to various factors which revolve around family crises and challenges which are faced within that unit, and some guidance was given by Allah ﷻ on how to overcome them with a God-conscious mindset. The previous verse spoke about sacrifice and struggling, and in this verse, the focus switches to a discussion in regards to sacrifice in the perspective of giving to others from what we have been blessed by Allah ﷻ. This giving consists of all of the blessings we have at our disposal, including wealth, time, talents, life, and so much more.

[249] *Mustadrak al-Wasā'il ash-Shī'ah,* Vol. 7, Pp. 262, 264, and 265.

Commentary

In this verse, Allah ﷻ begins by asking a rhetorical question that who is there from among the believers who will give Allah ﷻ a beautiful loan *(qarḍ al-ḥasana),* and who is willing to spend out of the wealth which Allah ﷻ has provided to them, so that in return Allah ﷻ can provide that person with a multifold return on their charity?

At the end of this verse, Allah ﷻ states that it is Allah ﷻ who limits or expands the provision of the servants, and the believers should recognize that almsgiving will never result in a reduction of a person's sustenance, but that ultimately everyone will return back to Him and attain their rewards according to their actions in this world.

This verse makes it clear that the believers must not think that giving to others in need will reduce their wealth because the expansion or limitation of their livelihood is in the hands of Allah ﷻ who gives us wealth and everything else in the first place.

Why the Phrase "A Loan to Allah ﷻ"?

When speaking about giving in the way of Allah ﷻ *(fī sabīlillāh),* there are several verses[250] in the Noble Qur'ān which use the phrase of 'giving a loan' or 'lending to Allah ﷻ.' On one hand, such phrases convey the ultimate grace of Allah ﷻ to His servants; while on the other hand, they present the readers with the importance of almsgiving.

In this regards, there is a statement from Imām ʿAlī ﷺ which has been recorded in *Nahj al-Balāghah* in which he is reported to have said: "He (Allah) does not seek your support because of any weakness, nor does He demand a loan from you because of (any) shortage. He seeks your help - although He possesses all of the legions of the heavens and the earth;[251] and He is the All-Mighty, the All-Wise.[252] He seeks a loan from you - although to Him belongs the treasuries of the heavens and the

---

[250] See Qur'ān: 2:245, 5:12, 57:11, 57:18, 64:17, and 73:20.

[251] Qur'ān, Sūrah al-Fatḥ (48), Verse 7:

وَلِلَّهِ جُنُودُ ٱلسَّمَٰوَٰتِ وَٱلْأَرْضِ...

[252] Ibid., Sūrah Ibrāhīm (14), Verse 4:

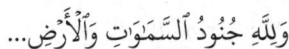

earth;[253] and He is the All-Sufficient, the All-Praiseworthy.[254] (Rather) He intends to test you as to which of you is the best in conduct.[255] You should therefore be quick in the performance of (good) acts so that you may be with His neighbors in His abode; He made His Prophet's companions of these neighbors, and made the angels to visit them. He has honored their ears so that the sound of the Hell fire may never reach them, and He has afforded protection to their bodies from weariness and fatigue. That is the grace of Allah, He bestows it upon whomsoever He wills; and Allah is the Lord of Mighty Grace."[256 & 257]

Keys of Guidance

- The mindset which Allah ﷻ wishes to instill in the believers is for them to recognize that they need to give back to others that which Allah ﷻ has bestowed upon them. In order to do this, Allah ﷻ motivates people with the follow three points:

  a. Human beings are, by their nature, business-minded and are always looking for profits in whatever they do. People want to invest somewhere where they can get the best profit - this reflects on the quantity.

---

[253] Qur'ān, Sūrah al-Munāfiqūn (63), Verse 7:

...وَهُوَ ٱلْعَزِيزُ ٱلْحَكِيمُ ﴿٤﴾

...وَلِلَّهِ خَزَآئِنُ ٱلسَّمَٰوَٰتِ وَٱلْأَرْضِ...

[254] Ibid., Sūrah al-Ḥajj (22), Verse 64:

...وَإِنَّ ٱللَّهَ لَهُوَ ٱلْغَنِىُّ ٱلْحَمِيدُ ﴿٦٤﴾

[255] Ibid., Sūrah Hūd (11), Verse 7:

...لِيَبْلُوَكُمْ أَيُّكُمْ أَحْسَنُ عَمَلًا...

[256] Ibid., Sūrah al-Ḥadīd (57), Verse 21:

...ذَٰلِكَ فَضْلُ ٱللَّهِ يُؤْتِيهِ مَن يَشَآءُ ۚ وَٱللَّهُ ذُو ٱلْفَضْلِ ٱلْعَظِيمِ ﴿٢١﴾

[257] *Nahj al-Balāghah*, Sermon 183. The initial portion of this tradition is as follows:

فَلَمْ يَسْتَنْصِرْكُمْ مِنْ ذُلٍّ، وَلَمْ يَسْتَقْرِضْكُمْ مِنْ قُلٍّ، اسْتَنْصَرَكُمْ...

b. People want their investment capital to be used to do good and in a good way, and for this reason, Allah ﷻ requests that we provide a good and pure investment - a *qarḍ al-ḥasana* - this reflects on the quality.
c. The last thing that people look for in their investments is that the returns should not be short-lived. Rather, they should continue to provide returns for as long as possible, and for this reason Allah ﷻ mentions that the returns from this investment will last for eternity.

- Another mindset which Allah ﷻ helps human beings create in the Qur'ān is the constant reminder that eventually, all creations will return back to Him. Therefore, whether a person invests in one's own hereafter or not, they will all have to make their way back to Him regardless - however, how they return and with what kind of an investment is up to the individual themselves. One can either choose to return to Him with full-hands and an impressive balance of good deeds, or go back to Him empty-handed and remorseful.
- Helping the creations of Allah ﷻ is equivalent to helping Allah ﷻ directly. In this and many other passages of the Qur'ān, Allah ﷻ uses the phrase of lending money to Him rather than saying lending money to people.
- If we recognize the fact that an increase in our sustenance, and a decrease in our sustenance are both in the control of Allah ﷻ and not in our efforts, then we will easily spend in His way.
- When a person recognizes that everyone will die and return back to Allah ﷻ, and that He can take back whatever He gives to His servants, these things will make it easier for an individual to spend in the way of Allah ﷻ.

Verse 246

أَلَمْ تَرَ إِلَى ٱلْمَلَإِ مِنۢ بَنِىٓ إِسْرَٰٓءِيلَ مِنۢ بَعْدِ مُوسَىٰٓ إِذْ قَالُوا۟ لِنَبِىٍّ لَّهُمُ ٱبْعَثْ
لَنَا مَلِكًا نُّقَٰتِلْ فِى سَبِيلِ ٱللَّهِ ۖ قَالَ هَلْ عَسَيْتُمْ إِن كُتِبَ عَلَيْكُمُ ٱلْقِتَالُ

أَلَّا تُقَٰتِلُواْۖ قَالُواْ وَمَا لَنَآ أَلَّا نُقَٰتِلَ فِي سَبِيلِ ٱللَّهِ وَقَدۡ أُخۡرِجۡنَا مِن دِيَٰرِنَا
وَأَبۡنَآئِنَاۖ فَلَمَّا كُتِبَ عَلَيۡهِمُ ٱلۡقِتَالُ تَوَلَّوۡاْ إِلَّا قَلِيلٗا مِّنۡهُمۡۚ وَٱللَّهُ عَلِيمُۢ
بِٱلظَّٰلِمِينَ ٢٤٦

Do you not consider what happened with the elders of the Children of Isrāʾīl after (Prophet) Mūsā once they appealed to a Prophet chosen for them (by Allah ﷻ) saying: "Set up for us a king and we will fight in Allah's cause." He (Prophet Ishmūʾīl ﷺ said: "Is it possible that you would hold back from fighting, if fighting was prescribed for you?" They (the Children of Isrāʾīl) said: "Why should we not fight in Allah's cause when we have been driven from our habitations and our children?" But when fighting was prescribed for them, they turned away, except for a few of them; and Allah has full knowledge of (such) wrongdoers.

Connection with the Previous Verses

Continuing on with the conversation of sacrifice, the Qurʾān focuses on one of the greatest topics which is standing up against oppression and sacrificing one's life for the greater good. In this verse under review, Allah ﷻ was providing the Muslims at the time of Prophet Muḥammad ﷺ and those who would come after them, a historical example in order to learn lessons from the past generations, and take admonition from them for the future.

Lessons from the History of the Children of Isrāʾīl

The Children of Isrāʾīl who had become weak and powerless under the rule of the Pharaohs in Egypt, were eventually saved from their miserable situation - thanks in part to the wise leadership of Prophet Mūsā ﷺ - and subsequently they reached levels of power and greatness. Through the blessings of Prophet Mūsā ﷺ, Allah ﷻ gave them many gifts - including the Ark of the Covenant.[258]

However, these same victories and blessings gradually made the Children of Isrāʾīl become proud, and led them to break the laws which Allah ﷻ had given them.

Eventually defeated by the Philistines,[259] they lost their power and

---

[258] The Ark of the Covenant or the sarcophagus *(tābūt)* is that same box which the mother of Prophet Mūsā ﷺ put him in as a baby and then let it sail in the river which the agents of the Pharaoh found in the water.

When those agents found the box, they took it and the baby, the infant Mūsā ﷺ, and passed both the box and the baby to the wife of the Pharaoh; so he was brought up and taken care of by the Pharaoh and his wife. Later, when Prophet Mūsā ﷺ grew older and left the palace, he took this box with him and eventually handed it over to the Children of Isrāʾīl.

The Children of Isrāʾīl honored this memorable box and would seek blessings from Allah ﷻ by means of it. In the last days of his life, Prophet Mūsā ﷺ placed the Sacred Tablets on which Allah's commandments were written, along with his armor, and other relics inside of this Ark, and handed it over to his successor - Yūshaʿ ibn Nūn ﷺ.

Therefore, the importance of this Ark increased for the Children of Isrāʾīl, and it was for this reason that they took it with them in wars because it had a unique psychological impact on them.

However, gradually the foundations of their religion weakened, and the enemies overpowered them and took that box from them. However, Prophet Ishmūʾīl (also known as Shamūʾī and Samūʾīl - or his Biblical name of Samuel) promised them that the Ark of the Covenant would return to them as a sign of the truthfulness of his word.

After the attack of Nebuchadnezzar upon Jerusalem and the destruction of the Temple, the Ark of the Covenant was lost. According to some *ḥadīth*, it is among the trusts of Imāmate and Imām al-Mahdī ﷺ will take out the Ark of the Covenant from a cave in Antioch upon his return.

[259] The Philistines were a group of people who arrived in the Levant (an area that includes Jordan, Lebanon, Syria, and Greater-Palestine) during the 12th century B.C. They came during a time when cities and civilizations in the Middle East and Greece were collapsing. The Philistines themselves left no texts, thus much of what we know about them comes from the people they encountered.

influence along with the Ark of the Covenant. As a result, they became so fragmented that the enemies drove large numbers of them out of their land and took their children captive. This went on for years until Allah ﷻ raised a Prophet from the Children of Isrā'īl named Ishmū'īl ﷺ to guide them and save them from their enemies. They rallied around him and asked him to choose a leader and commander for them so that they could all fight the enemy under his command in order to regain their lost honor.

Prophet Ishmū'īl ﷺ turned to Allah ﷻ and presented the request of his people, so Allah ﷻ sent Prophet Ishmū'īl ﷺ revelation that He has chosen Ṭālūt[260] to be their king and leader under whose command the Children of Isrā'īl will fight.

In this verse, Allah ﷻ directly addresses Prophet Muḥammad ﷺ and asks a rhetorical question if he saw a group from the Children of Isrā'īl who came after Prophet Mūsā ﷺ who said to their Prophet that he should choose a ruler for them so that they may fight in the cause of Allah ﷻ.

The word 'leaders' *(mala'ī)* means 'objects or people who fill the eye and amaze the onlooker.' For this reason, a large population that has one opinion and belief is referred to with this word; and in addition, the aristocrats and elders of a community are also referred to with this same word.

It is worthy to note that they stated that this struggle was 'in the way of Allah' *(fī sabīlillāh),* and this clarifies that when a person struggles to gain freedom and save others from the bondage of oppression, this is

---

260 Ṭālūt, or Saul as he is known by his Biblical name was one of the Kings appointed for the Children of Isrā'īl. He hails from the lineage of Prophet Ya'qūb ﷺ through his son, Binyāmīn ﷺ. Ṭālūt was known for his deep knowledge and powerful physique, and it was under the direct order of Allah ﷻ that he was chosen to preside over the Children of Isrā'īl; and as the Muslim scholars have stated, Prophet Dāwūd ﷺ (David) was his son-in-law, and he lived five centuries after Prophet Mūsā ﷺ. The story of the Children of Isrā'īl asking for a king to govern over them is also seen in the Old Testament in 1 Samuel 8 - for those who wish to compare and contrast the Biblical narrative with that of the unadulterated Qur'ānic story about this event.

considered as struggle in the way of Allah ﷻ.

In any case, their Prophet who was worried about their situation and did not see them as being steadfast in the covenant, said to them that if they are ordered to fight, they may disobey and will not strive or fight in the way of Allah ﷻ.

The Children of Isrāʾīl responded to their Prophet and asked him why he felt that they would not fight in the way of Allah ﷻ since they have been kicked out of their homes, and their children have been taken captive!?

However, none of these oppressions which had been meted out against them stopped them from breaking their pledge to Allah ﷻ and His Prophet, and this is understood from the portion of the verse in which we read that when fighting was ordained for them, all of the Children of Isrāʾīl except a few of them refused to fight - thus Allah ﷻ confirms that He is All-Aware of the evildoers, and He will recompense them accordingly.

As for the number of individuals from the Children of Isrāʾīl who remained loyal to Allah ﷻ and obeyed the commands of their leader to fight and defend themselves, the *ḥadīth* state that they were only 313 - the same as the number of loyal soldiers who took part in the first battle in the history of Islam - the Battle of Badr; and this is the same number of loyal followers who will be the first to join the movement of Imām al-Mahdī عجل الله تعالى فرجه الشريف after his occultation.

Keys of Guidance

- In many verses of the Noble Qurʾān, Allah ﷻ speaks about the Children of Isrāʾīl, and this is done so that Muslims will carefully study their history and endeavor that they do not follow in the footsteps of disobedience to their Prophets and his rightfully appointed 12 successors.
- When a person performs the sacred struggle to eliminate oppression and defend one's homeland, they are working in the way of Allah ﷻ.

Verse 247

وَقَالَ لَهُمْ نَبِيُّهُمْ إِنَّ ٱللَّهَ قَدْ بَعَثَ لَكُمْ طَالُوتَ مَلِكًا ۚ قَالُوٓاْ أَنَّىٰ يَكُونُ لَهُ ٱلْمُلْكُ عَلَيْنَا وَنَحْنُ أَحَقُّ بِٱلْمُلْكِ مِنْهُ وَلَمْ يُؤْتَ سَعَةً مِّنَ ٱلْمَالِ ۚ قَالَ إِنَّ ٱللَّهَ ٱصْطَفَىٰهُ عَلَيْكُمْ وَزَادَهُۥ بَسْطَةً فِى ٱلْعِلْمِ وَٱلْجِسْمِ ۖ وَٱللَّهُ يُؤْتِى مُلْكَهُۥ مَن يَشَآءُ ۚ وَٱللَّهُ وَٰسِعٌ عَلِيمٌ ﴿٢٤٧﴾

And he (their Prophet Ishmū'īl ﷺ) said to them: "Allah has set up Ṭālūt (Saul) for you as (your) king." They (the Children of Isrā'īl) said (to Prophet Ishmū'īl): "How can he have authority over us when we are more deserving of kingdom than him, seeing that he has not been given abundance of wealth?" He (Prophet Ishmū'īl ﷺ) said: "Allah has chosen him over you and increased him abundantly in knowledge and physical power (so that he can execute his decrees). Allah bestows kingdom on whomsoever He wills, and Allah is All-Embracing (with His Mercy) *(Wāsiʿ)*, All-Knowing *(ʿAlīm)*.

In any case, Prophet Ishmū'īl ﷺ fulfilled his responsibility and responded to their request, and appointed Ṭālūt (Saul) by the order of Allah ﷻ to rule over them. He also made it clear to the Children of Isrā'īl that Allah ﷻ had appointed Ṭālūt to rule over them, and that this was not the personal desire or selection of Prophet Ishmū'īl ﷺ.

From the interpretation of the word which is used in this verse of 'king' *(malik)*, it is understood that Ṭālūt was not only the commander of the army, but he was also the ruler of the country; and this is where the opposition from some of the Children of Isrā'īl began.

The Qur'ān quotes a number of the Children of Isrā'īl as asking how a person like Ṭālūt could rule over them, since the Children of Isrā'īl felt that they were better than him, and that he did not have much wealth so he was unfit for leadership and governance.

This was the first protest and breach of covenant which the Children of Isrā'īl made against this next Prophet of theirs, and by keeping in mind that although they were objecting to a Prophet, however since the choice of appointing Ṭālūt was from Allah ﷻ, in actuality they were objecting the command of Allah ﷻ.

The Noble Qur'ān narrates the response of Prophet Ishmū'īl ﷷ to the Children of Isrā'īl where he said to them that Allah ﷻ has chosen Ṭālūt as their leader, and that he has been granted knowledge *('ilm)* and physical strength *(jism)* by Allah ﷻ to lead the Children of Isrā'īl forward.

In other words, Prophet Ishmū'īl ﷷ was saying to his people that: This choice of Allah ﷻ is a wise one, and that you the Children of Isrā'īl are sorely mistaken and have forgotten the basic conditions of leadership. Having a certain familial lineage and vast amount of wealth are not indicators for leadership because both of these are superficial and extrinsic; whereas knowledge and physical strength are two real, intrinsic advantages which have a profound effect on leadership.

Going on to quote Prophet Ishmū'īl ﷷ, the Qur'ān adds that Allah ﷻ grants His Power and Authority *(Mulk)* to whomsoever He Wills, and the bounties of Allah ﷻ are vast.

The last portion of this verse may refer to the third condition for leadership which is the provision of the necessary conditions and means for leadership which are granted to a worthy individual by Allah ﷻ.

Keys of Guidance

- The positions given by Allah ﷻ are based on a person's own internal abilities and talents, and those merits must be aligned with the position that they are assigned to, as every position requires that the person has certain internal aptitudes in order to be able to execute their responsibilities. It is extremely important that when a person is seen to have certain unique talents they are given the opportunity to make use of them in order to obtain the best results. However, a completely incorrect mindset of people is that they see merits to be something external, such as wealth, popularity, family name, tribal or cultural affiliation, etc.
- When Allah ﷻ sees that a person has potential, is exhibiting the

abilities which one has, and is working hard using what Allah ﷻ has given them, then without a doubt He will continue to bless those individuals, provide them with increased bounties, and further assist them to persevere and hone their skills and talents.

- Through the chronicles of history which the Qur'ān narrates, it constantly shows us that people - meaning the companions of their respective Prophet - were **never** permitted to choose the successor of the Prophet whom they followed - this was based **solely** on revelation from Allah ﷻ.
- The Qur'ān clearly articulates that if a community of believers want to achieve freedom and salvation from their enemies, then they must accept the Divinely-appointed leaders.
- Leaders of a family, community, or society must ensure that they explain to people the reason why they are making certain choices and doing certain things, and not simply say that it is their right as the leader to do as they wish. In this passage we see that Prophet Ishmū'īl ﵇ clearly told the Children of Isrā'īl that the reason why Allah ﷻ chose Ṭālūt as the king over them was because of two unique traits which he had: knowledge, and physical ability to carry out the necessary tasks.

Verse 248

وَقَالَ لَهُمْ نَبِيُّهُمْ إِنَّ ءَايَةَ مُلْكِهِۦٓ أَن يَأْتِيَكُمُ ٱلتَّابُوتُ فِيهِ سَكِينَةٌ مِّن
رَّبِّكُمْ وَبَقِيَّةٌ مِّمَّا تَرَكَ ءَالُ مُوسَىٰ وَءَالُ هَـٰرُونَ تَحْمِلُهُ ٱلْمَلَـٰٓئِكَةُ ۚ إِنَّ فِى
ذَٰلِكَ لَءَايَةً لَّكُمْ إِن كُنتُم مُّؤْمِنِينَ ﴿٢٤٨﴾

And he (their Prophet Ishmū'īl ﵇ also) said (to the Children of Isrā'īl): "The sign of his (Tālūt's) kingdom is that the Ark (of the Covenant) will come to you in which there will be inward peace and assurance from your Lord, and a remnant of what the children of Mūsā and the children of Hārūn left behind, carried by the angels.

Surely in that, there is a sign for you, if you are (true) believers.

This verse shows us that it seems that the Children of Isrā'īl had not yet believed in the mission of Ṭālūt and him being deputed by Allah ﷻ, even though Prophet Ishmū'īl ﷺ clearly told them that this news was from Allah ﷻ. Unfortunately, they had not yet accepted his statement, so they asked him for a sign and further proof to validate that Ṭālūt was truly sent by Allah ﷻ.

Since the conviction of some of the Children of Isrā'īl in regards to the Prophethood of Ishmū'īl ﷺ was weak and they were questioning his status, they required a miracle to be fully convinced.

History tells us that the Ark of the Covenant had been lost for many years, and the Children of Isrā'īl were searching for it. The Ark was unique because it contained many special items such as a shirt, a walking stick, and other things which belonged to Prophet Mūsā ﷺ. These items were very important and held great spiritual significance for the Children of Isrā'īl.

If the Ark of the Covenant was to be miraculously found, then this would have been taken as a sign of the truthfulness of Allah ﷻ to them, and one more way of their guidance. Perhaps through this, the Children of Isrā'īl would have truly believed and reached inner peace and tranquility, and developed a stronger sense of commitment toward their faith.

In answer to their request, Prophet Ishmū'īl ﷺ said to them that the sign of the validity of Ṭālūt ruling over them is that the Ark of the Covenant will be miraculously brought to them, and in finally reclaiming it, they will find tranquility from their Lord, and inside it they will find the relics from the family of Prophets Mūsā ﷺ and Hārūn ﷺ.

Keys of Guidance

- From time to time, Allah ﷻ shows those who are willing to accept Him, His reality by the use of various signs. He does this to prove that if they accept Him and truly believe, then they too can have a life full of peace and tranquility. The signs which Allah ﷻ sends can be manifested in various ways such as: They can be provided with needed advice from someone; something may happen to an individual to jolt them; they could witness something extraordinary while performing *ziyārah*; or other such things. However, we should keep in mind that we must be extremely careful not to generalize, or make decisions based on such signs, especially haste decisions. Ultimately, Allah ﷻ advises us to always seek counsel with others and take advice from people who may be more experienced than us.

- The true source of peace and tranquility in the heart is Allah ﷻ - even if at times He may use physical devices to facilitate that peace - like he did for the Children of Isrā'īl in bringing them the Ark of the Covenant.
- If the Ark which touched the body of Prophet Mūsā ﵇ as an infant, carried him down the river, and later on housed the sacred Tablets which Prophet Mūsā ﵇ was given by Allah ﷻ was considered sacred and something which soothed and calmed people; then there is nothing wrong to say that the ornate silver box (known as a *ḍarīḥ*[261]) which rests above the graves of the saints (*awliyā'*) of Allah ﷻ - such as the Prophets of Allah, or the 11 Imāms of the Ahlul Bayt ﵇, or other noble personalities - does not go against the Qur'ān,

---

[261] A *ḍarīḥ* is a metal structure similar to a grille made of gold, silver, copper, wood, etc., which is placed on the grave of an Imām, the children of an Imām, or religious leaders. There is no exact information about the history of the emergence of the *ḍarīḥ* or its development into the current form; however *ḍarīḥ* which means 'a small room or box' has been commonly used since the first/seventh century. Apparently, the history of the *ḍarīḥ* with its current form (grille-shaped and made of silver or copper) dates back to the Safavid period.

Ḍarīḥ is an Arabic word meaning 'grave' or 'the cleft in the middle of a grave' and has been mentioned in Arabic dictionaries; however, in Farsi, it refers to 'a small room, a box, or a grille-shaped structure made of iron or wood placed on the grave of an Imām or the children of an Imām.' This is its common Persian meaning; but in Lebanon it is referred to as a *shubbāk* meaning 'a net-like enclosure made out of iron or wood;' and in Egypt it is called a *maqsūra* commonly referring to 'a place, room, or small house.'

because those who are buried in these sacred shrine cities of:

1. Mecca;[262]
2. Medina;[263]
3. Syria;[264]
4. Najaf;[265]
5. Karbalāʾ;[266]
6. Baghdād;[267]
7. Sāmarrāʾ;[268]
8. Mashhad;[269]

---

[262] The burial site of individuals such as: The Mother of the Believers, Lady Khadījah bint Khuwaylid and the uncle of Prophet Muḥammad ﷺ, Abū Ṭālib ibn ʿAbdul Muṭṭalib.

[263] The burial site of Prophet Muḥammad ﷺ; as well as four of the 12 Imāms of the Ahlul Bayt: the second one, Imām Ḥasan ibn ʿAlī al-Mujtabā; the fourth, Imām ʿAlī ibn al-Ḥusayn Zayn al-ʿĀbidīn; the fifth, Imām Muḥammad ibn ʿAlī al-Bāqir; and the sixth, Imām Jaʿfar ibn Muḥammad aṣ-Ṣādiq; as well as the only daughter of the Prophet ﷺ, Sayyidah Fāṭimah az-Zahrāʾ.

[264] The burial site of the granddaughter of Prophet Muḥammad ﷺ, Lady Zaynab bint ʿAlī; and the young daughter of Imām Ḥusayn, Ruqayyah (also known as Sakīna).

[265] The resting place of the first Imām, ʿAlī ibn Abī Ṭālib.

[266] The burial place of the third Imām, Ḥusayn ibn ʿAlī; his brother Abūl Fadhl al-ʿAbbās as well as the loyal companions of Imām Ḥusayn who sacrificed themselves on the Day of ʿĀshūrāʾ alongside him.

[267] The burial site of the seventh Imām, Mūsā ibn Jaʿfar al-Kāẓim; and the ninth Imām, Muḥammad ibn ʿAlī al-Jawād.

[268] The place of the martyrdom and burial of the tenth Imām, Muḥammad ibn ʿAlī al-Hādī; and the eleventh Imām, Ḥasan ibn ʿAlī al-ʿAskarī.

[269] The resting place of the eighth Imām, ʿAlī ibn Mūsā ar-Riḍā.

9. Qum;[270]

and many other places - contain the resting sites of the family of Prophet Muḥammad ﷺ.

Verse 249

فَلَمَّا فَصَلَ طَالُوتُ بِٱلْجُنُودِ قَالَ إِنَّ ٱللَّهَ مُبْتَلِيكُم بِنَهَرٍ فَمَن شَرِبَ
مِنْهُ فَلَيْسَ مِنِّى وَمَن لَّمْ يَطْعَمْهُ فَإِنَّهُۥ مِنِّىٓ إِلَّا مَنِ ٱغْتَرَفَ غُرْفَةًۢ بِيَدِهِۦ ۚ
فَشَرِبُوا۟ مِنْهُ إِلَّا قَلِيلًا مِّنْهُمْ ۚ فَلَمَّا جَاوَزَهُۥ هُوَ وَٱلَّذِينَ ءَامَنُوا۟ مَعَهُۥ قَالُوا۟
لَا طَاقَةَ لَنَا ٱلْيَوْمَ بِجَالُوتَ وَجُنُودِهِۦ ۚ قَالَ ٱلَّذِينَ يَظُنُّونَ أَنَّهُم مُّلَٰقُوا۟
ٱللَّهِ كَم مِّن فِئَةٍ قَلِيلَةٍ غَلَبَتْ فِئَةً كَثِيرَةًۢ بِإِذْنِ ٱللَّهِ ۗ وَٱللَّهُ مَعَ
ٱلصَّٰبِرِينَ ﴿٢٤٩﴾

Thus, when Ṭālūt set out with the armies and said (to them): "Allah will put you to test by a river: whoever then drinks from (the water of) it is not of my group, and whoever does not drink it, he is of my group; but forgiven will he be who takes thereof in the cup of his hand (a small amount of water to drink). But they drank (to their fill) thereof, all (of the Children of Isrāʾīl) except a few of them; and when he (Ṭālūt) crossed it (the river) with those who believed in him, (those who drank only a bit of the water of the river - as much as would fit in the cup of their hands) said: "Today we have no power against Jālūt[271] (Goliath) and his forces." But those who

[270] The burial place of Lady Fāṭimah Maʿṣūma bint Mūsā ibn Jaʿfar ﷺ, the sister of the eighth Imām.

[271] Jālūt or as he is known by his Biblical name of Goliath, was the name of a powerful Philistine warrior who was defeated by Prophet Dāwūd ﷺ. The name Jālūt is mentioned three times in the Noble Qurʾān (See Qurʾān, Sūrah al-Baqarah

had certainty of their meeting with Allah and felt as if they were always standing in His Presence said: "Many a small group has overcome a larger group by the permission of Allah." And Allah is with the patient and persevering ones.

Eventually, the Children of Isrā'īl accepted Ṭālūt's leadership and command over them, and they were able to mobilize many troops. Once they were prepared they set out together, and this new generation of people from the Children of Isrā'īl came face to face with a unique test from Allah ﷻ.

The Qur'ān presents their narrative in the following fashion by stating that when Ṭālūt was appointed as their King and Commander in Chief, they began to march toward the battlefront, and he said to them: Allah will test you by a river. You will get thirsty on this journey, and those of you who drink the water from it are not from me; and those who do not drink more than one measure of it by cupping their hands and taking only that amount of water, are from me and will pass this unique test from Allah ﷻ.[272]

---

(2), Verses 249-251) in the story of the battle between the Children of Isrā'īl and the people of Philistine. This story has been narrated with much more detail in the Old Testament. The victory of Prophet Dāwūd ﷺ over the large contingent of the Philistines reminds us that in the time of war, the victory belongs to the faithful ones, and Allah ﷻ will help them even if they are small in number and may lack the material means to be victorious.

[272] The word which has been translated in the introductory portion of this verse as 'set out' *(faṣala)* means 'to cut,' however in the context of this verse, it means 'separation' - such as the separation from a city or region where a person is from.

Another word which is used in this verse and has been rendered into English as 'the armies' *(junūd)* is the plural of the word 'army' *(jund)* and its root meaning is 'land that has large, stacked stones on it.' Later on, this word began to be used for 'anything dense and remarkable' - and it is for this reason that an army of soldiers, since they are densely packed when they march and are an astonishing sight to see, are referred to in the Arabic with this word *jund*.

At this juncture, the armies of Ṭālūt faced a great trial: battling the scorching heat and their extreme thirst. Such a test was necessary for this army, especially when we keep in mind the negative track-record of the Children of Isrā'īl in some of their previous wars, and their encounters with the Prophets sent by Allah ﷻ.

We must keep in mind that the victory of any group of people depends on their degree of discipline, the strength of their faith, endurance against the enemy, and their obedience to the orders of a leader and Commander in Chief.

However, the Noble Qur'ān states in this passage that most of the Children of Isrā'īl did not pass this test as they should have, so Allah ﷻ says that except for a few of them, the vast majority drank their fill from the river.

The Qur'ān continues and states that when Ṭālūt and the believers who were with him passed through the river which they were prohibited to drink from, they said to each other that today we are able to stand in opposition to Jālūt and his troops.

Allah ﷻ goes on to relate this story and states that those who knew that they would meet Allah ﷻ and believed in the Day of Resurrection modestly proclaimed: How many times has it been that a small group of people were able to overcome a large group of people by the permission of Allah, and indeed Allah is with the patient ones.[273]

The word which has been used in the English translation of this verse for 'those who had certainty' *(yazhunūn)* actually means 'they knew' *(yaʿlamūn)* - meaning that these were individuals who had complete belief and certainty in the Day of Resurrection.

Keys of Guidance

- Before a person can expect to deal with external enemies, one must

[273] The word which has been rendered into the English translation of this verse as 'company' *(fi'a)* comes from the Arabic root of *fai'* and its original meaning is 'to return' - and since a community which supports each other is always going back to help one another out in times of difficulty, it is for this reason that this word has been coined in Arabic for such people.

go through some training, certain hardships, and struggle against the inner enemy - the soul, the lower desires, and one's passions. If these can be overcome, then an individual can almost be certain that one will be able to defeat any external threat which comes up.

- Everyone is going through different tests in the life of this world, however there are only a few people who will come out of this exam victorious.
- Being revolutionary in spirit and deed is not important - what holds weight is to remain revolutionary and continuously carry this spirit. There are many people who simply scream the slogans of revolution, however very few actually act upon this, and continue down this path in life.
- Faith *(īmān)* has various degrees and intensities. When a person enters Islam and calls themselves a Muslim it is good, however one must realize that there are stages to perfection until one can graduate to being a true believer *(mu'min)*. Even in true faith there are multiple stages to traverse in order to get to the top-most level of faith.
- Although people tend to equate military might and a large force as being the key to "victory," however we must realize that it is much more important to have a qualitative force - which means people who are dedicated and truly believe in what they are standing up for. Human history has shown us that even when a small country is attacked by a larger superpower, as long as the army of the small country has dedication, conviction in their cause, and the will to sacrifice themselves for the greater good, they will eventually be able to defeat the superpower.

Verse 250

وَلَمَّا بَرَزُواْ لِجَالُوتَ وَجُنُودِهِۦ قَالُواْ رَبَّنَآ أَفۡرِغۡ عَلَيۡنَا صَبۡرٗا وَثَبِّتۡ أَقۡدَامَنَا
وَٱنصُرۡنَا عَلَى ٱلۡقَوۡمِ ٱلۡكَٰفِرِينَ ﴿٢٥٠﴾

And when they went forth against Jālūt and his forces, they (the Children of Isrā'īl) prayed (to Allah ﷻ saying): "Our Lord, pour down upon us steadfastness *(ṣabr)*, and make our feet firm, and help us (to be victorious) over those who reject the truth."

In this verse, Allah ﷻ mentions the event of the actual confrontation of the two armies, and says that when the Children of Isrā'īl under the guidance of their King Ṭālūt stood before Jālūt and his armies, they prayed to Allah ﷻ saying: Our Lord, pour down upon us a measure of patience and perseverance, and keep our feet steadfast; and make us victorious over those who reject the truth.

The word which has been rendered into English as 'went forth' *(barazū)* comes from the Arabic root word *burūz,* and the original meaning of this word is 'manifestation' or 'emergence,' since when a person is ready to fight and makes one's way onto the battlefield, he is said 'to emerge forth,' The next step in challenging the transgressors is considered as a struggle, thus it is from this same root that we get the Arabic word for competition, contest, dual, etc., which is *mubārizah.*

In fact, in this very short yet powerful supplication made to Allah ﷻ, Ṭālūt and his army requested three things from the Creator:

1. Patience and perseverance *(ṣabr).*
2. The ability to keep their feet steadfast *(thābit)* so as to not be distracted, nor run away from the battle.

If we analyze this supplication made by the Children of Isrā'īl, the first portion of it has an esoteric and internal aspect, while the second part of it has an external aspect, since steadfastness is one of the results of the spirit of perseverance and patience.

3. The final request which the Children of Isrā'īl made in this supplication was their appeal to Allah ﷻ to help them in this battle, and for them to be able to defeat those who reject the truth, and this is the final stage in the journey of patience and steadfastness.

Keys of Guidance

- Prayer and supplication to Allah ﷻ is always important, however it takes on an even greater urgency when on the battlefront - not only in the battlefield of a traditional war, but even in our daily lives when we wake up and are constantly being confronted with life in a secular system, surrounded by materialistic and irreligious teachings; so especially in such a scenario, we must constantly pray to Allah ﷻ for Him to pour down perseverance upon us and to assist us in our daily struggles.

- Patience *(ṣabr)* and victory *(naṣr)* are closely related - patience leads to victory, and victory cannot be achieved except with patience.
- During times of difficulties, the human being is in need of an intense amount of patience; and this is not only a logical statement, but it is also seen in this verse as Allah ﷻ uses the word 'pour down' *(afrigh)* which denotes a tremendous descent, while the word perseverance *(ṣabr)* has been mentioned as an indefinite noun which also denotes a great deal of patience which is being asked for.
- As servants of Allah ﷻ, our duty is to move forward, strive, struggle, and put forth our best efforts, but know that actual victory is only in the hands of Allah ﷻ. We will not be asked why we reached a certain outcome in our struggles, however we will be asked if we were fully committed to the cause and what we did.
- Victory in the struggles of our lives is only of value when the goal of those who are standing up is for the superiority of truth over falsehood - not for the conquest of one group or country over another.

Verse 251

فَهَزَمُوهُم بِإِذۡنِ ٱللَّهِ وَقَتَلَ دَاوُۥدُ جَالُوتَ وَءَاتَىٰهُ ٱللَّهُ ٱلۡمُلۡكَ وَٱلۡحِكۡمَةَ وَعَلَّمَهُۥ مِمَّا يَشَآءُۗ وَلَوۡلَا دَفۡعُ ٱللَّهِ ٱلنَّاسَ بَعۡضَهُم بِبَعۡضٖ لَّفَسَدَتِ ٱلۡأَرۡضُ وَلَٰكِنَّ ٱللَّهَ ذُو فَضۡلٍ عَلَى ٱلۡعَٰلَمِينَ ﴿٢٥١﴾

So they (the Children of Isrā'īl) defeated them (the army of Jālūt)

> by the permission of Allah, and (Prophet) Dāwūd[274] killed Jālūt, and Allah granted him kingdom and wisdom, and taught him of that which He willed. If it was not that Allah repelled people - some by means of others - then the (entire) Earth would surely be corrupted; but Allah is Gracious on all of the worlds.

Certainly, Allah ﷻ will not leave such dedicated and sincere servants all alone, even if they are few in number and the enemy are many, and this is why the verse says that the Children of Isrā'īl defeated the army of Jālūt by the permission of Allah ﷻ, and He goes on to confirm that Prophet Dāwūd ؑ, the strong and brave young man in the army of Ṭālūt, was the one who killed Jālūt.

A youth with a slingshot in his hand, Prophet Dāwūd ؑ threw one or two stones so skillfully that he struck Jālūt on his forehead, and screaming in pain he fell down dead. Terror gripped his entire army and they fled as fast as they could - seeing their seemingly fearless leader killed so quickly. It was as if Allah ﷻ wanted to show His Power, and how a kingdom with that greatness and mass of armies could be overthrown by a relatively inexperienced army with a young soldier in their midst, and that too with an apparently insignificant weapon.

---

[274] Prophet Dāwūd ؑ, son of Īshā, was from the progeny of Yahūdā, the son of Prophet Yaʿqūb ؑ. He was an Isrā'īlite Prophet to whom Allah ﷻ revealed the Zabūr (Psalms).

The verses of the Qur'ān mention that Prophet Dāwūd ؑ could understand the language of the animals (See Qur'ān, Sūrah an-Naml (27), Verse 16); he was bestowed the power of authority and was granted wisdom by Allah ﷻ; and he was taught by Allah ﷻ whatever he wanted to learn (See Qur'ān, Sūrah al-Baqarah (2), Verse 251). In addition, Prophet Dāwūd ؑ worshiped Allah ﷻ frequently and cried out of the fear of the Almighty ﷻ; and the mountains and birds exalted Allah ﷻ together with Prophet Dāwūd ؑ (See Qur'ān, Sūrah al-Anbiyā' (21), Verse 79).

Prophet Dāwūd ؑ is mentioned 16 times in the Qur'ān in the following passages: 2:251, 4:163, 5:78, 6:84, 17:55, 21:78. 21:79, 27:15, 27:16, 34:10, 34:13, 38:17, 38:22, 38:24, 38:26, and 38:30.

The Qur'ān then adds that Allah ﷻ granted him (Prophet Dāwūd ؑ) authority *(al-mulk)* and wisdom *(al-ḥikmah),* and that Allah ﷻ taught him whatever He wanted - meaning that He granted His servant Prophet Dāwūd ؑ Prophethood, and that it was announced to the people from this point in history.

At the end of this verse Allah ﷻ refers to a general law and states that if Allah ﷻ does not repel some people by way of others, then corruption would prevail over the entire Earth, however since Allah ﷻ has mercy on the worlds, He ensures that there is always a balance of peace on Earth through people standing up for their rights to help defend their own territory and that of others.

A similar statement has been mentioned in another place in the Qur'ān where Allah ﷻ states: "Those who have been driven from their homeland against all right, for no other reason than that they say: 'Our Lord is Allah.' Were it not for Allah's repelling some people by means of others, monasteries and churches and synagogues and *masājid,* where Allah is regularly worshiped and His Name is mentioned much, would surely have been pulled down (with the desire that Allah is no longer able to be worshiped and the Earth would become uninhabitable). And Allah most certainly helps whoever helps His cause. Surely, Allah is All-Strong, All-Glorious with irresistible might."[275]

These verses serve as good news for the believers, who are suffering under the severe pressures of the tyrants and despots, but they anticipate the Divine help and victory.

In speaking about this verse, the late 'Allāmah Ṭabā'ṭabā'ī states the following in *Tafsīr al-Mizān*: "This verse hints at a philosophical reality, which is as follows: The felicity and good of the human species is incomplete if there is no society and no mutual assistance. This factor depends on unity to a certain degree in society, so that various individuals

---

[275] Qur'ān. Sūrah al-Ḥajj (22), Verse 40:

ٱلَّذِينَ أُخْرِجُواْ مِن دِيَٰرِهِم بِغَيْرِ حَقٍّ إِلَّآ أَن يَقُولُواْ رَبُّنَا ٱللَّهُۗ وَلَوْلَا دَفْعُ ٱللَّهِ ٱلنَّاسَ بَعْضَهُم بِبَعْضٍ لَّهُدِّمَتْ صَوَٰمِعُ وَبِيَعٌ وَصَلَوَٰتٌ وَمَسَٰجِدُ يُذْكَرُ فِيهَا ٱسْمُ ٱللَّهِ كَثِيرًاۗ وَلَيَنصُرَنَّ ٱللَّهُ مَن يَنصُرُهُۥٓۚ إِنَّ ٱللَّهَ لَقَوِيٌّ عَزِيزٌ ﴿٤٠﴾

may join together to form a single group.

The group together becomes a unified unit; and metaphorically speaking it becomes as though it has a single body and a single soul. It acts and reacts like one individual.

Social unity and the place in which it occurs, that is the assembly of human individuals - is just like unity in creation, and the place in which it occurs meaning the universe.

We know that unity in this system of creation results from the action and reaction occurring in the components of the universe. The various creative causes struggle with each other - repel, or are repelled by opposing forces, and it is because of this constant action and reaction that various parts of this system remain connected with one another.

Otherwise, the universe would have ceased to exist.

Likewise, the system of human society is also based on action and reaction, on repulsion and overpowering; otherwise the various members of society could not remain bound to each other, and society would have ceased to exist; in short the felicity of the species would have vanished.

If we suppose that there was no repelling each other in this meaning (i.e., overpowering others and making them obey the victor's will), then every individual member would have done whatever one thinks is best, even if it goes against the interest of the other members (whether or not those interests are lawful or not is not our concern at this juncture); and the other members would have no means to prevent them from that course of action.

Thus, the unity of the members would cease to exist, and society would be finished.

This repulsion and overpowering are an overwhelming factor in human society.

Human beings try to make others do what they want, and repel them from what they do not like. It is seen in war as well as in peace, in comfort as well as in discomfort, in ease as well as in hardship. The human being does it instinctively; one becomes conscious of it only when someone opposes their will, and then they begin the process of the said repulsion as they think is necessary. That repulsion has degrees of strength and weakness.

War is one of those degrees.

This instinct is seen in action when a believer repulses one's oppressor in defense of one's lawful rights; and it is also seen when someone uses it to protect one's unlawful gains.

Nature bestows its bounties on the believers and the unbelievers alike. It is not that a believer has a nature separate from that of an unbeliever. If this trait of repelling and overpowering was not present in human nature, then nobody would have defended anything, whether it be a lawful right or an unlawful gain.

It is this natural trait from which a human being gains so many benefits - first of all, society is founded on it, and a person makes others follow one's own will, and through it an individual keeps what one has gained, lawfully or otherwise; and it is through this that one tries to get back what has been taken away from them unjustly; and lastly it is through this trait that a person makes the truth live after it has died, and tries to keep society on the path of eternal bliss.

In short, it is a natural factor from which a human being derives many more benefits than harm.

Perhaps it is these things which are referred to in this sentence: "And were it not for Allah's repelling some people with others, the Earth would certainly be in a state of disorder."

The next sentence supports this interpretation where the Qur'ān says that Allah is Gracious on all of the worlds.[276]

Keys of Guidance

- Although efforts and struggles are put forth by people, the defeat of the enemy lies in the hands of Allah ﷻ - it is very well possible that those who are trying to defend themselves from an aggressor will do everything in their power and still be 'defeated' - and some may ask why did Allah ﷻ allow the victim of injustice to 'lose' - however we must always look at the bigger picture and recognize that there are times when an apparent defeat is actually a victory.
- We must keep alive the names of the brave and courageous men and

[276] *Tafsīr al-Mizān*, commentary on this verse.

women who stood their ground throughout history and sacrificed everything to ensure that the flag of the truth stands tall.

- If there is no defense against an aggressor and oppressor - regardless of who they are and what religion or ideology they follow, then corruption and destruction will pervade the Earth, and it is for this reason that humanity needs to stand together to oppose injustice and tyranny - regardless of who is delivering it. However, before this, the victim and the aggressor both need to be clearly identified.

Verse 252

تِلْكَ ءَايَٰتُ ٱللَّهِ نَتْلُوهَا عَلَيْكَ بِٱلْحَقِّ ۚ وَإِنَّكَ لَمِنَ ٱلْمُرْسَلِينَ ﴿٢٥٢﴾

Those are the revelations of Allah and His signs that We recite to you (Muḥammad) in truth, for indeed you (Muḥammad) are one of the Messengers (sent with the Book and receive revelations).

This statement of Allah ﷻ points to the various stories which were related in the previous verses of the Noble Qur'ān in regards to the Children of Isrā'īl, and tells us that all of these are signs *(āyāt)* from Allah ﷻ which are revealed in truth, and that Prophet Muḥammad ﷺ is indeed one of the Messengers of Allah ﷻ *(Mursalīn).*

Each of these stories is a sign of the Power and Greatness of Allah ﷻ and are free from myths and legends. They have been revealed by Allah ﷻ to Prophet Muḥammad ﷺ and recount events which transpired hundreds and thousands of years ago, and are among the signs of the truth of his words and Prophethood - for surely how else could he have known about these events of the past?

Keys of Guidance

- The Qur'ān is a Book of guidance, and although Allah ﷻ brings evidence from history to teach us lessons, and even though for some people it may appear that these are merely historical accounts with no real value, however if you look closer, Allah ﷻ only highlights those areas of history which have lessons for us to learn from. That is why we do not see the historical narrations in the Qur'ān being presented in a chronological order. Rather, there are bits and pieces intertwined within the verses of the Qur'ān with moral lessons for us to reflect upon and then apply within our lives. In general, Allah ﷻ tells stories to help us wake up from our heedlessness *(ghaflah)* - unlike others who tell us stories to put us to sleep.

- Although some of the stories which Allah ﷻ recounts in the Qur'ān are also found in the Old Testament, we must realize that they are not copied from that Book. We may see some parallels between the two narratives, but at other times there are clear discrepancies, and this is where a Muslim must accept that the Qur'ānic narrative is the accurate description, whereas the Biblical account has been tampered with.
- Prophet Muḥammad ﷺ did not copy the stories of the Bible and place them into the Qur'ān. The Prophets of Allah ﷻ all come from the One Source, therefore there may be some narrations that are bound to be mentioned in the Final Testament, the Noble Qur'ān, that may be similar to stories in the previous Scriptures.

End *of* Section *(Juzʾ)* Two *of the* Commentary *of the* Noble Qurʾān

Volume Three of *The Qurʾān: The Clear Guidance* will feature the Commentary of Sūrah al-Baqarah - Verses 253-286 to Sūrah Āl ʿImrān - Verses 1-200

Personalities Mentioned

Throughout *The Clear Guidance*, we reference numerous Prophets and saints - either those mentioned directly in the text of the Qurʾān or those noted in the *ḥadīth* and have used the Arabic name for these individuals. Below are their English equivalents - where available.

Arabic	**English**
Ādam	Adam
Binyāmīn	Benjamin
Dāwūd	David
Ḥizqīl	Ezekiel
Ibrāhīm	Abraham
ʿIsā	Jesus
Ishmūʾīl	Samuel
Ismāʾīl	Ishmael
Muḥammad	Mohammed/Muhammad
Mūsā	Moses
Nūḥ	Noah
Ṭālūt	Saul
Yaʿqūb	Jacob

Glossary of Terms

ʿĀdil: This word means 'just' and has various meanings depending on which Islamic science it is used. In Islamic Jurisprudence *(Fiqh)*, it refers to a Muslim who does not perform the major sins, and does not persist in performing the minor sins. It is one of the necessary criteria for a person to lead the congregational prayers.

Ashhuru al-Ḥurum: This phrase means 'The Sacred Months' and refers to the four months of the lunar-based Islamic Calendar which are sacred in Islam. Amongst the unique rules of these months, one is that fighting is forbidden - except in response to aggression. These months are: Muḥarram (1st month), Rajab (7th month), Dhul Qaʿdah (11th month), and Dhul Ḥijjah (12th month).

ʿĀlim (Plural: ʿUlamāʾ): Literally means 'scholar,' or 'knower,' and is used in various ways. In the Qurʾān, Allah ﷻ refers to Himself as *ʿĀlim al-Ghayb* - the Knower of the Unseen; while for people, it is used to refer to 'one who has attained religious knowledge.'

Barzakh: Literally, this word means 'a barrier,' or 'a partition,' and it is also used to mean 'an obstacle,' 'a hindrance,' or 'a separation between things.' In technical terms, it denotes 'a place and/or the time after death which separates this world from the hereafter.'

Bayt al-māl: Literally means 'House of money' or 'House of wealth,' but is used to refer to 'the public treasury of an Islamic state' and the aparatus that was responsible for the collection and administration of taxes to the Muslim nation.

Bishārah: Means 'glad tidings' - such as the good news which Allah ﷻ provides in the Qurʾān for the coming of future Prophets, or the pleasures and benefits which await the righteous in the world to come.

Dhikr (Plural: Adhkār): Literally means 'remembrance,' 'reminder,' or 'mention.' It has various meanings depending on the context in which it is used, but is most often regarded as the remembrance of Allah ﷻ recited in a specific manner or number of times. It is also used in the Qur'ān to refer to the Scriptures which Allah ﷻ sent for the guidance of humanity.

Diyah (Plural: Diyāt): In Islamic Jurisprudence, it refers to the financial compensation paid to the victim or heirs of a crime in the case of murder, bodily harm, or any property damage.

Dunyā: This temporal, lowly world and its earthly concerns and possessions; as opposed to the *ākhirah* which is the hereafter, and the world to come.

Fidyah: A religious compensation that has to be made when a person is not able to keep fasts during the month of Ramaḍān due to one's health, old age, pregnancy, breastfeeding, or other justifiable factors. One can refer to the books of Jurisprudence for more information.

Fitnah (Plural: Fitan): Literally means 'test,' 'temptation,' 'trial,' 'sedition,' or 'civil strife.' It is a word which has extensive connotations based on the context in which it is used.

Ghaflah: Literally means 'to be negligent,' and in Islamic terminology it means to be in a state of forgetfulness of Allah ﷻ and not fulfilling one's responsibilities.

Ghusl (Plural: Aghsāl): Literally means 'to wash,' however in Islamic Jurisprudence, it refers to a full-body ritual purification which is mandatory when a Muslim enters into a state of spiritual impurity - such as after sexual intercourse, the completion of a woman's menstrual cycle, post-partum, and other occasions.

Ḥasanah (Plural: Ḥasanāt): Refers to 'honorable deeds' - positive and good actions which are deemed as such through revelation - either in the Qur'ān, or the teachings of Prophet Muḥammad ﷺ and his successors.

Ḥayḍ: The Islamic Jurisprudential term for a woman's regular monthly menstrual cycle.

Ḥā'iḍ: The term given to a woman who is in her regular monthly menstrual cycle.

Ḥikmah: Literally means 'wisdom' and is a term sometimes used in the Qur'ān alongside *'Kitāb'* - making it 'The Qur'ān, full of wisdom.' Some scholars have stated that *ḥikmah* refers to the *sunnah* - which are the teachings and practical methods of life of Prophet Muḥammad ﷺ.

Ḥadd (Plural: Ḥudūd): Literally means 'borders,' 'boundaries,' or 'limits,' however its meaning differs based on the context in which it is used. Although it can also refer to specific punishments which are under Islamic law - such as for murder, rape, etc.; it is used to mean limits that Allah ﷻ has set for humanity which they must not transgress. Doing so will entail consequences in this world and/or the next.

'Iddah: The waiting period that a woman she must observe after a divorce, or the death of her husband - during which time, she is not permitted to marry another man, and certain other requirements must be fulfilled. The length of the *'iddah* varies based on numerous circumstances.

Ifṭār: Also known as *fuṭūr* which means 'break fast,' it is the evening meal at *Maghrib* time that Muslims partake in to end their fast - either during the month of Ramaḍān, or at any other time of the year when they fast a recommended fast or when making up a missed fast *(qaḍā')* of the month of Ramaḍān.

Iḥrām: A term used in Islamic Jurisprudence which has two meanings: (1) The sacred state which a Muslim must enter in order to perform the rites of *Ḥajj* or *'Umrah*. This state must be entered before crossing the pilgrimage boundary known as the *mīqāt*; and (2) This word also refers to the physical attire that a Muslim must wear which the scholars of Islamic Jurisprudence have explained in various *Ḥajj* manuals.

Iḥsān: A term which means 'to do beautiful things,' 'perfection,' or 'excellence.' At one level, *iḥsān* is a matter of taking one's inner faith *(īmān)* a step further and ensuring that it is shown in both one's deeds and actions as a sense of social responsibility.

Ijtihād: This word comes from the Arabic word 'to struggle' *(jihād)*, and is used to describe the physical or mental efforts which a religious scholar - an expert in Islamic law - will employ to determine what Allah ﷻ expects from the believers.

Ikhlāṣ: Literally means 'sincerity,' and in addition to its being a name of one of the chapters of the Qur'ān (chapter 112), it is an overall quality which all Muslims strive to attain in which they perform all of their actions for the pleasure of Allah ﷻ and without any show of ostentation.

'Ilm al-Ghayb: Literally means 'Knowledge of the Unseen' and refers to knowledge that is reserved for Allāh ﷻ - however He can share it with His chosen servants or whoever He Wills whenever He wishes.

Imsāk: Literally means 'to stop' and has various uses in Islamic Jurisprudence. It is most often used to denote the time of the early-morning hours during the month of Ramaḍān (or any other time which a person wishes to keep a fast) in which they are recommended to stop eating, drinking, or performing any of the actions which would invalidate the fast. The timing of *imsāk* will vary based on one's geographic region and the time of year, but it is usually about 10 to 15 minutes before the time of *Fajr*.

Isrā'īliyyāt: In *ḥadīth* studies, this is a term used to denote statements attributed to Prophet Muḥammad ﷺ which are of foreign import - most notably events which were originally in Jewish sources which were imported into Islamic teachings. This was done by individuals of questionable character and for nefarious motives — usually to cause damage to the religious teachings and deviate the Muslims.

Istighfār: Literally means 'to seek forgiveness from Allah ﷻ for one's sins' that were done either intentionally or unintentionally.

Istiḥāḍā: Irregular vaginal bleeding which is not that of the monthly menstrual cycle, nor from post-partum. (For the specific rules related to a woman who is in this state, please refer to the relevant books of Jurisprudence.)

Īthār: Literally means 'self-sacrifice,' and is a noble ethical quality in which a believer forsakes one's own comforts and ease of life for the benefit and greater good of another person or society on a whole.

I'tikāf: A unique spiritual retreat in which a Muslim temporarily detaches oneself from worldly life, and spends a minimum of three full days and two nights in a Masjid engaged in prayers, worship, reflection, and contemplation.

Itmām al-Ḥujjah: Literally means 'Completion of the Proof.' This is a concept in Islam which denotes that religious truths have been completely clarified and outlined to humanity by Prophet Muḥammad ﷺ]. As the message has been made available to people, they are now considered to have no excuse to deny it and will be answerable to Allah ﷻ on the Day of Judgment. In Shī'ah Islam, this term is further extended to the 12 Imāms ؑ who are the *ḥujjaj* (proofs - plural of *ḥujjah*) of Allah ﷻ upon this Earth and will remain so until the end of time.

Izār: A part of the *iḥrām* clothing worn by male pilgrims during the Ḥajj or 'Umrah that covers the lower-half of the body from the navel downwards. In some Muslim cultures, this word is often used to describe the traditional clothing which Muslim women wear to cover the entire body.

Jāhiliyyah: Literally means 'ignorance' or 'decadence' - most often used in the term 'Era of Ignorance - *Jāhiliyyah*' to denote the period before the coming of Prophet Muḥammad ﷺ and the teachings of the Qur'ān. It is also used to describe the pre-Islamic time of the Arabs.

Jamā'at: Literally means 'congregation' and has various uses in Islamic Jurisprudence such as *Ṣalāt al-Jamā'at* - prayers which are recited in congregation.

Jumu'ah: Literally means 'Friday' - the sacred day in Islam when the Friday prayers (*Ṣalāt al-Jumu'ah*) are performed.

Kaffārah: A religious penalty - of either money or food - which has to be given to a needy person by an individual who intentionally missed or broke a fast during the month of Ramaḍān without a valid reason. One can refer to the books of Jurisprudence for more information.

Kitāb: Literally means 'book,' however it is most often used by Allah ﷻ to refer to the Noble Qur'ān, and this word is also used in the Qur'ān when Allah ﷻ speaks about the Scriptures given to past Prophets.

La'n: Literally means 'the removal of the special mercy of Allah ﷻ' from an individual. *La'n* is the opposite of *du'ā'* in that a person asks Allah ﷻ for Him to remove His special mercy from someone due to their vile actions, or flagrant breaking of His laws with no remorse or recompense.

Maytah: Literally means 'dead' and is used in Islamic Jurisprudence to describe an animal that has died on its own, such as an animal which died due to a drought, or fell off a cliff, and was then found dead. Such an animal is impure *(najis)*, and also impermissible to eat.

Mujāhid (Plural: Mujāhidīn): Literally means 'one who struggles,' and comes from the same root as *jihād*. It is used to refer to those individuals who struggle hard in every-day life, and can also be used to refer to those who defend their homeland on the battlefield.

Mukallaf: Literally means 'one who is legally responsible' and is a term used in Islamic Jurisprudence relating to a young man or woman who has reached the age of responsibility such that their actions are now all accountable. Based on narrations, scholars believe that girls reach this at age 9 in Islamic lunar years, while boys reach it at a maximum of 15 Islamic lunar years of age.

Musībah: Literally means a 'trial' or a 'tribulation' depending on its context.

Mustaḥab (Plural: Mustaḥabbāt): Literally means 'recommended' and in Islamic Jurisprudence it refers to actions which the Islamic law deems as being commended and highly recommended to perform. There is a reward if this action is performed, however there is no punishment if it is left out.

Mutawātir: A term used in *ḥadīth* studies which refers to the category of a narration. A *ḥadīth* is said to be *mutawātir* when it is a successively narrated statement from Prophet Muḥammad ﷺ, his daughter Sayyidah Fāṭimah az-Zahrā' ؑ, or one of the 12 Imāms ؑ which has been narrated so numerously such that it is not conceivable that the narrators would have agreed upon an untruth.

Najis: Literally means 'impure' and in Islamic Jurisprudence it refers to something which is unclean in itself such as urine, stool, blood, and some other items.

Nifās: One of the categories of blood which a woman sees, and is related to the blood which is seen post-childbirth or after a miscarriage.

Niyyah: Literally means 'intention' and it is the basis for all actions in Islam. A person must have an active and conscious intention behind each action of goodness that one wishes to perform in order to ensure the maximum rewards.

Qanā'ah: Literally means 'contentment' - to be satisfied with whatever Allah ﷻ apportions to an individual without being greedy or envious of what others have.

Qasam: Literally an 'oath' which one verbally takes. In Islam, an oath is legally binding and one must fulfill what one pledges when it is taken in the name of Allah ﷻ - such as when one says: *'Wallāhi,' 'Billāhi,'* or *'Tallāhi.'* For example, if someone says: *'Wallāh*, I swear that if I get a raise at work, I will give $1,000.00 in charity to a specific cause.' Such an oath is binding on the individual and if one gets the raise, then they must fulfill their pledge, and if one fails to follow through with their promise to Allāh ﷻ, then they have committed a sin.

Raḥmah: Literally means 'mercy' and is generally used to refer to a quality of Allah ﷻ, however it can also be seen in lesser degrees within humanity.

Rajab: The seventh month of the lunar-based Islamic calendar.

Rakʿah (Plural: Rakaʿāt): A unit of prayer. This term refers to a counting method in the *ṣalāh* (prayers). Each of the five daily prayers has a set number of units *(rakaʿāt)* that need to be performed, and within each unit there are a set number of actions and recitations which must be performed.

Riḍā: Literally it means 'pleased or content' and is one of the praiseworthy ethical traits in Islam in which a person is pleased with whatever Allah ﷻ gives or takes away from one's at that point in life.

Rukn (Plural: Arkān): Literally means 'pillar' and has various meanings based on its context. In Islamic Jurisprudence, it can be related to a fundamental aspect of an act of worship such as the *arkān* of *ṣalāh* - requirements which must be met in the prayers in order to ensure its validity. In Islamic Theology, it refers to fundamental beliefs which a faithful believer must have to be considered a Muslim

Ṣadaqah (Plural: Ṣadaqāt): The literal definition is 'righteousness' and comes from a root word which means 'sincerity,' 'to speak the truth,' or 'to fulfill one's promise.' The Qur'ān uses it extensively to refer to voluntary charity, however it can also be used to refer to obligatory charity. Ṣadaqah does not have to be monetary, but rather it can be any act of righteousness, including: administering justice between people, removing a harm from the road or path, speaking a kind word, and even smiling at others.

Saʿī: One of the rites of *Ḥajj* and *ʿUmrah* in which a pilgrim walks from the mount of aṣ-Ṣafā to al-Marwa seven times - starting at aṣ-Ṣafā and ending at al-Marwa.

Shaʿāʾir: Literally means 'a sign' or 'a symbol,' and it refers to individual rites of the *Ḥajj* pilgrimage, and various aspects or objects which are employed during *Ḥajj* such as the sacrificial animal.

Shukr: Literally means 'to show thanks or gratitude,' and it is used in respect to show thanks to Allah ﷻ or to other people when they provide some level of assistance.

Sīrah: Literally means 'to travel,' or 'be on a journey,' but the technical usage of the word refers to a biography. Although this word can be used for anyone, it most often refers to the biography of Prophet Muḥammad ﷺ.

Ṣubḥ: Literally means 'the morning,' and is used in Islamic Jurisprudence to refer to the morning/dawn time when the first prayers of the day, *Ṣalāt al-Fajr,* begins, this prayer is also known as *Ṣalāt aṣ-Ṣubḥ.*

Talbīyyah: A specific pronouncement by a *Ḥajj* pilgrim as a sign of conviction that they are intending to perform *Ḥajj* for the sake of Allah ﷻ. This phrase is repeated shortly after donning the specific clothing *(iḥrām),* and stops once the pilgrim reaches the city of Mecca. The prayer is: "Here I am [at your service] O Allah, here I am. Here I am [at your service]. You have no partners (other gods), here I am. To You alone is all praise and all excellence, and to You is all sovereignty. There is no partner for You. Here I am."

Taʿlīm: The act or process of education.

Tarbiyah: The act of bringing up, rearing, fostering, or nurturing.

Taslīm: Literally means 'submission,' and it comes from the same root word as Islam and salām, and its meaning differs based on the context in which it is used. It can refer to complete submission to Allah ﷻ via the religion of Islam, or can also be used for the final act of the *ṣalāh* to conclude the prayer.

Tayammum: One of the ways to enter into a state of purity. It is defined as a dry ritual purification which is done in place of *wuḍūʿ* or *ghusl* if water is not available, or if one is not able to use water due to medical reasons, or for certain other reasons as outlined in the books of Jurisprudence.

Ṭayyib: Literally means 'good,' 'pleasant,' 'agreeable,' and 'lawful.' In the Qur'ān, it is used to define the type of food which a Muslim should consume - *'ḥalāl'* (permissible) and *'ṭayyib'* (wholesome).

Tazkiyyah: Literally means 'to purify' and it refers to the process of purifying one's heart, soul, and character from negative traits, spiritual impurities, and sins. The goal of tazkiyyah is to acheive a higher level of spiritual consciousness and closeness to Allah ﷻ through eliminating negative moral traits and cultivating positive moral qualities.

Uṣūl ad-Dīn: Literally means 'The Fundamentals of the Religion,' and refers to those Theological concepts which a person must believe in to be considered a Muslim. For Shīʿah Muslims this is the following five: *Tawḥīd* (Monotheism), *ʿAdālah* (Justice of Allah), *Nubuwwah* (Prophethood), Imāmah (Divinely-appointed Leadership), and Qiyāmah (Resurrection and the Day of Judgment).

Wājib (Plural: Wājibāt): Literally, this word refers to things which are an obligation in the religious teachings, such as *ṣalāh, zakāh, ṣawm,* etc., and must be performed. Not performing them without a valid reason on time will entail a punishment.

Ẓālim: Literally, this word refers to 'a person who commits acts of aggression' and is 'an oppressor.'

Zuhd: Literally, this word refers to 'a lack of desire towards this material world.' *Zuhd* differs and should not be confused with monasticism in Christianity, as a believer who practices *zuhd* does not forbid oneself from the legitimate pleasure of this world, but rather does not attach oneself to it; and further to this they put their sole trust in Allah ﷻ, not on the material means and pleasures of this world.

Index

A

ʿAbdullāh ibn Jaḥsh 265, 266
ʿAbdullāh ibn Rawāḥa 300
ʿAbdullāh ibn Salām 21, 22
ʿAbdur Raḥmān ibn Zubayr 324
ʿĀlam adh-Dharr 52
ʿĀlam al-Barzakh 52
ʿĀlam al-Baṭn 52
ʿĀlam al-Khulūd 52
ʿĀlam al-Maʿād 52
ʿĀlam an-Nāsūt 52
ʿAmmār al-Yāsir 43
ʿAmrū ibn Ḥaḍramī 266
ʿAmrū ibn Jamūḥ 242
ʿArafāt 195, 196, 197, 198, 199, 200, 201, 202, 211, 213
ʿĀsim ibn ʿUday 329
ʿĀʾishah bint Abū Bakr 84
Abū ad-Daḥdāḥ al-Anṣārī 364
Abū Jahl 43
Ahl adh-Dhimmah 179
Ahlul Kitāb. See People of the Book
Akhnas ibn Sharīq 213
Allah
  Attaining His forgiveness 67
  Focusing on other 77
  His manifestations 73
  Possibility of seeing 224
Al-Marwah 55, 56, 57, 59, 61, 62
Angel 100, 104
  Jibrāʾīl 10, 12, 100, 201, 217, 218
  Mīkāʾīl 217, 218
Antioch 369
Arabian Peninsula 17, 18, 83, 84, 348, 350
Ark of the Covenant 369, 370, 374, 375, 376
Ashʿath ibn Qays 160
Aṣ-Ṣafā 55, 56, 57, 59, 61, 62, 402
Aṣ-Ṣafā and al-Marwah
  Historical Position of 59

B

Banī Isrāʾīl. See Children of Isrāʾīl
Barzakh 7, 44, 45, 53
Battle of Aḥzāb 240. See also Battle of Khandaq
Battle of Badr 42, 43, 265
Battle of Ḥunayn 179
Battle of Jamal (The Camel) 84
Battle of Khandaq 178
Battle of Mūʾta 178
Battle of Ṣiffīn 84
Battle of Tabūk 178
Battle of Uḥud 178
Bayt al-Muqaddas 1
Beautification of this temporal world 228
Blindly following one's forefathers 89
Breastfeeding 333
Bribes and Kickbacks 159
Buddhists 101

C

Certainity
  Levels of. See Yaqīn
Charity in the way of Allah 364
Children of Isrāʾīl 22, 360, 361,

371, 384, 388
Ark of the Covenant 375
Clear proofs given to 175, 225
Defeating the army of Jālūt 383
Fasting 144
Fasting as an atonement for sins 144
Guidance by Prophet Ishmū'īl 374
Lessons from the history of 368
Pride and arrogance of 369
Special mercy and forgiveness for 245
Standing up for war 378
Story of Ṭālūt (Saul) 372
Supplication of 382
The elders of 368
China 227
Concealing the Truth 64
Conquest of Mecca 169

D

Damnation 63
Upon Satan 63
Upon some of the people from the Tribes of Isrā'īl 63
Upon some of the People of the Book 63
Upon the followers of the Pharaoh 63
Upon the Tribe of ʿĀd 63
Upon those who disregarded the Sabbath 63
Day of Judgment 7, 44, 45, 71, 80, 81, 82, 84, 85, 100, 106, 146, 162, 202, 224, 233, 284, 299, 311, 362
Dhikr. See Remembrance of Allah
A Life of Remembrance 35
Avoiding Ghaflah 36
Dhikr in One's Life 38
Different Forms of Dhikr 37
What is Remembrance (Dhikr) of Allah? 35
Why do we Need Dhikrullāh? 37
Divorce
Before consumation of the marriage 343
Provisions after divorce 357
Remaryying after the waiting period 329
Rules relating to 309, 312, 317
Third pronouncement of 323
Types of 313, 321
Waiting period 312
Respecting women 326
Diya 113, 116, 117, 119
Duʿā'. See Supplication
Duʿā' Kumayl 148

E

Egypt 227
Eid al-Aḍḥā 199, 210, 211
Evangelical Right-Wing Christians 101

F

Fasting
As seen in previous nations 144
Choosing the month of Ramaḍān 145
Expansion of the rulings 153

Fixed number of days 136
Medical benefits of 143
Societal benefits of 142
Some of the rulings 140
Source of God-Consciousness (Taqwā) 134, 156
Types and history of 133
Various outcomes of 141
Fighting in the way of Allah 260
In the Sacred Months 265
Financial corruption 158
Focusing on other than Allah 77
Forbidden for Muslim consumption 94
France 227

G

Gabriel. See Angel Jibrā'īl
Gambling 272
God-consciousness 31, 93, 106, 109, 139, 158, 162, 163, 183, 194, 210, 212, 213, 216, 217, 234, 299, 300, 311, 329, 336, 337, 345, 346, 361
In marital relationships 297
In respect to marriage 291
In the sacred months 182
Related to fasting 133, 142, 152, 153, 156
The best provision 193
Writing a will 122
Goliath. See Jālūt
Gradual immorality 87

H

Hājar 59, 60, 61
Sent to Mecca 60
Ḥajj
Business during 196
Definition of 56
Entering the state of iḥrām 193
First stop in 200
Importance of 187, 190
ʿArafāt, Muzdalifah, and Mashʿar 197
Prohibitions while in iḥrām 193
Pronouncement of Talbīyyah 190
Rites in al-Muzdalifah 195
Rites in ʿArafāt 195
Rites of 188, 193
Second stop in 201
Various types of 190
When to perform 193
Hamzah Sayyid al-Shuhadā' 42
Ḥawwā 198
Hindus 101
Humanity as one nation 236

I

ʿIlm al-ghayb. See Knowledge of the Unseen
Iblīs. See Satan
Ibn ʿAbbās 42, 63, 83, 228
Iḥrām 61, 163, 187, 188, 189, 190, 191, 193, 195, 200, 201, 399, 403
Ijtihād 9, 33
Imām
ʿAlī ibn Abī Ṭālib 8, 13, 14, 22, 35, 36, 41, 42, 48, 54, 65, 84, 160, 161, 185, 218, 219, 224
Battle of Tabūk 178
Battle of the Camel 84
Burial site of 377

Du'ā' Kumayl 148
Helping Allah 365
Importance of Ḥajj 190
Night of migration 218
Seeing his Lord 224
ʿAlī ibn al-Ḥusayn as-Sajjād 7, 148
Ḥusayn ibn ʿAlī ash-Shahīd 54
Jaʿfar ibn Muḥammad aṣ-Ṣādiq 45, 145, 150, 354
Divorce ruling 313
Muḥammad al-Mahdī 176, 177, 369, 371
Muḥammad ibn ʿAlī al-Bāqir 79, 109, 131, 204
Importance of Ṣalāh 349
India 227
Infāq (Charity)
Benefits of 243
Increased proximity to Allah 244
Replenishment and increase in wealth 244
Reward in the world to come 246
Safety and stability of society 245
Special mercy and forgiveness from Allah 245
Spiritual purification of the soul 243
Spiritual tranquility 244
Conditions for the acceptance of 246
Based on moderation 249
From the permissibly-earned (Ḥalāl) 248
Given during times of ease and difficulty 250
Given in secrecy 249
Giving from that which a person loves 249
Intention of seeking proximity to Allah 247
Islam and Īmān 246
Not placing an obligation upon the recipient 248
In the way of Allah 184
Ranking of recipients 251
Dedicated to working for Islam 253
Freeing slaves 254
Immediate family members 251
Jihād (struggling) in the Way of Allah 255
Orphans 252
Poor and needy 252
Stranded travelers 253
Those who ask 254
Those who migrate in the Way of Allah 253
Winning over the hearts of the non-believers 256
Spending in charity for others 279
Intercession 82
Intoxicants 272
Isrāʾīliyāt 22, 398
Iʿtikāf 152

J

Jāhiliyyah 56, 92, 112, 114, 130, 163, 182, 196, 204, 276, 304
Jālūt 378, 380, 382, 383, 384
Jerusalem 1, 2, 3, 4, 5, 10, 11, 12, 13, 15, 16, 17, 25, 104, 369. See also Bayt al-Muqaddas

Jews and Christians
  Concealing the truth 98
Jews and Christians recognized Prophet Muḥammad 21
Jews and Christians will never be pleased 19
Jibrā'īl 10, 12, 100, 201, 217, 218
Jihād
  Defensive 166, 178
  Forgiving those who stop aggression 173
  In the Way of Allah 363
  Islamic concept 175
  Meaning of 174
  Supporting the oppressed 180
  Used to extinguish rebellions 176

K

Kaʿbah
  House of idolatry 5
  House of Monotheism 16
Khārijah ibn Zayd 63
Khums 108
KKK (Ku Klux Klan) 101
Knowledge of the Unseen 213

L

Last will and testament 122
  Inheritance for one's spouse 353
  Maintaining justice in the writing 131
  Making alterations after the fact 125
  Permission to ammend a will 126
Laylat al-Mabīt 218
Laʿn. See Damnation
Levant 360, 369

M

Marriage
  Not marrying polytheists 288
  Proposal to a woman 341
  Some of the rulings 290
Martyrs
  Are alive 44
Mashʿar al-Ḥarām 195, 196, 200, 201
Masjid al-Qiblatayn 11, 13
Maʿād. See Day of Judgment
Maʿqil ibn Yasār 329
Menstruation
  Rules of 292
Michael. See Angel Mīkā'īl
Minā 199, 200, 202, 211, 213
Misfortune/Trial (Musībah)
  What is a 51
Monotheism 5, 16, 29, 51, 61, 71, 94, 179, 180, 181
Month of Ramaḍān
  Importance of 140
  Sexual intimacy with one's spouce 151
Movements of Satan 85
Muslims
  A witness 4
  Balanced, Middle Nation 3
Muzdalifah 195, 197, 199, 200, 202, 211
Muʿādh ibn Jabal 63
Muʿāwiyah ibn Abū Ṣufyān 84

N

Namrūd ibn Kanʿan 175

Nebuchadnezzar 369
New moon 162

O

Oaths
  Sexual abstinence 300, 303
  Various categories of 303
Orphans
  How to deal with 283

P

Peace Treaty of Ḥudaybiyyah 84
People of the Book 11, 19, 23, 63, 98, 99, 105, 179
Pharaoh 369
Philistines 369, 379
Plague 361
Polytheism 5, 77, 85, 171, 175, 179, 289
Prayer in times of fear 351
Prophet
  Ādam
    First location to reside 197
    Reason for fasting 133
    Staying in ʿArafāt 198
  Binyāmīn
    Relationship to Prophet Yaʿqūb 370
  Dāwūd
    Defeating Jālūt 378
    Given authority and wisdom by Allah 385
    Given the status of Prophethood 385
    His intense worship of Allah 384
    His lineage 384
    His mention in the Qur'ān 384
    How he defeated Ṭālūt 384
    In the army of Ṭālūt 384
    Relationship to Ṭālūt 370
    Understanding the language of the animals 384
    Victorious 384
    Victory over the Philistines 379
    Worshiping Allah with the animals and nature 384
  Ḥizqīl
    One of the Prophets sent to the Children of Isrāʾīl 360
    Response to the supplication of 361
    Successor to Prophet Mūsā 361
  ʿIsā
    Birthplace of 4
    Concept of fasting in his teachings 134
    Fasting 144
  Ibrāhīm
    Brief history of 175
    Test 60
    Witnessing recreation of life 230
  Ishmūʾīl 368, 370, 373, 374, 375
    Children of Isrāʾīl speak to 372
    Conversation with the Children of Isrāʾīl 368, 372, 374, 375
    Fulfilling his responsibility 372
    Given power and authority by Allah 373
    Prophet for Children of Isrāʾīl 369
    Raised as a Prophet for the Children of Isrāʾīl 370
    Revelation sent to 140, 370

Ismāʾīl
Taken to Mecca 60
Muḥammad 7
A guide to world peace 220
Asked about Allah 148
Asked about giving in charity 242, 244, 247, 257, 278
Asked about how to deal with orphans 284
Asked about intoxicants and games of chance 272, 276
Asked about the importance of the new crescent moon 162
Asked about the new moon 163
Asked about the sacred months 267
Asked about the women's menstrual cycles 294
Asked for 'where' Allah is 147
Asked questions 165
Asked questions by the Jews 162
Asking the Children of Isrāʾīl 226
Aspects of the pilgrimage 192, 195, 196, 199
A witness 4, 8
Battle of Tabūk 178
Being connected to 6
Burial site of 377
Change of qiblah 13, 14, 15, 106
Change of the qiblah 13
Code of conduct in war 262
Condeming bribery 161
Condemned bribery 160
Conquest of Mecca 169
Defining the concept of dhikr of Allah 35
Denying his status 98
Details on choosing a spouse 299
Did not copy Biblical stories 389
Disbelieving in 268
Encouragement to fight in the way of Allah 363
Encouraging to perform prayers even in war 352
Excuses made by the Jews for not accepting him 225
Experience in congregational prayers 348
Explaining some of the rules of menstration 294
Explaining the rules of divorce 318, 324, 325, 329
Explaining the rules of marriage 288
Explaining the rules regarding the orphans 285
Falsely attributing things to 88
Follows the rulings as sent by Allah 18
Giving the permission to fight 166, 174
Gradual guidance from 153
Guiding people on what to spend in charity 252
Him and the twelve Imāms as witnesses 8
His participation in the Battle of Tabūk 178
His process of iʿtikāf 154
His role in society 32, 33
How he changed direction in the prayers 12, 15
Importance of fasting 142

In barzakh 7
Jewish scholars that denied his message 64
Jews and Christians recognize his status 21
Legitimacy of war 263
Mediating in marital disputes 300
Meeting the people of the Tribe of Thaqīf 83
Migration to Medina 218
Number of battles during his life 177
Ordered to turn toward the Sacred Mosque 10
Participation in the Battle of Tabūk 179
People of the Book upset with him 19
People will never be pleased with him 19
Praying facing Jerusalem 1
Qiblah is the 'middle' qiblah 3
Recognizing him 21
Reprimanding some companions 354
Revelation of the Quran to 145
Right to retailiate 183
Role model for humanity 4
Sent to his community and beyond 32
Sign of the Final Prophet 11
Some rules on fasting 141, 152, 153
Spiritual agenda of 32
Standing firm against the idolators 170
Stressing on the importance of prayers 349
Supplication 147
Tasks of 32, 33
The developer and administrator of rulings 309
The issue of the triple divorce 324
The Middle Nation 7
Trying to block people from following 98
Turning in the prayers 13
Turning toward the heavens 10
Turning toward the Sacred Mosque 27, 28
Various questions by the people 164
Wars during his lifetime 177
Will never follow the qiblah of others 19
Witness over humanity 7
Witness over the people 4
Women complaining about divorce issues 318
Writing a last will and testament 130
Mūsā 100, 133, 134, 175, 361, 368, 369, 370, 376
Contents of the Ark of the Covenant 375
Fasting 144
Interrogated by his community 17
Judaic law of retribution 121
Obligation to fast 133, 144
Placed into the tābūt 368
Qārūn ibn Yaṣhura revolts against 175
Spoken to through a burning bush 100

Nūḥ
Instruction to fast 133
Yaʿqūb 370
Children from his progeny 384
Punishment forever 70

Q

Qarḍ al-ḥasana 365
Qārūn ibn Yaṣhura 175
Qatar 227
Qiblah
Event of the Shift of 1
Praying facing Jerusalem 1
Reactions and consequences to the change 17
Reason for the change 4, 5, 15
Specifics on the Changing of 11, 12
Turn toward the Kaʿbah 10
Qiṣāṣ
Introduction to the system 112
Life in the law of retribution 114, 120
Philosophy of 118
Why blood-money? 116
Qunūt 207

R

Reality of death 51
Remembrance of Allah 34
During Eid al-Aḍḥā 210
During pilgrimage 204
Revelation of past Scriptures 145

S

Sacred months 182
Fighting therein 182
List of 182, 267
Salmān al-Muḥammadī (al-Fārisī) 8, 354
Samuel. See Prophet Ishmūʾīl
Satan
False promises of 88
Following the footsteps of 83, 219
Global influence of 213
Movements of 85
The worst creation 65
Tools used to deviate 86, 282
Tricks of 87, 278
Saudi Arabia 227
Saul. See Ṭālūt
Sayyidah Fāṭimah az-Zahrāʾ 54
Burial site of 377
Following the sunnah of 33
Performing the tasbīḥ of 38
Saʿd ibn Muʿādh 63
Saʿī
Definition of 57
Shafāʿah. See Intercession
Shayṭān. See Satan
Shirk. See Polytheism
Source of righteousness 105
Sufyān al-Thawrī 354
Sumayyah bint Khabāṭ 43
Sunnatullāh 50, 241
Supplication 147
Weapon of the believer 148

T

Ṭālūt 370, 372, 373, 374, 375, 378, 379, 380, 382, 384
Taqwā. See God-consciousness
Tarbiyah 33, 34, 40, 150

Ṭawāf
Definition of 56
Tawḥīd. See Monotheism
Tazkiyah 33
Taʿlīm 33, 40
Tests from Allah
Universal tests 48
The Middle Nation 6
The reality of 242
Those who die as disbelievers 68
Tribes
Banū Naḍīr 178
Banū Sālim ibn ʿAwf 13
Khuzāʿī 84
Thaqīf 83

U

ʿUmrah
Definition of 56
Importance of 187
United Arab Emirates 227
United States of America 227

V

Various Types of Ḥajj 190

W

Wahhābi movement 101
Waiting period after death of husband 337
Why does Allah test humanity 47
World peace 220

Y

Yaqīn
Ḥaqq al-Yaqīn 24
ʿAyn al-Yaqīn 24
ʿIlm al-Yaqīn 23
Yāsir ibn ʿĀmir ʿAnsī 43
Yūshaʿ ibn Nūn 369

Z

Zakāh 108
Zamzam 61
Zaynab bint ʿAlī 54
Zionists 101

About the Board ʿĀlim

Moulana Nabi R. Mir (Abidi) is a scholar, an educator, a father, and an enthusiast for creating educational infrastructure and Islamic resources for the benefit of the global community. Always wanting to think 'outside of the box' by supporting the creation of innovative materials to engage young readers to pick up Islamic books, interact with Qur'ānic games, learn from the Steps to Perfection Curriculum, and begin their life-long journey of holistic education.

Being a dedicated student and graduate of *Darse Khārij* (the highest level of Islamic Studies in the Seminary) from the *Ḥawzah*, Moulana Abidi knows the value of Islamic education. Also, having grown up in India, and now residing in the United States, he has had the honor of traveling to various communities and meeting many community leaders. He values the importance of collaboration and working together to optimize potentials, and to create open source platforms so that information and resources are available and accessible to everyone around the world.

You, dear reader, are now part of the Al-Kisa family.
Share the word, and join the mission.